Into the Sunset
Anthology of Nineteenth-Century
Austrian Prose

Studies in Austrian Literature, Culture, and Thought

Translation Series

Into the Sunset

Anthology of Nineteenth-Century Austrian Prose

Selected and Newly Translated
with a General Introduction and
Author-Specific Prefaces
by
Richard Hacken

ARIADNE PRESS
Riverside, California

Ariadne Press would like to express its appreciation to the Austrian Cultural Institute, New York and the Bundeskanzleramt – Sektion Kunst, Vienna for their assistance in publishing this book.

Library of Congress Cataloging-in-Publication Data

Into the sunset : anthology of nineteenth-century Austrian Prose /
   Selected and newly translated with a general introduction and
   author-specific prefaces by Richard Hacken.
         p.   cm. – (Studies in Austrian literature, culture, and
thought. Translation series)
   Includes bibliographical references.
   ISBN 1-57241-077-9
   1. Austrian prose literature--19th century--Translations into
English. I. Hacken, Richard D. II. Series
PT3626.P7I58   1999
838'.70808--dc21   98-48469
                                                                     CIP

Cover Design:
Art Director, Designer: George McGinnis

Copyright ©1999
by Ariadne Press
270 Goins Court
Riverside, CA 92507

All rights reserved.
No part of this publication may be reproduced or transmitted
in any form or by any means without formal permission.
Printed in the United States of America.
ISBN 1-57241-077-9

In memory
of
Leola Baldwin Jones Hacken
1920-1998

CONTENTS

Richard Hacken 1
Introduction:
Austrian Prose of the Nineteenth Century

Acknowledgments 11

Prose written before 1848:

Caroline von Pichler 12
The Love of Charlemagne's Youth
[*Carl's des Großen Jugendliebe, 1823*]

Ernst von Feuchtersleben 33
An Alpine Journey
[*Eine Gebirgsreise,* 1841]

Adalbert Stifter 45
Brigitta
[*Brigitta,* 1843]

Betty Paoli 93
Confessions
[*Bekenntnisse,* 1844]

Franz Grillparzer 118
The Poor Fiddler
[*Der arme Spielmann,* 1847]

Prose written after 1848:

Friedrich Halm 157
Marzipan-Lisa
[*Marzipan-Lise*, 1854]

Leopold Kompert 196
Isaac's Glasses
[*Eisiks Brille*, 1860]

Leopold von Sacher-Masoch 222
Don Juan of Kolomyya
[*Don Juan von Kolomea*, 1866]

Karl Emil Franzos 272
The Higher Law
[*Nach dem höheren Gesetz*, 1873]

Ada Christen 308
Kathy's Feather Hat
[*Käthes Federhut*, 1876]

Marie von Ebner-Eschenbach 321
The Gemperlein Barons
[*Die Freiherren von Gemperlein*, 1879]

Ludwig Anzengruber 366
The Love Child
[*Das Sündkind*, 1879]

Peter Rosegger 395
Mary in Misery
[*Maria im Elend*, 1881]

Ferdinand von Saar 420
Tambi
[*Tambi*, 1882]

INTRODUCTION

AUSTRIAN PROSE OF THE NINETEENTH CENTURY

RICHARD HACKEN

*No one writes like a god
who hasn't suffered like a dog.*

– Marie von Ebner-Eschenbach

In the last sentence of Stifter's *Brigitta*, the first-person narrator describes his literal exodus from Hungary into the Alpine twilight of his Austrian homeland. The prose works of the nineteenth century presented here can also, in a figurative sense, be regarded as a literary montage of departure into the sunset of the Austro-Hungarian empire. The stories and tales (most of them in novella format) are arranged in a chronological sequence from the earliest to the latest. A quick glance at the table of contents will reveal that the great watershed year for Austrian letters of the previous century was 1848, the year of upheaval and revolution: fictional works preceding the grand caesura of 1848 were significantly different from those that followed it. One thing both epochs offer in common, though, is a glimpse into the sunset.

Austrian Prose before 1848

Nowadays in the Anglo-American world, the term *Biedermeier* often refers to a style of furniture. Yet it signifies considerably more: for Austria it was an age that extended from the Congress of Vienna in the year 1815 – when Europe reconfigured itself following the defeat of Napoleon – until the unsuccessful revolution of 1848. It was during this time that one southeastern realm of German speakers first became truly and consciously "Austrian" in a political sense – no longer to serve as a mere German appendage. Former considerations of a large and all-inclusive German nation were abandoned for the time, and Austro-centered patriotism and pride flourished. It was a time when love of nature abounded (and with it passions for gardening, for alpinism, and for exploring the intricacies of human health and hygiene), a time when God was in the minutest of details and conspicuous Catholic piety was in vogue. One essential societal idiom of the age was a strengthened collectivism, both among individuals and among peoples, though the family and other small social units were most sacred.[1] In sociological terms coined by Ferdinand Tönnies in 1887, the *Biedermeier* age was able to retain its essence as a *Gemeinschaft* – an agrarian and cohesive society still unmarred by the industrial deluge to come – in direct contrast to the coming *Gesellschaft*, the urban society of estrangement and anonymity that capitalism and factories would bring in their wake. The Viennese theater was at its zenith. The middle classes began to participate in cultural pursuits previously reserved for nobility, such as chamber music and poeticizing.

In prose literature the age was epitomized by two master craftsmen, Stifter and Grillparzer. The moral authority of Stifter's *Brigitta*, as of his other tales, proceeded from the "gentle laws" of life, such as honesty and the joyful peace of mind found in harvesting the fruits of hard labor, forgiveness and love. The age was perhaps rounded to its completion by the fictional hero in Grillparzer's *Poor Fiddler*, a questionably talented musical amateur and humble little *petit bourgeois* beleaguered with financial woes and emotional inadequacies. Still, he was able to serve as a folk hero for *Biedermeier* tastes due to his long-suffering demeanor and deep-rooted spirituality. Some

---

[1] Cf. Friedrich Sengle, *Biedermeierzeit: Deutsche Literatur im Spannungsfeld zwischen Restauration und Revolution 1815-1848*. 3 vols. (Stuttgart: Metzler, 1971-1980), I, 1-78.

believe that this novella, first published in an almanac in 1848, signaled an end to the *Biedermeier* age.²

Nostalgia for the *Biedermeier* has run rampant in the Alpine regions. Yet such rosy visions of the past are incomplete. Running counter to the imperial glories, the cultural advantages, and the fictional encomiums to virtue were philosophical and literary strains of a deep pessimism – of doubts about God, doubts about the possibilities of a harmonious society, and even despair at the impediments to finding any sense in historical or contemporary existence. Censorship, political repression, and the stringent measures of secret police lurked behind the masks of cultural exhilaration. One reason the bourgeoisie flocked to the theatrical and music halls was as a consolation and an escape; they had been forced into exile from the political arena. Since the *Poor Fiddler* was modeled on Grillparzer himself, the hero who quietly accepts his fate embodies a poignant form of *Biedermeier* resignation. In his own day Grillparzer was accused of inventing a new system of fatalism.

The first five prose works anthologized here were penned prior to 1848, and the censors allowed them to be published because they avoided almost all references or allusions to the politics of the day. The masterworks of Grillparzer and Stifter represented in this collection – and the faux-romance novella of Betty Paoli for that matter – cast light upon personal issues or universally human struggles in *Biedermeier* presentations that are essentially stateless. Feuchtersleben's prose, the product of a humanistically versed physician, takes similar psychological concerns and juxtaposes the Alpine landscape against them – again without commenting on Austrian rule or devising any metaphors about the imperial form of government. Caroline von Pichler's novella, *The Love of Charlemagne's Youth* – a literary escape, a flight into a glorious past – may be the political exception that proves the rule, however, with the laudatory light it casts on the origins of empire. (Pichler was herself a cultural counselor – and apparently an occasional spy – to the *Vormärz* Powers-That-Were.)

---

² Cf. Richard Brinkmann, *Wirklichkeit und Illusion: Studien über Gehalt und Grenzen des Begriffs Realismus für die erzählende Dichtung des neunzehnten Jahrhunderts.* 3rd ed. (Tübingen: Niemeyer, 1977), pp. 143-144.

Austrian Prose after 1848

The abortive Viennese revolution of 1848, a crisis of the first magnitude in the socio-political as well as in the philosophical and cultural realms, was a shock to those with liberal or progressive impulses, but it did lead to a loosening of strictures that had been particularly harsh on writers. Only after coming to this crossroads did the narrative arts in Austria start to attain loftier levels of achievement on a broad scale. If decreased repression after the revolution led to a climate more conducive to writing, the repercussions of a failed revolution also gave some authors greater impetus to write. Literature and the arts in general became substitutes, to some extent, for religion and other havens of traditional assurance that had, in the past, supplied feelings of comfort and salvation.

To outward appearances, Austria was doubly entitled to happiness for the latter half of the century: not only was it enjoying an economic and cultural zenith, but it was also the center of an extensive multiethnic empire at the crossroads of Europe. From 1848 onwards, Franz Josef was to become a popular emperor and linger in the imperial palace for over sixty majestic years.

The Habsburg Empire, despite its glitter and pomp, was suffering in many respects from internal rot,[3] and its antiquated bureaucracy[4] had to effect changes and compromises – including the establishment of a dual monarchy with Hungary – to fan the dying embers of empire. The same multiethnic character that had served to diversify the empire also contained within it the seeds of its own demise – a demise that would later be sealed by the assassination in Sarajevo that plunged Europe into the First World War.

Another revolution, the Industrial Revolution, was also coming full term at around the same time, introducing further changes that were in many ways threatening to the traditional modes of Central European life. Despite the welcome conveniences increasingly being introduced in commerce,

---

[3] Wilhelm Mommsen, *Größe und Versagen des deutschen Bürgertums: Ein Beitrag zur politischen Bewegung des 19. Jahrhunderts* (Munich: R. Oldenbourg, 1949), p. 62.

[4] Cf. William M. Johnston, "An Empire of Bureaucrats" in *The Austrian Mind: An Intellectual and Social History 1848-1938* (Berkeley: University of California Press, 1972), pp. 45-50.

transportation and other aspects of daily life, there were darker sides to the industrial transition: even in a post-Marxist age we recognize that workers, young children among them, were shamelessly exploited. Labor-management conflicts became inevitable. The air and the water began to reel from proto-pollution, and even the sounds of life became more shrill. Most striking, perhaps, was the shift in public focus from an agrarian society – with its bucolic images of nature, images that had supplied authors with metaphors for peace and contentment since ancient times – to smokestacks, factories and other attendant sights of the urban cityscape.

Buffeted between phenomena of empirical reality and imperial royalty, Austrian writers after 1848 produced a literary landscape that was dotted, ever more richly as the century progressed, with prose that illuminated the problems of real-life human beings trying to cope in a society slowly turning away from its feudalistic beginnings. The literary tools of realism – tempered into a poeticized realism – began to craft fiction ever more removed from classical ideals and romantic flights of fancy. The writing of this age has also been characterized as a "bourgeois realism,"[5] i.e., one taken from the perspective of the middle-class citizen. In that regard, it is instructive to see the number of authors whose very names (by the addendum "*von*") indicate nobility: five of the writers represented here were of high birth, but those writing after 1848 were either critical of their own class or highly laudatory of the common folk. A sixth, Friedrich Halm, actually crafted a pseudonym to hide his aristocratic origins and to seek solidarity with the man on the street.

These tales of realism, centering around the common man, are also uniquely Austrian. Unlike the cool precision of Kleist's Prussian novellas, these Austrian works of prose display the literary legacy of an empire that was scattered from Poland and Ukraine to Italy and the Balkans: the Mediterranean humor and the Slavic warmth find themselves joined together in a unique amalgam.[6]

As with any twilight, the twilight of the dual monarchy of Austria-Hungary turned out to be an excellent time for clear and sober reflection. The reciprocal efflorescence of tradition and modernity that came together

---

[5] Cf. Fritz Martini, "Vorwort" in *Deutsche Literatur im bürgerlichen Realismus 1848-1898*, 4th ed. (Stuttgart: Metzler, 1981), p. vi.

[6] Franz Theodor Csokor, "Einführung: Die österreichische Novelle" in *Die schönsten Erzählungen aus Österreich* (Vienna: Volksbuchverlag, 1958), p. 7.

so uniquely in Vienna during the reign of Franz Josef led, in the phraseology of Hermann Broch, to the "cheerful apocalypse."[7] This anthology contains an assortment of sharply focused cultural snapshots from that era of decline. If each author was sketching out aspects of the sunset from his or her own unique vantage point, then the anthology can be regarded, on one level, as a collage of gradual farewells to the monarchy.

A Prime Vehicle for Prose: The *Novella*

During both halves of the nineteenth century, but increasingly in the latter half, a number of writers turned to writing shorter works – with a preference for the novella.[8] Indeed, the process of narrative compaction was typical for Austrian fiction of the entire century. The novella was a fitting form of narrative for the age: it sprang up in the face of societal insecurities as a sort of shrunken novel, a distillation down to individual case studies. It is "more specialized, . . . more pointed, . . . more limited than the novel, it is 'microcosmic' so to speak."[9] When the critical mass of change, transition and loss became too much for writers to comprehend and to represent in a connected way, what did remain for them was the individual, the local, the episodic.[10] If they felt themselves forced to agree with the sentiment expressed in the last line of Hebbel's play, *Maria Magdalena*: "I don't understand the world anymore," they did at least think they still understood their street, their neighborhood, their village, their countryside, or, to some limited extent, themselves. These topics became the unpretentious targets for their pens.

Frequently shared traits in the abundant novella literature of this time are the tendencies toward liberalism and open-mindedness, crossed with a lust for didacticism. The fictional personae of strong women and weak men proliferated; this confrontation arises with varying definitions and

---

[7] In his novel trilogy, *Die Schlafwandler* (Zurich: Rhein-Verlag, 1931).

[8] Cf. Sengle, *op. cit.*, II, 840-841.

[9] Excerpted from Theodor Mundt, *Aesthetik: Die Idee der Schönheit und des Kunstwerks im Lichte unserer Zeit* (Leipzig, E. J. Gunther, 1845), p. 342. The translation is mine.

[10] Martini, *op. cit.*, pp. 481, 488.

degrees of "strong" and "weak" in almost every work presented here, but especially in *The Poor Fiddler* and *The Gemperlein Barons*. One oft-expressed mood that holds steady from the *Biedermeier* to the end of the century is the attitude of resigned melancholy: the novellas of Betty Paoli and Ferdinand von Saar share it despite their separation in time of six decades. Underlying the melancholic frame of mind, character exposition often reveals the common man to be in a state of repressed passion, struggling inwardly between having certain benefices in life – love, respect, peace of mind – and doing without them. The plot leading up to the resolution of that struggle is frequently set in a framed tale once removed from present-time narration.[11]

While the stages of narrative action are broad and varied – ranging from the Slavic provinces to the cosmopolitan streets of Vienna to the bleak Alpine heights – the motifs seldom hearken back to grand figures of history (with Pichler's early work again presenting the lone exception), perhaps because the intellectual focus was so concentrated on the crises of the moment that a preoccupation with history, after the revolution at least, seemed to be escapist if not downright reactionary. As a result of the shortened focal length, psychological novellas set in their own present time, often critical of contemporary institutions, became one pole of the accepted fictional norm. At the other pole, parallel to the first, were the village tale and its Jewish variant, the ghetto tale, both of which rose to prominence at this time. Having arisen from the heart of the folk, so to speak, such tales signified a democratization of literature and a growing rapprochement between the writer and that writer's public.

Those works in this volume that hail from the second half of the century embrace tales fashioned around such humble rallying points as a feather hat (Ada Christen, *Cathy's Feather Hat*), a pair of glasses (Ludwig Kompert, *Isaac's Glasses*), or a brown dachshund (Ferdinand von Saar, *Tambi*). Yet these outer analogues to an inner state – since the novella traditionally involves a single unprecedented occurrence represented or epitomized by a recognizable material object – function as narrative tools attempting to guide the reader towards an emotional insight, intellectual point, or even spiritual epiphany. Likewise, the motifs of murder (Friedrich Halm, *Marzipan-Lisa*), of adultery and alienated affections (Leopold von Sacher-Masoch, *Don Juan of Kolomyya*, and Karl Emil Franzos, *The Higher Law*), of suicide

---

[11] Martini, *op. cit.*, pp. 482-483.

(Ferdinand von Saar, *Tambi*), and of men of the cloth tempted by the flesh (Ludwig Anzengruber, *Love Child*, and Peter Rosegger, *Mary in Misery*) rise above the physical denominators of sex and violence, pointing the way to emotional, intellectual or spiritual values – even when these values may reduce down to resignation and acceptance.

Why These Particular Fourteen Prose Writers?

It is both the joy and the agony of an anthologist to decide which authors will be included in the collection and thus be deemed representative of their age (that's the joy) and which will be left out (that's the agony). Given space restraints and time limits, which novellas will best illustrate the diversity as well as unity of the past century? Which prose texts will best survive the outrage of translation into the foreign tongue of American English? Which criteria at the cusp of the Third Millennium serve to help us render qualitative judgments on literary images from yesteryear?

My deliberations were twofold: not only did I want to translate works that were recognized by critics to be artistic creations and that touched on universal human concerns, but I wanted them to be highly readable as well. They should be engaging on the simplest – even popular – level, all the while allowing for deeper registers of thought and reflection.

In this quest I was immeasurably aided by an author and fellow anthologist who was himself a Nobel Prize winner for literature in 1910, namely Paul Heyse. Though unavailable for personal consultation, Paul Heyse was a welcome guide to me. For forty years, from 1871 until the year he received the Nobel Prize, Heyse oversaw the publication of numerous editions of his *German Treasury of Novellas (Deutscher Novellenschatz)* and *New German Treasury of Novellas (Neuer deutscher Novellenschatz)*. These contained the finest novellas written in the German-speaking world, among them a good representation of Austrian prose fiction.

After reading and analyzing all of the Austrian works honored by inclusion in Heyse's anthology, I realized that the Prussian theoretician and author was extremely reliable as an arbiter of novella quality. Agreeing with most of his choices, I selected eight of the same works that he anthologized; the novellas of Grillparzer, Stifter, Halm, Sacher-Masoch, Franzos, Ebner-Eschenbach, Anzengruber and Rosegger.

Introduction 9

For tactical and practical reasons, I was unable to translate the specific works that Heyse selected for Kompert and Saar, but, knowing that these authors were important enough to be included, I chose alternate texts. In the case of Saar's *Tambi*, the choice seems particularly fortuitous and well-suited to a comparison with Grillparzer's *Poor Fiddler*.

The other four selections, by Pichler, Feuchtersleben, Paoli and Christen, were not found in Heyse's anthology, but help greatly, in my opinion, to illuminate the era. Caroline von Pichler offers a baseline of where Austrian literature had been at the first of the century, permitting a measurement of how it was to change, and how much. The work of Feuchtersleben, not arguably a novella or even totally recognizable as fiction, grants us a glimpse into the philosophical and cultural milieu of the *Biedermeier*. The novellas of Paoli and Christen, besides introducing women writers who have been forgotten and underappreciated up until now, open up vistas to world-weary society and grinding poverty, respectively, that expand our picture of what at least one scholar has called the "Austrian century."[12]

Each of these works serves as an individual scene or vignette capable of standing on its own, but also lends itself to accumulation with the others as a compendium of impressionistic fragments. Thus, the collection of short prose found here – of necessity limited – can be regarded in its entirety as a varietal exercise in literary pointillism. With colorful points and dots of nineteenth-century Austrian life presented on one canvas, we – the viewers of the scene, the mental filters through which the impressions must pass – can view a panorama of bygone Austrian life relatively clearly from the objective distance we enjoy.

Notes about the Translations

Many of these authors had a predilection to crafting extremely long sentences, reveling in phrases held together by series after series of commas, semi-colons, and hyphens. I have attempted to hold to the authors' word flow in order to retain their original energy and tone, though at times, where it appears not to detract from the intent or cadence, *e.g.*, where a semi-colon

---

[12] Hellmut Andics, *Das österreichische Jahrhundert: Die Donaumonarchie 1804-1918*. (Vienna: Molden, 1974).

in the original signifies not only the semantic equivalent of an English period but also allows for a lull in the ongoing rhythm, I've divided that sentence as deemed necessary for English usage. It should be equally clear, though, that certain of the sentences were retained in the splendor of their fullness.

Another literary device often found in these stories is the shift of verb tense in ways that make, at times, no grammatical sense, but which could give insight into artistic intent. For that reason, I have caused the English to shift tenses when the German original does the same: one good example for this can be found when Stifter's *Brigitta* narrator observes the sunset over the steppe with his host after his arrival at Uvar (p. 60), and we find ourselves suddenly transported to the present tense. Though idiomatic usage between German and English does not always match up neatly, I have tried to retain original imagery as closely as possible where word play is important.

There is a use of hyphens (--) or dashes (–) in certain of the original dialogues as a means of indicating the staccato cadence of incomplete phrases, and I've inserted ellipses (. . .) in their place where that seems to agree more with English usage. In other instances, particularly in rendering the unique style of Sacher-Masoch with its almost naturalistic telegram-style, it seemed proper to retain the dashes.

Acknowledgments

I wish to thank my dissertation advisor of almost a quarter-century ago, Professor Clifford A. Bernd of the University of California at Davis, for having kept in touch with me all these years, for having encouraged me to translate these works, and for his constant support and advice throughout the selection, translation, and editing process.

My working relationship with Richard H. Lawson, Jorun B. Johns, and the rest of the editorial staff at Ariadne Press was smooth and rewarding. Heidi Hutchinson of the U.C. Riverside library has been through the same process herself, and was able to give me inside tips.

My supervisors at Brigham Young University, Susan Fales and Julene Butler, were generous and understanding in allowing me time and materials to complete this anthology.

Colleagues from Vienna to Los Angeles assisted in filling needs that arose as I translated various of these prose works, needs ranging from procurement of rare texts and insights into authors' motives (and motifs) to the explanation of arcane allusions that needed to be footnoted. These colleagues are acknowledged in the respective prefaces.

Marianne Siegmund – who, having left Pfaffenberg and the wild strawberries of the Traun meadows behind her, one day became my wife – was a help and an inspiration with suggestions and loving support. Thanks also to my children – Kristin, Lisa, Michael, and Juliana – for their interest and their love.

Thanks are due and gratitude is given.

Richard Hacken
Provo, Utah
May 15, 1999

Caroline von Pichler

There were few literary phenomena on the Viennese cultural scene in the first decades of the century more conspicuous than **Caroline von Pichler, née von Greiner (1769-1843)**. Even before her marriage in 1796 to the government counselor Andreas Pichler, she had been raised in well-connected Viennese circles, educated in the best Josephinian[1] spirit of enlightenment, and had taken music lessons from both Mozart and Haydn; at the time of her marriage she was considered one of the premiere piano virtuosi of Vienna. Today her portrait peers down from its prominent place on the wall at the Vienna Historical Museum, a statuesque lady dressed in a blue silk dress and a fashionable red turban.[2]

She is best known for having sponsored and conducted for decades the most important Austrian literary salon of the day, all made possible through her own family contacts and cultural acumen: it was frequented by such figures as Beethoven, Schubert, and Grillparzer. Metternich[3] is said to have used von Pichler as an informant through her salon contacts, and, through her writings, as a solicitor for cultural policies that favored the patriotic Austrian cause he espoused. As a consequence – but also in accordance with her own well-delineated attitudes – Pichler's literary efforts are based on Catholic and Holy Roman/Habsburg Imperial models that trump and overshadow ancient classical motifs.

---

[1] During the reign of Joseph II (1741-1790), who was emperor of the Holy Roman Empire from 1765 on as co-regent with his mother, Maria Theresia, and also emperor of the Habsburg realm after her death in 1780 until his own in 1790; a brother of the ill-fated French queen, Marie Antoinette.

[2] Cf. Walther Killy, *Literatur-Lexikon. Autoren und Werke deutscher Sprache*, vol. IX (Gütersloh: Bertelsmann, 1991), pp. 161-162. This encyclopedia of German-language authors has been consulted, and in some cases paraphrased in English, for other of the prefaces as well.

[3] Prince Klemens Wenzel Nepomuk Lothar von Metternich (1773-1859) was the central Austrian diplomat of the age and the most influential European statesman of the early nineteenth century.

The basic idea behind ***The Love of Charlemagne's[4] Youth*** was taken from *Sei Giornate* (*Six Days*), a prose work written in 1567 by the Italian Renaissance writer Sebastiano Erizzo (1525-1585). Though the original plot was sketched out in only two pages of text, Pichler expanded upon the concept and embellished the surrounding legend in a manner that clearly owes nothing to empirical reality but is squarely set in a narrative frame of imperial royalty. Her self-proclaimed goal in this historical novella – as in other, multivolume historical novels featuring the Holy Roman and Habsburg empires – was to make Austrians aware and proud of their fatherland and its institutions, its Christian and patriotic literature, its scholars and their accomplishments,[5] a goal that was largely successful.

This novella owes its atmosphere to certain favorite genres and themes of the late Romantic literary movement as well. The realms of fairy tale and legend are mixed with Medieval chivalry, with uncontrollable effusions of emotion, with dark forests and even darker mysteries punctuated by the forces of darkness and black magic. The narrative style owes very little to dialogue and very much to extended and flowery description. The resultant literary ambience serves as a backdrop from which the author wished Christian enlightenment and patriotic enthusiasm to shine forth, especially in contrast to the humiliations of the recently endured Napoleonic wars.

---

[4] Charlemagne (742-814) was king of the Franks and later king of the Lombards as well, having united nearly all the Christian realms of Europe with his conquests, and he ruled as emperor from 800-814. The Holy Roman Empire he formed was the first German *Reich* and included what was to become the Habsburg realm as well, but Charlemagne was also considered a founder of the French nation. Numerous legends sprang up around his personality immediately upon his death.

[5] As paraphrased in translation from *The Love of Fatherland* [*Über Vaterlandsliebe*], taken from Pichler's *Contemporary Images* [*Zeitbilder*], 1839, vol.1, p. 315.

THE LOVE OF CHARLEMAGNE'S YOUTH

Caroline von Pichler

Old stories, minstrels of early days, even monuments and ruins from earlier centuries tell us of the special love that Charlemagne felt for the city of Aachen.[6] It was his favorite residence. From thence it was that he traveled throughout the widely scattered empire whose boundaries his victories had pushed out to the far reaches. It was thither he returned from glorious battle campaigns and enjoyed the pleasures of a short rest in the bosom of his family and with learned and well-versed[7] men of his age between the strenuous activities of a military life. There also his bones are laid to rest, there his imperial vestments and gems were stored for long centuries, there many of his successors received the German crown; and Aachen, the old imperial residence and city of royal coronations, has remained standing to our day, a dignified memorial of olden times, a representative of the German Empire[8] in a way; and Charlemagne's spirit seems to float over it, extolling it still.

Later generations were well aware of the great emperor's fondness for this locale, a town otherwise blessed with no conspicuous attractions.

---

[6] The city of Aachen (French: *Aix-la-Chapelle*), located in present day Germany near the intersection of the Belgian and Dutch borders, became, after Charlemagne, the coronation city of German kings for centuries (936-1531).

[7] The German term is literally "knowledgeable in songs" and refers to those who were well "versed" in the minstrel songs of the Middle Ages through which legends and historical lore were preserved and passed down to later generations. It's not inconceivable that Charlemagne was interested in the propagation of his own lore through glowing reports from such Medieval public relations agents.

[8] That is, the Holy Roman Empire of the German Nation, which included Austria.

The Love of Charlemagne's Youth   15

It's easy to understand that the Roman baths, known from ancient times and used even up to our own day, could not have been the only reason, since the robust war hero didn't need to seek out healing for his body or invigoration for his mind from those beneficial waters in the course of his campaigns, military marches and far-flung travels, given the simple way of life back then. The emperor's love stemmed from completely different causes, and there were secret and marvelous bonds that drew him so firmly to this place.

Childeric, the last king of the Merovingian dynasty,[9] had been deposed by the approbation of God and by the immeasurably increasing power of his palace mayor[10] Charles Martel; the empire had been wrested away from him and his sons and given over to Martel's own sons Pepin and Carloman,[11] who, with a strong hand, were able to keep not only the Franks in a state of obedience and order, but also the German dukes who reluctantly endured the sovereign rule of former servants of the dynasty.

Carloman renounced the throne soon after and retired to the solitude of Monte Cassino,[12] where he was to live and die as a Benedictine monk; Pepin continued to administer the widely scattered empire with insight and power, watching with joy as his youthful son developed and justified the grandest hopes he had for him.

Then suddenly the Holy Father[13] himself appeared in France to plead with the pious and powerful king of the Franks for protection and help against Aistulf, king of the Lombards, who was laying heavy siege on the Holy See[14] from his stronghold in Pavia[15] and clearly revealing his intentions – after having already torn many a nice possession away from the inheritance

---

[9] A dynasty established by Clovis, of the Frankish line, that ruled over Gaul and Germany from 476 to 751.

[10] Palatine, or important palace official, in this case a hereditary position.

[11] This occurred in the year 750. Pepin III, younger of the two brothers, also known as Pepin the Short, was the father of Charlemagne.

[12] A monastery founded by St. Benedict in the early sixth century A.D. at Cassino, Italy. It was destroyed by Allied bombs in 1944.

[13] The Roman Catholic pope.

[14] The papal dominions.

[15] A city in northern Italy, located in the area still known as Lombardy.

of Peter[16] – of now taking the rest of it into his power, along with Rome itself. Pepin received the Holy Father with all the joy and respect that such a visit deserves, did not need to be asked a second time to enter the fray as a protective steward to the besieged church, and armed himself with all the resources of his extensive empire for battle against the savage king of the Lombards. Charles,[17] in his youthful courage, rejoiced at the opportunity to test his swordsmanship and show his distinguished father that he knew how to use it in serious battle, not just for play and show at tournaments.

When Aistulf heard of Pepin's war preparations against him, he dreaded the thought of measuring his own might against the powerful king of the Franks. He had Carloman called in from Monte Cassino and asked him to go to France, intervene as an emissary for peace, and offer Aistulf's only daughter, beautiful Florabella – the reputation of whose charms had resounded throughout the entire known world of the day and for whom many hundreds of lances had already been broken – as a bride to Pepin's son Charles and as a pledge of peace.

It was with this mission that Carloman had left Pavia. He had been forced to swear allegiance to the king whose subject he had become; but his heart was far from this mission, and he considered a union between Florabella and his nephew to be an abomination. Yet out of monastic duty he had quickly passed the message along, had even counseled and requested it as if his mind were completely in accord with Aistulf's thoughts. But when he saw that his brother was firm and could not be swayed from his plans, when he heard young Charles' expression that he had no wish at all to be united with the proud Lombard woman, when he had fulfilled all the requirements of his promise and his conscience, then he joyfully took his brother and his nephew in his arms, thanked them for their courage and their loyalty to the Holy Father, and returned to his cloister cell in Italy.

Pepin moved across the Alps and his son accompanied him. They laid siege to Pavia. At the time Charles was still very much a blossoming youth, full of exuberance and anxious to do battle, his mind on nothing but the

---

[16] That is to say, stolen from the papal state. At this time, and well into the first centuries of the Holy Roman Empire, the papacy and the empire, the two strongest powers of the Middle Ages, were closely allied with each other.

[17] In references to Charlemagne during his youthful years, he will be referred to as "Charles," since he had not yet earned the title that means "Charles the Great," or *Carolus Magnus* in its official Latin form.

deeds and fame his weapons could earn him, and gentler inclinations had not yet found their way to his heart. Now, as the siege was proceeding slowly due to the courageous resistance of those besieged, the royal youth went roaming in the surrounding region, sometimes on battle maneuvers, sometimes just for pleasure or hunting.

On one of these outings, when he had distanced himself quite far from the army accompanied only by a weapons bearer, he came upon a number of the enemy and, in his exuberant thirst for battle, challenged them to fight despite the warnings of his weapons bearer. Contemptuously the leader of the group listened to the challenge of the lone warrior, thinking to silence him or send him to eternal rest for his audacity. But things turned out differently: Charles guided his strokes with such force and, at the same time, with such calm calculation that a very serious battle grew out of what the others had taken to be a simple joke. Finally most of the enemy were vanquished, but Charles had grown so exhausted and weak from several wounds that he still would have been lost if it hadn't been for the message of some of his own people who had seen the odd battle from afar, hurried back to the Frankish camp to bring him help – full of respect and sympathy for the heroic warrior – and if a small troop of his people had not hurried out to assist him just in time, just as he was defending himself with his last gasp of strength, threatening to fall from his horse. At the appearance of the Frankish squadron the foreigners took flight, and the rescuers recognized with horror and wonderment that the unknown heroic knight was the son of their king.

But there was no possibility of returning to the rather distant camp with the exhausted youth. Fortunately a small villa revealed itself, half hidden behind olive trees in the bottom of a valley not too far from there, under whose peaceful roof perhaps could be found hospitality and rest for the wounded prince. The Franks braided a stretcher out of branches, laid the prince on it and slowly walked towards the house. An elderly female doorkeeper opened the tightly locked door, but she shrugged her shoulders at the mention of taking in a wounded knight in a house that was only occupied in monastic seclusion by a widowed noblewoman and her daughters. The name of the royal Frankish son made her stop short; she hurried off to call her mistress. An elderly, dignified lady appeared, the gates were immediately thrown open, and everyone rushed to receive the son of the prince who had filled the entire western world with his fame and now had drawn his sword in the cause of the besieged church.

Charles was laid on a luxurious bed and a young woman was summoned, one well experienced in treating wounds. The door opened. Two noble-appearing women stepped into the room, each of whom was already beyond the first blossom of youth. Dark hair and eyes, proud and noble figures and an unmistakable similarity with the features of the matron showed at first glance that these were the daughters of the lady of the house; the cut and types of clothing also pointed to southern European customs and a high standing. But they were followed by a third figure in a white nun's habit, veiled in white, carrying linen and boxes of healing salves. She approached with hesitant steps; the matron asked her to take up her post and to lift the veil which would hinder her in carrying out her duties. She did so without saying a word, and the young knight caught sight of a woman's deathly pale but infinitely beautiful face, delicate and blue-eyed, serious and gentle at the same time: he thought he'd never before seen anything so lovely, so touching. A bright crimson spread across his cheeks, his eyes were riveted on her quiet, serious features, but the nun appeared to notice none of it. Her eyes noticeably avoided meeting those of the patient, and a quiet tremble passed through her hands as she examined and bound his wounds: they were certainly numerous, but so insignificant that only loss of blood and the exertions of battle could have brought on his exhaustion.

She still hadn't spoken a word and was just carrying out her work grimly and busily. Now, however, once she was finished, one of the ladies asked her how things stood with the prince.

"He's in no danger," she said coldly and in a tone that seemed to be characterized more by annoyance than by pleasure: "The son of Pepin will be able to return to camp in a couple of days." With these words she turned, dropped her veil, gathered her utensils together, and left the room.

Charles felt irritated at the cold displeasure with which he found himself treated by a person he had never seen before and therefore could not have insulted. He felt the affront all the deeper since this person had won his tenderest sympathies in the first few moments by the paleness and silent worry in her features as well as by the charming impression of her entire manner. Her image was constantly before him; it was the first time that a woman had made an impression on his heart, and it was partly her beauty, partly her cold pride that occupied his mind unceasingly. Also her phrase, "the son of Pepin," reverberated in his soul strangely, as if spoken contemptuously. To no avail did the lady of the house and her daughters try to distract their distinguished guest through conversations, lute playing, or songs; the only thing on his mind was the nun and her behavior, and at last he couldn't help from asking who the monastically dressed girl was, and whether she was of southern European origins and a relative of the family with her blue eyes and light skin?

Marozia, such was the name of the matron, looked at the prince dubiously and was quiet for a moment. Then she said: "You're not wrong, gracious Sir! Engelberta is not from here; she is from Frankish territory and of very noble blood; she has been entrusted by her relatives to me for her education."

"Engelberta?" Charles repeated to himself and thought: "She is perhaps an angel[18] when it comes to the way she looks and to her helpful service, but not when it comes to sympathy and delicacy of feelings." Yet the name seemed familiar to him, and bit by bit all sorts of half-erased ideas and memories came together. Childeric had fathered not only a son, who was exiled to the cloister with him, but a very young daughter as well, about whom no further thoughts had been made and whose traces had been lost. It seemed more and more likely to him, the more he thought about it, that this daughter's name had been Engelberta. "Oh God!" he thought: "If this pale young woman turns out to be Childeric's daughter — and so unhappy, suffering so much because of my father and me! And if she hates me because of that — and yet she was required to take care of me as a practice of childlike obedience and Christian love!"

These thoughts wouldn't leave him for the rest of the day; they agitated his innermost soul, they brought his blood to a fever pitch, they chased the sleep from his eyes. When Marozia came into his room early the next morning, she found him noticeably worse and quickly sent for the healing young woman.

Engelberta came just as hesitantly, just as silently as the day before. She approached the bed, cast her veil aside, and today Charles found the unmistakable similarity of her features with those of the Frankish royal house, not without consternation, something he hadn't observed the day before. Marozia made her aware of the worsened condition of the patient. She appeared not to believe it, yet she wanted to start unwrapping the dressing. "Don't bother!" said Charles while respectfully but earnestly pushing her hand away: "Make no further efforts, noble young woman! I feel that things are worse with me, but the camp of my father is not so far, and it won't

---

[18] *Engel*, the German word forming the first part of her given name, means "angel."

cost me my life to be taken there." Now Engelberta lifted her large blue eyes; her gaze met that of the patient for the first time. She blushed; she quickly cast her eyes down at the floor again, and confused, quaking, she said: "Please permit me, Sir Knight, to look after your wounds first, lest you make a decision that could perhaps be dangerous for you!" – Once again Charles wanted to prevent her, once again she lifted her blue eyes up to him, but this time with such a beseeching expression that he let his raised hand fall back down, and, turning away with a sigh, he let her examine him.

She found his wounds visibly worsened; a tender stirring of sympathy moistened her blue eyes and her hand trembled for the pain she must be causing him as she bound up his wounds. The voice with which she answered the matron, who asked her about the condition of the prince, betrayed her inner emotions. Charles turned to her: "And do you have so much as a trace of feeling for me in your heart?" Engelberta broke out in tears. Charles, beside himself, reached for the beneficent hand that had touched him so protectively, their eyes met, and Engelberta forgot that she was standing in front of the son of her family's enemy. "You don't hate me?" he asked once again. Engelberta looked at him with her faithful blue eyes. – He never asked her again.

In a short time the young hearts had found each other, had come to an understanding, and, before the few days of Charles' recovery were over, had made wordless declarations. Engelberta came to love the son of her enemy and in Charles the thought had ignited vividly and joyfully of offering her his hand, lifting Childeric's daughter to the throne of her ancestors, and thus partially making restitution for the injustice that his heart could not overlook in the dealings of his father.

He was restored to health; he had to leave the house of hospitality and return to his father in camp. Engelberta trembled at the thought of separation; Charles feared it less for he saw in it the means of explaining things to his father and winning him over to his wishes, in whose fulfillment his youthful courage had no doubts. In the wistful hour of separation he told as much to Engelberta. He urged her to delay taking on the monastic veil she had earlier decided upon . . . until he could report back to her on the success of his discussion with Pepin. He swore eternal faithfulness to her and received the same sacred assurances from her. And so they parted, Engelberta mourning and with little hope for improving her life, long since given over to pain and self-denial; Charles full of cheerful courage and with the sacred promise to see her again soon.

His father received him joyfully and with a feeling of pride for his brave son; yet he didn't forget to add a few serious admonitions about the excessive boldness of the undertaking. The siege had meanwhile progressed significantly: everything was in lively motion, and the arrival of the knightly prince, the favorite of all the army, gave renewed fire to the souls of the warriors. Pepin had every reason to hope for attaining his goal of humiliating proud Aistulf. Charles saw him in this good mood and he risked unburdening himself of his love and his wishes. But Pepin's brow darkened at the very name of his enemy's daughter. He became violently angry when his son told him that he had pledged faithfulness to her, and he forbade him with a curse to even think of this love, indeed he made it unmistakably clear that Engelberta's fate would depend on his obedience.

The youth's love remained unshaken. In the presence of his father he didn't mention a word of what had transpired; nor could his father, in fact, discover any trace of the relationship continuing. Nevertheless, Charles continued to see the young woman in secret from time to time; but he spared her delicate emotions from the full weight of the danger threatening them. He only let her fear a slight resistance on the king's part, one that could soon be overcome, and he still hoped with silent courage and faithful patience to attain his goal at last.

But if his hidden love could escape the eyes of the king and warlord, it wasn't secret enough to escape the eyes of jealousy. Lovely Florabella, Aistulf's proud daughter, had, with furious rage, taken note of Pepin's refusal and of the fact that Charles, in agreement with his father, had rejected a marriage alliance with her – for whose hand and love so many noble knights of the Occident and Orient would have gladly served all the days of their lives and would have vied with blood and honor. She swore bitter hatred to the king of the Franks and even more to his proud son, challenging the knights who were serving her – without hope of earning her love, and yet faithfully – to take revenge against the unworthy wretch for having heaped disgrace upon her beauty.

Thus had matters stood until Pepin and Charles appeared with their army outside Pavia. The Frankish prince had already fought many a skirmish with the knights of proud Florabella and had tilted many of them into the sand without a single one of them having succeeded in making him feel the superiority of Florabella's charms. Finally, when the army of the Franks had drawn up in front of the city and their knights were leaping to and fro before the ranks of foot soldiers, curiosity and a thirst for vengeance lured

Florabella and her ladies onto the city wall to observe the enemy squadrons from afar. At her side she had the old man Catenides, a Greek by birth, the tutor of her youth in all the sciences and arts of this civilized nation, having been sent by the Byzantine Emperor to Aistulf for precisely that purpose and used by the latter, besides for the education of his only daughter, in all sorts of important affairs due to his experience and political shrewdness. Thus Catenides had also been in Paris with the emissaries of the Lombards and had come to be acquainted with the court of Pepin, the knights, the princes, their customs, and their war fame; learning half with regret of their dubious crudeness, half with fear of so much power and simple virtue. This man now accompanied the princess and had to name at her request those of the battle princes and other knights he knew.

Twice already, one of the youngest knights – through whose opened helmet visor peered a face full of youthful exuberance, knightly valor, and faithfulness – had attracted their attention, twice already she had asked the old man, and each time the latter had appeared not to hear her question. Florabella became impatient. She asked the question one more time, and in a tone that let the old man know he mustn't let it pass unnoticed again. So he bowed deeply and said : "You command it, noble lady! Very well, then, you shall be told! The young knight whose noble figure and chivalrous conduct appears to please you so much is none other than the son of the Frankish king himself, *Carolus*, or Charles in your tongue."

Florabella went pale, and a glowing crimson immediately covered her face. So this was the son of her enemy, the lone man among all his generation who dared to give scant regard to her charms and to reject a possession for which others, rejoicing a thousand times over, would have risked their very lives? From then on her eyes, as if enchanted, followed each movement of the young prince, and the resolve grew ever brighter and clearer in her soul: He is to become mine.

No sooner had all those small events transpired, no sooner had Florabella learned that Charles was back in his camp than she was able to send a clever and trusted slave past the guards into the enemy camp to bring the Frankish royal son news of the victory which he had unknowingly gained over the heart of his enemy, of his good fortune, and of cheerful hopes. But Charles listened to him untouched; indeed, it required all the courteous consideration he could muster – as was the knight's duty to every lady, even unknown ones – not to erupt in annoyance when the entrusted slave handed him Florabella's picture and he saw what voluptuous, passionate charms he was expected to receive in exchange for the quiet, reverent image that lived in his heart.

Florabella began to glow with rage and shame when the slave brought back to her a respectful but ice-cold greeting along with her returned portrait. But there was too much love in this surge of blood for it not to master the shame and rage and impel her to make new attempts. She was able to bring her father to the point of sending yet another message of conciliation with even more advantageous conditions to the camp of the Franks; and since precisely at that time news had come to Pepin that the Wends[19] and the Saxons[20] were in uneasy movement at the borders of his empire, the feeling in Pavia was that these circumstances should motivate the king to give a favorable reply.

In actuality it appeared as if Pepin would not have been opposed to entering into talks; but Charles declared firmly and definitely that he would never give his hand to Florabella; he was ready to fight his father's battles with his blood, with his life, but never to submit to being a tool and pawn of a treaty that he could not approve and that would never bring honor to his father and himself. Charles' refusal was supported by a legation that came from Rome counseling the king not to enter into peace talks with an enemy of the church. Pepin found the courage to exhibit new resistance; Aistulf's petitions were denied, and the siege efforts that had been suspended for a few days began with renewed energy.

Florabella had scouts too talented everywhere, in the Frankish camp as well as in the region round about, for her not to learn that Charles' defiant refusal had been the main cause for the renewal of hostilities. She quickly also learned from whence this youth's coldness towards her, something incomprehensible to her vanity, actually stemmed. She learned of his secret love for beautiful Engelberta; and injured pride, jealousy, and vengeance agitated her heart into a state of wild ferment. She now recognized that there was no hope for the normal course of events, and she decided to risk everything, even the most unnatural and horrifying measures, to obtain satisfaction for her love and her wounded pride.

---

[19] A Slavic tribe from the east of Germanic lands, also called Sorbs.

[20] A Germanic people that lived near the mouth of the Elbe in ancient times and after invading Britain became part of the hyphenated phrase Anglo-Saxon.

Pepin, who knew the true reason for his son's refusal just as well as Florabella did, but, taking Florabella in consideration, hadn't asked for his obedience, did threaten him anew with the harshest of treatments and even a paternal curse if he didn't give up his foolish love for the daughter of deceased Childeric. The proud king of the Franks had either not been in love in his youth or had already forgotten how he had felt at the time. Charles' affections for the unfortunate young woman who bore her own misfortune and that of her family with so much dignity and reverent humility, who had been drawn by her tender sympathies to her bitterest enemy, and whose heart had been won over by his virtues, could not be banished by the king's threats and oaths. Rather, those affections continued to glow quietly and to grow stronger after each such storm with which Pepin thought to tear them out by their roots.

More secretively, less often than before, but all the more longingly and tenderly did Charles see his Engelberta. The lonely country house under the olive trees was the kingdom of heaven for him, and every surreptitious hour that he spent at Engelberta's side, happy to the very depths of his soul in demure and delicate discussions of their reciprocal love, seemed to him a foretaste of those joys awaiting him some day in the angelic choirs.

A battle mission, for which his father needed him and which he wouldn't have wanted to avoid at any price, kept him away from camp and from his love for many days. But he returned, gave his father a report to the latter's complete satisfaction, and hurried off to the little olive orchard as soon as it was possible. He had reached it; he dismounted from his horse and gave it to the squire[21] who always accompanied him. At the place in the woods where Engelberta had always come to meet him before . . . was no one. He went on; nobody was there to greet him. Even when the house itself was showing through the nearby shrubbery, there was still no Engelberta to be seen. An anxious premonition that his beloved could be ill gripped the youth's heart. The gate was locked; he knocked, the old female porter appeared: her gloomy mien signaled nothing good. Charles blanched as he saw her. "Where is the girl? What's wrong with Engelberta?" he asked quickly. The old woman silently shrugged her shoulders and directed him to her ladies, who were gathered together, sitting in the front room. Engelberta was not among them, and Marozia stood up when she saw the Frankish royal son,

---

[21] A knight's assistant, a young apprentice learning the knightly ways but also assisting with armor, weaponry, etc., even accompanying the knight into battle.

The Love of Charlemagne's Youth 25

went towards him with a gloomy manner, and said: "Merciful Sir! I know why you have come; I know what you're looking for, but Engelberta is no longer with us." Charles stepped back in consternation. "And where is she? Why is she gone from here?" Now the matron broke down in tears and both her daughters began weeping as well. "For the sake of the Savior, noble lady, what has happened? How could Engelberta leave you, leave me?" asked the deathly pale youth, holding on to the doorpost, quaking.

Marozia had gathered her wits; the daughters crowded in around her. After some questions and explanations, Charles finally learned that Engelberta, while taking an evening walk through the olive orchard some days before, as was her custom, had not returned; and country folk from the area had said that they had seen several well-armed riders in unrecognizable sets of armor dashing through the woods that same night. One of them was holding a thickly veiled woman in front of him on the horse, and she seemed to be struggling in his arms.

Engelberta was abducted. By whom? Nobody knew. Charles' first suspicions fell on his father. He didn't say a thing about it, but after a hollow silence he suddenly arose, offered Marozia his trembling right hand, and said: "I'll bring Engelberta back to you or at least news of her, so help me God!" He turned around and quickly left the house. Then he swung up on his horse and rode to camp while continually trying to force back his tears. The more he thought about the matter, the less likely it appeared that his father's hand had been involved. He had known about this love for a long time! He could have resorted to other less violent, less unchivalrous measures a long time ago if he thought he had to fear Engelberta's presence that much! But if his father was not the one who had her stolen away, his thoughts stood totally still, and he didn't know what to think.

Having arrived at camp, his first path was to Pepin; and with the humility of a son – but with the valor of a knight and the fear of a loving heart – he asked him directly whether he had found it necessary to have Engelberta abducted. Pepin's astonishment, his rising indignation, and in fact a stirring of sympathy for the fate of the unfortunate princess which Charles thought he saw arising from the midst of the grim statements of his father, immediately disarmed the suspicions he had been nurturing at first. As he held out his right hand to his father and said: "If you are innocent of the abduction of the unfortunate woman, then shake on it," and Pepin shook his hand without guile, the youth fell weeping at his father's feet, begged forgiveness for his suspicions and his bold interrogation, and wept at the heart of his father, who lovingly embraced his mourning child and lifted him up in his arms.

Pepin himself gave the strictest orders that he wanted the abductor of the young Frankish woman to be found, for as far as his army camp extended and wherever Frankish guards were standing watch, innocence should be safe and feminine honor should be secure.

Three anxious days passed. Charles was everywhere. No bush, no house remained unsearched. On the fourth morning some knights and squires returned with news they thought could shed some light on the disappearance of the young woman.

Quite far from Pavia, concealed by a thicket in the woods, was a cave overgrown with moss, ivy, and shrubbery, the lair for poisonous snakes and grisly nocturnal fowl of all descriptions; hikers who might have otherwise sought protection in its cool darkness from the hot afternoon rays of the sun had been scared off by hissing sounds and a terrible beating of wings. Nobody neared this grotto anymore; as long as anyone could remember, in fact, every traveler had avoided even coming near it, for a horrifying aura surrounded it and all manner of awful creatures confronted whoever was careless enough to approach it, punishing such bold curiosity. Legend had it that a terrible witch pursued her nefarious trade in the murky bowels of the cave, and that she prepared slow-acting lethal poisons, love potions, or other terrible and irreversible magic concoctions from the blood and hair locks of murdered children or young people that she was somehow able to bring under her spell. Mutilated bodies and traces of blood were sometimes found; but, in order to bring to justice the criminal who housed there, the punishing arm of the law had never dared venture to the center of her lair, defended as it was by the powers of hell.

Not far from this cave, Charles' knights had come upon the corpse of a magnificently beautiful young woman dressed in a nun's habit. Her long blonde hair had been cut off on one side; in her bosom, right above the heart, was the death wound; and her delicate wrists bore the marks of chains. The knights brought back the body and Charles threw himself across it in excruciating pain, for it was Engelberta. Pepin rushed to his side as well, full of sympathy, and the field marshals of his army stood around the group in respectful silence, honoring with their sadness the pain of their beloved lord. Then Engelberta's beautiful corpse was lifted up, laid on a magnificent bed in accordance with her high birth, surrounded by burning candles and the fervent prayers of priests; and on the next day she was interred with full ceremonies in the church at the nearest cloister.

Charles had followed the corpse in dull anguish, and only with some effort could his father persuade him to leave the crypt in which the dearest thing to him on earth was resting, now to be hidden from his view forever. But scarcely had he arrived back in camp than a new, incomprehensible emotion stirred in his heart. A fierce longing gripped him and drew him to the walls of Pavia. There — there, he thought, must dwell the bliss of his life! It was there he was drawn with an inexpressible and totally miraculous power!

He didn't understand himself, and if an illusion had been possible in the clear light of day, he would have thought some deceiver was tricking him and that Engelberta was still alive and living in Pavia, for that was where the power of love was pulling him. Two days passed in such baffling suspense with only the activities of camp, the battles and dangers of besieging and storming the walls, able to relieve a portion of the painful effect it had on the prince. But on the third day, as he was sitting in his tent deep in thought about this mysterious yearning . . . he suddenly sees something shining on the ground in front of him.[22] It is the portrait of a very beautiful woman. He looks at it more closely; it is Florabella's picture that he'd already had in his hands once before, and which, as he thought, he'd already returned to its owner. All at once it leapt into his soul like a hot flame. It became clear to him; he understood himself completely. This was the object to which his incomprehensible yearnings were drawing him, the quintessence of all his desires, the goal of all his efforts. He loved Florabella, the image source for the portrait he held in his hand, and he had to go to her, see her, declare his passion to her, or die.

When the first storm of intoxicated feeling had passed, he stood there grimly sunken in thought, bitterly reproaching himself for his capriciousness of heart, for having betrayed the memory of his beloved – now scarcely cold – and he punished himself with the severest of accusations. But oh, Engelberta was still precious to him; his old love was mixing miraculously with his yearning for the newly beloved, and both Florabella and Engelberta melted together in his bewitched mind to become one incomprehensible whole!

---

[22] This sudden leap to the present tense reflects Pichler's original wording.

Humiliated and reluctant, he deeply hid the shame of his vacillating heart from every human eye and ear. No one, no one was to know what had transpired within his breast and how damnably fast the tenderest love for his quiet angel had transformed into a consuming passion for a creature to whom he had once been more than indifferent and whom he had even found repulsive. He was a puzzle and an abomination to himself, but he could not resist the torrid urge that drew him to Florabella.

Pavia, meanwhile, found itself more beleaguered with each passing day; and Aistulf, no longer able to entertain hopes of help or replacements, whose warriors became less in number with each battle – even as the foodstuffs were diminishing and hunger and epidemics began to rage – finally decided to accept Pepin's hard conditions and to hand back everything he had taken from the Holy Father. The king of the Franks had never asked anything for himself. So with joy he agreed to the proposals of the Lombardic emissaries: the treaty was signed, the gates of the city were thrown open, and Aistulf himself, accompanied by beautiful Florabella and many luminaries of his court, paraded out to the Frankish camp in royal splendor to welcome his vanquisher.

Charles caught sight of the object of his passion; he flew to her, paying no heed to the courtly protocols, and Florabella, who had long burned with passion for the son of her enemy, let him know by the looks she gave and the words she spoke that this was no unresponsive woman he loved.

Now both of them had attained what they seemed to have craved so fiercely. But the joy expressed itself in a totally different form in Florabella's than in Charles' heart.

If the satisfaction of long-nourished desires filled Florabella with a joyful sense of composure and even pride, if she could now rest at the goal of her long struggle with the feeling of assuredness and even high spirits, a painful disquietude was tormenting her unhappy lover. An incomprehensible longing was drawing him to Florabella whenever he couldn't see her; a much more understandable indifference or even a form of repulsion frightened him away from any closer intimacy, from any effusions of the heart when he was in her presence. It was no sweet harmony of connected souls; it was no gentle inclination of close and loving hearts, no tender understanding of the deepest and quietest, wordless emotions, as it had been with Engelberta. A consuming passion was blazing inside him, expressing itself through intoxicated stares that held him inescapably near the passionately cherished object; but no satisfaction followed this desire: no look, no tone of voice, no vocal expression of either beloved and passionately loving creature corresponded to what the other had expected. Charles reacted to it with a harrowing aversion to himself. Remorse at his changeability and a somber, secret feeling – repressed and hidden, drawing him with doleful power to the memory of his deceased beloved – split his soul into a number of contentious power factions that battled among themselves.

Florabella, triumphant at having finally defeated the proud opponent and at holding him in her bonds, now sought through her father to arrange for a solemn bond of marriage to chain the beloved to her before all the world, inextricably, and to secure for herself with his hand the crown of the Frankish queens. But Pepin would have nothing to do with it, having been extremely upset at the quickly altered mind-set of his son. Aistulf and his daughter, the conduct of the Lombardic court during the whole time, the customs of the Southern Europeans in general, were totally at odds with him, and what he had not accepted before out of respect for the Holy See he now rejected from his own distaste. Indeed, he broke camp and left Pavia soon after, hoping that an attraction that had come about so quickly and unexpectedly would now just as quickly disappear with time and distance. But he hadn't reckoned on the manner of this love and the astuteness of the beloved woman. Charles felt, or indeed knew for certain, that he couldn't live without Florabella, and she had put her mind to nothing less than still attaining her desired goal someday – Charles' hand and crown.

So she instructed the youth, who was new at such arts, what he should do. Without contradiction he followed his father and the army. Not one complaint seemed to show regret at the separation; but at the end of the third day a cute little Moorish boy found his way among the supply carriers of the army. His friendliness, his adroitness soon recommended him everywhere. Charles heard of it and immediately took him into his services. Florabella followed her beloved to Germany in this disguise and was able to shunt aside the suspicions of Pepin and the rest of the observant courtly retinue with a thousand tricks and schemes. When she had arrived in Aachen, Charles took her into the house of a noblewoman devoted to him. There she put on her normal clothing again, befitting her gender and rank, and the peculiar love bond continued for a while as it had begun outside Pavia.

But not for long was Florabella able to rejoice in her laboriously earned advantage. She started to become ill; she began to wilt visibly away without anyone being able to find an actual cause for this malady. Charles, in utmost despair, ascribed it to the tribulations of travel and to the unaccustomed, harsh climate that had a destructive effect on the weak Mediterranean constitution. All his pain, all the medicinal aids that were applied, all the best attention and tender care were not sufficient to stem the inexorably draining away of this life. The complaints of unhappy Florabella – who saw herself fading toward death at the height of her youth and beauty – violently repulsed devout Charles from her, as did her blasphemous attitudes and her violent mood swings between unchristian despair and then furious accusations directed at her Creator. On the other hand, though, an inexplicable attraction still held him firmly to the withered, almost charmless beloved. Finally death took mercy on his torment and her suffering.

Florabella died, but even her pallor couldn't loose the bonds of this powerful love. Charles remained just as single-mindedly attached to the lifeless remains as he had formerly embraced the living woman. He had the corpse embalmed with the most precious spices, decorated with royal jewels, and sat at the open coffin day and night. He didn't want to allow her to be buried and wouldn't allow himself to be separated from the corpse by any persuasions, not even at the strict command of his father, who had finally been made aware of the raging passion and foolish actions of his son. Pepin himself then appeared in the room where the idolized beloved, embellished with the costliest jewels of profound love, lay on magnificent sheets; and he recoiled with dismay at the hideous sight of this figure upon whom death had already begun to express its destructive powers. All those present felt the same horror as he; only the blinded son appeared to notice none of it, only continuing to view this object of abhorrence with the same love he had shown the flourishing beauty.

Then the archbishop of Cologne – a man of devout spirit, a God-fearing man walking in the ways of holiness, whom all the deceptions of heaven and hell could not blind – stepped up to the corpse and spoke, after looking at it for a long time: "It seems to me as if something unnatural were the cause of all this. With God's help it will be revealed." Thereupon he left the room with all the others and remained at his prayer stool all the following night in persistent, reverent prayer to God for enlightenment.

As he sought out his place of slumber and rest towards morning, a marvelous but clear dream descended on him. He saw himself in the gaping chasm of a deep and dark cave, illuminated only by the light of a fire over which a kettle was swinging, while a frightening witch was pacing around it, mumbling incantations. On the ground, not far away, lay a dead young woman – murdered, white and pale, as charming and demure as a lily that's been snapped from its stalk. The witch was gathering snippets from the blonde hair locks and blood from that innocent heart to prepare a terrible potion in the kettle over the flame. Thick clouds of smoke were curling up, enveloping the witch, the corpse, the whole picture. They dissolved away bit by bit. A magnificently beautiful royal lady, whom he recognized right away as Aistulf's daughter, was then standing in front of the witch, receiving from her a wide, golden bracelet which she put on and which then encircled her left arm near her heart.

Here the devout archbishop awoke, but he had seen enough and thanked God fervently for the illumination. Then he returned to the house where the dead woman lay; he was able, because of the esteem he enjoyed with the lovelorn prince, to convince him to be left alone for a few moments with the body, searched along her richly ornamented arm until he found the bracelet, took it off, and left the room. Charles entered it again immediately, but he was paralyzed with horror when he saw the corpse. "Take away this gruesome sight!" he cried: "Bury this image of destruction!"

He was obeyed quickly and gladly. Charles took a deep breath, looked around like someone awakening from heavy slumber; and the first utterances of his rediscovered heart were tears for Engelberta and laments for her death. The entire time period between her loss and this moment seemed to have sunk into forgetfulness. Florabella, his raging passion for her, everything that had transpired with him from Pavia until here in Aachen just floated before him now like images of a nightmare.

But the devout archbishop, when he noticed how the young prince was following him everywhere with tremendous love and devotion (ever since he had been carrying the magic bracelet with him), threw the ornamental band into a pond not far from Aachen in order to rid himself of any sort of diabolical contact.

The shore of that pond became Charles' favorite resting spot from then on. Often the image of his transfigured beloved appeared to rise up from its quiet waters. Here it was that he most preferred to rest from his heavy cares and matters of government, delighting himself with remembrances of his first love. Here it was that Engelberta's gentle memory finally surrounded him and whispered with angelic charity for him to treat Emma and Eginhart[23] with consideration and mercy, for they with their own fond looks

---

[23] Charlemagne's own children by a subsequent marriage.

of love reminded him of the times when he had made mistakes in the name of love and had been disobedient to an honored father.

This is the true cause of Charlemagne's uniquely strong attraction to the famous old city. It was the magic of a first, ill-fated love that bound the royal hero so strongly to this region as long as he lived, that drew him there with quiet yearning, and that allowed him, after his death, to find his final resting place near where the miraculously preserved remains of his first beloved were resting in the watery depths.

Ernst von Feuchtersleben (1806-1849) was equally at home in the worlds of medicine and of literature. He was the son of Austrian nobility: his father was a counselor to the Habsburg court. His mother died when he was very young, and he spent his childhood in rural surroundings and then as a pupil in Vienna. Following a nine-year-long study of medicine at the University of Vienna contrary to his father's wishes, Feuchtersleben married and opened up a medical practice in a suburb of the capital. More importantly, he became involved in literary and artistic circles: he was the private physician, as well as friend, of both Friedrich Hebbel and Franz Grillparzer. After publishing a collection of poetry and proving himself adept in the field of literary criticism, he became famous at one stroke with the publication of a monograph that perfectly combined his expertise at medicine and literature, *Dietetics of the Soul*.[1]

The Alpine Journey, as much a philosophical as a physical excursion, was written as a literary counterpoint to Feuchtersleben's treatise on the relationship between body and soul. It would be hard to give a generic classification to this piece, as it shows elements of a short story – albeit with little plot development – but also elements of an essay, a debate, a travelogue, and a guidebook to meditation. Perhaps the closest description would be that of a literary/philosophical sketch. At any rate, this work offers an enthusiastic description of nature, specifically the Alpine heights, from the pen of a Biedermeier prose artist.

The mid-nineteenth century was a time when psychology as a discipline was in its infancy, and this work exhibits proto-psychological approaches to what might be termed a buffer zone between the material body (where Doctor Feuchtersleben had certain expertise) and the imaginative mind (where Literary Critic Feuchtersleben was making explorations). There is a constant interplay between the two as the physical senses and the metaphysical sensibilities interweave. On another level, time and space are seen as inconstant and ever-changing.

The narrator seems to advocate a Zen-like stance: observation, acceptance (resignation), and meditation are keys to enlightened living. Spiritual mastery does not come so much through denial, indifference, or repression of life's experiences as it does through the process of lifting oneself above both pleasure and pain, through achieving a perspective that is elevated above

---

[1] Original German title: *Zur Diätetik der Seele*.

the mundane happenings of everyday. Placing oneself at the physical elevation and uplift of the mountain tops is shown to be an appropriate catalyst for the figurative elevation that can only come in a spiritual or psychological sense.

The two hiker/protagonists of the sketch, Julius and Theodore, represent different world views, and thus their dialogue becomes a benign struggle between perspectives. Julius is the impetuous romantic while Theodor is the conservative moralist. The resultant prose narrative moves beyond earlier depictions of nature that had oozed with artificial sentimentality and in a direction that was to prefigure realism.

Observations and proverb-like sayings are presented on every page within the matrix of a journey, and in literature a journey is often – as it is here – a vehicle for illustrating human progress. What could have been a dull series of abstract nouns and comparative ideas is here transformed into a work of art whose constant backdrop and arena of learning is punctuated with Austrian mountains and lakes.

THE ALPINE JOURNEY

Ernst von Feuchtersleben

>Blue mountains, emerald meadows,
>Rushing streams and woodland shadows
>Tempt my eyes intoxicated.
>Soon, alas, they are abated!
>Is there a way for scribbled lines
>To call back the lost from previous times?

The loveliest season had unfolded in all its glory. The storms of the past days had moved on to the river valley, and the contours of the wooded mountains were sharply outlined against the azure of the pristine heavens. A mild, balsamic warmth refreshed the newborn vegetation, and the song of early morning worshipers on pilgrimage was lost behind the richly planted hills.

Two friends marched resolutely onward. The rains had scattered thousands of white butterflies on the furrows of the small mountain path, where they clung to the moist soil like joyous living seed. Warmed by the sun, they tore loose in clumps and fluttered up as the wanderers came past them. And so the travelers hiked through the friendly valleys, surrounded by scores of delightful sights.

They spoke little and gave themselves over to quietly enjoying the last vestiges of evaporating morning dreams, those vestiges with which sensitive individuals – by lazily entertaining them for a while after rising – prepare themselves for the day's work. Their feelings were still in a state of pleasant uncertainty as they waited for the effects of what was to follow. Theodore, more accustomed to being resigned to life and to filling out the self-drawn boundaries of his activities in definite directions, had decided for once to let down his guard and give himself over to the balsamic blue of the air and the restorative green of the mountains. He needed it, for where seriousness is afoot, considerable worries accompany it. So it was that he chose fun-loving Julius as a companion for these days. Julius, accustomed to living in the moment, mediating between the self-contained spirit and luxuriously free nature, was merrily strolling along, always a few steps ahead of his friend. The two complemented each other, and both, no matter the differences in their natures, were motivated by a reverence and love for nature. They had undertaken this Alpine journey as a cult experience in that sense. Nothing enlivens life as much as traveling in a beautiful region; nothing brings people closer together, and – who was it that said it? – you should plan a trip with whomever you wish to become fond of.

"Slower, slower my friend!" Theodore called, chuckling at the one rushing on ahead, "He who runs in the morning will limp by evening!"

"Forgive me, my dear man," came the reply, "But you have something of the foolish wisdom of Eulenspiegel,[2] who always thought of rain when the sun was shining and of sunshine when it was raining. I stick to the wiser foolishness: I think of sunshine when the sun is shining and again of sunshine when it's raining.

Be that as it may, this time Theodore's warning proved true, for soon the trail got steeper and Julius had cause to regret his wasted steps. Theodore felt more comfortable and at home the steeper it got. Steeply-angled meadows stretched between tall-trunked forests; signs of sturdy mountain dwellers' industry became visible on all sides. On one slope, precipitous enough to give an onlooker vertigo, a woman was harvesting hay for her cattle. The wind whipped even stronger through the dark pines, attuning Theodore's mood to seriousness. The plain and valley address more the sensual needs of man. He plucks and enjoys his fruit; nothing stands in his way. Mountains provide more for the needs of the spirit. Man has to wrestle a living from the poor soil, measuring himself in the process against the heights that loom unshakably into the clouds. Nature, by dispensing to man the greatest fullness of inner strength precisely where she acts as a stepmother to the plant world, seems to want to teach us that she takes greater pleasure in the fruits of his labor than in those of his soil.

---

[2] Till Eulenspiegel was a legendary German peasant of the 14th century who reveled in practical jokes and became the center of numerous stories.

Meanwhile the sun rose higher, illuminating scattered brown huts that clung to the rocks round about and making the climb more difficult. Soon the last traces of human activity were lost as well. There was not one furrow more to indicate the path of the plowshare, not one enclosure more to show ownership, and even the regions of the hardiest hunter were lost in sadly proliferating scrub timber. The sound of footsteps echoed across unsurveyable scenes of loneliness: creation seemed to go silent, and by way of a mountain ridge on whose mossy stones only deep blue gentian flowers were blossoming, the friends made their way to the peak.

What a feeling! If you've never stood on Alpine heights, if you've never made contact with the heavens on cloud-intoxicated peaks where the senses reel, then you will never comprehend the homesickness of mountain dwellers that always draws them back from the shallow flatlands with painfully pleasant insistence to the mountains of their birth. Those of little faith down there on the plains – shuttling trivially back and forth between squat dwellings, enmeshed in the labyrinth of cold calculations and driven from faith by the pitiful affairs that they neurotically pursue – they've been punished enough already since they don't know the feeling of rapture. Our friends savored it to the full. Now liberated, their view swept across the lower regions from which they had climbed and where the last sparsely scattered fields of agriculture could still be identified, across the central chain of mountains towering over one another like waves in a stormy sea, over valleys winding around the mountains in various directions with silver threads snaking through them, onto the plain on the far side of the country where villages and cities seemed like dark dots cast from the sower's hand until, ominously, the view faded into the indistinguishable blue haze of the mountain range rimming the distant plain.

"My friend!" cried Julius, enthusiastically grabbing the hand of his quiet companion, "I'm so happy here! Any worry that bothered me down below seems so trivial and petty. Like a man saved, I stretch my arms – on which shortly before the chains of life were still clanking – up to the heavens, which are closer to me here. My soul is filled, and I wish nothing more than to see my fellow man contented. Here the world belongs to me. That Alpine flower pleases me; it seems to me more magnificent than all the treasures of town, and I reach my hand out for it. Here I don't just exist . . . I live. Look! On the shore of that river winding shimmeringly from sunrise to sunset lies our yesterday, the city from which we escaped, and here, between dark wooded heights, the lake we will be crossing by boat later today is flowing from the veiled depths like an illuminated wisp of fog. The past recedes behind me. I can't grasp the present; but the future, I feel the future. I sense her flapping her wings as she encircles us! Yes, it is the future that lays nature open to our soul and interprets it if only we can understand her language, the morning, the Alps."

Theodore also felt the same, perhaps even more deeply than his talkative friend. He warmly squeezed the hand offered him and was silent. His spirit, attuned to the duties of the moment, was used to seeking relief from the exhaustions of life at the bosom of memory. He had forgotten how to lose his way in the provinces of dream into which youth cram so much hope. The experienced climber enjoys the view from a peak in silence. Those in the valley can't hear his cry, those at the foot of the mountain can't understand it at best and would be agitated in vain. He doesn't want to confuse those climbing after him or to spoil the pleasure of their own hard-earned, gradually-widening views into the distance. He has nothing to say to those standing up there with him. And could this place even be expressed? Isn't nature herself silent there, such that the sounds of wind through the branches, the bubbling of the waters, and the twittering of the birds don't even reach up that far? . . . The sun was already quite high, and it was time to leave. Julius expressed it sadly: "Oh, why does all beauty leave us or we leave it?"

"My friend!" replied Theodore disapprovingly, "Leaving is a significant word that shouldn't guide us to our weakness but to our strength. Only to the weak does it bring despair; only to the weak does it mean testing and transition. How often does such a moment throw a crucial ray of light into the future? How often is separation the blossoming of something eternal? Do we hope anything different of our own lives as they close? A man buries the ashes of what's been lost in the depths of his heart, and only then does the loss become for him a true and holy possession."

These words moved the procrastinator . . . and infinity had faded from their view.

An ominous stillness continued on the heights. Only a vulture cried out through the solitude. The path led ever lower. One mountain ridge after the other was left behind. The echo of lost sounds and the distant clouds of smoke sometimes rose up, mixed with quiet, distant notes of the wind and of birds; but all that soon disappeared again, for the back side of the mountain was rugged and uncultivated and sank down into a rocky ravine. Fountains sprang up at the hikers' feet. The path, precipitously steep and sometimes wet, often seemed to be lost between the moss and the cliffs.

And so they continued on among tall, lone firs into ever quieter shadows. It was a region as is often found not far from waterfalls, and in fact a deep roar announced that one was near. A dark grove opened up, and the friends were standing in front of a magnificent cataract. The rushing sounds of the forest went mute as the hikers entered this sanctuary. A forest stream, having been fed by the last rainfall, poured its foaming masses of water into a rocky basin, where they collected and surged over the gray rocks to the depths in single shining threads like flowing silver. Down below on the moss, the atomized shower of pearls, released as fine mist in the sunshine, spread an invigorating freshness over the luxurious ferns. Thin branches of larch, hanging over the weathered stone, tried in vain to mirror themselves in the excited floods. Individual boulders, undermined by the elements and then torn from between the shattered greenery, lay scattered about, and a reddish wall magically lit by the sun through narrow fissures completed the backdrop. The hikers stood there, gripped by the powerful language of nature, while the thundering seemed to develop more and more into distinct beats the longer they stayed. The scene fit in with what had gone before. The glorious feelings first called forth on the mountain top compounded themselves. The clarity of their thinking was swallowed up in the foam and ferment of sensations that fill the soul with a great and omnipotent power in which no single thing can be distinguished anymore. That form of unmanliness that thinks itself wise for resisting all powerful impressions is despicable: it takes on the thin veneer of some ambiguous quietude at the cost of going without those things most beautiful and magnificent. It is great to overcome pleasure and pain; it is petty and animalistic to be without pleasure or pain.

It is midday. We find our friends on the surface of that lake they had greeted from the mountain tops in the full glow of the sun. They are sitting in the back of a small rowboat. In front of them is the oarsman, whose powerful rowing at a regular beat induces the waves to a uniform lapping sound while a long, shifting shimmer follows the vessel. Peacefully they glide over the still, blue-green surface that seems to cover their desires as well as their losses. The roar of the waterfall doesn't carry this far, and with that the surging feelings it called from slumber are pacified. A deep peace lies over all of nature and insinuates itself into the friends' mood; they, sunk in the feeling of the moment, enjoy it. Just as the value of the present moment is not properly appreciated and savored by most, it is the same with the beauty of midday. The ancients – the true ancients who lived in an intimate understanding with nature – comprehended that better, since they deified the hour when Pan sleeps and when a soft magic spins all of nature in a web; her pulse seems to skip a beat in order to gather up all the powers at her core and to infuse them with the balsam of life. So the present gleans the fallen fruit of the past where the seeds of development lie concealed, enveloping and brooding them with maternal love. The young, completely devoted to this process, don't dissect its causes and connections. Julius sometimes dips his hand in the flood for fun, and Theodore watches the clouds passing by as floating shadows over the luminescent waters. From time to time the boat stops and hangs over the depths a few moments, rocked by the swelling flood. Then a refreshing breath wafts across to them from the richly verdant tongue of land whose blossoming trees are reflected in the smooth surface, stirring up the dewy, vibrant air, and the boat moves on even more resolutely. Fish shoot apart as quick as arrows when the boat glides over them and reassemble behind it. Rich agricultural fields, wreathed with villages, gardens and chapels, flee past at times. A pealing of bells from shore and voices sometimes carried over by the wind announce that the worshipers on pilgrimage from that morning had covered the same route, and soon the little red banner shows itself,[3] and the procession prayerfully follows. A gentle touch of fog veils the stark bay behind the lake, allowing the bare walls of snow and bright green meadows of the tall distant mountains to shine brightly through ... and above the entire friendly spectacle is vaulted the deep, peaceful blue of a cloudless heaven.

    The true present moment provides a pleasure that doesn't merely reverberate in memory but, when called forth ever anew, creates an eternal present. Likewise in our travelers, the happy midday attitude kept reverberating as they left the small town – where they had eaten a rustic meal – and strolled with slow steps toward the village they had chosen for their night's rest. The exertion of climbing and the subsequent grand scenery had made them silent that morning. Now close camaraderie, fair daughter of the evening, was drawing near, moving them to cordial discussions. It was the value of the past that they discussed, and, as with the pleasures of that day, they let the pleasures of former days glide past their souls in review, and they rejoiced in what they had experienced. They had fruit to gather now since they had blossomed earlier. Woe to others of us who now bear fruit so seldom ... because our blossoms have been nipped in the bud. Only hope remains

---

[3] A religious banner of the pilgrims.

faithful to us – "hope, which always finds a way to deceive itself"[4] – but memory remains faithful to those more fortunate as well, as it holds fast to beauty and immortalizes what actually was. And what would be more lovely, and at the same time more true, than the joy that Mother Nature grants us? Remember the meaningful whisperings of the forest brook, the green light filtering through the branches that covered you, the eloquent silence of midday on the lake, the singing of the seldom-trod forest, the unfathomable, smiling bed of waves in the shadowed bay, the veiled peaks of high country . . . remember them when in the sterile flatlands; with them in mind hide yourself inside your four walls from the shrillness and clatter ringing in your ears! Amidst discussions of similar content the two walked on, and the sun, as they walked, sank deeper and deeper and more and more golden onto the mountain pinnacles. And just as our observations were threatening to get lost in drearier earnest, it appeared to be the same with Theodore, who was visibly feeling more serious. Man, a son of time and space, is subject to the effects of a situation. The moment governs the moment, and life is composed of moments. This minute forces tears from us, and the next one laughs at them. Blessed is he who is aware at every fleeting moment of the past one and the future one! Thus we continually illusion and disillusion ourselves until, finally, we disillusion ourselves of the greatest illusion of all, life itself. When such feelings come over us like dark forebodings, when the gradations of our thought dissolve, and nostalgia and melancholy flow together into one grand shadow, then it becomes twilight in our soul, and we yearn for rest as did Theodore and Julius.

"You are getting more serious," said the latter, who had become the same himself. "Give yourself over to soft feelings, though you're always the one advising me to avoid them. Should I repeat your own lovely maxims about courage?"

"My friend!" replied Theodore, "Believe me, what has moved me is not the melancholy that I criticize in others. Just let me say: the little pains from which the narrow hearts of most bleed, the sufferings of physical and moral egotism, have no claim on me. My sadness goes deeper and wider . . . to the grand scale, to everything. I'm not mourning any loss. I'm mourning the condition of the world that makes it not feasible to carry out the purest and loveliest intentions, even though all the means are at our disposal. I

---

[4] Cf. Cicero, *De Oratore*, III, 2.

mourn with the poet that 'man is denied not only the impossible, but also so much that *is* possible,' that nature, love, truth remain misunderstood by hearts that are made for them but which impose an eternal ban on themselves; that humans, who all want and need the same things deep down, can never understand each other. All those who have the power to liberate one another, whose quiet sighs beg each other for liberation . . . they keep pulling the chains tighter and more slavishly around themselves. Will it never come, the Age of Understanding? Julius! This is a pain that can only be felt by someone who has put off the other pains. How many sing and talk about the duality between idealism and life, thinking of some fantasy that is rightfully repugnant to both nature and life? But someone clearheaded and powerful knows what he can demand. It is not the head-hanging of the crotchety; it is the yearning and power of bliss that feels itself both strongly evoked and, at the same time, poisoned at its source. Nothing remains for us but to endure the small sufferings happily and the great ones quietly, always with repressed defiance. That's what I call the task of life . . ."

"Admit it, Theodore! You dream sometimes, too . . . in your way, as everyone does things his way. You're dreaming right now. And in the final analysis, the worst evil is only in your imagination!"

Theodore: "And this imagination itself is the worst evil, that's how I would answer. But no! Leave me my pain, and I'll be satisfied with it; I'll praise it. This sadness of the loftier sort is the seed of heaven within us, the pangs of an inner birth. How often I've said to myself: 'Don't avoid looking into this chasm or that; suffer that too, even if it breaks your heart. It's all in the cause of the highest good: truth! And truth rewards you with the left hand what the right hand takes away. Sufferings suffered for their own sake become ecstasies.' And, in fact, that's the way it's been . . . The individual has to die so that love can encompass the whole. That's the way it is with people and with nations . . . And so I love my pain, since it's given me the great teaching that I expressed earlier, perhaps a little too harshly, that the task of life is active resignation.

Julius: "Maybe you've set a tougher resignation for yourself than someone else might need, but I don't want to try to talk you out of it. Whatever someone makes as the purpose of his life, that seems to me to characterize him. What you wrestle with determines your character."

Theodore: "Certainly! Just as you recognize the saints in illustrations by the signs of their martyrdom, nothing expresses the personality of someone more, there's nothing he may call his own so much as the pain with which finishing life has become his unique life's test. We are different according to how our sufferings are different. Instead of asking 'How's it going?' we could ask someone: 'What's torturing you?' and a sincere answer would reveal his personality."

Julius: "You're infecting me with your mood. Or is it the evening that's making me more serious? As the region around us grows quieter, as the detail of objects is lost, as foreboding takes the place of certainty and the moon rises up over that black highland forest, nature herself seems to be joining in with your lament, and those mountains decked in evening gauze seem like petrified melancholy to me."

Theodore: "Dear Julius! I've just held a eulogy to sadness, but let me admit that nothing is more disgusting to me than when people attach their pitiful feelings to eternal and vast nature. Even if the pain we spoke of were the noblest one . . . nature doesn't feel it, and from her lap flowers blossom on our graves. I find it so petty of the poets that they have thought, since Ossian,[5] that they were doing something right by lending rocks and rivers their human language, the language of their pains. If poets want to approach nature, then let them copy her down in a straightforward and simple way, without interpretation, without a moral. That produces a completely different effect on those who have seen her than anything you could add! 'Nature is a silent gospel,' one of you has said. Well, you won't be able to give that gospel a voice. Consider yourselves lucky if, by heaping a palisade of dark, dead gray letters and punctuation marks on the page, even a quiet breath of that mood you were in when you wrote is transmitted to the reader. An atom of life, as nature strews them out amongst the grasses by the millions! It is the highest achievement that an author can reach. With this in mind, I will simply write down the scenes from today once we've arrived. May such a breath blow across my sheet!"

While Theodore was saying this, a startled deer fled to the bushes encircling the edge of the woods. At the end of the woods could be seen – between richly plowed and planted hills – the village toward which they were headed. The graveyard with its crosses and headstones lay in the moonbeams before them. The evening bell was calling the tired folk together, and a friendly star shone above the house designated to give them lodgings.

---

[5] Ossian (or Oisin) was the son of Finn, both of whom lived in the third century A.D., according to Irish legend, and formed the center of an extended circle of sagas in Southern Ireland and Scotland.

"Even if all the days of our short journey contain so little that might be of interest to our friends in the bustle of the city, as today," said Julius, "there is still material enough for us to remember on New Year's Eve."

"For anyone accustomed to contemplating his actions," replied Theodore, "every evening is New Year's Eve."

Adalbert Stifter (1805-1868) is today considered by many the premier Austrian prose writer of the nineteenth century. He was born in the quiet of the Bohemian Forest, a circumstance reflected in his textual output: Stifter's prose is marked less by dynamic external events than by hints at the inner life of the soul. The actual incidents themselves are not as important as what happens in the heart and mind of his protagonists and are accompanied by descriptions of a beneficent natural order. This proceeds from what Stifter called the "gentle law" of life: the allegedly "small events" of life overshadow the grand and violent experiences. To some extent, the outer world portrayed in Stifter's novellas – whether deep in the Austrian Alps or, in the present work, on a Hungarian country estate – seems to parallel the human psyche. Thus, idyllic and almost utopian landscapes point to the possibility of happiness, while, conversely, dangers confronting man in nature – wolves, heavy snows, barren deserts – may suggest misery and unhappiness, but any evil intent is negated by the very fact that these forces are natural and indifferent: wolves attack humans only when hunger drives them to it, snows are life-giving and beautiful as well as treacherous, and deserts are harsh and unfeeling but amenable to being irrigated. Consequently, there appears to be no calculated evil in Stifter's world – only the opportunity to join the natural order.

Brigitta first appeared in the year 1844 and was reworked for the fourth volume of Stifter's collection, *Studies,* in 1847. The reworked version is the one translated here. The story itself moves between a number of inner (psychological) and outer (natural and societal) levels: on the outside are such things as wolves, stony wastelands, nineteenth-century family values and the benefits of agricultural cooperation. On the inside, mirrored by outer events, are the power of forgiveness and the constancy of love. The two sides are woven together in a central conflict between apparent outer beauty and true inner beauty. The title figure, Brigitta, may seem plain or even ugly to the casual observer, but her beauty is revealed to those who look into her soul.

The story unfolds slowly and meticulously, with many a glance sideways at cultural artifacts of the Magyar people, the wonders of viticulture and animal husbandry, and the stark beauty of the *puszta* (Hungarian steppe). The resolution of the story is gradual as well: the entire third section (*The Steppe in Times Past*) represents a digression necessary to round out the cycle of human connectedness that comes to fruition in the fourth section.

Despite a paucity of references to God or religion, there are clues that one of Stifter's aims was to depict the possibilities of reconciliation or re-binding to which the word "religion" originally referred. One direct reference comes in the first paragraph – a philosophical template or spiritual guide to the story following it. There Stifter mentions an abyss where God and the spirits dwell that is at once serene (or even cheerful) and at the same time unfathomable. Thus the import of what follows is not to be analyzed in objective, scientific terms, he suggests, but is discernible to emotional interpreters of the heart or spiritual receptors within the soul. Metaphorically – both with agricultural descriptions bordering on the Garden of Eden and with human relations no less utopian – he is describing a return to paradise.

BRIGITTA

Adalbert Stifter

1.
Traveling on the Steppe

In our life as humans there are often events and feelings which are not clear to us right away, the root causes of which we're not able to get at quickly. So their effect on our soul comes mainly from a certain alluring and gentle charm of the unknown. In the face of an ugly person we often see an inner beauty whose worth we're not able to trace objectively on the spot, while the features of another, said by all to possess the greatest beauty, seem cold and empty to us. Likewise, we sometimes feel drawn to someone we don't actually know at all: we like the way he moves, we like his mannerisms, we're sad when he's gone and feel a certain longing or even love when we think of him in later years. Yet with another, whose value lies manifest in numerous deeds right in front of us, we feel alienated even if we've associated with him for years. There can be no doubt that moral causes are at work here, ultimately, and that the heart senses them; but we can't always pull them out into the open and weigh them on the scales of reason and logic. Psychological studies have illuminated and explained many things, but they still leave a great deal murky and remote. So we believe it's not too much to say that for us there still exists a serene, unfathomable abyss in which God and the spirits dwell. The soul, in moments of ecstasy, often soars across it; poetry unveils it at times with childlike naivete; but science with its hammer and yardstick is often only perched at the rim and may, in many cases, contribute nothing at all.

I've been moved to these observations by an event I once experienced on the estate of an old Major in my early years, back when I still had a great wanderlust driving me out into the world, here and there, because I still hoped to experience and to study God knows what.

I had gotten to know the Major on a trip, and at that time he invited me more than once to visit him in his homeland sometime. I considered this to be mere rhetoric and courtesy, however, such as travelers customarily exchange with each other. I probably wouldn't have given the matter any further thought if a letter from him hadn't arrived the second year after our separation in which he took the opportunity to inquire about my health and finally reiterated the old request to come visit him and to spend a summer, a year, or five or ten years with him, whatever would be my pleasure; for now at last he was of a mind, he said, to stay attached to one solitary, tiny point on this globe, not allowing any other dust to touch his foot than that of his homeland. He said he had finally found the destination there for which he had been searching the earth in vain.

Since it was spring just then, since I was curious to learn about his destination, and since I just didn't know where I should travel next, I decided to give in to his request and to accept his invitation.

He had his estate in Eastern Hungary, and for two days I muddled around with plans about how best to make the journey; by the third day I was sitting in the stagecoach rolling eastward, already contemplating sights of plains and forests in this country I had never seen, and by the eighth day I was on a *puszta*[1] as glorious and desolate as Hungary alone may have to offer.

In the beginning, my entire soul was gripped by the enormity of the landscape: the way the boundless air caressed me, the fragrance of the steppe, and how a shimmer of solitude fanned out everywhere and over everything. But when it turned out to be the same the next day, the same again the day after next – still nothing at all but the fine ring where heaven and earth kissed – then my spirit got used to it, my eye began to surrender and to become as sated with the nothingness as if it had loaded masses of substance upon it. It retreated into itself, and various lone thoughts wandered through my soul as rays of sunlight danced and the grasses gleamed; old memories came swarming across the plains, and among them was the vision of the man I was traveling to visit. I gladly accepted it, and in the desolation I had time

---

[1] Hungarian: "steppe" or "plain."

enough to collect and refresh in my memory all the features I had known of him.

It was in Southern Italy, in a desolation almost as solemn as the one through which I was traveling today, that I had first seen him. At the time he was celebrated in all the social circles, and, though he was almost fifty years old already, he was the target of many lovely eyes, for never was a man seen whose form and face could be called more handsome, nor one who knew how to bear this external grace more nobly. I would say it was a gentle majesty that surrounded all his motions, so simple and so winning that he even turned the heads of men more than once. On women's hearts, though, so went the legend, his effect had once been truly mind-boggling. Rumors spread about successes and conquests he had made, and they were magnificent enough. But there was one failing, they said, one part of his constitution that made him decidedly dangerous: no one yet, not even the greatest beauty on earth, had succeeded in holding on to him any longer than his whim would have it. It was with sufficient charm to win any heart that he acted, with charm to fill the chosen woman with victorious ecstasy until the end; then he took leave, went on a trip and never returned. But this failing, instead of frightening women off, only won them over to him more, and many a rash Mediterranean lady yearned to throw her heart and happiness into his arms as soon as possible. It was very appealing as well that no one knew where he came from, nor what standing he had in society. Although people said that the Graces flitted about his mouth, they also noted that some sort of sadness rested on his brow – the indicator of a significant past, but it was ultimately most alluring that nobody knew this past. It was said he had been wrapped up in affairs of state, he had been unhappily married, he had shot his own brother, and more such rumors. What everyone knew for certain, though, was that he was now very heavily involved in the sciences.

I had already heard a lot about him and immediately recognized him when I once had occasion to see him hammering out rock samples on Vesuvius, then moving on to the new crater and smiling as he watched the blue spirals of smoke rise up thinly from the opening and from the cracks. I walked across the uneven, glistening yellow deposits toward him and greeted him. He was happy to respond, and one word led to another. At the time, in fact, there was a terribly chaotic, ominous desolation around us which seemed all the harsher for being set against the unimaginably pleasant, deep-blue southern sky directly overhead with the puffs of smoke cozily streaming up sideways into it. We spoke together for a long while, but then each of us went down the mountain separately.

Later we found occasion to meet again; we visited each other more and more often until finally, up till the time I left for home, we were together almost constantly. I found that he was more or less innocent of the effects others blamed on his appearance. From inside him, so often, something primal and spontaneous erupted just as if he had been saving himself up until now, though he was already nearing fifty, because his soul hadn't really found itself yet. I recognized at the same time, as I was around him longer, that his soul was the most vibrant and poetic one I had ever come across, which might also explain its childlike, natural, simple, secluded, and even naive aspects. He was unaware of these gifts and spoke, as a matter of natural course, the loveliest words I've ever heard from any tongue. Never in my life, not even later when I had the chance to spend time among poets and artists, did I ever come across such a sensitivity for beauty as his, which could be provoked to the point of impatience by any type of deformity or coarseness. It may also have been these subconscious gifts that made all the hearts of the opposite sex flock to him, since such playfulness and radiance are so very rare in men of advanced years. That might also be the reason that he liked to be in my company so much, in the company of someone so young. By the same token, I was not yet able to appreciate the true value of these things at the time, and they didn't really start to make sense to me until I was older and went about compiling the narrative of his life. The extent of his legendary prowess with women was something I was never able to discover, since he never talked about it and I never had the opportunity to observe it. Neither was I able to perceive any of that sadness others claimed to see mantling his brow, just as I learned nothing of his earlier life except that he had once taken constant trips but had now been in Naples for years and was collecting lava samples and antiquities. He told me himself that he had land holdings in Hungary and, as I said above, he repeatedly invited me to visit there.

We lived close to one another for a rather long time and finally separated when I left, not without emotion. But so many different images of countries and peoples crowded through my memory afterwards that it wouldn't have occurred to me in my wildest dreams that someday I would be underway across the Hungarian plains to visit this man, as was now actually the case. I kept embellishing my mental picture of him and got so wrapped up in it that I often had trouble believing I was not in Italy: it was as hot, as silent on the plain I was hiking across as it had been there, and the blue layer of haze in the distance was like a mirage of the Pontine Marshes.[2]

I did not head directly for the Major's estate as he had mapped it out in his letter, but took several crisscross excursions to view the countryside. Just as my image of the land had always run together earlier with that of Italy because of my friend, now its tapestry wove itself more and more uniquely into something independent and complete. I had crossed over a hundred brooks, streams, and rivers; I had often camped with shepherds and their shaggy dogs. I had drunk from those solitary wells of the steppe that point to heaven with their frightfully tall draft poles, and I had eaten under many a low thatched roof – the bagpiper resting at one spot, the quick coachman flying across the plains, the white coat of the horse herdsman glistening. Often I wondered how my friend would look to me in this country, for I had seen him only in society and in the tumult of everyday life where all people look as much alike as bits of gravel in a stream. There his exterior had been that of the smooth, sophisticated gentleman – but here everything was different, and often, when I saw nothing for days at a time but the distant reddish-blue twilight over the steppe, dotted with a thousand of the country's cattle as little white spots, or when I saw the deep black soil at my feet and so much wildness, so much abundance, so much that was primitive and primordial here despite the long history, I wondered how he would behave here. I traveled around in the country, accustomed myself more and more to its ways and its peculiarities, and I seemed to hear the beat of a hammer forging the future of this people. Everything in this land points to coming ages: everything about to die is tired and worn; everything growing is passionate, and so it was with gladness that I saw its endless villages, saw its vineyards rising up, saw its marshes and reed thickets, and its light-blue mountains stretching into the distance.

After months of wandering, I finally thought one day that I had to be very close to my friend's estate, and, a bit tired of so much sightseeing, I decided to set a destination to my pilgrimage and to turn directly toward the property of my future host. I had been walking across stony ground all afternoon; to the left of me rose peaks of distant blue mountains to the sky

---

[2] An area southeast of Rome that was formerly marshy, but which has now been drained.

– I thought they were probably the Carpathians[3] – to the right of me lay a rifted landscape with that peculiar reddish coloring that the breath of the steppe so often leaves behind. The two did not unite, however, and between them the endless vision of the plains continued on. Finally, as I was just coming up out of a hollow with a dry stream bed running across it, a chestnut forest and a white house sprang into view to the right of me, a sand dune having previously hidden both from me. "Three miles, three miles" – that's what I'd heard almost all afternoon when I inquired about Uvar, for that was the name of the Major's residence – "three miles." But since I was acquainted with Hungarian miles from personal experience, I knew I had walked at least five and I greatly hoped that the name of the house might be Uvar. Not too far away, fields rose up toward an earthen embankment on which I saw people. Intending to go ask them, I walked through one corner of the chestnut forest. Here I saw what I had immediately suspected, having been instructed by the many optical illusions of this country: the house was not right at the edge of the forest but out in the open beyond the chestnut trees, and it must be a very large building indeed. I saw a figure on horseback dashing across the plain straight toward those fields where the people were working. All the workers gathered around this figure when it arrived, as they would around their master – but this person didn't look like the Major at all. I slowly walked up toward the earthen slope, which was also more distant than I had thought, and arrived just as the full flame of the setting sun was already blazing behind the dark waving fields of corn and the groups of bearded farm hands and the rider. This rider, however, was none other than a woman around forty years of age, who, curiously enough, was wearing wide Magyar pants and also sitting on her horse like a man. Since the workers were already dispersing and she was almost alone there, I directed my inquiry to her. Bracing my knapsack on my hiking stick and looking up at her while shielding my eyes from the slanting rays of the setting sun, I said to her in German: "Good evening, Ma'am."

"Good evening," she answered in the same language.

"Would you be so good as to tell me whether that building is called 'Uvar?'"

"The name of that building is not Uvar. Are you expected at Uvar?"

---

[3] A Central European range that extends from Slovakia to Romania.

"I am indeed. I'm to visit the friend I met abroad, the Major. He's invited me there."

"Well, walk beside my horse for a ways then."

With these words she urged her horse to a walk, and then, so I could follow her, she rode slowly up the slope between the tall green cornstalks. I walked along behind her with the chance to cast my gaze at the surroundings and, in fact, I found more and more cause to be astounded. As we went higher, the valley opened up in full view behind us; a whole gigantic plantation ran from the mansion to the mountains beyond, roads stretched out to the fields, and one agricultural field after another revealed itself, each appearing to be in excellent condition. I'd never seen the long, fresh, and juicy leaf of the corn plant before, and not a single weed was to be found between the rows. The vineyard along whose edge we were just passing reminded me of those on the Rhine, the only difference being that I've never seen such robust exuberance and abundance of leaf and grape along the Rhine as I saw here. The plain between the chestnut trees and the mansion formed a meadow as pure and gentle as if it were spread with velvet; it was intersected with enclosed pathways along which the white cattle of the countryside were ambling, yet they were smooth and lean, like deer. The whole image stood out magnificently from the stony stretch of ground I had hiked through that day and which lay behind us in the evening air now, peering across, hot and dry in the reddish twisting rays, to this cool green freshness.

In the meantime we had reached one of those small white cottages I had noticed scattered throughout the greenery of the wine-growing region, and the woman said to a young man who, despite the hot June evening, was wearing his shaggy fur coat and working at various tasks in front of the cottage door, "Milos, the gentleman wants to reach Uvar today, if you would perhaps take the two bay horses from the pasture, give him one, and guide him as far as the gallows."

"Yes," replied the youth, and stood up.

"Now just go along with him, he'll lead you right," the woman said, and turned her horse to ride back the way she had come with me.

I thought she was some sort of steward and tried to give her a good-sized coin for the services she had just given me. She just laughed, though, displaying a set of beautiful teeth in the process. She rode slowly down through the vineyard, but then soon after we heard the fast hoofbeats of her horse as she flew across the plain.

I put my money away and turned to Milos. He had meanwhile put a wide-brimmed hat on above his fur coat, then he led me some distance through the vineyards until we went around a bend in the valley and came across some farm buildings from which he took two of those small horses often found on this country's plains. He saddled mine; then he mounted his just as it was, and off we rode in the twilight toward the dark eastern sky. It must have been a strange sight: the German[4] hiker sitting on a horse with his backpack, walking stick, and cap, beside him the slender Hungarian with his rounded hat, mustache, shaggy fur, and broad, fluttering white pants – both riding through the desert at night. In very fact it was a desert that we entered into beyond the vineyards, and the settlement had been like an oasis in it. Actually, the desert was once again that old stony ground, so uniformly the same that I would have imagined we were riding back the same path I had come if the darkening red glow in the sky behind my back hadn't proven to me that we were really riding eastward.

"How much further is it to Uvar?" I asked.

"We still have one and a half miles," Milos answered.

I accepted the answer and rode behind him as best I could. We were riding past the same innumerable gray stones I had counted that day in the thousands. In the bad light they glided past me on the dark ground, and, because we were actually riding on a dried and compacted bog, I couldn't hear the hoofbeats of our bay horses except when a horseshoe by chance struck one of the stones which the animals, accustomed to such terrain, were otherwise adept at avoiding. The ground was level everywhere but for two or three hollows that we climbed in and out of, within each of which lay a bed of pebble debris.

"Who owns the property we've just left?" I asked my guide.

"Maroshely," he answered.

I didn't know, since he had pronounced the words quickly while riding along in front of me, if this was the name of the owner or if I had even understood him correctly, since the riding motion made speaking and listening difficult.

Finally a blood-red slice of moon arose, and by now I was able to see in its weak light a narrow scaffolding that stood on the plain, presumably the point to which I was to be accompanied.

---

[4] That is, German-speaking citizen of Austria.

"Here is the gallows," said Milos. "Down there, where you see a glimmer, there's a stream flowing along; next to it is a black shape. Go towards it; it's an oak tree where the criminals used to be hanged. That's not the way it's done anymore, since there's a gallows. A trail leads from the oak, and it's lined with young trees on both sides. Follow that trail a little less than an hour, then pull the bell cord at the gate. Now pay attention: even if it isn't locked, don't go in; that's on account of the dogs. Just pull on the bell cord. Well now, climb down and close up your coat a little better so you don't catch cold."

I got off the horse and, even though my tip hadn't been well received by the woman steward, I did offer Milos another one. He accepted it and put it inside the fur coat. Then he reached for my horse's bridle, turned, and flew away in a rush before I could even ask him to thank the owner of the horses who had allowed me to ride off into the night just like that. Obviously he wanted to get away from there just as quickly as possible. I looked up. There were two pillars with a crossbeam. It loomed up in the yellow moonlight. There was something lying on top, like a head, which, in fact, may have been some sort of extension. I walked on, imagining that the steppe grasses were whispering behind me and that something was moving at the foot of the gallows. Not the slightest sound was coming from Milos's direction, as if he had never been there in the first place. I came to the executioner's oak right away. The stream was shimmering and gleaming and curling around the reeds like a dead snake. Next to it was the black expanse of tree. I went around it, and on the other side was a straight white trail, illuminated by the moon. The pathway had been tamped down and had ditches and a row of young poplars on either side. It felt good to hear the sound of my own steps again, just like it was on the trails back home in my own country.

I went slowly along. The moon rose more and more and finally stood out clearly in the warm summer sky. The steppe fell away like a pale slab beneath it. At last, when a good hour may have passed, dark lumps rose up before me, like woods or a plantation, and in a short time the path butted up against a gate set in a wall running around the forest; the treetops behind it were enormous and stretched up, deathly silent, into the silver night air. At the gate was a bell pull; I tugged at it, and it rang from the inside. There wasn't exactly a bark right after that, but rather two expulsions of that deep, determined, and curious panting of noble dogs – the sound of a muffled leap – and the largest, most handsome dog I've ever seen in my life stood on the other side of the gate. He got up on his hindlegs, grasped the iron bars with his forelegs, and looked out at me without making even the slightest sound, as is the solemn manner of such animals. Soon, two smaller and younger dogs of the same breed, shorthaired bulldogs, came growling and chasing, all of them watching me attentively. After a while I heard human steps coming closer, and a man in his shaggy fur came up and asked me what it was I wanted. I replied by asking if I was at Uvar, then told him what my name was. He must have had instructions, for he immediately calmed the dogs in Hungarian and opened the gate.

"My master has letters from you and has been expecting you for a long time," said the man as we walked on.

"Well, I did write him that I intended to take a look at your country first," I replied.

"And you've looked at it for a long time," he said.

"I certainly have," I responded. "Is the Major still awake?"

"He's not even home at all; he's at a meeting. He will be riding back home tomorrow morning. He's had three rooms set up for you and said we should take you to them if you showed up while he was gone."

"So please take me to them now."

"Gladly."

These words were the only ones we exchanged on the long way we took through what seemed to me more primeval forest than plantation. Huge pine trees stretched to the sky, and oak branches as thick as a man's torso reached out. The larger dog went along quietly with us; the others sniffed at my clothing and chased each other from time to time. When we had thus crossed through the grove, we came to an elevated clearing on which the mansion stood – a large rectangular building as well as I could see at the moment. The most radiant moonlight was gazing down on wide stone steps leading up the hill. Beyond the steps was a fairly level area, then a large front door laced with iron bars instead of a normal entryway to the house. When we had reached the door, my guide spoke a few words to the dogs and they shot back into the plantation. Next he opened up the door and led me into the building.

On the stairs the lights were still on, and they cast light on some strange, tall stone figures with wide boots and trailing robes. They were probably Hungarian kings. Then, on the second floor, a long hallway covered with reed matting received us. We walked along it and then went up one more flight. There was another such hallway here, and, opening up one of the double doors from the hall, my guide told me these were my rooms. We went in. After he had lit several candles in each room, he wished me a good night and left. Wine, bread, and cold cuts were brought after a while by another, whereupon I was wished a good night, as from his predecessor. I realized from this and from the complete room furnishings that I would be alone now, and so I went to the doors and locked them.

Subsequently I ate and, while doing so, looked around my lodgings. The first room, where the food had been placed on a large table, was very spacious. The candles were burning brightly, illuminating everything. The utensils were different from the ones customary in my homeland. In the middle stood a long table, at one end of which I ate. Oak benches had been placed around the table, not actually looking very comfortable but more as if meant for meetings. Other than that, a chair could be seen only here and there. On the walls hung weapons from various periods of history. They may well have been a part of Hungarian history themselves at one time. There were still many bows and arrows among them. Besides the weapons there was clothing hung there as well, Hungarian pieces preserved from earlier times as well as those loose silk garments that may have belonged to the Turks or even the Tartars.[5]

When I was finished with my night meal, I moved into the two adjoining rooms. They were smaller, and, as I had noticed at first sight on being led in, they were more comfortably furnished than the larger room. There were chairs, tables, closets, toiletry supplies, writing utensils – everything that a solitary wanderer could ever wish for in his lodgings. There were even books lying on the night stand, and they were all in the German language. There was a bed in each of the two rooms, but, instead of a bedspread, each had spread over it the traditional wide folk mantle that they call a *bunda*. This is usually an overcoat made from skins, where the hairy side is turned to the inside and the smooth white side is turned out. The outside is frequently decorated with colorful lacework and appliqued patterns in colored leather.

Before going to bed, I went to the window, as is my custom in foreign places, to see how it looked outside. There wasn't much to see. The one thing I could make out in the moonlight, though, was that the landscape was not German. Like yet another *bunda*, but an enormously large one, the dark expanse of forest or plantation was spread out below me on the steppe.

---

[5]Also called Tatars. A Turkic tribe, fierce in battle, that had once extended from southeastern Europe into parts of Central Asia.

Beyond it shimmered the gray of the plains, then still further out were all sorts of strips; I didn't know if they were objects of this earth or layers of clouds.

After I had allowed my eyes to wander over these things for a while, I turned back away again, closed the windows, undressed, went to the nearest bed and lay down for the night.

As I pulled the soft fur of the *bunda* over my tired bones, and when I was about to close my eyes, I had one final thought: "Well, now I'm really curious about what sort of friendliness or ugliness I'll find in this house."

Then I fell asleep and all of my previous life was dead – along with everything I fervently hoped might someday be a part of it.

2.
The House on the Steppe

I don't know how long I slept, but it was neither deeply nor well; that much I do know. It must have been the fault of being overly tired. All night I was walking around on Vesuvius; first I watched the Major sitting in his traveling gear at Pompeii, then I saw him standing among the cinders in his formal wear, looking for stones. Into my morning dream were infused the sounds of whinnying horses and barking dogs; then I slept deeply for some time and when I awoke, there was broad daylight in the room and I looked out into the large room where the weapons and clothing were hanging, lit by the sun. Down below, the dark woods were reverberating with the loud chatter of birds and after I had gotten up and stepped to one of the windows, the steppe beyond was glowing in a web of sunbeams. Before I had quite finished dressing, there was a knock at my door. I opened it, and my friend entered. I had been curious, in all the days preceding, to know how he might look, and he didn't look any different than he had to look: that is, so in accordance with the whole region round about that it seemed as though I'd always seen him this way. On his upper lip he had the customary mustache that made his eyes seem to sparkle all the more; a wide, round hat covered his head, and from his hips hung the broad white pants. It was completely natural that he had to be like this; I suddenly couldn't even remember how he had looked in a tailcoat; his costume seemed so charming to me that my plain German wool coat, lying dusty and tattered on a bench beneath the faded silk skirts of a Tartar, appeared almost contemptible to me. His jacket was shorter than they generally are in Germany, but it fit in well with the whole outfit. It's true that my friend seemed to have aged some: his hair was mingled with gray and his face was full of those short, fine lines that finally betray increasing age among healthy people who have taken care of themselves for a long time. Still, he appeared to me as pleasant and captivating as ever.

He gave me a very friendly greeting, very heartfelt, almost intimate, in fact, and after we had chatted together for a half hour we were as familiar with each other again as we had been before. It felt as if we hadn't even separated at all since our trip to Italy. As I was dressing and happened to remark that a suitcase with my other things would be arriving soon, he suggested I might like to wear Hungarian clothes until then or, if I wanted, for the whole length of my stay. I consented to the idea, and the essential pieces of clothing were soon brought to me; at this point he remarked that he would arrange for a full change of clothing in the next few days. Then, as we went down into the courtyard to the farm hands dressed the same as us, and as they looked out at us so approvingly from their dark mustaches and bushy eyebrows and brought us horses for a morning ride, there was something so noble and soothing in the sight that I felt refreshed to the core by it.

We rode around on the Major's estate, accompanied by the great and gentle bulldog. The Major showed me everything and from time to time gave orders and praise to workers. The woods through which we first rode formed a pleasant wilderness, very well tended and maintained, intersected with pathways. When we came out into the fields, they were undulating in the darkest green. Only in England have I seen anything like it, but there, it seemed to me, the green was softer and more delicate while here it appeared more robust and sun-drenched. Beyond the woods we rode slowly uphill; along the ridge of a gentle rise stretched the long vineyards, facing the steppe. Dark, broad leaves were everywhere; the vines took up quite a wide area. There were peach trees scattered all over and from their appropriate locations could be seen, as in Maroshely, the luminous white dots of caretakers' cottages. Having ridden down to the steppe, we saw his cattle: a large, scattered, almost boundless herd. An hour's ride took us next to the stud farms and sheep camps. As we were crossing the plain, he pointed far off to the west at a narrow black strip cutting into the gray expanse of the steppe and said, "Those are the vineyards of Maroshely where you borrowed the horses yesterday."

We made our way back from another side, and here he showed me his garden, his fruit orchards, and his greenhouses. Before we got there, we rode past a very unattractive plot of land on which a significant number of people were working. Responding to my inquiry, he told me that these were beggars, transients, even petty criminals that he had won over to working for him by giving them their wages promptly. They were draining a swampy area and building a road.

At noon, after we had returned home, we ate with all the workers, male and female, in some sort of entranceway or rather under a huge overhanging roof next to which stood a huge nut tree. On a wooden platform surrounding the fountain, visiting gypsies were making music. There was a stranger who had come to lunch as well, a youth in the first throes of adolescence. He caught my attention because of his extraordinary handsomeness. He had delivered letters from the vicinity, then had ridden off again after the meal. He had been treated very attentively by the Major, almost tenderly.

We spent the hot afternoon in our cool rooms. In the evening, my host showed me the sunset over the steppe. We rode out expressly for that purpose after he had advised me to put a fur coat around me, as he was doing, for protection against the fever-inducing air of the plain even though the air itself, still warm, seemed to make it superfluous. We waited, once we had reached the spot he'd designated, until the sun had set. And in fact it was a dazzling sight that followed next: the gigantic cupola of flaming yellow heavens was perched above the whole darkened platter of the steppe, lulling and mesmerizing the eyes so much that everything on the ground turns alien and black. A leaf of steppe grass stands out like a post against the blaze, an animal occasionally passing by forms the silhouette of a black monster against the golden background, and paltry juniper and wild plum bushes paint images of distant cathedrals and palaces. After a few moments then, the cold deep-blue moisture of night begins to rise up in the east, cutting off the uniform glow of domed sky with its opaque and gloomy haze.

This phenomenon lasts a very long time, especially on June evenings when the sun is so far north. After we had arrived home again, after we had eaten our evening meal and chatted together for some time, I was in my bedroom standing at the window with midnight already approaching, and there was still a dreary patch of yellow light in the west even as a red disk of half-moon was already shining in the deep-blue east.

I resolved that evening to ask the Major on the next day, the day after, or whenever the occasion arose in the following days, about the destination he had written about, the one he had found at last, the one that bound him forever to his homeland.

The next morning he woke me before sunrise and asked whether I wanted to spend the day by myself or share it with him. I would be at liberty to do either from now on, he assured me. On any day I wanted to take part in the business affairs and endeavors of the house, I could get up when the courtyard bell rang, as it did each morning, and make my way to the communal breakfast. But if I had my own plans on a certain day, and in case he weren't there himself, his people had been directed to provide me with horses, with a companion, or with anything else I needed. It would be a favor to him, he said, if I would let him know about any such plans ahead of time, particularly if it involved long distances from the house, so he could save me from detours, difficulties, and perhaps even from small dangers that could arise. I was grateful to him for his hospitality and told him that I wanted to share time with him for today and tomorrow and for just as long as nothing else occurred to me.

So I got up, dressed, and went out under the overhanging roof for breakfast. The people were almost finished already and were leaving to go to their various jobs. The Major had waited for me and stayed until I had finished eating breakfast. Then the saddled horses were brought to us. I didn't ask what he was about to do but just followed him where he was riding.

On this day we didn't ride around the estate for him to show me his properties and activities in general, but he said he wanted to do what the day demanded of him and I might watch if it didn't bore me.

We came to some extensive meadow lands where hay was being harvested. The lovely Hungarian bay that the Major was riding carried him dancingly across the beautiful, soft-mown green grass. He dismounted and, while a worker held the horse, he examined the various stacks of hay. The worker commented that it was going to be gathered into the sheds that day. The Major ordered that a number of ditches ought to be dug to help drain off extra water and at other places to collect it, all while the fields were being mown. From the meadow he took the path to the greenhouses which were not, as is the usual case, situated near the residence but rather at their own suitable place where a gentle slope of ground allowed for a southern and an eastern exposure. There was a small clean stable available next to the greenhouses where the Major and those in his company, if there were any by chance, could put their horses; for it was not seldom the case that he would have to stay here for some time, and if he had visitors who wanted to examine the plant nursery, several hours might pass as well. We put our horses, still saddled, into the stable, and he first started looking at a number of bushes and plants that were being processed for on-demand shipments. Then he went into the gardening office, where the paperwork lay, and spent a rather long time at the desk with it. I looked at the things around me, meanwhile, about which I understood about as much or as little as an eternal traveler examining countless greenhouses can understand. As I browsed through some books and illustrations about this subject in his library later, though, I realized how little I actually knew about the essence of it.

"If you really want these charming things, which can get so complicated, to bear fruit," the Major was to say on another occasion, "then you have to tend to them from the ground up and try to improve significantly on what others are achieving."

Returning from the gardening office, he watched several women for a while who were busy dusting and cleaning the evergreen camellia leaves. This plant was still rare and expensive at the time. He also inspected those that had been cleaned and made his comments. From there we walked past the many pure white beds of sand in which the new seedlings were planted, then over to all the flowers and bushes whose cultivation he was overseeing. At the opposite end of the complex our horses were waiting; a gardener's apprentice had led them around to the back at the appropriate time. It was here that the preparation and mixing of soils took place; the constituent soils were brought here all year round by mule-train from various regions and often from distant stands of evergreens. There were even designated places for scorching the soil, and nearby were the piles of oak wood that served for heating in the winter.

Since it wasn't far from the greenhouses to the steppe, as I had already noticed the day before, we now rode out onto it. The steady lope of our lean horses soon carried us so far out onto the monotonous plain, fragrant with morning air, that all we could see of the mansion and the woods was a dark spot in the distance. Here we came across his herders. A few poles, so thin that there was no question of them providing shelter, formed a hut or perhaps just a sign that could be easily seen and located on the steppe. Beneath these poles burned, or rather glowed, a fire, kept alive with tough branches or roots of juniper, wild plum and other scraggly bushes. Here the herders, who took a lunch break at eleven o'clock, were already preparing their food. Tanned figures, whose furs lay around on the ground, were standing around the Major in dirty white pants and shirtsleeves, answering his questions.

Others, having seen his arrival from far out across the plain, came racing up on small, insignificant horses with neither saddle nor saddle cloth and often with only a piece of rope instead of bridle and halter. They dismounted, held their horses, and surrounded the Major, who had also dismounted and given someone his horse to hold. They talked with him not only about their work, but also about other things, and he knew almost all of them by name. He was as congenial as though he were one of them, and this, it seemed to me, evoked a kind of enthusiastic rapport among the men. Just as in the mountains of my homeland, the livestock here stayed outside in the elements all summer long. They were those long-horned white cattle indigenous to the country that nourish themselves from the steppe grasses, grasses with an aroma and a floral fragrance that we Alpine dwellers would scarcely find credible. The men also stay outside with the animals assigned to them; they often have nothing over their heads but the sky and the stars of the steppe, or perhaps, as we had just seen, a few lone poles or a sod dugout. They stood in front of the Major, or "lord of the estate" as they called him here, and listened to his instructions. As he mounted up again, one of the herdsmen, with sparkling eyes shining from his dark face and brows, held the horse while another with long hair and a dense mustache bent down and held the stirrup for him.

"So long, fellows," he said while riding off, "I'll come visit you again soon, and when the neighbors come over to visit we'll relax on the steppe some afternoon and eat with you."

He had said these words in Hungarian and then translated them for me at my request.

As we rode off, he said to me, "If you would find it pleasant to take a closer look at this cattle herding on the steppe sometime, and if you wanted to come out here on your own to live together with these people, you really ought to watch out for the dogs they have. They aren't always as tame and as patient as you saw them today; they would be savage towards you. You'd have to tell me ahead of time so I could come with you or, if I couldn't, then I would send a herder along with you, one that the dogs know and love.

As a matter of fact, I had marveled at the uncommonly tall, slender, shaggy dogs while we were at the herders' campfire, dogs such as I had never come across during my entire journey. They sat around us and among us so timidly at the fire that it seemed as if they understood the discussion and were taking part in it.

We changed directions, once we had ridden away, to turn towards the mansion again, since the time for the noon meal was approaching. As we were passing, just as the day before, close to the piece of land where people were working to drain the swampland and to mark out the path for a road, he said, pointing to a nearby wheat field on which the crop looked extremely rich: "These good acres of loam, if they do their duty, will have to earn us enough money so we can get the job done at other locations. The people over there work in wastelands all year round. They get their day's wages and cook out in the open right next to their work. For sleep, they go into those wooden cottages you see. In the winter, when ice builds up, we move to the lower-lying areas that we can't get to now because the soil is too soft, and we fill them in with rock debris from the plain and with stones removed from the vineyards."

When I looked over at the curious layout, I did in fact spot the wooden cottages he had spoken of, and I saw weak smoke rising at various places along the ridge, indicating perhaps the unsophisticated hearths on which the people were cooking their noon meal.

Just as we were riding through the woods, with the large bulldog and the smaller ones leaping around us, the dinner bell rang at the mansion, calling us and the others to dine.

I did not ask my friend about his destination that evening, as I had so firmly made up my mind to do before going to bed the night before.

The afternoon passed as usual at home, but around five o'clock the Major rode out, I don't know where, along the groomed trail with the rows of poplars where I had arrived by night. In the meanwhile, I surveyed the ever-increasing number of books he had ordered brought to my room from his library.

The following day the Major had a lot to write, and I spent nearly all day looking at the horses he kept at the mansion and getting acquainted with his workers.

On the day that followed I was with him at the sheep farm, a two-hour ride away, where we spent the whole day. He has some people there that display signs of considerable training and appear capable of exploring their beloved occupation with him in depth. Here I also learned, when he lent the sheep operations a sum of money taken from another area of operation, that all the branches of his enterprise have their own separate financial management. The transaction was correctly documented by a precise contractual agreement in the books. The operations are very wide-ranging and the agricultural disciplines are organized to meet their needs best.

Another time I saw the stud farms, and we were on the meadow where his foals and young ponies of ordinary breed were being herded, as were the cattle elsewhere.

In this way I gradually got to know the full extent of his activities, which was truly not insignificant. I was surprised that he would devote such attention and care to these things, since earlier I had known him more as the dreaming type, as someone meditating on the sciences and researching them.

"I believe," he once said, "that the place you have to start is with the soil of a country. Our constitution, our history is very old, but there is still much to be done; we've been preserved in it just like a dried flower pressed in a memorial album. This large country is a greater jewel than one might think, but it still has to be put in a better setting. The whole world is struggling to make itself useful, and we must also. But above all, what blossoming and what beauty this land is capable of, and both must be coaxed out! You must have seen it on your way to visit me. This steppe is made of the richest black soil; in these hills, full of glittering stone all the way to those blue mountains you see to the north, slumbers the fiery flow of wine, and the gleam of metal shimmers through, slightly veiled by the earth. Two grand waterways course through our land. Above them the air is still dormant, so to speak, and just waiting for the time when countless banners will flutter in it. There are many races of people in this country; many of them are like children who have to be shown what to do. Since I've been living in the midst of my people, over whom I actually hold more rights than you might think, since I've been going around with them in their own dress, sharing in their way of life, and earning their respect, it truly seems to me as if I had attained the very type of happiness I'd always been looking for in some distant place or other."

From this point on, I didn't ask the man anything more about his destination, the one he had mentioned in his letter to me.

He had devoted his attention, as a matter of first priority, to the various types of grain. And they were growing with such plumpness and splendor that I was already curious when the ears would start to ripen and when we would harvest them.

The solitude and vigor of these activities frequently reminded me of the powerful ancient Romans, who had also loved agriculture so much and who, at least in their earlier period, also liked to be solitary and vigorous.

"How lovely and primeval," I thought, "is the calling of a farmer if he understands and exalts it. In its plainness and variety, in that basic cohabitation with nature, which is free of passion, it borders on the very legend of paradise."

When I had been on the Major's estate for a considerable time, when I had assessed its various parts and had come to understand them, when living things were growing in front of me and I took an active interest in their flourishing, then the uniformly gentle passage of those days and activities had spun such a web around me that I felt healthy and balanced and I forgot our cities just as though what goes on in them were of little consequence.

After we had been among the horses on the steppe once again, and after their herdsmen had been joined by those responsible for tending the cattle, so that by chance a large group of these workers were together with us on the steppe, the Major said to me while we were driving home – for this time he had harnessed a handsome team to a wide-axled wagon now rolling safely along on the grass of the plain: "I would even be able to lead these men into war just by putting myself at their head. They are bound to me, without question. The others as well, the servants and workers I have at home, would rather have every bone in their body shattered than to allow one hair of my head to be disturbed. If I count in the ones that are subject to me by a feudal relationship as well and the ones emotionally bound to me from the bottom of their hearts, as I've been able to learn on many occasions, then I could gather together, I do believe, a rather large number of people that love me. Just imagine; and I didn't come to them until my hair had already turned gray and after I had forgotten them for many years. How would it be to lead hundreds of thousands like that and to lead them toward good, for when they trust someone, they are mostly like children and will follow toward good as well as toward evil."

"Once," he continued after a while, "I thought about becoming an artist or a scholar. I came to see, though, that such people have to deliver a deep, serious message to mankind in order to inspire others and to make them greater and nobler – or that the scholar, at least, has to reveal and create things that enhance and improve people in their earthly goods, in their means. In both cases, though, it's necessary for a man like that to have first of all a simple and great heart himself. But since I don't own that, I let it all go, and now that's behind me."

It seemed to me as if a gentle shadow fell across his eye after he said these words, and as if, at that moment, his eye were still looking out into the distance with the same passionate zeal he showed once, back when we sometimes sat leisurely on Epameo,[6] a whole sea of blue sky rejoicing around us, while the ocean glistened below and he would talk about all sorts of wishes and dreams that come to young hearts. And so, suddenly, the thought came to me that perhaps the happiness he told me he had found was still not quite complete yet.

That had been the only time during our acquaintanceship that he had referred to his past; he had never done so in all of our previous association. I also never asked, just as I was never to ask later. Whoever travels a lot learns to protect others and lets them repose in the sanctuary of their own private life, which won't open unless by voluntary means. By now I had been at Uvar for a considerable time and enjoyed being there, since I took part in the local activities to the extent of watching and often also by doing the actual work myself, and since at other times I was continuing to write about the travels and experiences in my diary. But I thought I could see that in the tidy, busy life of the Major some sediment was floating, preventing it from reaching full clarity, and it seemed to me as though some sort of sadness were indeed there, which in a man, of course, expresses itself only in quiet, solemn ways.

Other than that, he was quite straightforward in his life style and in his dealings with me, and there was never the slightest hint of reticence or duplicity. Sitting on the table in his office, for instance, where I frequently visited and where we chatted about various things on hot afternoons or on candlelit evenings before going to bed, was a picture beautifully framed in gold, the miniature portrait of a young lady of around twenty to twenty-two years old, but it was also strange that, no matter how the painter may have masked the subject's features, it was not the picture of a lovely young lady, but that of an ugly one. The darkened facial coloring and the shape of her forehead were peculiar, but there was a certain something inside of her, like power and strength, and her look was savage, like that of someone very determined. It became clear to me that this young woman had at some point played a role in his earlier life, and the question came to mind why this man had never married, just as I'd wondered when I'd known him in Italy; but following my principles, I hadn't asked him then and I wasn't asking now. He could leave the picture on his desk without any qualms, of course, since

---

[6] A mountain on the island of Ischia, which is located southwest of Naples in the Tyrrhenian Sea.

none of his servants came into the study but had to wait out front in the reception area, where a little bell rang as they entered whenever they had something to tell him. None of his acquaintances or visitors entered the study either, since he always received them in his other rooms. So there was some degree of trust involved: I was permitted to enter there and I could see everything sitting there or lying about. I might attribute such trust to the fact that I never asked questions or snooped around.

Meanwhile the time of harvest had come, and never will I forget those cheerful, joyous days!

Around this time the Major had to make occasional short trips in the vicinity and he invited me to go along. In no country are the distances between populated points often as great as they are here, but they can be covered in a relatively short time by riding with fast horses or driving light wagons across the plain. One time the Major put on his snug-fitting Hungarian folk outfit; he was smartly adorned with a saber at his side. It looked very good on him. He gave a speech in Hungarian about common concerns at a meeting of his regional colleagues. Since it had been my custom from the start, in every country I'd visited, to learn as much of the language as possible, I had also learned some Hungarian from the Major's workers and from all those around me; as a result, I understood much of his speech, which drew intense praise from one part of the audience and intense criticism from another part. While driving home, he translated all of it into German for me. At the afternoon meal that day I saw him in formal wear, as I had once in Italy, just as most of those present had changed from their folk dress and were dressed in the standard European tailcoats.

I had accompanied him on other visits he'd made in the vicinity as well. From these I discovered that four such great estates existed, of which the Major had one. A few years before, the owners had formed an alliance to improve agriculture and the use of natural resources by first achieving it with high standards on their own estates and thus setting an example for others, particularly when others saw that prosperity and a better life could come from it. The alliance also had its rules, and the members held agricultural meetings. Apart from these four large model farms, which had been the only actual members of the alliance to that point, a few smaller owners had already begun imitating the procedures of their larger neighbors without actually joining the alliance. All the farmers and other people were allowed to attend the sessions if they had preregistered for them, but then only to listen or to ask advice now and then. And their interest was not slight, as

I deduced from a meeting held at the estate of Gömör, a four-hour ride away from Uvar. The Major and Gömör were the only members there, but a considerable audience was present.

I visited Gömör twice more all by myself after that, and the second time I even spent several days with him.

As the harvest was nearing its end and the work was decreasing somewhat, the Major said to me one day: "Since we're going to get a little rest from our duties now, we'll ride over to my neighbor, Brigitta Maroshely, next week and pay her a visit. You'll get to know the most marvelous woman on earth in my neighbor Maroshely."

Two days after this utterance, he introduced Brigitta's son to me, who had come over by chance. This was the same young man who had eaten the noon meal with us on the first day of my stay at Uvar, the one who had caught my attention back then by his extraordinary good looks. He stayed with us nearly all day and was with us at various places on the estate. He was, as I had already noted the first time, in the earliest years of youth, scarcely past the transition from child to adolescent, and I liked him very much. His dark, gentle eyes spoke most agreeably to me, and whenever he was sitting so powerfully yet modestly on his horse, my whole being felt drawn towards him. I had known a friend like him, one who had gone to the grave in the earliest years of adolescence. Gustaf, as Brigitta's son was called, vividly reminded me of him.

Since the Major had made that pronouncement about Brigitta, and since I knew her son, I was very curious to meet her personally as well.

I had learned a little about the past of my host, the Major, from Gömör when I stayed with him. Gömör has an open and friendly tongue, like so many of his friends that I got to know there, and he told me what he knew without my asking. The Major, he said, wasn't born in this area. He had come from a very rich family. Since his youth he had almost always been on journeys; nobody really knew quite where, just as nobody knew in whose service he had earned the rank of Major either. He had never been on his estate at Uvar in all his earlier life. A few years ago he had arrived, settled at Uvar and joined the alliance of agricultural associates. At that time there were only two members of the alliance: Gömör himself and Brigitta Maroshely. Actually, he had gone on to say, it wasn't an alliance then, for the gatherings and the rules didn't come until later, but the two neighbors, he and Brigitta, had agreed to start cultivating their holdings better in this barren region. In essence, it had been Brigitta who had made the start. Because she could more easily be called unattractive than pleasing, her husband, a young, irresponsible man to whom she had been married at a young age, had left her and never returned. Then she had shown up with her child at Maroshely, her estate, had begun to make changes and to run the farm, and even up until now she still dressed and rode like a man. She kept her workers together and actively managed the estate from morning to night. Here, Gömör said, you could see what constant labor was capable of, for she had nearly created miracles on the stony ground. After getting to know her, Gömör became her imitator and introduced her ways on his own properties. Up until the present day, he had never regretted it. The Major, in the first few years after settling at Uvar, hadn't gone over to visit her. Then she fell deathly ill; at that, he rode across the plain to her and made her well again. From that time on, he regularly came to visit her. The people said at the time that he had used the healing powers of magnetism he had at his command, but no one really knows how to say accurately what happened. There had developed an unusually intimate and friendly bond between them – the woman was certainly worthy of the loftiest friendship, but whether the passion which the Major had embraced for the ugly and already aging Brigitta was natural, that was another question – and everybody who visits there, he said, recognizes that it is most assuredly a passion. The Major would certainly marry Brigitta if he could – he is obviously deeply upset that he can't – but because nothing is known about her legal husband, no certificate of death or divorce can be brought into evidence. This fact speaks very well for Brigitta and as a judgment against her spouse, he said, the one who once deserted her so irresponsibly, while now such a serious man was yearning to have her.

Gömör had told me these things about the Major and Brigitta and, on the occasion of visits we made at various of the neighbors, I came together with her son Gustaf a few more times before the day arrived on which we had arranged to ride over to see his mother.

On the evening before this day, as the thousandfold nocturnal chirpings of the steppe crickets were falling on my sleepy ears, I thought of her one more time. Then I dreamed all sorts of things about her: in particular, I couldn't escape the dream that I was standing on the steppe in front of the strange woman rider who had lent me the horses earlier, that she was casting a spell with her lovely eyes so that I had to remain standing there, that I couldn't raise either foot, and that I wouldn't be able to leave this spot on the steppe again for all the days of my life. Then I slept more soundly, awoke refreshed and strengthened the next day; the horses were brought, and I looked forward to seeing the woman face to face who had been with me in so many different forms in my dream that night.

3.
The Steppe in Times Past

Before I describe how we rode to Maroshely, how I got to know Brigitta, and how I visited on her estate quite often afterwards, it's necessary for me to relate a portion of her earlier life without which the following would be incomprehensible. The way I was able to get such thorough knowledge about the circumstances depicted here will emerge from my relationships to the Major and to Brigitta, and at the end of this story it will become self-evident, without it being necessary for me to disclose beforehand what I didn't even find out beforehand myself but only learned through the natural course of events.

Integral to the human race is the marvelous notion of beauty. We are all moved by the sweetness of the phenomenon and can't always tell the source of that appeal. It's found in the universe. It's found in an eye. Then again it's not found in features formed by any laws of the wise or rational. Often beauty is unseen because it's in the desert or because the correct eye hasn't seen it yet. Often it is worshiped and idolized even though it isn't there, but it must never be totally missing whenever a heart beats with fervor and ecstasy or when two souls are aglow for each other; otherwise the heart stops and the love of those souls is dead. The soil from which this flower blossoms is, however, different a thousand times in a thousand cases; but if it is there, it can be deprived of every possible germination point and it will still sprout from another where it was least expected. It is peculiar to humans and it only makes us noble that we kneel before beauty, and it alone pours everything worthwhile and praiseworthy into our quivering, blissful hearts. It is sad for someone who doesn't have it or isn't acquainted with it or in whom the eye of a stranger can never find it. Even the heart of a mother turns away when she is no longer able to discern even a single glimmer of this ray in her child.

That was what happened to Brigitta as a child. When she was born, she didn't prove to be the lovely angel that a child usually appears to her mother. Afterward she lay under snowy white linen in the beautiful, resplendent golden cradle with an unpleasant, gloomy little face, just as if a demon had breathed on her. Her mother unwittingly turned her eyes away and fixed them on two pretty little angels cavorting on the thick floor carpet. When strangers came to visit, they didn't approve or disapprove of the child; they asked about her sisters. This was the way she grew up. Her father often passed through the room looking for some task or other to finish, and when her mother, sometimes as if out of sexual frustration, hugged the other children, she never saw the staring black eyes of Brigitta fixed on her as though the tiny child already understood the insult. If she cried, they took care of her needs; if she didn't cry, they left her lying there. They all had things to do themselves, and she turned her big eyes toward the gilding on the cradle or the decorations on the wallpaper. When her arms and legs had gotten stronger and her habitat was no longer in the narrow cradle, she sat in a corner, played with rocks, and made sounds she hadn't learned from anybody. As she advanced in her game playing and became more agile, she often spun her large, wild eyes around in their sockets the way boys do who are already playing out evil deeds inside them. She hit her sisters whenever they tried to interfere in her games, and when her mother, in a show of belated love and compassion, would take the little creature into her arms and shed tears over her, little Brigitta didn't show any happiness but cried and turned away from the enveloping hands. This made her mother simultaneously even more loving and more embittered, for she didn't know that the shallow little roots which had once sought the warm soil of maternal love, and hadn't found it, were being forced to plant themselves in the stone of Brigitta's own heart and to turn defiant.

And so the desert kept expanding.

As the children grew and beautiful clothes were brought into the house, Brigitta's were always acceptable, while her sisters' were altered a number of times until they fit. The others were given rules of conduct and praise; she wasn't criticized, even if she got her dresses dirty or wrinkled. When the time for lessons came, filling the morning hours, she sat behind the others at the back and stared with the only beauty she had – her truly beautiful, dark eyes – at the corner of some distant book or at the map, and when the teacher asked her a rare, quick question, she panicked and couldn't come up with an answer. But on long evenings or any other time the others sat in the family room and forgot about her, she was lying around on the floor reading the hodgepodge of books strewn around her or looking at pictures and torn maps that the others no longer needed. It must have been a twisted fantasy world she was creating in her heart. Since her father always left the key in his bookcase, she had read nearly half of his books without anyone knowing it. Most of them she couldn't understand. The parents often found pieces of paper lying around the house that must have been hers, with odd and crazy drawings on them.

When the girls had become young ladies, she stood out like a weed among the flowers. Her sisters had grown soft and beautiful; she was merely lean and strong. In her body was a practically masculine strength; this was evidenced by the fact that if one of her sisters tried to murmur sweet words to her or to hug her, she could easily brush her aside with her angular arm, or by the fact that Brigitta would set to work at laborers' heavy chores, as she liked to do, until the beads of sweat stood out on her forehead. She never learned to play a musical instrument, but she rode boldly and well, like a man; often she lay around on the lawn in her prettiest dress, making broken speeches and exclamations into the leafy bushes. About this time, her father also began giving her warnings about her stubborn and sullen behavior. Then, even if she had just been talking, she suddenly stopped and became even more sullen and stubborn. It was of no help when her mother made signals, wringing her hands in bitter helplessness to announce her displeasure. The girl wouldn't talk. Once, when her father lost control to the extent that he physically spanked her, his grown daughter, because she refused to join the others in the family room, she simply looked at him with her dry, piercing eyes and still wouldn't go, let him do what he might.

If only someone had been there to see beyond her masked soul and to see her beauty so she wouldn't despise herself! But there was no one: the others couldn't do it, and she couldn't do it herself either.

Her father was living in the capital city with his family, as he had done most of his life, where he surrendered himself to a glittering life of ease. When his daughters were grown, reports of their beauty spread across the land; many came by to see them, and the gatherings and parties at the family house became more numerous and more lively than they had ever been before. Many hearts beat fast and sought to take possession of the jewels sheltered in this house – but the jewels themselves paid no heed, or else they were too young to understand such attentions. All the more did they give in to the pleasures that such soirées brought with them, and a party dress or the preparations for a celebration could keep them busy, most grippingly and intensely, for days at a time. Brigitta, as the youngest, was not asked to contribute, as if she didn't understand what was going on. She was sometimes present at the gatherings – on those occasions always wearing a full, black silk dress that she had sewn herself – or else she avoided them altogether, sat in her room during that time, and nobody knew what she was doing there.

A few years passed in this way.

Toward the end of that time, a man who had stirred a sensation in the various social circles appeared in the capital city. His name was Stephan Murai. His father had raised him in the country in order to prepare him for life. When his education had been completed, he first had to travel and then he was to become acquainted with the most exclusive society of his homeland. This was the reason he had come to the capital. Here he soon became almost the only topic of conversation. Some extolled his intelligence, others his conduct and his modesty; still others said they had never seen any man as handsome. Several claimed he was a genius; and since there was no lack of slander or character assassination either, some said that he showed the signs of something timid but savage and that you could tell by looking at him that he had been raised in the woods. A few thought, too, that he had false pride and, if it came down to it, deceit as well. Many young female hearts were curious to see him once at the very least. Brigitta's father knew the family of the new arrival very well; in earlier years when he was still making one-day social calls, he had often visited on their estate, and only later did they lose contact, for he lived in the capital from then on and the Murai family never did. When he investigated the state of the family's holdings, which had once been superb, and learned that it was now even considerably better and that, given the family's simple life style, it was improving all the time, he thought that if the man's character were also acceptable to him personally, he could deliver a highly desirable bridegroom for one of his daughters. Since many other fathers and mothers were thinking the same thing, however, Brigitta's father hurried to seize the advantage. He invited the young man to his house; the latter accepted and had already been at several of their soirées. Brigitta hadn't seen him, since this was just at the time she'd been avoiding social gatherings for quite a while.

Once she went to see her uncle, who had organized some sort of celebration and invited her to it. In earlier years, it hadn't been without enjoyment that she had visited her uncle and his family. On this evening, she sat there in her usual black silk dress. Around her head she wore a headdress she had made herself, one that her sisters had pronounced ugly. In all of this city, at least, it wasn't customary to wear one like it, but it matched her dark coloring quite well.

Many people were present, and once when she looked through a group of them she saw the two dark, gentle eyes of the young man riveted on her. She looked away again immediately. Later, when she looked over again, she saw that his eyes had been directed her way again. It was Stephan Murai looking at her.

About a week later there was a dance at her father's house. Murai had been invited too, and he arrived when almost everyone was there and the dance had already started. He watched, and when partners were being chosen for the second dance, he went over to Brigitta and asked her in a modest voice for a dance. She said that she had never learned how to dance. He bowed to excuse himself, then mixed in among the spectators again. Later on, he was seen dancing. Brigitta sat down on a sofa behind a table and watched the activities. Murai spoke with various girls, danced and joked with them. He had been particularly kind and obliging on this evening. Finally the entertainment was over; people scattered in all directions to find their night's shelter. When Brigitta had entered the bedroom in which she lived alone, a concession she had wrested from her parents with incessant pleading and pouting, and as she was undressing there, she shot a glance at herself in the mirror while passing and saw her brown forehead float past with the raven-black curls framing it. Then she went over to her bed and pulled down the covers – since she never tolerated a maid either while she was dressing or undressing – turned back the snowy-white linens from her resting place, which she always required to be made up very hard, lay down, put her slender arm under her head and looked at the ceiling of her room with sleepless eyes.

As there were now parties often after this and Brigitta attended them, she was again noticed by Murai; she was greeted very respectfully by him, and as she was leaving he brought her shawl to her, and right after she was gone his wagon could be heard down below, rolling away to take him home.

This lasted for a long time.

One night she was at her uncle's house again, and after she had stepped outside, because of the great heat in the ballroom, onto the balcony, whose doors always stood open, and dense night lay around her, she heard him walking toward her and then saw in the dark that he was standing next to her. He didn't say anything other than normal things, but when she listened for his tone of voice, it seemed as though something bashful were in it. He spoke highly of the night and said that people who cursed it did it an injustice; it is actually so full of beauty and peace that it alone encompasses, softens, and soothes the heart. Then he was silent, and she also was silent. After she had stepped back into the room, he too went in and stood at a window for a long time.

After Brigitta had gotten home that night, after she had retired to her room and taken off her party clothes piece by piece, she stepped in front of the mirror in her nightgown and looked at herself for a long, long time. Tears came to her eyes; they didn't run dry but just made way for more to well up and run down her cheeks. These had been the first tears in her life that came from the depths of her soul. Her weeping grew longer and longer and became more and more passionate; it seemed as if she had to make up for all of her wasted life, as if everything would have to get much better once she had wept her heart out. She had fallen to her knees, as she was used to doing often, and was sitting on her own feet. On the floor next to her, by chance, lay a little picture: it was an illustration for children depicting the way one brother sacrifices himself for another. She pressed this little picture to her lips until it was wrinkled and wet.

Even after the wellsprings had run dry and the candles had burned low, she was still sitting on the floor in front of her dressing table, thinking, just like a child who had cried herself out. Her hands were lying in her lap; the bows and ruffles of the nightgown were damp and hanging down around her virgin breast with no particular appeal. She grew quieter and less agitated. Finally she took a couple of deep breaths, wiped her eyes with the palm of her hand, and went to bed. As she was lying there and the night lamp, which she had put behind a small shade after the candles had burnt out, was burning dimly, she said to herself, "It just isn't possible; it just isn't possible!"

Then she fell into slumber.

When she was with Murai again after that, it was as it had been earlier, except that he singled her out even more; other than that, his behavior was shy, almost reticent. He said almost nothing to her. She herself gave him no encouragement, not even the slightest.

When the occasion presented itself after some time to speak with her alone, after having failed to seize many such opportunities before, he found the courage to talk to her and said that it appeared to him she harbored a dislike for him, and if this were so, then he only wanted to make one request: that she might try to get to know him. Perhaps he was not totally unworthy of her attention; perhaps he had qualities, or could develop some, that would gain her respect for him. There was nothing that he wished for more deeply.

"It's not dislike, Murai," she replied, "Oh no, not dislike; but I also have a request for you: don't do it, don't do it! Don't try to win me over; you'll only regret it."

"But why, Brigitta, why?"

"Because," she answered quietly, "I can't ask for any other love but the very greatest. I know I'm ugly, so I would demand greater love than would the most beautiful girl on earth. I don't know how great, but it seems to me it should be without measures or limits. So you see, since this is impossible, don't try to win me over. You are the only one who's even inquired if I have a heart, so I can't lie to you."

Perhaps she might have said even more if others hadn't joined them right then, but her lip was quivering with pain.

That Murai's heart was not calmed by these words but only grew more inflamed is understandable. It was as an angel of light that he worshiped her. He retreated into himself, his eye passed over the grandest beauties that surrounded him in order to seek hers with gentle pleas. So it continued on, inevitably. In her own impoverished soul now the dark power and immensity of feelings also began to tremble. This became obvious in both of them. The people around them began to suspect the unbelievable and were openly aghast. Murai unmistakably opened up his soul for all the world to see. One day, in a room alone, as others were gathered elsewhere to listen to music now resounding from afar off, as he stood before her and said nothing, as he took her hand, gently drawing her to him, she didn't resist, and when he bent his face down toward her and she suddenly felt his lips, her lips responded sweetly. She had never before felt a kiss, since she had never even been kissed by her mother or her sisters, and Murai said once, years later, that he had never experienced such pure joy as then, when he had felt those untouched, deserted lips on his mouth for the first time.

The curtain between the two of them was now torn, and fate took its course. In a few days Brigitta was declared the fiancée of the celebrated man; both sets of parents agreed to the marriage. Now came a time of congenial relations. From the depths of the previously unknown girl came forth a warm personality, improbable and insignificant in the beginning, but then unfolding abundantly and cheerfully. The instinct that had drawn this man to this woman had not led him astray. She was strong and virtuous like no other woman. Because she hadn't sapped the power of her heart prematurely by thoughts and dreams of love, the breath of fresh life could flow into her soul. The way she related to Murai was charming as well. Because she had always been alone, she had constructed her own world, and now he was introduced into a new, remarkable kingdom that only belonged to her. As her personality was unfolding before him, he also came to realize that her intense and passionate love was surging like a golden river between full but lonesome banks, for just as others share their hearts with half the world, she had kept hers intact, and since only one man had recognized that, her heart was also the property of this one man. Thus he lived through the days of engagement in joy and high spirits.

Time flew on rose-colored wings and, with it, fate on wings of darkness.

The wedding day had come at last. Murai, once the religious ceremony was over, had taken his silent bride into his arms just outside the church, had lifted her into his wagon and driven it to his house. Since the young couple had decided to live in town, he had commissioned the house to be furnished in a most elegant and glittering fashion from the wealth of his father, who had put his life savings at his son's disposal. Murai's father had traveled to the wedding from his country estate, the one he had chosen as his permanent place of residence. His mother could not share in the joy, unfortunately: she had already died long before. From the bride's side, both father and mother were present, along with the sisters, the uncle, and several other close relatives. Murai, as well as Brigitta's father, had wanted the day to be celebrated publicly and with great pomp, and that is precisely the way it went.

When the last guests had finally left, Murai led his wife through a series of lighted rooms – though up until then they had always had to make do with just one – and then back to the living room. There they remained sitting for awhile, and he said these words, "How splendidly everything has gone, and how wonderfully it's come true. Brigitta! I realized at once what you meant to me. When I saw you for the first time, I already knew then that I would never stay indifferent to this woman, but I didn't know yet whether I would have to love you infinitely or hate you infinitely. How fortunately it's turned out to be love!"

Brigitta said nothing; she held his hand and let her glowing eyes wander in gentle tranquility around the room.

Then they ordered the servants to carry off the leftovers from the celebration, turn off the mass of superfluous lights, and change the festive halls into an ordinary residence. This was carried out; the servants went to their rooms and the first night descended on the new house and the new family just a few hours old, consisting of two.

From this point on they lived in their own house. Just as they had seen each other only in social groups when they were getting to know one another, and just as they had only met in public while they were engaged, now they always stayed home. They didn't think that any external thing was required for their happiness. Although the house was generally equipped with everything necessary, there were still so many details for improving or beautifying the surroundings. They made subtle adjustments, they pondered what they could place here and there, they lent each other advice and help until the living space took on an increasingly sophisticated organization; anyone entering was met with clear convenience and simple beauty.

After the space of a year she bore him a son, and this new miracle kept her at home even more. Brigitta cared for her child; Murai looked after his business, since his father had transferred a portion of his landed holdings to him, and he managed them from town. This made a number of compromises necessary and caused a number of difficulties to accumulate that could have been solved had he been on location.

When the child had developed to the point that immediate care was not so necessary any more, when Murai had gotten his business affairs in order enough that they ran smoothly, he began to take his wife out more frequently than he had otherwise been accustomed: to public places, to social events, on walks, to the theater. On these occasions, she noticed that he treated her even more tenderly and considerately in front of other people than he did at home.

She thought, "Now he knows what's wrong with me," and kept her suffocating heart to herself.

The following spring he took her and his child along on a journey, and when they returned towards autumn, he suggested that it might be preferable for them to live permanently on one of his properties in the country: it would be more convenient and pleasant than in the city.

Brigitta followed him to the country estate.

Here he began to manage the agricultural concerns and to make changes; he spent his spare time going hunting. And here fate led him to a completely different woman than he was used to seeing every day. During one of the solitary hunts that he went on frequently now, hiking or riding alone through the area with his rifle, he had seen her. As he was slowly guiding his horse through a break in the willow thicket, down a slight slope, he had suddenly seen two startled, beautiful eyes peering across through the thick bushes at him like those of an exotic gazelle, and her cheeks glowing as sweetly as the blush of dawn beside the green leaves. It was just an instant; before he was able to take a good look, the figure, who was also sitting on a horse behind the bushes, turned her horse and flew away between the scraggly bushes and across the plain.

It had been Gabriela, the daughter of an elderly count who lived in the vicinity, a wild creature her father was raising in the country, giving her all possible freedom, since he thought this was the only way to have her unfold naturally and not turn into the sort of artificial doll he couldn't stand in other women. Gabriela's beauty had already become well known far and wide, only her repute hadn't reached Murai's ears because he had never been on his country estate before and had recently been on his extended journey.

Several days later the two met again at almost the same place and then more and more frequently. They didn't ask each other who they were or where they came from, but the girl, just like a bottomless source of uninhibited nature, joked, laughed, teased him, and usually challenged him to daring, boisterous horse races in which she flew along beside him like a heavenly, maniacal, radiant mystery. He joked with her as well and usually let her win. One day, though, when she was breathless with exhaustion and only able to let him know that she wanted him to stop by repeatedly reaching for his reins, and when she had achingly whispered, while being lifted down off the horse, that she was vanquished – and after he had repaired the strap on her stirrup where something was broken and he saw her standing by a tree trunk, her passion smoldering – then, he suddenly pulled her into his arms and embraced her. Before he could see if she was angry or ecstatic, he jumped on his horse and rode away. It had been done out of high spirits, but a jumble of indescribable joy was in him for that moment, and as he rode home the image of the soft cheek, sweet breath, and shining eyes hung in front of him.

They didn't seek each other out anymore from then on, but when they saw each other once by chance for a moment in the room of a neighbor, both their cheeks were flooded with deep crimson.

Murai then went to one of his distant land holdings and reorganized all the working conditions he found there.

But Brigitta's heart was broken. A lump of shame as large as earth itself had metastasized in her bosom; she didn't say a word, and she went around the rooms of the house in a cloud of gloom. Finally, she took her swollen, shrieking heart in her hands, so to speak, and crushed it.

When he returned from reorganizing the distant estate, she went into his room and, in gentle words, asked him for a divorce. When he reacted with acute shock, when he begged her, when he offered her his objections, she just kept on saying the same words, "I told you that you would regret it; I told you that you would regret it." Then he jumped up, took her hand and said in a fierce voice, "Woman, I can't tell you how much I hate you; I can't tell you how much I hate you!"

She didn't say a word, but just looked at him with her dry, inflamed eyes. When he had packed and shipped his luggage three days later, though, and had ridden off in his travel outfit that evening, she lay down, just as she had done as a girl when she had loudly recited the poetry of her heart to the bushes in the garden, but this time it was in pain on the carpet in her room, and such hot tears were flowing from her eyes it seemed they would have to burn through her dress, the carpet, and the floor boards. They were the last tears she would ever weep for the man she still dearly loved, then no more tears. Meanwhile he rode out onto the dark plain and had in mind a hundred times to blow his simmering brains out with his saddle pistol. During his ride, while it was still light, he passed by Gabriela standing on the balcony of her mansion, but he didn't look up. He just rode on.

After half a year, he sent back his consent to the divorce and also granted custody of the son to her, whether it was that he thought the boy would be better off in her hands or whether it was still his old love that didn't want to deprive her of everything – her, Brigitta, who was now completely alone while the wide world lay open before him. With regard to finances, he had provided for her and their son in the most generous manner possible. He enclosed papers documenting all this. This was the first and last sign of life that Murai had sent; after that, nothing else arrived and he never showed up again. The sums of money he needed had been transferred to an Antwerp bank. This is what his financial trustee said; he didn't know any more than that himself.

Around this time Brigitta's father, her mother, and both sisters died one right after the other. Murai's father, who was already very old anyway, also died a short time after.

And so Brigitta was, in the strictest sense of the word, completely alone with her child.

Extremely far from the capital city, she had a residence on a barren plain where nobody knew her. The estate was called Maroshely, from which the name of her family had come. After the divorce, she took her maiden name of Maroshely again and moved to the house on the plain to hide.

Just as once when someone, probably out of pity, had given her a lovely doll, and she tossed it aside after enjoying it a short while and then brought back crude things to her bed like stones, pieces of wood, and such, she now brought the greatest possession she had, her son, to Maroshely with her; she looked after him and protected him, and the only place her eye would turn was toward his cradle.

As he grew and his range of vision and his heart expanded, so did hers; she began to look at the steppe around her, and her spirit began to deal with the desert encircling her. She put on men's clothes, got back up on the horse again as she had in her youth, and showed up for work with her laborers. As soon as the boy was able to stay on a horse, he was with her everywhere, and the active, creative, demanding soul of his mother gradually flowed into him. Her soul reached out further and further; a heavenly touch of creation flowed into her. Green hills plumped up, wells flowed, grape vines whispered, and on the barren, stony ground was composed the powerful beat of a heroic saga. And the saga brought, as poetry will do, its own blessing with it. Many imitated her; the agricultural association came to life. Those even further away became enthused, and here and there on the gloomy, barren steppe the free rein of humanity opened up like a lovely eye.

After Brigitta had been living at Maroshely for fifteen years, the Major arrived, moving into his country estate at Uvar, where he had never been before. From this woman he learned, as he told me himself, to work and to work effectively – and it was for this woman he developed that deep and belated affection I told of earlier.

Now that this part of Brigitta's earlier life has been told, as was mentioned at the beginning of this section, we will move on to develop the situation as we left it.

4.
The Steppe at Present

We rode to Maroshely. Brigitta was indeed that woman rider who had loaned me the horses. She remembered our meeting with a friendly smile. My cheeks turned red as I thought of the tip I'd offered her. There was no one else visiting there but the Major and I. He introduced me as someone he had met on his travels, someone he had spent a lot of time with and whom, he flattered himself to say, he was in the process of turning from an acquaintance into a friend. I felt the joy – truly not insignificant to me – that she knew almost all the details relating to the time I had spent with him earlier, which meant he must have told her a lot about me, that he still liked to dwell on those days, and that she considered it worth the effort to remember such things.

She said she didn't intend to show me around her mansion and her fields. I would see them in the natural course of things as we went walking, if I would come over from Uvar often enough in the future, which she politely invited me to do.

She accused the Major of not having come over to visit for a long time. He excused himself by saying how busy he'd been, but mainly by saying that he didn't want to ride over without me and that he first wanted to find out how well or how poorly I would be suited to her.

We went into a large room where we rested for a bit. The Major pulled out a notepad and asked her about several things, to which she gave clear and simple replies, some of which he wrote down. Then she, too, asked about various things related to some of the neighbors, to my friend's present activities, and even to the next session of regional parliament. I saw on this occasion the deeply earnest way she had of dealing with these matters and the kind of attention the Major paid to her opinions. When she was unsure of something, she admitted her ignorance and asked the Major for a solution.

After we had rested and the Major put his notepad away, we stood up to take a walk through her properties. The talk was frequently about the changes that had just recently taken place in her household. While Brigitta was speaking about matters of *his* house, it seemed to me that there was some sort of tenderness in how truly concerned she was. She showed him the new wooden colonnade opening onto the garden from the house and asked him if she should let grapevines grow up the columns. Just such an arrangement could be made by his own courtyard windows as well, she said, making a delightful place to sit in the late autumn sun. She led us out into the park, which had been a wild stand of oaks ten years earlier, but trails now passed through it, enclosed fountains were flowing, and deer were grazing. By inexpressible persistence, she had seen to the construction of a high wall around the huge circumference of the park as a protection against wolves. She had taken the money for this project slowly from her cattle proceeds and from the cornfields, whose productivity she had greatly increased. When the enclosure was completed, there had been an organized hunt, step by step through every portion of the park, to make certain that not a single wolf, possibly with a future brood, had been walled in. But not one was there. Only then were deer introduced into the enclosure, and other precautions were taken. The deer, it appeared, knew all that and were grateful to her: whenever we saw one during our walk, it wasn't shy and just looked across at us with its dark, shining eyes. Brigitta liked to take her guests and friends for tours through the park, because she loved it herself. At the far end we came to the pheasant sanctuary. As we were hiking the trails like this, with white clouds peeking through the tops of the oak trees, I had an opportunity to observe Brigitta. Her eyes, it appeared to me, were even blacker and shone more brightly than those of the deer, and they may have been beaming with particular brilliance that day since there was a man walking at her side who knew enough to appreciate the results of her work and creativity. Her teeth were snowy white and her figure, still supple for her age, bore witness to indomitable power. Since she had expected the Major, she was dressed in women's clothing and had set her work aside to devote the day to us.

While discussions of various types were underway about the future of the country, about elevating and improving the lot of the common man, about preparing and profiting from the soil, about controlling and restricting the flow of the Danube, about outstanding Magyar patriots, we walked through most of the park, since, as I already said before, she didn't want to take us on a tour of her estate but just wanted to keep us company. When we returned home, it was time to eat supper. Gustaf, Brigitta's son, also came to supper with his cheeks somewhat sunburned, a delightfully slender young man in the bloom of health. He had visited the fields and assigned the tasks that day in place of his mother, and now he briefly reported on various things. At the table he sat listening modestly at one end; in his handsome eyes were excitement for the future and infinite kindness for the present.

Since here, as at the Major's estate, the workers were seated at the table, too, I noticed my friend Milos, who greeted me as a sign that we knew each other.

The largest part of the afternoon passed as we inspected a number of changes new to the Major, spent an hour in the garden, and walked through the vineyards.

Toward evening we took our leave. As we were looking for our overcoats, Brigitta reproached the Major for having ridden home from Gömör in the night air recently with only light clothing – didn't he know how treacherous the misty air of this steppe was that he should leave himself exposed like that? He didn't defend himself but said he would be more careful in the future. I knew very well, though, that he had forced his own *bunda* on Gustaf that night, who had come without one, and had lied by saying that he had another one in the stable. This time, though, we both departed adequately outfitted and safe. Brigitta herself saw to everything and only went back into the house once we were seated astride our horses in our thick overcoats and the moon was rising. She had given the Major a few more instructions and then took her leave with simple but noble friendliness. The conversation between these two had been calm and cheerful all day, but it seemed to me as if a secret intensity were quivering between them, one that they were both ashamed to yield to, probably because they thought themselves too old. On the way back, though, the Major said to me, after I had been unable to hold back some truthful, sincere words of praise for this woman: "Friend! I have often been passionately desired in my lifetime – whether I've also been loved like that, I don't know – but the companionship and the esteem of this woman have become greater sources of happiness for me in this world than any others I've imagined in my life."

He had said these words without any passion, but with such a calm assurance that I was totally convinced in my heart of their truth. Something nearly came over me at that moment that is otherwise not typical of me: I was very nearly envious of the Major for this friendship and his domestic activities. At that time, I had nothing solid to hold onto in the whole wide world apart from my hiking stick, perhaps, with which I had set off to see this country or that, but it was nothing that was truly lasting.

As we were going home, the Major asked me whether I might like to spend at least the next summer and winter with him. He had begun to treat me with greater confidence and trust, allowing me deeper glimpses into his heart and his life such that I was forming a great love and affection for the man. So I accepted. And once I had done that, he said he wanted to entrust me with one of the branch operations of his estate for which I would be permanently responsible. I would never regret it, he said, and it would certainly be of use to me in the future. I likewise agreed to that, and indeed it was to be of use to me. Entirely to the major I attribute the fact that I now have a household, that I have a loving spouse whom I support with my own efforts, that I now coax one blessing after another, one achievement after another into our sphere of influence. Once I became a part of the harmonious operations he had developed, I wanted to do my part as well as I could; and as I kept practicing I started doing it better and better. I myself was worthwhile and esteemed; and as I got to know the sweetness of work I also realized that anything that causes good is much more valuable than the life of loitering I had previously spent in the name of gathering experiences. So I grew accustomed to the active life.

Thus time passed slowly, and I was infinitely glad to be in Uvar and in the surrounding lands.

I visited Maroshely often under these circumstances. I was respected and I was almost like one of the family members and got to know the inner workings better and better. There was no trace of any foreboding passion, of any feverish lust, or even of magnetism as I had heard. The relationship between the Major and Brigitta was, on the other hand, of a very strange type such that I'd never seen anything like it. It was, without a doubt, what we would call love between two persons of opposite sexes, but it didn't appear to be such. The Major treated the aging woman with a tenderness, with an adoration reminiscent of worship toward a Higher Being. She was visibly filled with intense joy from it and this joy blossomed like a late flower on her face, laying a breath of nearly incredible beauty across it, but it also cultivated the hardy rose of cheerfulness and health. She reciprocated the same respect and adoration for her friend, except that a touch of worry about his health or about his minor needs and such was commingled with it at times, all of which was a part of the woman and of her love. The behavior of both of them didn't exceed these bounds by a hair's breadth – and so they kept on living this way, side by side.

The Major once said to me that the two of them, in one of those moments when they were discussing their personal relationship in an intimate way that rarely occurs between people, had come to the conclusion that friendship of the most graceful sort should reign between them, as should sincerity, cooperation, and communication, but nothing more: they wished to stand before this altar of unimpeachable virtue, possibly happy until the end of their lives – they didn't intend to ask any further questions of fate so that it might not sting them and might not be fickle again. This is how things had gone on for a number of years and how they would remain.

That is what the Major had said to me, but it was some time later that fate unbidden offered its own answer, solving everything quickly and in an unexpected manner.

It was very late in autumn, you could say the beginning of winter, and a thick fog was lying over the already frozen steppe one day as I was riding along with the Major on the recently built road between the rows of young poplars. We were thinking about hunting a little when we suddenly heard two muffled shots ring out through the fog.

"Those are my pistols and none other!" the Major cried out.

Before I could comprehend or ask what was happening, he already had his horse leaping down the road at a more frightening gallop than I have ever seen. I followed since I suspected some tragedy, and as I caught up to him, I came upon a spectacle so gruesome and so magnificent that even now my soul simultaneously shudders and rejoices: at the spot where the gallows stands and the stream shimmers through the reeds, the Major had found the boy Gustaf defending himself at the point of exhaustion against a pack of wolves. Two of them he had already shot; with his knife he was warding off one that had leapt at his horse from the front, and the others he was keeping at bay for the moment with the fury of his eyes sparkling with fear and wildness, boring into them, but they surrounded him, patiently waiting and panting, so that a turning away, a blink of his eye, a trifle could give them all a reason to spring on him at once – then, in the moment of greatest need, the Major appeared. When I arrived, he was already in the midst of them like a miracle of destruction, like a meteor. The man was almost terrifying to behold: with no regard for himself, almost like a predator, he attacked them. I hadn't seen how he got off his horse, since I arrived too late, but I had heard the roar of his double-barreled pistols, and when I appeared on the scene, his hunting knife was flashing out at the wolves, and he was on foot. Three or four seconds it may have lasted; I only had time to fire my hunting rifle once into the midst of them, and the menacing beasts vanished into the fog as if swallowed up by it.

"Load your weapons!" cried the Major, "they'll be right back!"

He snatched up the pistols that he had cast aside earlier and was inserting cartridges in them. We loaded up as well, and as soon as it was relatively quiet again we heard the ominous trotting around the oak near the gallows. It was obvious that the hungry, frightened animals were circling around us until they could find enough courage to attack again. Actually, these animals are cowardly when they're not spurred on by hunger. We weren't equipped for a wolf hunt and the accursed fog lay thick around us, so we headed straight toward the mansion. The horses shot along in deathly fear, and as we were riding, I saw a shadow chasing along beside me more than once, gray in the gray fog. With infinite patience the pack hurried along beside us. We had to be in constant readiness. Once the Major fired off a shot to his left, but we didn't see anything. There was no time for talking, and in this way we reached the park gate. As we pushed our way inside, the wonderful, noble bulldogs waiting behind it broke loose and charged past us, and in that instant their enraged howls and barks resounded through the fog, coursing down along the plain behind the wolves.

"Mount up, all of you!" cried the Major to his men rushing up to us, "Let all the wolfhounds loose so my poor bulldogs don't take the brunt of it. Muster up all the neighbors and hunt for as many days as you like. I'm offering twice the usual bounty for every dead wolf, except for those lying at the gallows oak, since we killed those ourselves. Near the oak could also be one of the pistols that I gave as a present to Gustaf last year. I see only one in his hand, and the saddle holster for the other one is empty. Go see if it's there."

"For five years," he said, turning to me as we rode on through the park, "no wolf has dared come so close to us and in general it's been very safe here. It must be a very hard winter, and it must have already started in the northern countries for them to have pushed their way down south already."

The servants had heard their master's order and, in less time than seemed possible to me, a group of hunters had been outfitted; that race of beautiful shaggy dogs peculiar to the Hungarian steppe and so indispensable was with them. The servants talked about means for recruiting the neighbors, and then they went off to initiate the hunt from which they wouldn't return for one week, two weeks, or even more.

We had watched most of these preparations, all three of us, without getting off our horses. But when we left the area of the barns and headed toward the house, we saw that Gustaf had indeed been wounded. As we reached the archway, where we wanted to dismount and go to our rooms, a rush of weakness came over him and he was in danger of falling off his horse. One of the workers caught him and lifted him down, and then we saw that the horse's flanks were red with blood. We took Gustaf into one of the suite of rooms on the ground floor, opposite the garden. The Major commanded that a fire be lit in the chimney right away and that the bed be made ready. Meanwhile the sore spot was exposed, and the Major examined the wound himself. It was a slight bite wound in his thigh, not dangerous, but the loss of blood and the preceding emotional shock now left the young man fighting to stay conscious. He was taken to the bed, and immediately a messenger was sent to the doctor and one to Brigitta. The Major stayed at his bedside and prevented the fainting spells from becoming too serious. When the doctor arrived, he gave a boosting drug, pronounced the boy's condition to be not at all serious, and said that the blood loss in itself had been beneficial, since it reduced the severity of inflammation that usually follows such bite wounds. The only bad effect, he said, was the psychological trauma, and a few days' rest would completely relieve the fever and exhaustion. We were reassured and glad, and the doctor left after being thanked by all, for there was no one there who did not love the boy. Brigitta appeared around evening and, in her decisive way, would not rest until she had examined her son's body limb by limb and had convinced herself that there was nothing else besides the bite wound that could put him in further danger. When the examination was over, she still kept sitting by his bed, dispensing the medicine according to the doctor's prescription. A hastily prepared bed was made up for her to spend the night with her sick son. The next morning she was sitting beside the youth once again, listening to his breath while he slept, while he slept as sweetly and refreshingly as if he might never want to wake again. Then came a heartrending scene. I still clearly see that day in my mind's eye. I had gone down to inquire about Gustaf's condition and entered the room adjacent to the one where he was recuperating. I've already said that the windows looked out on the garden; the fogs had lifted and a reddish wintry sun was streaming into the room through the leafless branches. The Major was already there; he was standing at the window, his face turned toward the glass as if he were looking out. In the room with Gustaf, with the door ajar so I could look into it and the windows somewhat shaded by very light curtains, sat Brigitta, looking at her son. Suddenly, a joyful sigh escaped her lips; I looked more closely and saw that her eyes were resting with sweetness on the face of her son, who had opened his own eyes now, for he had awakened from a long sleep and was looking cheerfully around.

But I also heard a slight sound from the spot where the Major had been standing, and as I looked over I saw that he had turned halfway around and that two frozen teardrops were hanging from his eyelids. I went towards him and asked him what was wrong. He replied softly: "I have no child."

Brigitta with her sharp hearing must have heard his words, for she appeared under the doorway between the rooms at that moment. She looked at my friend very cautiously and then with an expression in her eyes that I can't describe – seemingly restrained by the meekest trace of worry, scarcely daring to ask for a favor – she said nothing but the single word: "Stephan."

The Major turned completely around, and each stared at the other for a second, just a second. Then, bounding forward, he threw himself into her arms, which closed around him with immeasurable passion. I heard nothing but the deep, quiet sobbing of the man while the woman embraced him even tighter, pulling him closer to her.

"No more separation, Brigitta, not now or in eternity."

"None, my dear friend!"

I was greatly embarrassed and wanted to leave as quietly as I could, but she raised her head and said, "Please stay; please stay."

The woman I had always seen as serious and strict had been weeping in his arms. She lifted her eyes, still glimmering with tears – this is how magnificent forgiveness is, the loveliest thing that poor, error-ridden man is capable of this side of heaven – so that her features radiated as with inimitable beauty in my eyes, and my soul swam with deep emotions.

"My poor, poor wife," he said in turmoil, "for fifteen years I had to do without you, and for fifteen years you had to suffer."

But she folded her hands and looked beseechingly into his eyes as she said: "It was my mistake; please forgive me, Stephan, for the sin of pride. I had no idea how good you are. It was just natural; there is a gentle law of beauty that draws us together."

He held her mouth shut and said: "How can you talk like that, Brigitta? Yes, the law of beauty draws us together, but I had to wander all over earth until I learned that it lies in my own heart, and that I left it at home in a heart that had always wanted the best for me, a heart faithful and true that I thought I had lost, but one that moved with me through all those years and all those countries. Oh Brigitta, mother of my child, you were on my mind day and night!"

"I was never lost to you," she replied, "I lived out years of sorrow and regret! How good you've become. Now I know the real you. How good you've become, Stephan!"

And again they threw themselves into each other's arms, as if they could never get their fill of it, as if they couldn't believe the happiness they'd gained. They were like two people from whom a great load had been lifted. The world stood open again. A joy such as only children find was with them – and at that moment they were as innocent as children – since forgiveness is the most purifying and beautiful flower of love, the highest form of love: that explains why it's found in God and in mothers. Good hearts forgive frequently; evil ones never do.

The couple had forgotten me again and turned toward the room where Gustaf, who had a vague sense of all this, lay like a blossoming rose aglow, waiting breathlessly for them.

"Gustaf, Gustaf, he is your father, and you didn't know it!" cried Brigitta, as they entered across the threshold into the darkened room.

As for me, I went out into the garden and thought: "Oh, how sacred, how sacred must married love be, and how poor am I, not having realized it up till now, letting my heart be touched at most by the dim flames of carnal passion."

I didn't return to the house until late, and found everything aired out and resolved. Bustling joy, like bright sunshine, permeated all the rooms. I was received with open arms as the witness of that glorious scene. They had sent people to search for me everywhere after they had gotten so involved in themselves and I had vanished. They told me everything that had taken place, including what I've noted before, partly in broken sentences on the spot and partly in the proper sequence during the following days.

So the friend I had met in my travels had been Stephan Murai. He had traveled under the name of Bathori, actually the name of one of his female ancestors. That was the way I had known him, too, but he had used the title of Major, a rank he had earned in Spain, and everyone else also called him "the Major." After he had been all over in the world, he moved – bearing the same name and drawn by an inner need – to the barren Uvar estate where he had never been before, where no one knew him, and where he would become, as he very well knew, the neighbor of his estranged wife. Despite that, he didn't ride over to visit Brigitta, who was already doing such a good job of administering the Maroshely estate, until he learned of her life-threatening illness. Then he set out, rode over to her estate, went into her room where fever prevented her from recognizing him, stayed at her bedside day and night, watched over her and tended her until she recovered. At that point, touched at seeing each other again and driven by that quiet love, but still anxious about the future because they didn't really know each other now, and because something terrible could take place again, they agreed on that strange pledge of mere friendship which they kept for many years and which neither of them had dared to be the first to tamper with until now, when fate itself broke it by a sharp stab into both their hearts, reuniting them in the grander, more natural bond.

Everything was fine now.

Two weeks later it was announced in the region round about, and the irritating well-wishers came from far and near.

As for me, I stayed with the family all winter – at Maroshely in fact – where everyone was living for the time being and from which the Major had resolved never to take Brigitta, since she was in the midst of her own creation there. Nearly the happiest of all was Gustaf, who had always been so fond of the Major, who always passionately and single-mindedly called him the greatest man on earth, and who was now able to adore him as his father, a man on whom his eye was riveted as on a god.

I got to know two hearts that winter, hearts that only then truly opened up into a full, if somewhat belated, blossom of happiness.

I will never, ever forget those hearts.

In spring I put on my German travel outfit again, took my walking stick, and started hiking toward my German homeland. On the way I saw Gabriela's grave; she had died twelve years before at the peak of her youthful beauty. On the marble were two large white lilies.

With wistful, gentle thoughts, I moved on until the Leitha River had been crossed and the dear blue mountains of home were darkening in the twilight before me.

Overwhelming financial need forced **Betty Paoli,** pseudonym for **Barbara Elisabeth Glück (1814-1894)** to work as a governess in Russia and Poland at age sixteen. She published her first poems in Prague and Vienna two years later. Strongly influenced by Lenau,[1] she dedicated a volume of poetry to him in 1841. From 1843 until 1848 she served as a social companion for Princess Maria Anna Schwarzenberg,[2] a multi-year engagement that served to make her known in Viennese cultural circles. Grillparzer came to consider her, simply, as the "premiere lyricist of Austria." But she was a prose writer as well.

Paoli wrote the 3-volume collection of novellas, *The World and My Eye* [*Die Welt und mein Auge*], in the early 1840s. The approaching literary wave of realism was contradictory to her artistic sense of idealism, and she never fulfilled Stifter's expectation that she would come to terms with the social and political conditions of the age in a novel.[3]

Confessions, one of the novellas found in the 3-volume collection, shares a common trait with several of Paoli's other novellas in that it is a framed tale whose main action is revealed in a confidential discussion (while some of her other novellas take on the epistolary form).The description of the main female character, Countess Benna T., parallels the principal characters from other novellas: she has strikingly dark eyes and dark hair. Thus, as we can deduce from portraits and written descriptions of the day, most of Paoli's heroines resemble the author herself. Many of her novellas deal with the psychological aftermath and defense mechanisms called forth by an unfulfilled or forbidden love. The heroine of this novella, Benna von T., is unique among Paoli's female characters in that she does not effect an atonement through great suffering nor does she pay for a mistake in love with her life. Rather, she reacts with mockery and sarcasm to the destruction of her own illusions. These are the same moods with which Paoli was to

---

[1] Nikolaus Lenau [pseudonym for Niembsch Edler von Strehlenau], 1802-1850, Austrian poet known for his expressions of melancholy.

[2] Two minor female characters in Adalbert Stifter's 1857 novel, *Nachsommer,* were modeled after Paoli and Schwarzenberg.

[3] This and the following paragraph have been abstracted and translated, with permission, from a letter written by my colleague Karin Wozonig, doctoral candidate at the University of Vienna. I am grateful to her for her critical observations and for having provided me with a copy of the original novella itself (which is, unfortunately, hard to find in North America).

become a critic herself after 1848, especially in writing newspaper essays critical of contemporary society. For her contemporaries' taste, many of her female characters were too passionate, too dour, too nonconformist; but the way Paoli represented the social standing of women in her novellas was retrograde in comparison to the theoretical discourse of the day, to which Paoli also contributed (after 1848).

There are a number of thematic notes introduced within the heroine's long monologue or illustrated by her behavior. Prime among these are the following themes: inner emotions and personal hopes versus external appearances and social expectations; the validity of sympathy versus its uselessness; the joys of the imagination versus its dangers; the appreciation of great art; the deluded eyes of "love"; the dangers of being put on a pedestal; and, ultimately, cynical and bitter overreaction to pains of the heart.

Confessions

Betty Paoli

*En amour tout est vrai et tout faux;
c'est la seule chose, sur laquelle
on ne puisse pas dire des bêtises.*
Chamfort[4]

Two young women, the widowed Countess Benna von T. and her friend Augusta, were sitting together one evening embroidering and chatting. Though neither of the two was strikingly beautiful, they did form a very charming contrast as they sat beside each other like that. The countess may well have been close to thirty; her features were sharp and distinct, her movements quick and lively; her bearing had the stamp of strong decisiveness. Remarkable were her somewhat deep-set but large and wonderfully beaming eyes. If there were black diamonds, that's what they could have been compared with. There was something angelic and at the same time demonic set in them; in fact, they seemed less like eyes than souls. Mostly they looked out proudly, boldly and freely; but often flashes of mockery or tragicomedy escaped from them, and again there were moments when they looked up toward heaven with passionate devotion, as if despairing of this world. The personality of this woman was a curious tone of enlightening clairvoyance mixed with an indestructible freshness of spirit. She was considered cold since many

---

[4] Nicolas-Sébastien Roch de Chamfort (1741-1794), a French playwright and critic known for his cynical and ironic maxims. The quotation translates: "In love everything's true and everything's false: it's the only topic you can't say stupid things about."

things that deeply moved others went right past her without a trace, and the sentimental element in her nature appeared to be totally missing. No one cared to notice that her calmness only originated from her awareness of power, from her contemptuous aversion to everyday happenings.

Augusta was younger by some years and by far the more charming of the two; at least she had the advantage that her beauty could be perceived by earthly senses while that of the countess was only there for the eyes of the soul. There are physiognomies that you have to get to know before you find them beautiful; others, on the other hand, reveal their easy charm at first sight, and Augusta was one of the latter. Her light brown hair flowed down in rich waves around her gently colored cheeks; her eyes were of indeterminate color, admittedly, but they were very beautifully shaped and capable of the most endearing expressions; her forehead and nose were conspicuous for their strict symmetry, her dazzling white hands for their admirable delicacy. It was unmistakable that this mouth, always in readiness to smile, had not yet had any great questions of fate to answer. When you saw Augusta next to the countess, the question spontaneously arose how these two women could be friends – with such great character differences that had to be evident to everyone; the answer to that, however, was not hard to find. It's true that Benna was far superior to her "favorite person," as she usually called Augusta, in intellect, thinking power and a splendid scope of outlook; on the other hand, the latter, Augusta, had at her command so much ease, naturalness and cordial grace that the countess felt attached to her as to a well-behaved, dear child. It wasn't necessary for her to use any force around her, and even if Augusta didn't understand everything that her friend expressed in what was, at times, a rather Baroque manner, still Benna had complaints at the most about a lack of comprehension but never about any sorts of insulting misunderstandings. Augusta loved the countess with all her heart, insofar as she was able to grasp her personality, and where that stopped, unconditional and devout worship took the place of love.

After theater productions and the current fashions had been sufficiently discussed, Augusta asked, looking up quickly: *"A propos,*[5] what do you think about the breakup between Fernheim and Sidonia?"

"I don't see anything so very unusual in it," Benna replied, smiling.

---

[5] French: "By the way . . . ."

"You can't be serious!" Augusta retorted in her eager, vivacious way. "Two people who made every sacrifice for four or five years in their hopes of being together, who shunned no battle, defied all the odds, broke with their own families: to see these two people voluntarily back off just when their union had finally become possible, that seems like watching one of those plays where we're even losing assurance of our own hearts anymore. Don't you think so?"

"Assurance?" asked Benna with slow emphasis. "I'd like to know what kind of assurances there are in the world at all."

"Their feelings for each other seemed a sure thing to me, since I thought they had been strengthened by all the pain. Just think how much they suffered for each other, what obstacles they had to fight!"

"It was the obstacles that they loved. Sidonia is effusive enough and Fernheim vain enough to enjoy, tremendously, being cast in the roles of Romeo and Juliet. They suffered just as much as was necessary to be considered interesting, and they certainly wouldn't have wanted to suffer any more than that. For my part, I can hardly believe in broken hearts that go out to dine twice a day, that go to the theater and to parties and carry their sighs to places where they're least appropriate. True passion is coy and true pain rejects the openly bitter shows of emotion. When those obstacles dropped off, their imagined feelings for each other also fell away; the only thing that amazes me is that the two characters were smart enough not to act out their antecedents to love and to get married on account of *qu'en dira-t-on*."[6]

"No, no," said Augusta, shaking her head, "that's not the way I'd care to explain the disconcerting breakup; something major must have happened. Fernheim or Sidonia must have discovered something that suddenly sent their inner souls off in different directions. What that might have been, of course, I can't even begin to guess. . . perhaps some unfaithfulness, perhaps a contentious secret came between them, but in any case I insist: something major must have happened."

"Possibly; but it could just as easily have been something trivial," responded Benna with her usual cold smile. "Maybe she noticed that he dyes his beard; maybe he found out that she gives an artificial boost to her uneven complexion – to the extent that's possible. Solomon says that love

---

[6] French: "What will people say?"

is stronger than death. . . I'll admit that; but it's not strong enough for both of them to put up with discoveries like that."

"All you do is mock people."

"Me? That didn't even occur to me. My whole wit consists in understanding the wit of life. I'm not the one who made the joke; I'm just trying to understand it. I was born with the tendency to do that; multiple experiences have developed it to the point of virtuosity. Just as Hogarth[7] unwittingly perceived the quietly emerging caricature in the loveliest face: likewise, every feeling and every relationship reaches out to me and bellows its own irony before I have to go looking for it. Each of us was given a role in the bold comedy of the Eternal Playwright. To those who don't find it egotistical of me I would say that my role is that of the *gracioso*[8] who knows how to detect the comical side of passions that he doesn't feel himself."

"No, Benna! You do yourself a great injustice. If people believed what you say, they'd have to think of you as a cold, sealed-up creature that only feels with her head; that is truly not the case with you. On a thousand occasions you've proven that you are good, generous, ready to help, and that any human suffering finds a rapid response in your own soul."

"And why shouldn't it? Does a wound bleed any less when it's caused by a smaller toy sword? Is a pain any less severe when I recognize its source as foolish? On the contrary! I have more sympathy for people when I realize more clearly how many unnecessary loads they voluntarily pile on themselves even though their unavoidable burdens alone would be completely sufficient; and when I see such things, I exclaim from the depths of my heart: *pauvre humanité!*[9] I know that they call me a female Mephisto[10] now and then; that's not at all what I am. If I encounter true misfortune, then I do what's in my power to bring relief to those who are suffering; but when a twisted mind and a deceitful imagination bear children together that they prefer to call 'pain,' and people expect me to take these horrid, counterfeit creations fondly in my arms and hug them compassionately as if they were the loveliest of human forms, then that's something I refuse to do. That certainly doesn't make for a character defect in me; I believe, in fact, that people would

---

[7] William Hogarth, 1697-1764, English painter, engraver and caricaturist.

[8] Spanish: "jester, clown."

[9] French: "poor humanity!"

[10] Mephistopheles, the character representing the devil in Goethe's *Faust*.

generally have more authentic goodness to spread around if they didn't mindlessly waste so much unnecessary sympathy. So all these soft-hearted folks – who close their hearts to real misery and ignore the most visible types of suffering – have felt sorry for Fernheim and Sidonia for years and years on account of their silly passion, until the two have now played a trick on everyone by turning the whole maudlin melodrama into a prank. The reason they act that way is easy to guess: such sympathy looks good and doesn't cost you a cent. Of course, it doesn't help anybody either."

"So you'd only like to give credence to the type of sympathy that can be expressed through tangible assistance?"

"Oh, God, don't talk to me about that! All human comfort-giving seems to be a strange thing. Where it's most needed it can't be given, and where it can be given, it's not really needed. Small pains don't need it; the great ones despise it. Whatever strikes at the innermost soul of a person, every struggle, every storm, he has to wrestle through on his own and nobody can help him with it. Beyond that it seems to me that our paltry sympathies are, as emotions go, much too pathetic in the face of any true and extensive misfortune; and the reverential shudder of horror with which the ancients avoided the spot where a consuming and sanctifying bolt of lightning from heaven had struck earth is, for my sense, far more dignified and truly religious. People only enjoy expressing their sympathies so much because it lends them a certain superiority. As for myself, I would institute a lawsuit against anyone who felt sorry for me, no matter the reason. For internal suffering such weak-kneed lamentations are totally superfluous, and for external suffering they shouldn't be expressed in rhetorical phrases of melancholy, as they usually are, but in rapid action, in willing and joyful sacrifice. Charitable acts I consider to be the very highest things that a person has at his disposal, effusive verbal eruptions the very lowest."

The countess seemed to sense that she was speaking more for her own sake than for her listener; she stopped talking but kept on embroidering furiously. Augusta was one of those women who can only talk about people, never about ideas, and who are only able to pay attention when they can concentrate their thoughts on a fixed topic. Benna's verbal offensive had only marginally touched her, nor could the general views that Benna expressed make Augusta forget the topic she had introduced, and so she said after a while: "This sudden breakup is still incomprehensible to me, no matter whether the thing that caused it may have been important or trivial."

Benna stared in front of herself pensively, then she said in a serious tone: "When I consider that a situation so trivial it bordered on the ridiculous decided my own entire fate, it seems to me almost a crime to call any happening insignificant. Either we see life as vain and futile or else everything in it as important and richly manifold. The choice is left to us."

"You were in such a situation yourself?" asked Augusta, not concealing her thirst for more exact details.

"I was, and I'm at your service if you want to hear my story. I don't need to ask you not to tell anyone about it, since nothing happened that was particularly angelic or devilish, but even if that were the case . . . ."

"I wouldn't abuse your trust."

"I know that."

Both women laid their work aside. Augusta looked attentively into the large, dark eyes of her friend, and Benna began her tale.

"For an exact understanding of the story that follows, I have to repeat a few facts for you that you may have forgotten or that you've never known at all. I was born, as you know, a Countess Reichau; my parents, whose only child I was, died very young and immediately after their death I was sent to a boarding school that I wasn't to leave again until I was sixteen years old, after which I lived in the house of my uncle. I had been looking forward to this time very much and had woven together a thousand images in my mind of the colorful and exciting life waiting for me. When my arrival at the home of my uncle actually took place, the reality didn't seem to want to deliver what my dreams had promised. My uncle was employed in an important position that took up most of his time. In his few free moments, he sought out the habitual amusements he had long since come to enjoy and in which I couldn't participate. He didn't concern himself with me very much, although he was very favorably inclined towards me in his way. Perhaps he would have made significant sacrifices in order to set me up advantageously in society, but to play one less round of whist[11] on my account went beyond his abilities. We usually only saw each other in the mornings when I would go visit him in his office, but was soon chased out of it again with the arrival of a horde of subordinate bureaucrats, supplicants, and so forth; then at the dinner table along with the servants; and sometimes in

---

[11] A card game, a precursor to bridge in which there is no bidding.

the evenings when he was already preparing to go out and came to see me beforehand in the greatest hustle and bustle for a few moments.

"My contacts were limited to the unmarried aunt who lived in the house with us and a few teachers kept there to complete my education. Aunt Laura possessed many admirable qualities, but leniency and kindness were not among them. She had experienced a lot of misfortune in her own life, and her character hadn't been strong enough to refuse entry to the bitterness and severity that greatly enjoy injecting their poison into betrayed hearts: the wounds of her soul had become disfiguring scars. If you add the fact that she was almost continually sick, that on many days going to the theater, listening to music, or even the simplest discussion demanded painful efforts on her part, you can easily guess how poorly suited the aging, well-traveled, and sickly woman was as company for a young girl gazing out into the fresh world with fresh eyes and anxious to learn about life. It would be hard to say whether Aunt Laura suffered more from my impetuosity or I suffered more from her deadened spirits: one thing that's certain is that we made each other's life miserable.

"The isolation and loneliness in which I lived finally reached the point where my own powers, not being permitted to develop outwardly, worked their way all the more forcibly inside me, and bit by bit a dreamlike fantasy world took over. At first this had been totally alien to my personality, and only under the circumstances was it smuggled into my soul. Instead of flying up to the sky in total awareness of my youthfulness, now I could just barely flap my wings: my current life offered me so little that I went begging for morsels from the past. The efforts of longing to leave my boarding school, where I had friends and companions in abundance, had, so it seemed, been rewarded by living in my uncle's hotel like a nun.

"We saw almost nobody. Aunt Laura's sickliness and her incessantly bad moods kept her from going out or from receiving visitors. Her acquaintances were limited to three or four like-minded old ladies, and as venerable as this company may have been, it held very little attraction for me when it was assembled *in corpore*.[12]

"If I expressed the wish to associate with persons of my own age, she told me I should just be patient – in two years they would introduce me at court; it wouldn't be appropriate for me to go out into the world before my

---

[12] Latin: "all together," literally "as a body."

formal debut. 'Why should I have to wait so long?' I asked, at times quite annoyed.

"The answer was: 'Because it isn't advantageous for a girl to be introduced so early; in later years it's just too easy for people to say: My God, how long have we known her now! without calculating how young she was when they got to know her. By our social plan, though, you'll still be able to look sixteen years old when you're eighteen.'

"There was no appeal possible: I held my tongue and kept on unwrapping my life like an enormous ball of yarn. I wasn't really bored since my studies kept me busy enough to fill in the hours of the day, but inside me I recognized that stifling emptiness that fertilizes the soul for any foolishness – just like Nile mud fertilizes the agricultural fields. I didn't think I would ever see that time pass by. Once you're older the years rush past with uncanny, ghostly swift flight; the impatience of early youth, though, sees two years as an eternity *en miniature*. I kept on vegetating. The most raucous and colorful life holds not half the dangers for a girl's heart as does the uniformity with which I half sighed away, half yawned away my days: the former meant that one impression could be wiped away by the next, but the latter gave me time to devise the most intricate scenarios.

"Six months had slipped by and a quite a lump of fuel had gathered in my head, when, by way of public notices, I found out about the arrival of an artist, painter R., who was known at the time and has since become famous: he was passing through our city on his way to Italy, and, to meet numerous demands, had agreed to spend some time in town. The praise lavished on his work even found its way into our isolated circle; Aunt Laura's lady friends as well as my uncle spoke with lively appreciation about the portraits of the duchess and of some ladies that R. had masterfully painted. Painting had always been my favorite form of art. Everything within its realm aroused my liveliest interest; I had wished a thousand times that I lived in a metropolis where my art sense could find more satisfaction in galleries and magnificent collections than in this small town of D., and since it wasn't within my control to change where I lived, at least I tried to make up for it by learning to draw and paint to my heart's content under the tutelage of a somewhat mediocre teacher. You can just imagine the effect on me of the news that a major artist was in the vicinity. I didn't stop asking and pleading until Aunt Laura promised me, if only to have some peace, that she would visit R.'s studio with me. The joy caused by her promise was so great that even her grouchiness couldn't stand up to it. I hugged her around the neck, kissed her hands and did all kinds of crazy things until she had to laugh along with me and exclaim, half angrily: 'How childish you are!'

"'What better thing can I be?' I asked, totally uninhibited, and had no idea what a true statement I was making.

"Our visit at R.'s studio was set for three days later; until then I wouldn't let Aunt Laura out of my sight. I brought her tea and aperitifs, protected her from drafts and overheating, asked her every fifteen minutes how she was feeling, and treated her, in short, as an impresario would treat a soprano who could dash all his hopes by getting ill. Finally the long-awaited hour arrived. Full of impatience to have everything ready, I helped my aunt dress, wrapped her carefully in her coat and feathered scarf, almost carried her down the stairs, and was in the coach with one joyous leap.

"My heart hammered almost audibly as I entered the studio where I hoped to receive new revelations about art. My first glance fell on the portraits of Princesses Louisa and Helena,[13] and I stopped right in my tracks, numb and breathless. Great God! Everything I saw was light, radiance, flowing life! The pictures I had seen up until now were, in comparison to these, just colored marble statues. Here you could see the blood coursing beneath their translucent skin, the sunshine filtering through their soft hair; you felt the warm breath of their smiling mouths. The royal daughters were both of great beauty but in totally different ways: Princess Louisa bore in her serious features – touched with a wisp of spectral melancholy as from moonbeams – the very premonition of her early demise; while her younger sister, a blonde-haired, rosy girl, was peering out at life with cheerful openness, trustingly, without a care in the world. The former was sublime – almost horrifyingly beautiful, like the angel of death – while the latter was charming and pleasant, like the spirit of life. With magnificent faithfulness and mastery, the painter had been able to grasp the characteristic features of these phenomena and then reproduce them; he hadn't merely made slavish copies of physical features but had delivered portraits of the soul, inner biographies. And what perfected technique, what a feel for beauty and elegance in the depiction, what fine taste even in the insignificant minor details! I was barely able to tear myself away from these pictures when I fell into even greater

---

[13] The first of these fictitious princesses may have been modeled on Louisa of Saxe and Coburg (1800-1831). The mother of Queen Victoria's consort, Prince Albert, she died at the young age of 30. Yet she was an only child.

ecstasy at seeing R's historical sketches. One of them depicted Tasso's first meeting with Leonora,[14] and the impression that this composition made on me was so deep, so overwhelming, that I folded my hands, forgetting everything and everyone around me, and exclaimed: 'Oh, how lovely!'

"'I thank you, *Fräulein*,' said a male voice behind me. I turned around quickly and saw a young man, whom, with his artist's smock, long hair, and that indefinable something that art imprints on its disciples, I immediately recognized as R. It was really him. In my ecstasy I hadn't noticed him stepping into the studio and silently observing me for a while. My enthusiasm flattered him so much that he put aside his anonymity to express his gratitude to me.

"I turned crimson red and scarcely knew what to say; everything at my poor head's command seemed much too trivial and insignificant in the presence of such a genius. I thought it best to be silent so as not to have to say anything. Aunt Laura made a sweet and sour face. She sincerely found it inappropriate and presumptuous that an ordinary painter was taking it upon himself to address the niece of Count Reichau without having been introduced first; but she was too much of a *grande dame* to let herself be enticed by her displeasure into breaching external etiquette. She responded in my stead, offered R. a pleasantry about his talent and excused my inconsiderate behavior by saying I was ignorant of cosmopolitan life; her tone of voice at the same time, though, despite all the correctness, was rather curt and communicated her wish to end the conversation. R. paid no particular heed to this, but asked me: 'So you're an art lover?'

"'Oh, very much so!' I exclaimed.

"'And are you a practicing artist yourself perhaps?'

"'My niece pursues art for her own amusement,' interjected Aunt Laura before I could say another word, "but at least that puts her in a position of being able to judge the accomplishments of others better than I can; all I can do is get bad headaches from every gallery I go to. Today as well, my head is already swimming from all the looking and viewing. So I'm truly sorry not to be able to remain here any longer, but that just won't do. Come along, Benna, let's go home.'

"I cast one final, sad look at the pictures, said my farewells to the painter, who was standing there in front of us, cold and proud, and left with my aunt. At home I had to endure another long punitive sermon about my tactless

---

[14] Torquato Tasso (1544-1595), an Italian poet. The unattainable love of his life was Leonora.

behavior, but I scarcely paid any attention to it; the impressions I had gained that morning were too strong to leave room for any others. With that poetry in pigments, the full glory of art that I had only vaguely suspected till now blossomed before me for the first time. Correggio's statement: *Anch'io son pittore!*[15] suddenly became clear to me. Don't misunderstand me: in no way did I think that I myself had attained any valuable goal worth mentioning. What I had done till then seemed thoroughly awful and disgusting, but the humiliation of that realization was soothed somewhat as I felt that the power for higher things dwelt within me and that my receptivity for beauty hadn't failed me. I let Aunt Laura complain while I thought of other things.

"As luck would have it, my uncle was unusually cheerful on that particular day. This was something so uncommonly rare that Don Philip's courtiers[16] certainly couldn't have shouted out with greater astonishment: 'The king wept!' than did I say to myself in secret: 'My uncle's laughing!' I wanted to take advantage of his good mood before it passed. As young and inexperienced as I was, my feminine instincts did teach me to take proper use of circumstances. My uncle was a declared enemy of anything that smacked of hyperbole. If I had described the powerful impression I'd experienced, his response would probably have been to poke fun at me. So I kept that to myself and merely listed for him which ladies' portraits R. had already painted. I lingered purposefully on the portraits of the royal sisters, and, playfully wrapping my arms around his neck, I whispered quietly and bashfully in his ear: 'Uncle-kins! I'd love to be painted by R., too!'

"'Oh, female vanity!' he smiled. 'Do you imagine you'd end up looking as beautiful as the princesses?'

"'Maybe not,' I retorted cheerfully, 'but in R.'s picture I'm sure I would be quite pretty.'

"' You mean, he'd flatter you quite a bit?'

"'And what if he did? ' I joked. 'In any case there's something to be gained when somebody's not-so-pretty niece can at least provide for a beautiful painting. Don't you think so?'

---

[15] Antonio Allegrida Correggio (1494-1534), Italian artist. His statement translates: "And I, too, am a painter!"

[16] Philip II (1527-1598), Habsburg king of Spain at the time of the Spanish Armada's defeat, was known for his stoic demeanor.

"'Well, all right!' he replied after thinking it over for a short while, 'that's a good enough reason. This thing has become fashionable, and there's no reason why you shouldn't join in; besides, I've wanted for a long time to have your portrait over my desk for . . .'

"'For being able to love me *en effigie*?' I interrupted.

"'You're such a clown,' he said, laughing. 'But to get back to the subject at hand, I'll send over Herr Reiser (that was the name of his private secretary) to see the painter so he can let me know if he has the time and the interest to fit you in. We can't put it off very long, since I hear he'll be leaving D. fairly soon. You'll get an answer tomorrow. *Adieu* for now!'

"I had consciously chosen a time for this discussion when Aunt Laura wouldn't be around. She had quite a great influence over her brother and would have been able to spoil my tactics if she'd been in a grumpy mood. But now I was safe from that, for among the good qualities of my uncle was the fact that he never went back on his word under any circumstances. I soon came to realize how wise my precaution had been. When I reported the decision he'd just made to my aunt, she shrugged her shoulders and said things would have been different if she'd been there. The whole matter seemed too trivial, however, for her to seriously fight the decision. Herr Reiser fulfilled his assignment with his usual quickness, R. agreed to it, and a few days later I had my first sitting in his studio.

"If you ask me if R. was handsome, witty, educated, then I have to answer quite honestly with a triple 'no.' Imagine a rather tall person with drooping posture whose arms and legs looked like they'd been haphazardly attached to his body; *les attaches*[17] – as they call them in French, but I can't think of how you'd say it in German right now – were that inelegant. His features were irregular, without harmony or nobility."

"So he was definitely ugly?"

"Definitely; but I wrestled with this ugliness as with an enemy, and my imagination came out victorious. I understand the fairy tales quite well where the most horrendous of monsters are suddenly transformed into beautiful princesses or handsome princes by a kiss. Even now the same thing happens every day, for ugliness is a spell that love can break very easily, and there is no magic that can withstand the power of the heart."

---

[17] French: "wrists and ankles," i.e., points of attachment.

"But to be able to break that spell, love has to be there in the first place, and how can it even get started with a person like that?" Augusta asked, full of doubts. "It has to have some source from which to grow."

"It forms its own source," replied the countess. "If love were reasonable enough to look for causes, it would necessarily have to be attracted to the most exalted beauty every time, to the most striking endowments of mind and heart. But this is not the case by any means; I've often found, in fact, that the most ardent and glowing passions are wasted on very mundane persons in whose entire being that passion won't find the slightest justification. It's as if a gigantic pride were inherent in the passion, as if it wanted to prove its power by granting nobility to even the commonest object. Conscious of its power, it refuses to reach for the stars, but instead picks up any old thing from the dark masses down below and lifts it up to the reeling heights where shortcomings and imperfections are no longer visible to the eye. But God save us all from being the object of such passion! I wouldn't want to be standing up on a pedestal at any price. Just think how uncomfortable it would feel up there! If you move even a little, you risk losing your balance; and if you actually fall, you're lost forever, since passion is like the wild pagans who don't hesitate to throw their discredited idols into the fire. No! I'd rather stay down below here and go for relaxing walks along with everyone else. Comfort is a wonderful thing, and the continuation of a pleasurable existence is preferable to good fortune that comes and goes. But I notice I've gotten completely away from my story, so I'll get right back to it.

"Now you know how R. looked; as far as his intellectual capacities go, they were largely undeveloped; his manners were clumsy; and as with all uneducated people he leaped back and forth between awkward bashfulness and inappropriate familiarity. This person, whom I would certainly just walk past with total indifference if I happened to meet him now, was the one to whom the full enthusiasm of my young heart turned. I raised up the good qualities that he actually had to unnatural heights; I either overlooked his faults or was able to look at them in such a favorable light that they seemed to be hidden virtues. Thus his nonobservance of societal norms came to mean for me the types of elevated sensibilities that don't bother with earthly paltriness; his defiance that bordered at times on hostility was, in my eyes, a noble artistic temperament; and his sunken features which had faded so early – as a result of strenuous work and, as I was to learn later, a rather wild lifestyle – seemed to me mute witnesses of his painful genius. I think if he'd had a hunchback I would have viewed it as a harmonious wave-form. With cold disgust I would have turned my back on anybody who uttered the same judgment then that I'm making now. Having been born under a lucky star myself, I saw in him a truly unusual person singled out by fate; there was no good quality I didn't bestow on him; and with an enthusiasm that would have done justice to a more exalted object, I knelt before the idol that I had constructed. My imagination asked for nothing more than to allow its riches to unfold: it strewed flowers and precious jewels all across that dismal little town. I didn't know I was the one distributing these valuables, for I considered them to be his property.

"The story of R.'s early life helped to inflame my imaginative powers further. He had been the son of very poor parents and originally designated for a trade; only a stroke of luck had brought to light his great talent for painting. An outstanding artist had taken him under his wing, influential patrons had supported him, and so he suddenly found himself in a new situation that fit neither his education nor his habits. His truly extraordinary abilities allowed him to reach a glittering goal in such a relatively short time that he didn't consider it necessary to fill in the great gaps in his education. His sense of beauty, color and light, the gift for depicting what was mirrored in his eyes powerfully and vividly with his hands, was inborn; everything else seemed useless or at least very dispensable to him. His talent was not at all united with the rest of his character, but remained something apart, something inexplicable that didn't have the slightest thing to do with his true self. Just as I claim of a poet that it's not him but someone else, something higher, making poetry through him, likewise I would say it wasn't R. who painted those wonderful pictures dipped in fire and aroma, but it was the pure spirit of beauty who sank down upon him at times.

"My portrait was completed and extraordinarily well done. As you can clearly see, the vain possession of beauty was not exactly bestowed on me in rich measure, but in R.'s picture I was almost beautiful, not because he had flattered me, but because he'd been able to bring the full youthfulness of my soul into my physical features. My uncle, generally very spare with words, poured exaltations of praise out upon the artist and accepted with gratitude R.'s proposal that he guide my painting studies during his stay in D. I stood there gaping when this decree was brought to my attention. Did R. sense my love? Did he feel the same? Was that tutoring assignment just an excuse he was using to see me more often? I was egotistical enough to answer all these questions with 'yes,' though this 'yes' went against all probability since he had always acted totally indifferent towards me, and my attempts to initiate a deeper, more serious discussion with him had always been dismissed very prosaically with a curt: 'Please, *Comtesse*,[18] turn more to the left,' or 'Don't hold your head so low.' You would have to possess my sense of exaggeration not to stumble upon the natural explanation that the offer only came from R.'s enthusiastic love for his art: he thought he'd discovered a significant talent in me and didn't want to let it shrivel up by being misdirected.

"The instruction began. At first Aunt Laura chaperoned the sessions; but she soon found that R.'s clothes reeked horribly of tobacco, and, since the smell was unbearable to her, Madame Rigaut, a cross between a lady's companion and a housekeeper, took her place. Although she'd been living in German-speaking lands for more than twenty years, the good woman still hadn't gotten to the point of learning our language. She had developed a type of *lingua franca*[19] with the servants and made herself sufficiently understood around them; she had only a very incomplete understanding of good German, on the other hand, especially when it was spoken fast. For that reason I preferred having her around, rather than Aunt Laura. Of course the things being discussed between me and R. could have been heard by anyone on earth, but I was expecting a formal declaration of feelings from one visit to the next and was only curious that it was taking so long. Even this fact wasn't able to sway me from my convictions: my blindness was so great that, to quote Börne,[20] 'its magnitude almost excused me.' I convinced myself that R. was just keeping silent out of noble-mindedness, that he intended to sacrifice his happiness for the sake of my peace of mind, that his heart had to be mute before the command of duty, and other such lovely things that a sixteen-year-old conjures up.

"It was my total ruin that R. was so natively monosyllabic. Such a silent man, as long as he's not fat and ruddy-complexioned, has already won half the battle with imaginative women, for they fantasize that he would say the profoundest things if he wanted to talk, and they credit him with thoughts that he probably never had in his life. On top of that, unfortunately, R. was

---

[18] French: an unmarried "countess."

[19] Italian: "commonly intelligible language."

[20] Ludwig Börne, pseudonym for Juda Loew Baruch (1786-1837), Jewish-German journalist, essayist and literary critic.

very pale, and since he painted all day and sketched halfway through the night, it was unavoidable that he often had red eyes. These I unquestioningly assumed to be the unmistakable signs of great heartache and nights filled with weeping. Only the natural shyness of my youth and my gender prevented me from confessing that I loved him and thus that his heartache was without foundation. However, I did hatch a thousand schemes how I might bring happiness and joy to his soul some day. Dante's Beatrice,[21] Buonarotti's Vittoria Colonna[22] were constantly in my mind's eye: like these women, I intended to grant my utmost and loftiest consecration to the life of an artist. As with all ardent and rapturous souls, I loved R. more for what I imagined him to be than for what he actually was. I think that people aren't aware enough that most of the foolish and mistaken things women do arise more from their good qualities than from their bad ones.

"I need to make it short since it's almost eleven and I think I saw you looking at the clock once already. That doesn't speak very well for my storytelling abilities!

"Completely contrary to habit, R. came to visit one evening. Aunt Laura was bedridden with violent headaches. Madame Rigaut wasn't allowed to leave her alone; I was alone with him in the sitting room. My heart was beating almost audibly: the decisive hour, so I thought, had arrived. After the usual greetings, R. told me that he had come to say good-bye; certain circumstances had suddenly changed and he was forced to depart earlier than planned: he would be leaving D. within the next twenty-four hours.

"The image of lightning striking out of the blue is an old cliché, but I can't find anything more accurate with which to compare the terror that paralyzed me when I heard the news. 'God! My God!' I finally stammered, 'So you're really going to leave us?'

"'That was already decided long ago,' he replied.

"'But so quickly!'

"'I've already been here too long,' he responded, and my deluded heart allowed me to read a hidden meaning into his words.

"'No!' I cried out violently, 'I don't want to lose you!'

---

[21] A youthful Florentine girl loved by the Italian poet Dante Alighieri (1565-1321). She died young and became a central figure in his *Divine Comedy*.

[22] Member of a Roman royal line and poetess (1492-1547) who figured prominently in the love life of the great sculptor and artist Michelangelo Buonarotti (1475-1564).

"'What is it you'd be losing, *Comtesse*?'

"'Oh, don't call me by that title! Are you using that word to remind me of the imaginary difference that holds us apart and that I refuse to recognize? Your pupil is what I want to be, and nothing else on earth.'

"He was taken aback by my intensity. Perhaps he sensed what was really going on, but he limited himself to saying: 'It *is* truly a pity that you won't be able to get the proper training for your great talent. If your circumstances were different, I would tell you . . . .'

"'What?' I asked in breathless anticipation.

"'I would tell you: come with me to Italy,' he replied, laughing. 'But since you have the enviable misfortune of having been born a countess, you would surely refuse such an offer most graciously.'

"'Try me,' I said very seriously.

"'So that you could laugh at me? Oh, no!'

"His uninhibited joking only served to put me in a more tragic mood. Even if it couldn't heal the delusions under which I was laboring, at least it didn't allow them to erupt. I was convinced that R. was suffering from the bottom of his heart, like me, and that I could put an end to all these tortures with a single statement; yet my senses were still with me enough to realize that it wasn't my place to pronounce that statement first. Instinctively I felt that a breach of femininity could never be forgiven – even by the one to whose advantage it's done. I grew silent, but an indescribably fearful pain fluttered in my breast, and it was only my desire not to be outdone by R.'s own magnificent self-denial that lent me the power to speak about trivial things while my inner soul bled.

"At R.'s request I sent someone to ask Aunt Laura if she cared to receive him; her answer was a 'No' convoluted with excuses. She was, in fact, actually in pain, not to mention the fact that R. was not at all in her good graces: the profane tobacco smell and his sometimes brusque, sometimes too familiar manner had engendered in her a sort of physical repugnance towards him, and so she was glad to have some pretext not to receive him. R.'s request had been a mere matter of courtesy as well, and he asked for nothing more than to see himself relieved of that visit.

"After a while he stood up. I followed his lead, but I was scarcely able to hold myself up, for everything was reeling before my eyes and my arms and legs were shaking. The dreaded moment had arrived. 'Farewell; I wish you all the best!' said R., offering his hand in parting.

"I turned away to hide the tears streaming down my cheeks.

"'Are you angry at me?' he asked, with unusual gentleness.

"'God be with you!' I cried, overcome by my emotions, turning my weeping face towards him.

"'You are a good and dear child,' he said, 'and thinking of you will always make me happy. Don't cry; and just think: maybe we'll see each other again soon.'

"'Really?' I asked, holding up my folded hands pleadingly.

"'Certainly,' he replied. Before I knew it, he kissed me quickly on my forehead and left the room in haste to foreshorten the bitterness of our farewell.

"I remained behind in an indescribable state; it's true that I'd never doubted R.'s love for me, but now for the first time I'd come to the fullest, most unshakable conviction of it. His kiss was still burning on my forehead and he was gone – maybe I'd never see him again. Never! And this soul, whose life I'd wanted to illuminate, had only been plunged into deeper darkness because of me! What had I left unspoken? What demon had imprisoned the words of salvation inside my breast? No! R. couldn't ask anything of me... but I should have spoken; it was my duty to lay myself at his feet as a love sacrifice he could accept but never demand. Oh, the cowardice, the miserable weakness that held my mouth sealed shut! My tears were flowing ever more passionately and bitterly. Now everything was over and done with. 'Done?' I repeated, and the exuberance of my youth caught flame again; why 'over and done with?' R. still hasn't left town yet; I can still make good what I'd transgressed by my silence. Yes, I will speak to him, lay my entire fate in his hands, follow him as his spouse, no matter where it may lead! . . . .

"The decision was made. My place was at R.'s side: there my life had a reason, a purpose; there I could make someone joyous and happy. I recoiled from the bliss that suddenly poured into my heart like an ocean of light, blinding me, overpowering me. Sweet shudders reverberated through me at the thought of the ecstasy with which R. would receive my confession of love. Now it seemed right to me that I hadn't declared myself that evening. We were meant to feel the most lacerating pain in order to be receptive for the loftiest bliss. The darker and more hopeless the night, all the brighter a red dawn to end it.

"I realized that my relatives would never agree to such a marriage, so our nuptials would have to be held in secret. In my childish inexperience I didn't think about the fact that more is required for a legal union than the acquiescence of a loving couple. I felt liberated and entitled to anything, since no actual bonds of the heart tied me to my relatives. My uncle's whole life consisted in writing memos and playing whist, my aunt's in complaining, arguing and medicating herself. They could accomplish all this full well without me, and all too often I had painfully sensed just how totally dispensable I was to them. I was good to them, since my child's soul was incapable of wishing them ill, but I had never found in them the tenderness, caring, or inner connectedness that are the only means of winning someone's heart. I breathed easier after I had come to that decision: my whole life seemed clear to me now – organized, set – and my gushing high spirits led me up and away to realms where no storm clouds could gather.

"Aunt Laura had me called. I had to spend the rest of the evening with her, God knows why. My presence or absence should have been a matter of indifference to her, for no word could be spoken on account of her headaches. The lamp was shaded over, and so it was too dark in the room for anyone to read or work. I sat down in a corner, and soon I lost myself in a thousand hopes and dreams. I was already strolling in spirit with R. along the ocean beach, in the valleys of the Apennines, in the laurel groves of Naples; I heard people calling out his name in admiration and declaring me fortunate for being his. Art and nature offered us up their richest, most beautiful blossoms; love transfigured our earthly happiness, lending it the shimmer of eternity.

"Now let me tell you, Augusta," Benna interrupted her tale, "it almost seems to me that the hour I spent in the dark and dreary room of my morose aunt that evening was the most blissful hour of my life. Oh God!" she continued, and her eyes were lifted up with an indescribable expression of grief and hopelessness, "Isn't it terrible that the most magnificent things we're capable of imagining never come true? That dreams are the sum of our wealth, fantasy our only true possession? That a jewel is broken from our crown of joy with every delusion that robs us of life, and that it goes on like that until at last we don't own anything anymore and die as beggars? . . . But let's finish the story.

"My aunt let me go; I hurried to my room and began writing to R. while tears flowed that had sprung up from a number of various feelings. Unfortunately, I don't have such a good memory as most novel heroes – who are able to repeat word for word the content of letters they'd written ten or twenty years before – but that's not necessary here. You can easily imagine the contents of my letter and can thank the Lord that you don't need to ingest that extract of effusiveness. After I had finished my letter and sealed it, I walked back and forth for a long while in feverish excitement. Anxious warnings came to me, but I fought them off as whisperings of cowardice and spurred my fantasy onward until it found in my distorted image of life the perfect ideal. Finally I felt so exhausted that I needed to rest; I rang for my maid to help me change.

"Jenny was a rather vain and forward know-it-all. These shortcomings were amplified under the circumstances of my totally isolated state: I gave her more attention than would have been the case if things were different. It wasn't exactly that I got involved in discussions with her, but as she dressed and undressed me I did tolerate her blabbering all kinds of things, to which I often paid no heed. Today she made use of her usurped privileges as well.

"'Dear God!' she said, taking my hair down, 'how pale and exhausted you look, *Mademoiselle Comtesse*! But of course it's no wonder, given the life we all lead here in this house. His Excellency we hardly ever see anymore; Countess Laura has more moods than there are hours in the day; nobody comes to visit, and now Herr R. has to leave, too.'

"Even the most common voice can take away none of the magic of a beloved name: I quickly looked up at the mention of R.'s name, and, in order not to have this discussion topic dropped, I replied: 'Yes, he's planning to leave D. Did you already know about it?'

"'He told me himself when he left *Mademoiselle Comtesse* this evening. I was just going down the corridor; he came up to me, bid me a friendly "Good evening," lit his cigar from the candle I was holding in my hand, and . . . .'

"'He did *what*?' I screamed more than I said it.

"She looked at me, taken aback. 'Nothing more,' she continued, 'than this: he just took a cigar out of his case and lighted it. At the same time he was gallant enough to tell me that my eyes could do the job just as easily as the candle could. Then he told me about his imminent departure, and . . . .'

"She kept on talking, but I didn't comprehend another word. God All Righteous! In the very moment when I was down on my knees with the bitterest of tears flowing, when I imagined him to be consumed through and through by the same tortures, when I was battling my way through to the decision to sacrifice every grace of my being for him, even my life itself . . . he was standing outside calmly lighting a cigar; and the very same lips that had just touched my brow were joking with my chambermaid two minutes later! I can laugh about it now, but at the time I was still too innocent, too childlike to be able to laugh at the irony of life. I didn't cry, either, but an ice-cold hand reached down into my heart at that moment, and it hasn't warmed up since. Anger, contempt, injured pride, insulted vanity, the most hostile feelings imaginable sprang up from inside me, armed for battle. I couldn't be objective enough to recognize that the totality of R.'s transgression consisted of not having guessed my love or of not having returned it. I felt humiliated, debased, trampled.

"With curt and harsh words I left Jenny. No sooner was I alone than I held my letter to R. over the candle flame until the last trace of it was destroyed. With cold and dry eyes I watched the mute witness of my delusion flicker out; then I threw myself on my bed and quickly put out the light itself as if even that flame mustn't see my flush of shame and degradation.

"The night was long, hard, decisive. By the next morning I was a changed woman; in those few hours my soul had turned gray, for only delusion is youthful. R. was a matter of indifference to me from then on. If I'd only had to lift a finger to win his love, I wouldn't have done it: I felt that he'd never understand me. I had sown the best and noblest within me onto stony ground, and now I was determined not to waste the celestial seed anymore. I've faithfully kept my word."

"And how did it come about that you married Count T.?"

"Very simply and completely naturally. This match was deemed acceptable by my relatives: and it truly was, Aunt Laura having served me as an admonition against the lot of an old maid. The social position of a *vieille fille*[23] is the most unbearable, most humiliating that I can imagine, particularly if she's not rich, which was the case with me. If she's wise at all, she won't go out into the world where her appearance can only put herself and others in an embarrassing situation, nobody knowing exactly where she belongs. Loneliness can't offer her any joys, for solitude can only be sweet to a full and satisfied heart but not to an empty one that's languishing in vain. I also didn't feel at all that I was born to be alone: I need social contacts, entertainment, radiant surroundings, convivial get-togethers to feel at home, and since I've given up any demands of an ideal life, I'm probably justified to make all the greater demands of reality. I clung tightly to the earth and actually wrested from it whatever I desired.

---

[23] French: "old maid."

"T. offered me a pleasant existence that met my needs. As a man he was respectable in every regard, in some ways even charming; not weighty enough to gain influence over me, but also not weak enough to force me into an absurd and bothersome position of having to rule over him. Sooner or later I would have had to marry. So I gave my approval to this union and never regretted it."

"Were you happy?"

"And what good would it have done me if I hadn't been? We led a quiet life that resembled the month of October: even if there weren't any flowers, at least there weren't any storms, either. I was cordially good to my husband and sincerely mourned his death. At any rate, I was happier with him than I would have been with R., whose social standing, education, habits and views were so comletely different from my own that only if he'd been a demigod would it have made up for the incredible sacrifices I would have been forced to make; as it was, he was just a common, rather crude and limited person. What saved me from the immeasurable disaster that I was ready to inflict upon myself? Nothing but that fateful cigar: its smoke wafted all my illusions away with it, and as a grateful reminder I've been smoking Spanish cigarettes ever since. The stupid people around here think I do it to imitate George Sand.[24] Not at all: I do it out of pure gratitude."

"And don't you think that love, even if not R.'s love, would have provided you with a richer, more substantive existence?"

"There are two things I'd like to say to you in response. You see, I passionately love to go riding, but if I were undertaking a long journey, then I would certainly rather sit in my comfortable coach than on the best riding horse, even if it came directly from Arabia. What's more: if I knew that the end of my love would be simultaneously the end of my life, that we could break the emptied glass . . . then yes, of course, in God's name. But to drag around later in a shattered existence that had lost its dignity, lost its color; to have to live on like a flower whose petals had been torn out or a butterfly whose wings had been pulled off . . . never! I don't even want to think about it! What is a bond of this kind, anyway, when you really

---

[24] Pseudonym for Aurore Dupin, baronne Dudevant (1804–1876), a popular female French novelist of the day. As a biographical aside, the author Paoli herself was a smoker, unusual for women of her time.

think about it? It's clever Karr,[25] witty with sheer truthfulness, who can answer better than I can: '*C'est une personne qui aime et une autre qui se laisse aimer.*'[26] And *that* is supposed to be the most magnificent thing in life?" she added, almost scornfully.

"Who tells you you're safe from that feeling that you seem to despise? What if love happens to slip into your heart after all?"

"Never! Never!" cried the countess, terrified. "I'm not old enough yet to be childish; I'll never be that old," she added, laughing at her own terror.

A few more insignificant words were exchanged; then Augusta stood up, packed away her needlework, thanked the countess for having shared her confidences, and left with a friendly "Good night." Benna remained seated for a while, not moving. Her whole life seemed to pass before her eyes; a light grimace of pain contorted her otherwise smiling lips. She bowed her head and whispered quietly to herself: "Oh sure, some things could have turned out differently, a lot of things!" Maybe a thousand images were dancing before her, luringly, enticingly; for her own good, though, she felt that it would mean her ruination if now, after it was perhaps too late, she were to grant those gentle voices admission into her heart. She didn't want to be a party to viewing her life as a mistake, and so, quickly standing up, she shut off her mute monologue with the words: "It's better that things happened as they did."

Then she rang, got help in undressing, lay down in bed, and read from a new novel until she fell asleep.

And even if it causes her to institute a lawsuit against me, all I can do is to say: "Poor Benna!"

---

[25] Alphonse Karr (1808-1890), French novelist and journalist known for the biting satire of his aphorisms and epigrams.

[26] French: "There's one person who loves and another person who puts up with being loved."

Franz Grillparzer (1791-1872) is best known as a dramatist whose plays are still regularly performed on the stages of Austria. It is by no means an accident that the fictional narrator of *The Poor Fiddler*, when attempting to explain his curiosity about the common folk, refers to himself as a dramatist. As highly regarded as are the dramatic productions in verse that propelled Grillparzer's name to the theater marquees of Vienna, though, recent scholars – particularly in the Anglo-American world of criticism – have insisted that it is in this novella, rather than in his plays, that Grillparzer's finest art and innermost self are most clearly displayed.[1]

The Poor Fiddler, begun as early as 1831, was completed in 1846 and is considered a prime example of the *Biedermeier* style of literature, an era for which the emblematic image remains that of a poor artist garreted in his miserable attic apartment, an image congruent with this novella. A thematic triad associated with the earlier era of Romanticism – music, love and death – still marks out the psychological and artistic borders of the tale, however. If "hell is full of musical amateurs," as George Bernard Shaw put it,[2] then the title character, Jacob, makes listeners infernally miserable by his fiddle even as he himself suffers by his amateurish approach to affairs of the heart. Though an apparent loser in the domains of music and love, the poor fiddler is revealed to have a transcendently redeeming character at the approach of death – well foreshadowed by the narrator's descriptions of Viennese crowds flooding in waves to St. Bridget's folk festival.

Central to the unfolding of the tale is the narrator's fascination with psychological motivation. The fiddler is a curious study in defense mechanisms. Does he turn the other cheek at verbal abuse because he dimwittedly feels he deserves it or because he's a veritable saint? He does indulge in his own selfishness, but only within the bounds of music; he quickly glosses over any dissonances – even necessary modulations – and dwells with rapture on the harmonic epiphanies. This is no way to play the works of a classical composer, but the question remains whether it's a courageous way to live a life: overlooking the disharmony caused by others.

---

[1] Clifford A. Bernd, "From Neglect to Controversy . . . ." in: *Grillparzer's Der arme Spielmann: New Directions in Criticism*, ed. C.A.Bernd (Columbia, SC: Camden House, 1988), pp. 4-5.

[2] *Man and Superman*, act 3.

The Poor Fiddler 119

Deep tension exists here between the poor fiddler's art and his daily existence. He loses himself totally in his art, lapses into trancelike states during worse-than-mediocre musical performances, all the while showing scant attention to the needs and demands of life. He becomes a target for financial hucksters, office pranksters, and general derision. Jacob's absent-mindedness seems neither a virtue in the realm of music nor in the demands of everyday life, where a figure like Barbara's suitor, the sturdy butcher, serves as a contravening metaphor for the practical ideal.

In the last analysis, though, Jacob's lack of sophistication in music as in life appears more than compensated for by his lack of guile. If he seems not to be mindful of others imposing pain on him, he is equally indifferent to his own ego. At the same time, he has remained true to himself and never pretends to be more than he is. For those who decry and mock his true self – such as his own father or Barbara, the object of his affections – Jacob can only exhibit appreciation, forgiveness, understanding, and love. The target of ridicule presents himself, in the end, as a paragon of saintliness even as his instrument, the fiddle, is elevated to the status of a house shrine, a souvenir of salvation mirrored by a crucifix.

The Poor Fiddler

Franz Grillparzer

In Vienna, the Sunday after the full moon in July of each year – along with the following day – is an honest-to-goodness folk festival if ever a festival deserved that name. The common folk both come to it and sponsor it themselves; and if any from the upper classes appear, they do so only in their role as part of the folk. There is no possibility of special privileges; at least there wasn't some years back.

On this day the district of Brigittenau[2], linked in an unbroken chain of merrymaking with Augarten, Leopoldstadt and Prater[3], celebrates St. Bridget's Day[4]. The working class counts its good times from one St. Bridget's Day to the next. Long awaited, the Saturnalian festival finally arrives. Pandemonium breaks loose in the quiet, good-natured town. A surging throng fills the streets. The sound of footsteps, the murmur of passers-by, punctuated here and there by a loud cry. All class differences have disappeared; civilians and soldiers share in the tumult. At the gates of the city the congestion grows. The way to the gate is found, lost, and found again until the exodus is finally achieved. But the Danube Bridge poses new difficulties. Flowing along successfully here as well, two streams cross over and under each other, the old Danube and the even more swollen tide of people; the Danube along its ancient bed, while the river of people – released from the confinement of the bridge – pours out like a wide, raging lake to

---

[2] Viennese district located between the Old Danube and the Danube Channel, named for St. Bridget.

[3] Viennese districts adjacent to Brigittenau.

[4] Kermis festival in honor of St. Bridget, celebrated on July 23rd.

flood everything. Anyone new to the scene would find the signs ominous. But this is the pandemonium of joy, the unshackling of pleasure. Wicker carriages are lined up at the bridge and even before it for the true hierophants of this festival: the children of service and labor. Though crammed full, the wagons fly along at a gallop through the crowds of people, which open up right before them and close up after them, unconcerned and unharmed. For in Vienna there is an unspoken rule between carriages and people: the former won't run people over even at full tilt and the latter won't be run over even when oblivious. From second to second the distance between one carriage and the next decreases. Then private coaches of the privileged class mingle in with the oft-interrupted procession. The carriages aren't flying along anymore. Five or six hours before dark, finally, the single horse-and-buggy units have congealed into a compact lump, impeding itself by its own mass and further impeded by new arrivals from every side street, clearly subverting the old proverb: "Any ride is better than going by foot." Stared at, pitied, mocked, the finely dressed ladies sit in carriages that seem to be standing still. Unaccustomed to the perpetual stopping, a black Holstein stallion rears up as if to fight his way through the blocked path by going up and over the wicker carriage in front of him, something the screaming women and children in the plebeian vehicle obviously fear. The fast-driving coachman, untrue to his nature for the first time, grimly calculates his loss at having to spend three hours for a trip that he would usually make in five minutes. Arguments, yelling, each coachman attacking the other's honor, now and then the crack of a whip.

Just as every standstill on this earth, no matter how inert, is nothing but an imperceptible move forward, a ray of hope does finally appear in this *status quo*. The first trees of the Augarten and of Brigittenau come into view. The countryside! The countryside! All the hardships are forgotten. Those who came by carriage climb down and blend in among the pedestrians. The sounds of distant dance music resound, answered by the jubilation of the newcomers. And then onward until at last the wide harbor of amusement opens up before them: forest and meadow, music and dance, wining and dining, shadow plays and tightrope walkers, festival lighting and fireworks combine in a *pays de cocagne*,[5] an *Eldorado*,[6] a pleasure land that

---

[5] French: "a land of feasting," hence a Utopia.

[6] Spanish: "a land of gold," hence a Utopia.

unfortunately – or fortunately, whichever way you take it – only lasts one day and the next and then disappears like a midsummer night's dream and only remains in our memories or at best in our hopes.

I don't take lightly to missing this festival. As one who passionately loves mankind, particularly the common folk, I as a dramatist have always found the uninhibited outburst of an overcrowded theater ten times more interesting and instructive than the fabricated judgment of some literary matador crippled in body and soul, bloated like a spider with blood he has sucked from authors. As one who loves mankind, I say, I find any folk festival to be a festival of the soul, a pilgrimage, an act of worship, especially when people in crowds forget their individual goals for a while and feel part of a larger whole, wherein ultimately lies the divine spark. As if a gigantic Plutarch has leapt from the pages of its book and unfolded before me, I gather the biographies of undistinguished men and women from their cheerful and secretly concerned faces, their lively or depressed way of walking, the interplay between family members and their detached, half involuntary remarks. Truly, you can never understand famous people unless you've gotten a good feel for those who are obscure. From the exchange between cart pushers, tipsy with wine, is spun an invisible but unbroken thread up to the feuds of the demigods, and in the young maiden who follows her insistent lover away from the bustle of the dance, half against her will, is found in embryo a Juliet, a Dido, or a Medea.[7]

Two years ago, as usual, I had once again joined in the foot traffic of the pleasure-seeking festival crowd. The main obstacles of my journey had already been surmounted, and I found myself at the end of the Augarten with the destination of Brigittenau right before me. But here there is one more battle, a final battle, to be fought. A narrow, elevated causeway with impenetrable barriers on either side forms the only connection between the two amusement parks, their common border marked by a gate of wooden latticework in the middle. For those out for a normal stroll on normal days, this connecting path offers more than ample room. On festival days, though, even if expanded to four times its width it would still be too small for the endless crowds violently pushing forward and stymied by those returning

---

[7] Heroines taken from myth and literature: Juliet from Shakespeare's *Romeo and Juliet*, Dido as the legendary daughter of a King of Tyre, and Medea from the Greek tragedy of the same name by Euripides.

home in the opposite direction. Only the good nature of all the entertainment seekers allows them to pass by in a reasonable manner.

I had surrendered to the pull of the crowd and was halfway along the embankment – already on hallowed ground – but unfortunately forced again and again to stop, move to one side, and wait. So there was time enough to observe what was going on next to the thoroughfare. Lest the fun-loving crowd miss out on a foretaste of the impending bliss, individual musicians had lined up along the left slope of the elevated causeway. Probably fearing the heavier competition, they wanted to harvest the first fruits of the still-untapped generosity here at the temple gates. A female harpist with disgustingly bulging eyes. An old invalid with a wooden leg, trying – on an atrocious instrument he had obviously devised himself, half hammer-dulcimer and half hurdy-gurdy – to make bystanders sympathetic to the pains of his injury by means of analogy. A lame, hunchbacked boy indistinguishably knotted together with his violin, playing an uninterrupted medley of waltzes with all the furious intensity of his misshapen chest. Finally, my full attention was drawn to an old man, easily seventy years old, wearing a threadbare but not untidy woolen overcoat and smiling to himself as if applauding his own performance. His head bald and uncovered, he was standing there as these musicians do with his hat lying before him on the ground as a collection plate. He was belaboring an old, badly cracked violin, keeping time to the music not only by tapping his foot up and down but by simultaneously swaying his whole stooped-over body to the same beat. Yet all this effort to harmonize his performance was fruitless, for what he was playing seemed to be a disjointed sequence of notes without rhythm or melody. At the same time he was completely immersed in his work: his lips were quivering and his eyes were riveted on the sheet music in front of him – yes indeed, sheet music! For while all the other, much more appreciated musicians relied on their memory, the old man had set up a small, easily portable music stand in front of him with dirty, tattered sheets of music that no doubt contained in proper order what he was offering up out of context. It was the quaintness of his paraphernalia that had drawn my attention to him, just as it now evoked the mirth of the passing crowd who laughed at him and left the old man's hat empty while the rest of the orchestra pocketed hoards of copper coins. In order to observe this eccentric undisturbed, I stepped down the slope of the embankment a little distance from him. He played on for a while longer. At last he stopped and, like someone waking from a trance, he looked into the sky which by now was starting to show the signs of approaching evening.

Then he looked down at his hat, found it empty, and put it on with undiminished cheerfulness. Placing the bow between the strings, he said, *"Sunt certi denique fines,"*[8] picked up his music stand, and laboriously worked his way through the crowds streaming toward the festival but in the opposite direction, like someone returning home.

Everything about the old man's personality seemed designed to whet to the extreme my appetite for studying human behavior: his pathetic yet noble bearing, his invincible cheerfulness, so much artistic zeal combined with so much clumsiness, the fact that he was going home precisely at the time when the actual harvest was just starting for others of his kind, and last but not least the few Latin words spoken with correct accent and total fluency. The man had evidently received a good education, had acquired a store of knowledge, and was now . . . a musical beggar! I was anxious to know how it all fit together. But a thick human wall had already closed in between me and him. Small as he was, and bothering people on all sides with the music stand he was holding, he was shoved from one person to the next and out the exit gate while I was still battling my way upstream against the human wave in the middle of the causeway. So he disappeared, and when I finally made my way into the peaceful open spaces myself, there was no fiddler to be seen far and wide in any direction.

The lost adventure had spoiled my enthusiasm for the folk festival. I crossed through the Augarten in all directions and at last decided to go home. When I'd reached the little gate that leads from the Augarten to Taborstrasse,[9] I suddenly heard the familiar sound of the old violin again. I doubled my pace and behold! . . . the object of my curiosity, playing with all the strength he could muster, was standing in the circle of a few boys who were impatiently demanding a waltz from him. "A waltz! Play a waltz!" they shouted, "Can't you hear?" The old man kept on playing as if he weren't paying attention to them until the little swarm of listeners went away, cursing and jeering, to gather around an organ grinder who had set up his hurdy-gurdy close by.

"They don't want to dance," the old man said sadly while gathering up his music gear.

---

[8] Latin quoted from Horace: "There are limits to everything."

[9] German: "Tabor Street."

I had stepped up quite close to him. "Children don't know any other dance but the waltz," I said.

"I was playing a waltz," he retorted, indicating with his bow the notes of the piece he had just been playing. "You have to keep such things in the repertoire to please the masses. But the children don't have an ear for it," he said, shaking his head wistfully.

"Let me at least compensate you for their ingratitude," I said, taking a piece of silver from my pocket and offering it to him.

"Oh, please! Please!" cried the old man, warding me off anxiously with both hands, "In the hat! In the hat!" I put the coin in the hat in front of him, whereupon the old man immediately took it out and put it in his pocket, satisfied. "For once I'll go home with a healthy profit," he said chuckling.

"That reminds me," I said, "of something that made me curious earlier. Your day's earnings don't appear to have been all that good, and yet you leave at a time when the actual harvest is just beginning. The festival lasts all night, as you probably know, and you could easily earn more there than you normally would in a week. How can I make sense of that?"

"How can you make sense of it?" the old man replied. "Excuse me, I don't know who you are, but you must be a generous man and a patron of music." As he said this, he pulled the piece of silver from his pocket one more time and pressed it between his hands in front of his heart. "So I'll tell you the reasons, though I've often been laughed at for them. Firstly, I never was a enthusiast of late-night activities and don't find it right to incite others to such repulsive behavior by music and song. Secondly, a man has to set a certain orderliness for himself in everything he does so that he doesn't fall into wildness and addictions. And last but not least, thirdly, Sir! I play all day for the clamoring people and scarcely earn enough for my meager daily bread, but the evening belongs to me and my poor art. In the evenings I stay home and then . . ." His voice got quieter and quieter, his face turned red, he looked down at the ground and said: "Then I play from imagination, just for myself without a score. 'Improvising' is what they call it in the music books, I think."

We had both grown silent, he from shame at having betrayed an inner secret, I from amazement at hearing a man speak about the highest pinnacles of art who was incapable of playing the easiest waltz recognizably. He was preparing to leave.

"Where do you live?" I asked. "I would like to visit one of your solitary music sessions."

"Oh no," he retorted, almost beseechingly, "you know that the prayer of the heart must be offered up in private."

"Then I'll come visit you during the day," I said.

"In the daytime," he replied, "I go out among the people to make my living."

"Well then, early in the morning."

"It almost appears," the old man said with a smile, "as though you, dear Sir, were the recipient and I were the philanthropist, if I'm permitted to say so; you're being so friendly and I'm the one objecting and trying to back out. Your distinguished visit will be an honor to my residence; I would only ask that you do me the favor of setting the day of your arrival in advance so that you won't be left waiting unceremoniously, and I won't be forced into the predicament of interrupting something I might have started. My mornings are also planned out, you see. At any rate, I consider it my duty to offer my supporters and benefactors something a bit decent in return for their donation. I don't want to be a beggar, dear Sir. Indeed I know that the rest of the public musicians are content to play a few memorized street tunes, Viennese waltzes, or even melodies taken from indecent songs over and over again *ad nauseam*, so that people give them money either to get rid of them or because their playing awakens the memory of dance pleasures or other disorderly amusements they've enjoyed. So those musicians play from memory and at times, or even frequently, they hit the wrong notes. Far be it from me to deceive people, though. For that reason – partly because my own memory isn't the best, and partly because it would be difficult for anyone to keep in mind the intricate works of respected composers note by note – I've copied the music into these notebooks." He pointed to his music book, leafing through pages on which, to my astonishment, I saw tremendously difficult compositions of famous old masters in careful but repulsively stiff notation, completely black with passages and double-stops. And such things the old man played with his clumsy fingers! "By playing these pieces," he continued, "I show my reverence for esteemed and honored master composers long since departed, satisfy my own needs, and entertain the pleasant hope that the gift most graciously given to me might not fail to reciprocate by ennobling the taste and the heart of the listening public – which is disturbed and misguided from all sides as it is. Since such things, or . . . to stick to the issue at hand," and at this point a self-satisfied smile spread across his face, "since such things need to be rehearsed, my morning hours are reserved exclusively for this *exercitium*[10]: the first three hours of the day for practice, the middle ones for earning my bread, and the evening for myself and the dear Lord. That's not a dishonest way to divide up the day," he said with his eyes glistening as if with moisture; yet he was smiling.

"Well then, good," I said, "I will surprise you some morning. Where do you live?"

"On Gärtnergasse[11]," he said.

"Which house number?"

"Number 34, one flight up."

"Really?" I asked, "On the fashionable floor?"

"The house," he said, "actually only has a ground floor. Up next to the attic, though, there's a small room where I live together with two workmen."

"One room for three?"

"It's partitioned," he said, "and I have my own bed."

"It's getting late," I said, "and you want to get home. *Auf Wiedersehen!*" Meanwhile I reached in my pocket in order to double – at the very least – my earlier donation, which had been much too small. But he, picking up his music stand with one hand and his violin with the other, hastily exclaimed: "I must decline most humbly. The honorarium for my playing has already been paid in full, and I'm not aware of having rendered any further services just now." With some parody of aristocratic elegance, he then gave me a rather stilted bow and left as quickly as his old legs could carry him.

As I've said, I had lost any further desire to attend the folk festival that day, so I headed towards home in the direction of Leopoldstadt. Exhausted by the dust and the heat, I went into one of the many garden taverns there which are overcrowded on normal days but today had lost all their customers to Brigittenau. The stillness of the locale, in contrast to the noisy crowds of people, felt good to me. I yielded to various thoughts, not the least of which concerned the old fiddler. It was late at night when I finally thought about going home; I left my tavern payment on the table and starting walking toward town.

---

[10] Latin: "exercising," "practicing."

[11] German: "Gardener's Lane."

Gärtnergasse was where the old man had said he lived. "Is there a Gärtnergasse near here?" I asked a small boy who was running across the street.

"Over there, Sir!" he replied, pointing to a side street that extended away from the mass of suburban houses and out toward the open fields. I went in that direction. The street consisted of individual houses scattered amongst large vegetable gardens that presented clear evidence of the residents' occupation as well as the origin of the street's name. In which of these miserable cottages might my eccentric friend be living? I had blithely forgotten the house number, and in the darkness there wasn't the slightest chance of reading any kind of sign anyway.

At that point a man, heavily loaded down with vegetables, came towards me and passed me. "The old man is scratching away at it again," he grumbled, "keeping decent people from their night's rest." As I went on, the soft, drawn-out tone of a violin immediately caught my ear, seeming to come from the open attic window of a hovel not far away. The house was low and single-storied like the rest but distinguished from the others by its gabled window at the roof line. I stood still. A quiet but solidly sustained note strengthened to the point of a violent fortissimo, sank back down, faded away, only to rise up again soon after to the loudest shriek – always the same note, repeated over and over with a kind of hedonistic single-mindedness. Finally came a change of pitch to an interval, the fourth. If the player had relished the sound of the single note before, now the almost voluptuous savoring of this harmonic relationship was all the more palpable. Jumping between notes with the bow still moving, he connected even the intervening notes on the scale in fits and jerks, played the third, then repeated everything. Next the fifth was added to it, played once with a tremolo like a silent weeping, sustained until it faded, then the whole series was repeated over and over at a whirlwind tempo, the same harmonics, the same notes. And this was what the old man called improvising! It was a basic form of improvising phantasies for the player perhaps . . . but certainly not for the listener.

I don't know how long that may have lasted or how torturous it had become, when suddenly the door of the house opened, a man clad only in shirt and partly buttoned trousers stepped from the threshold out into the middle of the street, and yelled up to the gabled window: "Is there going to be no end to it tonight?" His tone of voice was irritated, but not hard or insulting. The violin went silent even before he had finished speaking. The man went back into the house, the gabled window went shut, and soon an uninterrupted, deathly silence prevailed around me. I started to walk home, finding my way with some effort through the unfamiliar streets while I too was improvising, not disturbing anyone but just improvising for myself in my head.

The morning hours have always held their own unique value for me. It seems as though I have a need to dedicate myself to something uplifting or significant in the first hours of the day in order to sanctify the rest of the day to some degree. So only with difficulty can I make up my mind to leave my room in the early morning, and if I do force myself out without some valid reason, then for the rest of the day I have only the choice between mindless amusement or self-castigating depression. Thus it came that for quite a few days I put off my visit to the old man, which according to our agreement was to take place in the morning hours. At last my impatience got the better of me, and I went. Gärtnergasse was easy to find, as was the house. Violin notes could be heard this time too, but muffled to the point of being indistinguishable through the closed window. I entered the house. A gardener's wife, half speechless from astonishment, showed me the stairs to the attic. I stood in front of a low and badly fitting door, knocked, received no response, finally pressed down on the door handle and entered. I found myself in a rather spacious but otherwise exceedingly wretched room whose walls followed the contours of the steep roof from all sides. Right next to the door was a dirty bed, repulsively disarrayed, surrounded by all the accouterments of slovenliness; on the opposite side, next to the narrow window, was a second sleeping place, pathetic but cleanly and most painstakingly arranged and made up. In front of the window stood a small table with note paper and writing implements, on the window sill some flower pots. The middle of the room was marked with a thick chalk line from wall to wall, and you can scarcely imagine a more glaring contrast between filth and cleanliness than prevailed on one side and the other of the drawn dividing line, the equator of a world in microcosm.

Next to the equalizing line the old man had set up his music stand; he stood in front of it, fully and carefully dressed, practicing. So much has already been said to the point of cacophony about the disharmonies of this favorite of mine – and, I fear, mine alone – that I will spare the reader any further description of this hellish concert. Since the practice consisted mainly of passages, there was no conceivable way of recognizing the pieces from which he was playing excerpts, and even the actual pieces would have been obscure. After listening for some time, I was finally able to recognize the guiding path through this labyrinth, the method in his madness. The old man was playing for his own enjoyment. At the same time, his interpretation distinguished only two things *per se*, melodious and unmelodious sounds, of which the former pleased and even delighted him while he avoided the latter whenever possible, even when they were part of a harmonic progression. So instead of emphasizing sense and rhythm in a piece of music, he exaggerated and prolonged the notes and intervals pleasing to the ear; in fact, he didn't hesitate to repeat them arbitrarily, his face often taking on an expression nothing short of ecstasy. Since at the same time he was passing over the dissonances as quickly as possible – and since he would conscientiously not skip over a single note when performing passages too difficult for him at a tempo much too slow in relation to the work as a whole – you can easily get an idea of the chaos that resulted. It almost became too much even for me.

To bring him out of his trance, after having fruitlessly tried several other means, I intentionally dropped my hat. The old man gave a start, his knees shook, he could hardly hold the violin he had lowered to the floor. I stepped forward. "Oh, it's you, dear Sir!" he said, as if coming to his senses. "I hadn't counted on you keeping your kind promise." He made me sit down, tidied up, put things away, cast a few embarrassed glances around the room, then suddenly picked up a plate from a table by the door and went out with it. I heard him speaking outside the door with the gardener's wife. Soon after, he came back in the door, embarrassed, hiding the plate behind his back and secretly putting it back in its place. He had obviously asked for fruit to offer me as hospitality but hadn't been able to get it.

"This is a nice living arrangement you have here," I said to relieve him of his embarrassment.

"The chaos is on its way into exile. It's making its retreat through the door, even if it hasn't quite reached the threshold yet. My residence only extends as far as the boundary," the old man said, pointing to the chalk line in the middle of the room. "Over there on the other side live two workmen."

"And do they respect your line of demarcation?"

"They don't, but I do," he said. "Only the door is common ground."

"And aren't you disturbed by your neighbors?"

"Hardly ever," he said. "They come home late at night, and if they disturb me in my sleep a little, the pleasure of falling back asleep again is all the greater. In the mornings I wake them, though, when I'm cleaning up my room. Then they complain a little bit and leave."

I had been observing him meanwhile. He was dressed very neatly, his build was decent enough for his age, only that his legs were somewhat too short. His hands and feet were strikingly delicate.

"You're looking me over," he said, "and what might you be thinking?"

"That I am anxious to hear about your past," I replied.

"Past?" he repeated. "I don't have any past. Today is like yesterday and tomorrow like today. The day after tomorrow, of course, and beyond – who can know what's coming? But God will take care of things; he knows best."

"Your present life may well be predictable enough," I continued, "but what about your earlier strokes of fate? How did it come about..."

"That I became one of the street musicians?" he finished the question where I had subconsciously paused. Then I told him how he had caught my attention when I first saw him, how the Latin words he'd spoken had impressed me. "Latin," he repeated. "Latin? Certainly I studied it once, or rather should have and could have studied it. *Loqueris latine?*"[12] he said, turning to me, " but I couldn't continue with it. That's been way too long ago. So that's what you call my past? How it happened? Well yes, all kinds of things happened, of course – nothing special, but still all kinds of things. I wouldn't mind going over the whole thing again sometime for my own sake. I wonder if I haven't completely forgotten it. It's still early in the morning," he continued, reaching into his vest pocket where there was no watch. I pulled out mine; it was scarcely nine o'clock. "We have time and I'm almost of a mood to chat," he said. By now he had become visibly more at ease and he straightened to his full height. Without making a fuss, he took my hat from me and laid it on the bed, sat down, crossed his legs, and generally took on the bearing of someone narrating in comfort.

"No doubt you've heard," he began, "of Counselor X . . .," naming the name of a statesman who, under the modest title of a bureau chief, had enjoyed a gigantic, almost ministry-level influence around the middle of the previous century. I affirmed that I knew of the man. "He was my father," he continued. His father? Father of the old fiddler? Of the beggar? The highly influential and mighty man was his father? The old man didn't seem to notice my astonishment but went on weaving the further thread of his tale, visibly pleased. "I was the middle brother of three. The other two rose high in the

---

[12] Latin: "Do you speak Latin?"

national civil service but are now dead; I'm the only one left living," he said as he looked down and picked at his threadbare trousers, pulling off scattered little flecks from them. "My father was domineering and ambitious. My brothers measured up to his standards. I was considered slow-witted, and in fact I was slow. If I remember rightly," he went on, turning to one side as if looking out into the distance and propping his head up in his left hand, "if I remember rightly, I might have been capable of learning all sorts of things well, if only they'd given me time and systematic training. My brothers leaped like mountain goats from peak to peak in their courses, but I was totally incapable of leaving anything behind, and whenever I missed a single word, I had to start over again from the beginning. And so I was pressured more and more. Some new subject was supposed to take over where the old one hadn't left off yet, and I began to get stubborn. They managed to make music – which is now the joy and also the staff of my life – into something I despised. At twilight, when I reached for my violin to entertain myself in my own way without any music sheets, they took my instrument away from me. They said it spoiled the proper fingering, complained about the tortures of listening, and confined me to the music class instead, where the torture began for me. All my life I've never hated anything or anyone as much as I hated the violin back then.

"My father, dissatisfied to the extreme, frequently heaped reproach on me and threatened to make me into a day laborer. I didn't dare say how happy that would have made me. Only too gladly would I have been a woodworker or a typesetter. But he wouldn't have allowed it anyway, out of pride. The final straw was a public examination at my school, where, to appease him, the examiners had persuaded my father to watch. A dishonest teacher had told me ahead of time what he would ask, and so everything was going smoothly. At one point, though, when I had to recite some memorized verses of Horace, there was one word that wouldn't come to me. My teacher, who had been nodding his head and smiling at my father as he listened, came to my assistance by whispering the word to me. But I was struggling to find the word inside myself and in context with the rest of the passage, and so I didn't hear him. He repeated it several times, all in vain. Finally my father lost his patience. '*Cachinnum!*'[13] he yelled to me in a thundering voice: that had been the word. Now I was done for. Once I knew that one word,

---

[13] Latin: "loud laughter".

I panicked and couldn't remember any of the others. All the efforts to put me down the right track were in vain. I had to stand up in shame, and as I went over to kiss my father's hand as was customary, he pushed me away, stood up, gave a curt bow to those assembled, and left. '*Ce gueux*'[14] he called me: something I wasn't then, but now I am. Parents prophesy when they speak! By the way, my father was a good man, just domineering and ambitious.

"From that day on, he didn't say another word to me. His orders were passed along to me by others in the house. Thus I was told the very next day that my studies were finished. I was severely shaken because I knew how bitterly this had to grieve my father. I did nothing all day but cry and, in between, I recited those Latin verses that I now knew by heart, along with the preceding and the following verses. I promised to make up for my lack of talent with hard work, if only I would be allowed to go back to school. But my father never changed his mind once he had made a decision. Then for a while I stayed in my father's house with nothing to do. At last they took me to an accounting office on a trial basis. Mathematics had never been my strength, though. I rejected with horror an offer to go into the military. Even now, I can't look at any uniform without shuddering to the core. To defend beloved family members – even, if needs be, at the peril of your own life – is fine and understandable, but bloodshed and mutilation as a way of life, as a profession: No! No! No!" And saying this, he stroked each arm with the opposite hand as if feeling the stabbing pains of his own and other's wounds.

"Next I went into a government office as one of the copyists. There I felt right at home. I had always enjoyed writing, and even today I can't think of any more pleasant amusement than linking together narrow hairline strokes and wide shadowy strokes into words or even just into letters, using good ink on good paper. When it comes to musical notes, they're the most beautiful of all. But back then I wasn't even thinking of music. I worked very hard, but I was just too scrupulous. An incorrect punctuation mark, a word left out in the draft even though anyone could fill it in from the meaning, would trouble me for hours. In a dilemma whether I should hold exactly to the original or correct what I thought was a mistake, the time slipped by and I got the reputation of being lazy, despite the fact that I was more

---

[14] French: "that fool"

conscientious at the work than anyone else. I spent a few years like this – without a salary – since when I came up for promotion, my father gave his council vote to somebody else and the others went along with him out of deference.

"Around this time . . . Well, just look," he interrupted himself, "there is a kind of past after all. Let's tell the story! Around this time two events occurred: the saddest one of my life and the happiest one. The banishment from my father's house and my return to the sweet art of music, to my violin, which has been faithful to me right up to the present day.

"I lived in the house of my father, unheeded by others in the house, in a little back room with an entrance out to a neighbor's yard. At first I ate at the family table, where no one said a word to me. But when my brothers were promoted and moved out of town, and my father was invited out to dinner almost every day – my mother had been dead for a long time – it became inconvenient to keep a kitchen going just for me. The servants received a food allowance and I did too; it wasn't handed to me but paid out to a boarding house each month. I was only rarely in my room, as a result, except for the evening hours since my father insisted that I be home a half hour after the office closed. Then I would sit around at dusk with the lights off because of my eyes, which were already going bad back then. I would think about this and that and wasn't sad and wasn't happy.

"As I was sitting like that, I heard a song being sung in the neighbor's yard one day. Several songs, that is, of which I liked one in particular. It was so simple, so touching, and accented in just the right place so that you didn't really need to hear the words at all. I think the words just spoil the music anyway." Now he opened his mouth and issued forth some hoarse, croaking sounds. "I'm not gifted with a voice," he said and reached for his violin. He played, this time with the correct expression, the melody of a little song – cheery and pleasant but otherwise not at all exceptional – while his fingers shook on the strings and tears finally began running down his cheeks.

"That was the song," he said, laying his violin aside. "Whenever I heard it after that, it was with renewed delight. As lively as it was in my memory, though, I never managed to hit even two notes of it right with my voice. I almost grew impatient from listening. Then I noticed my violin, the one from my youth, hanging on the wall unused like an old piece of armor. I took it in my hands, and – perhaps the servant had been using it while I was gone – it turned out to be perfectly tuned. Then as I drew the bow across the strings, Sir, it was as if God's finger had touched me. The sound penetrated into my soul and back out again. The air around me seemed impregnated with drunkenness, the song below in the yard and the notes rising from my fingers to my ear, co-inhabitants of my solitude. I fell on my knees and prayed aloud and could not comprehend that I had once scorned and even hated this blissfully divine instrument in my childhood: I kissed the violin and hugged it to my heart and played on and on.

"The song outside in the yard – it was a woman singing – continued unabated all the while, but sorting out the melody to play wasn't so easy for me. You see, I didn't have the song written down. In addition, I noticed that I had very much forgotten the little bit of the fiddler's art that I had once known. I couldn't play anything in particular but just played what I could. I've always been uninterested in the latest musical trends anyway, with the exception of that song, and I've kept that attitude up till now. They play Wolfgang Amadeus Mozart and Sebastian Bach, but nobody plays the dear Lord above: the eternal blessing and mercy of tone and sound, its miraculous accord with the desperately eager ear, such that…" he continued with a lowered voice and blushed, "the third tone attunes itself with the first, as does the fifth, and the *nota sensibilis*[15] climbs upward like the fulfillment of a hope. Dissonance is subjugated as premeditated evil or arrogant pride, and by the miracles of phrasing and inversion even the second is bestowed with grace in the luxurious lap of euphonic sound. A musician explained all this to me, though much later. And then there are the *fuga*[16] and the *punctum contra punctum*[17] and the *canon a due*,[18] *a tre*,[19] and so forth – about which I understand nothing – an entire celestial edifice, one part joining with the other, bound together without mortar, and held in the hand of God. Nobody wants to hear about such things, except for a few. Instead, they disturb this inhaling and exhaling of the souls by adding words to it, words worthy of being spoken at best. Thus they try grasping and poking their way into calloused spirits, just as the children of God once united with the daughters of earth. Sir," he concluded at last, half exhausted, "speech

---

[15] Latin: "leading tone."

[16] Latin: "fugue."

[17] Latin: "counterpoint."

[18] Italian: "canon for two parts."

[19] Italian: "canon for three parts."

is as necessary to mankind as food, but the nectar that comes from God should be kept pure."

I could hardly recognize this man any more; he had become so full of life. He paused to reflect a little. "Now where was I in my story?" he asked finally. "Oh yes, that song and my attempts to play it. It didn't work out, though. I stepped to the window to listen more closely. Just then the singer was walking across the yard. I saw her only from behind, and yet she seemed familiar to me. She was carrying a basket with what appeared to be pieces of cake dough. She went through a little doorway at the corner of the yard, where I suppose there was an oven for baking, since I heard the scraping of wooden implements as she kept singing, and her voice sounded alternately muffled – like she was bending down and singing into a hollow enclosure – and then clear, like she was standing up again. After a while she returned and then I noticed for the first time why she had seemed familiar to me before. I had actually known her for a long time, from the office in fact.

"This is the way it was. Our office hours began early and lasted past noon. Several of the younger officials, who were either genuinely hungry or else wanted to take a half-hour break, had the habit of going out around eleven o'clock to eat a little something. The tradespeople, knowing how to turn everything to their advantage, made it easy for those with a sweet tooth by bringing their merchandise into the office building itself and setting up shop in the stairways and corridors. A baker sold little loaves of white bread, the fruit lady sold cherries. But especially popular were certain cakes that a neighboring grocer's daughter baked and brought to sell, still warm. Her customers went out to meet her in the corridor, and only rarely, when bidden, would she come into the office proper. Whenever the somewhat grumpy supervisor would see her there, he just as likely showed her the way to the door, an order that she obeyed only begrudgingly, murmuring angry words as she left.

"The girl was not considered pretty by my fellow workers. They thought she was too short and couldn't describe the color of her hair. Some didn't think her eyes were catlike, but everyone agreed on her pock-marked complexion. Only her buxom figure met with everyone's approval, though they complained of her crudeness, and one of them liked to tell about a slap on his face that he supposedly felt for a week. I wasn't one of her customers myself, partly because I didn't have the money, partly because I've always had to recognize food and drink as a necessity – often too much so – but to see them as sources of enjoyment and delight never occurred to me. So we didn't take notice of each other. Once to tease me, though, my colleagues made her think I had asked for her baked goods. She came up to my desk and held out her basket.

"'I'm not buying anything, Miss,' I said.

"'Well then, why did you send for me?' she asked indignantly. I apologized and explained the practical joke to her as best as I could, since I'd seen right through it. 'Well, at least give me a piece of paper to lay my cakes on, then.' she said. I pointed out to her that this was office paper and not mine to give away, but at home I had some of my own I would bring for her. 'At home I've got plenty myself,' she said sarcastically and left with a short laugh.

"That had happened a few days before, and I planned to take advantage of this encounter for my own needs right away. So the very next morning I strapped a whole ream of paper under my coat – something never lacking at our house – and went to the government office. In order not to betray my plans, I left the harness on my body with great discomfort until I noticed around noon, by the comings and goings of my colleagues and the sounds of their eating, that the cake salesgirl had come, and I could surmise that the main rush of customers was past. Then I went outside, took out my paper, fortified my courage, and went up to the girl, who was standing there with the basket on the floor in front of her and her right foot on a stool she would normally sit on; she was humming softly and tapping out the rhythm with the foot she had resting on the stool. She looked me over from head to toe as I approached, which made me even more embarrassed.

"'Dear Miss,' I finally began, 'you recently asked for paper from me at a time when none of mine was available. Well, now I've brought some from home . . .' and with that, I held the paper out to her.

"'I already told you,' she replied, 'that I have paper at home myself. Still, I can always use it.' With that and a slight nod of the head, she took my present and put it in her basket. 'Don't you want a piece of cake?' she said, looking around among her baked goods, 'though the best of it is already gone.' Turning down her offer, I said that I did have a different request. 'Well, what is it?' she said, putting her arm through the basket handle and standing up straight, her eyes fiercely flashing at me. I quickly chimed in to say that I was a music lover, even though I hadn't been one long, that I had heard her singing such lovely songs, especially one of them. 'You? Me? Songs?,' she flared up, 'and where was this?' I went on telling her that I lived in her neighborhood and had listened to her while she'd been working in the yard. I especially liked one of her songs, so much so that I had already tried to repeat the tune on my violin. 'Might you be the fellow,' she exclaimed, 'who scratches around on the fiddle?' I was only a beginner back then, as I've already said, and not until later was I able – by great effort – to put the right skill in these fingers," the old man interrupted himself, fingering around in the air with his left hand as if fiddling. "A flush," he continued with his tale, "was rising to my face, and I could tell by looking at her that she too regretted the harsh words.

"'Honored Miss,' I said, 'the scratching comes from the fact that I don't have the song written down, which is why I wanted to ask most respectfully for a copy.'

"'For a copy?' she said. 'The song is in print and they sell it on the street corners.'

"'The song itself?' I answered. 'That's probably only the words.'

"'Well, of course: the words, the song.'

"'But what about the melody you sing it in?'

"'Do they write stuff like that down?' she asked.

"'Certainly!" was my answer, 'that's the whole point. And how did you learn it yourself, honored Miss?'

"'I heard it being sung, and I sang what I had heard.' I was astounded at the natural genius, at how unlearned people often possess the most talent. But it's still not quite the right thing, not the art itself. I was in desperate straits once again. 'But which song is it?,' she asked. 'I know so many.'

"'All without the notes?'

"'Well, of course; so which one was it?'

"'It is just so beautiful,' I explained. 'It rises up high right at the beginning, returns to an inner soulfulness, and then ends very softly. It's the one you sing most often.'

"'Oh, then it's probably this one,' she said, set the basket down again, put her foot on the stool, and then sang the song with a very soft and yet clear voice, bobbing her head so beautifully, so endearingly, that before she had finished, I reached for her hand. 'Aha!' she said, pulling her arm back, since she probably thought I wanted to touch her hand in some unseemly manner; but no, I wanted to kiss it, even though she was just a poor girl. Well, now I am a poor man myself.

"Since I was all but tearing out my hair from eagerness to have the song, she comforted me and said that the organist from St. Peter's Church often came to her father's shop for nutmeg; she would ask him to write it all down in notes. Then I could pick it up there in a few days. At that, she took her basket and left, and I accompanied her as far as the stairs. As I was making my last bow on the upper step, my office supervisor surprised me, told me to get back to work, and called the girl names, saying she was totally worthless. I was extremely upset at that and was about to respond back that with all due respect I was convinced to the contrary, when I noticed that he had gone back to his room already. So I pulled myself together and likewise went back to my desk. But from this point on he was convinced that I was a poor worker and a debauched human being.

"For that day and the next few days, in fact, I was scarcely able to do any decent work, since the song was going around in my head and I was like a lost soul. A few days passed and I wasn't sure if it was time to go pick up the music or not. The organist, the girl had said, came to her father's store to buy nutmeg; he could only be using that with beer. For some time now it had been cool weather; so it was probable that the stout musician was keeping to wine and wouldn't be needing any nutmeg very soon. To ask too quickly seemed like a discourteous intrusion, while waiting all too long could be interpreted as indifference. I didn't dare speak with the girl in the corridor, since our first meeting had been gossiped among my colleagues and they were just itching to play a trick on me.

"Meanwhile, I had taken up the violin again with passion and was thoroughly practicing my way through the basics, yet from time to time I allowed myself the luxury of playing from my head. I carefully closed the window when I did, though, since I knew people didn't like my playing. But even when I had the window open, I wasn't able to hear my song again. The neighbor girl sometimes sang nothing at all, or sometimes so quietly behind closed doors that I couldn't tell one note from another. Finally, when about three weeks had passed, I wasn't able to stand it anymore. It's true that I had been sneaking down to the street for two evenings, hatless so the servants would think I was just looking for something in the house, but as soon as I came near the grocery store, I started trembling so much that I had to turn back whether I wanted to or not. But finally, as I've said, I couldn't stand it any longer. I gathered my courage and one evening, hatless again, I went down the stairs from my room and out along the street with sure steps all the way to the grocery store, where I stood for awhile and thought about what I might do next. The store was lit up and I heard voices inside. After some hesitation, I bent forward and peeked in from the side. I saw the girl sitting at the counter next to a light, sorting peas or beans in a wooden bowl. Standing in front of her was a stout, robust man, his jacket thrown over his shoulder, some sort of club in his hand like a butcher might have. The two of them were talking, obviously in a good mood: the girl laughed out loud a few times without interrupting her work or even looking up. Whether it was my strained, bent-over position or whatever else, my trembling began to come back, when suddenly I felt myself being roughly grabbed from behind and pushed forward. In an instant I stood inside the store and, when I was let loose, I looked around and saw it was the proprietor himself who had been returning home from somewhere, had caught me spying, and wanted to detain me for interrogation. 'By thunder!' he shouted, 'now we see where the plums have disappeared and the handfuls of peas and rolled barley that are swiped from our display baskets in the dark. I think lightning is just about to strike!' And with that he came at me as if he really wanted to strike.

"I felt destroyed, but the thought that someone doubted my honesty brought me quickly back to my senses. So I made a very short bow and told the discourteous man that the object of my visit was not his plums or his rolled barley, but his daughter. At that, the butcher standing in the middle of the store laughed out loud and turned to leave after first whispering a few words to the girl, who laughingly answered with a resounding clap of her palm on his back. The grocer saw the departing visitor to the door. I had meanwhile lost all of my courage again and stood facing the girl, who was sorting her peas and beans indifferently, as if the whole thing had nothing to do with her. Then her father stormed back through the door again. 'Blazing tarnation,' he said, 'what do you want with my daughter?' I tried to explain to him the context and reason of my visit. 'What song? I'll sing you a song or two!' he said, waving his right arm up and down threateningly.

"'There it is,' the girl said, leaning sideways in her chair and pointing at the counter without setting aside the bowl full of legumes. I hurried over and saw a music sheet lying there. It was the song. But the old man had gotten there first. He picked up the fine paper, crumpling it in his hand.

"'I asked what this is all about!' he said. 'Who is this fellow?'

"'He's a gentleman from the government office,' she answered, tossing one wormy pea a bit farther away than the rest.

"'A gentleman from the office?' he cried, 'in the dark? Without a hat?' I explained my missing hat by the fact that I lived very close by, pointing to the house. 'I know that house,' he cried. 'Nobody lives there but the Counselor X . . .,' here he said the name of my father, 'and I know all the servants.'

"'I am the son of the Counselor,' I said quietly, as if it were a lie.

"I've seen many changes come about in the course of my life, but never any as abrupt as transformed the whole personality of the man at these words. His mouth, opened to humiliate me, hung open. His eyes were still threatening, but around the lower part of his face a sort of smile began to spread, wider and wider. The girl remained indifferent, bent over, just brushing some loose strands of hair back behind her ears as she worked.

"'The son of the Honorable Counselor?' cried the old man at last, his face now completely cheerful. 'Would Your Grace perhaps like to make himself comfortable? Barbara, a chair!' The girl shifted reluctantly on her own stool. 'You just wait, you coward!' he said, lifting up a basket himself and dusting off the stool beneath it with his apron. 'I'm deeply honored,' he continued. 'As Honorable Counselor – or His Honorable Son, I meant to say – you're a musical practitioner as well? Perhaps you sing, like my daughter does, or rather from written notes like a true virtuoso?' I explained to him that by nature I had no singing voice. 'Or perhaps you tickle the ivories, as high-class people so often do?' I said that I played the fiddle. 'Me too; I used to scratch around on the fiddle when I was young,' he cried. At the word 'scratch,' I looked over at the girl involuntarily and saw her sneering sarcastically – something that upset me very much.

"'You should take an interest in the girl, that is to say: in her music,' he continued. 'She sings with a good voice and has other fine qualities, but as for refinement, dear God, where's that supposed to come from?' While saying this, he was repeatedly rubbing the thumb and index finger of his right hand together.

"I was completely ashamed that such significant musical abilities were being undeservedly attributed to me and wanted to fully expose the true state of affairs, when someone passing by outside cried out: 'A good evening to all of you!' I was terrified, for it was the voice of one of our servants. The grocer had recognized it as well.

"Extending the tip of his tongue and hunching his shoulders, he whispered: 'It was one of your gracious papa's servants. You couldn't tell, though: you had your back to the door.' The latter was actually the case. But a feeling of uneasiness, of something wrong, tormented me. I stammered just a few words of farewell and left. I would have even forgotten the song if the old man hadn't run out to the street after me and put it in my hand.

"I made it home in this state, went to my room, and waited for things to come. And they didn't take long. The servant had recognized me all the same. A few days later, the secretary of my father came to my room and told me that I had to leave the family house. All my pleas to the contrary were fruitless. A small room had been rented for me in a distant suburb, and thus I was exiled from my family. Nor did I see my songstress again, either. They had forbidden her to sell cakes at the office, and I couldn't resolve to enter her father's shop since I knew it displeased my own father. In fact, when I met the old grocer once on the street by chance, he turned away from me with a furious expression and I felt shattered. Then, alone for entire mornings or afternoons, I took out my fiddle and played and practiced.

"There was still worse to come, though. The fortunes of our house were declining. My youngest brother, an impetuous and stormy officer with the Dragoons, tried, while still overheated from a hard ride, to swim across the Danube deep inside Hungary with his horse and armor on an ill-considered bet. He had to pay for it with his life. The oldest one, the favorite, was employed as a counselor in one of the provinces. At continual odds with his immediate superior and, as people verified, secretly encouraged by his father, he took the liberty of making libelous statements to damage his opponent. This led to an investigation, and my brother fled the country in secret. The enemies of our father, of whom there were many, used the opportunity to topple him from power. Attacked from all sides and enraged at his decreasing influence besides, he made the most vituperative speeches daily in the council. In the midst of one of them, he suffered a stroke. He was brought home unconscious. I myself learned nothing of it. The next day at the office, I did notice people secretly whispering and pointing their fingers at me. I was already used to such treatment, though, and thought nothing of it. The following Friday – it had happened on Wednesday – suddenly, a black suit with crepe for mourning was brought to my room. I was surprised and asked why and found out. My body is generally strong and resilient, but that was too much for me. I sank to the floor, unconscious. They carried me to bed, where I had high fever and talked delirious nonsense all through the day and all night. By the next morning my strong constitution had the upper hand but my father was already dead and buried. I hadn't been able to talk to him again, to ask his forgiveness for all the trouble I had caused him, not able to thank him anymore for his undeserved favors – yes, favors! For he meant well, and I hope to meet up with him again some day in a place where we are judged by our intentions and not by our works.

"I stayed in my room for several days, scarcely able to eat any food. Finally I did go out, but I returned home again right after eating, and only in the evenings would I wander around in the dark streets like Cain, murderer of his brother. My father's residence was an image of terror that I carefully avoided. One time, though, thoughtlessly staring in front of me, I suddenly found myself near the dreaded house. My knees shook so much I had to steady myself. Groping around for the wall behind me, I recognized the door of the grocery store and Barbara sitting inside, with a letter in her hand, the light on the counter beside her, and her father standing right there, who seemed to be exhorting her. And even if my life had been at stake, I had to enter. To have nobody to tell my woes to, nobody to sympathize! The old man, I did know, was angry at me, but the girl would give me a kind word. Yet exactly the opposite occurred. Barbara stood up when I entered, threw an arrogant glance at me and went into the back room, locking the door behind her. The old man shook my hand, asked me to sit down, comforted me, and then said that I was a rich man now and didn't have to worry about anybody anymore. He asked how much I had inherited. I didn't know. He asked me to inquire at court, and I promised I would. There was nothing more for me in the government office, he said. I should invest my inheritance in a business venture. Spices and fruits made good profits; one of his friends, who knew the trade well, could change pennies into guilders. He himself, said the grocer, had once put a lot of effort into it. At the same time he called repeatedly for his daughter, but she gave no response. Still, it seemed to me as though I heard a rustling noise at the door from time to time. But since she wouldn't come out and the old man would only talk about money, I said goodbye at last and left. The man said he regretted not being able to accompany me a ways, since he was alone in the store. I was sad at my dashed hopes, yet wonderfully comforted.

"When I stopped on the street and looked over at the house of my father, I suddenly heard a voice behind me, muffled and with an indignant tone, that said: 'Don't be so quick to trust people; not everybody means you well.' Even though I turned around quickly, I couldn't see anybody: only the rattling of a window on the ground floor, part of the grocer's house, told me – even if I hadn't recognize the voice – that Barbara was the one giving the secret warning. So she had heard what had been said in the store. Did she want to warn me about her father, or had she heard that right after my father's death colleagues from the office and other total strangers had approached me with pleas for support and emergency help? I had agreed to assist them once I came into money. What I had promised I would keep, but in the future I vowed to be more careful. I did the paperwork necessary for my inheritance. It was less than people had thought, but still quite a lot, nearly eleven thousand guilders. Never, all day long, was my room empty of those asking favors or seeking help. I had gotten nearly hard-hearted, though, and only gave where the need was greatest. Barbara's father came as well. He complained that I hadn't visited in three days, whereupon I answered truthfully, saying I feared becoming a nuisance to his daughter. He said I shouldn't worry about that, though, and that he had set her straight about things, laughing in such a malicious way that I was frightened. Reminded of Barbara's warning, I concealed the amount of my inheritance when we got to speaking about it shortly after. I also skillfully evaded his business proposals.

"In actuality, other ideas had already entered my head. In the government office, where they had only put up with me because of my father, my position had already been filled by someone else. That didn't bother me much, since no salary was attached to it. But my father's secretary, who had lost his job to these last events, shared with me his plans for creating an agency for information, written copies and translations, for which I was to advance the set-up costs. He was willing to take over the day-by-day operations himself. At my insistence, the copy work was also extended to include musical manuscripts, and now I was in heaven. I gave him the necessary money, but since I had become wary, I also saw to it that the legal papers were drawn up. The security bond for the business – which I advanced as well – scarcely seemed worth mentioning, though it was considerable, since it had to be deposited with the Commerce Court and remained my own property there as if I had it locked away in my own vault.

"The deal was done and I felt relieved, elated, self-reliant for the first time in my life, a man. I scarcely thought of my father anymore. I moved into a better apartment, changed the way I dressed a little, and passed through well-known streets toward the grocery store when evening had come, strolling along and humming my song between my teeth, but never quite right. My voice was never able to hit the B-flat near the end. Cheerful and in bright spirits, I arrived, but an ice-cold look by Barbara threw me back into my accustomed trepidation again. Her father received me most heartily but she acted as if nobody were there, continuing to assemble paper bags and not joining in our conversation with a single peep. Only when the discussion came around to my inheritance did she rise up halfway and said, almost threateningly, 'Father!' at which the old man immediately changed the subject.

Other than that she didn't say a thing all evening, didn't give me a second look, and when I finally took my leave, her 'Good night!' almost sounded like a 'Thank God!'

"But I came again and again, and she gradually gave in. Not that I had done anything that she appreciated. She criticized me and called me names continually. Everything I did was awkward: God had given me two left hands, my coat made me look like a scarecrow, I walked like a duck with just a touch of rooster. Especially repugnant to her was my courtesy toward the customers. Since I didn't have anything to do until the opening of the copying agency and was mindful that I would have to work with the public there, I took active part in retail sales in the grocery store as a way to practice, often staying busy at it for a morning or an afternoon at a time. I weighed spices, counted out nuts and prunes to little boys, and made change – not without frequent mistakes, at which point Barbara would always barge in, forcibly take away what I was holding, deride and ridicule me in front of the customers. If I bowed a bit to one of the customers or commended myself to their kind consideration, then she would say gruffly, 'The merchandise recommends itself!' before the people were even out the door, and turn her back on me. Sometimes, on the other hand, she was full of goodness. She listened to me when I told her what was going on in town, about my boyhood years, or about life at the office where we had first met. At the same time she always let me do all the talking, and only with a single word or two did she show signs of her approval or, as was more often the case, her disapproval.

"We never did talk about music or singing. First of all, she believed people ought to sing or else keep their mouth shut; it was nothing to talk about. There was no singing either. In the store it was inappropriate, and I wasn't allowed to go into the back room where she and her father lived together. But one time when I came in unnoticed, she was standing on her tiptoes with her back turned to me and her hands raised up, feeling around on one of the top shelves as if she were looking for something. And she was singing softly to herself. It was the song, my song! She was chirping like a warbler that cleans her throat at the brook's edge by tossing her head about while ruffling and smoothing her feathers with her beak. It seemed to me I was walking across green meadows. I sneaked closer and closer and got so close that the song didn't seem to be coming from outside me, but from within me, a song of our two souls. Then I couldn't hold back any longer, and as she was bending forward at the waist with her shoulders leaning back down toward me, I took hold around her waist with both hands. Then the storm broke. She whirled around like a top. Her face fiery red with anger, she stood right in front of me; first her hand twitched, and then before I could apologize....

"At the office, as I reported earlier, they had often told about a slap that Barbara had given some pushy fellow while she was still selling cakes there. What they had said there about the strength of this rather short girl and the motive force of her hand seemed highly exaggerated for the sake of a joke. But that's the way it turned out to be in reality: it was monstrous. I stood there as if thunderstruck. Lights danced before my eyes, but they were celestial lights like the sun, the moon, and the stars, or like little angels playing hide-and-seek and singing at the same time. I saw visions; I was ecstatic. But she, scarcely less startled than I was, gently stroked the place she'd slapped as if to soothe it. 'Maybe that was too hard,' she said, and then – like a second bolt of lightning – I suddenly felt her warm breath on my cheek and her two lips, and she kissed me, just softly, ever so softly; but it was a kiss on this cheek of mine, here!"

At that the old man clapped his hand to his cheek and tears welled up in his eyes. "What may have happened next, I don't know," he continued. "Only that I threw myself at her, and she ran into the living room and held the glass door shut while I pushed from the other side. Then as she was pushing back with all her might as if glued to the glass panel, I took courage, dear Sir, and passionately returned her kiss ... through the glass.

"'Aha, what a merry scene we have here!' I heard someone calling out behind me. It was the grocer just returning home. 'Well now, flirting is the first stage of love ...' he said. 'Come on out here, Barb, and don't act so silly! An honest kiss is nothing to miss.' But she wouldn't come out. As for myself, I left after a few half-unconsciously stammered words, then I took the grocer's hat instead of my own, which he laughingly switched in my hand. That was, as I called it earlier, the happiest day of my life. I was half tempted to say the only happy day, but that wouldn't be true, for humans enjoy many mercies from God.

"I didn't really know what the girl thought of me now. Was she still angry or had she been calmed down? My next visit only came after a hard struggle with myself. But she was amiable to me. Modestly and quietly, without flaring up as she usually did, she sat there at her task. She motioned with her head to a stool next to her, indicating I should sit down and help her. And so we sat there and worked. The old man wanted to leave. 'Stay here, father,' she said, 'What you wanted to take care of is already done.' He stamped his foot hard on the floor and stayed. Walking to and fro, he talked about this and that, but I didn't dare to enter into the discussion. Then the girl suddenly let out a little cry. She had cut one of her fingers while working, and even though she wasn't usually so sensitive, she was shaking her hand back and forth. I wanted to see if I could help, but she motioned that I should keep on working.

"'Foolishness; this is nothing but foolishness,' the old man growled, and – stepping in front of the girl – he said in a loud voice: 'What had to be taken care of isn't done yet at all!' and then, his steps clattering, he went out the door.

"Just as I was starting to excuse myself for what happened the day before, she interrupted me and said: 'Let's forget about that and talk about more important things.' She raised her head up, looked me over from head to toe, and continued in a quiet tone of voice: 'I can hardly remember anymore how we first got acquainted, but for some time now you've been coming more and more often, and we've gotten used to you. No one will deny you have an honest heart, but you're so weak, always paying so much attention to trivial things, that you're scarcely able to take care of your own affairs. So then it becomes the duty and responsibility of friends and acquaintances to look out for you so you don't get hurt. You sit around in the store here for days, counting and weighing, measuring and marketing, but nothing comes from it. What are you thinking of doing in the future to make a living?' I mentioned the inheritance of my father. 'That may be very sizable,' she said. I told her the amount. 'That's a lot and a little,' she answered. 'A lot to get started with, but very little to live on. My father did make a suggestion to you, but I advised you against it. Once, you know, he lost money at things like that himself, and thus,' she added in a lower voice, 'he's so accustomed to making a profit from strangers that maybe he wouldn't give a better deal to a friend. You have to have somebody on your side with honest intentions.' I pointed at her. 'Yes, I am honest,' she said. At that, she laid her hand on her breast, and her eyes, usually gray, were sparkling bright blue, blue as the heavens. 'But I've got my own concerns. Our business isn't earning much, and my father is toying with the idea of setting up a tavern. There'd be no room for me there. All I would have left would be needlework, because I don't like the idea of being a maid.' And as she was saying this, she looked like a queen to me. 'It's true that another proposal has been made to me,'

she continued, pulling a letter from her apron and throwing it half reluctantly on the counter, 'but for that I'd have to go away from here.'
"'Far away?' I asked.
"'Why? What does that matter to you?'
"I explained that I wanted to move to the same place.
"'Don't be such a child!' she said. 'That wouldn't do and would be completely inappropriate. But if you do trust me and like to be near me, then go buy the clothing shop next door that's for sale. I know how to do that kind of work, and you wouldn't need to worry about good honest profits for your money. You, too, could have a decent job yourself with the accounting and writing. What else might come from it, we can't really talk about yet. But you would have to change yourself! I hate effeminate men.'
"I had jumped up and was reaching for my hat. 'What's happening? Where are you going?' she asked.
"'To cancel everything,' I said with a quick breath.
"'Cancel what?'
"I told her my plan for creating an agency for giving out information and making written copies. 'You won't get much from that,' she said. 'Anybody can get his own information, and everybody learned how to write in school.' I mentioned that musical scores would be copied as well, which isn't something everyone can do. 'Are you going to start up with that foolishness again?' she asked me abruptly. 'Forget about music and think about your needs! You wouldn't be capable of running a business yourself anyway.' I explained to her that I had found a partner. 'A partner?' she cried. 'Someone who wants to cheat you, no doubt! I hope you didn't give him any money yet?' I shivered without knowing why. 'Did you give him any money?' she asked one more time. I admitted to the three thousand guilders for setting up shop. 'Three thousand guilders?' she cried, 'so much money!'
"'The rest,' I continued, 'is deposited at court and so at least it's safe.'
"'So there's even more?' she shrieked. I mentioned the amount of the security deposit. 'And did you deposit that yourself with the court?' That was something my partner had taken care of. 'You certainly have a receipt for it, don't you?' I didn't have a receipt. 'And what is the name of your trustworthy partner?' she asked. I was somewhat relieved to be able to name my father's secretary."
"'God All Righteous!' she yelled, jumping up and clapping her hands together. 'Father! Father!' The old man came back in. 'What was it you read in the newspapers today?'

"'About the secretary?' he said.

"'Yes, yes . . . .'

"'Well, he's skipped town; he left a pile of debts behind and embezzled from people. Warrants are out for his arrest.'

"'Father,' she cried, 'Jacob trusted him with his money too. He's ruined.'

"'What a fine specimen of an idiot!' yelled the old man. 'Didn't I always tell you? But then you always had excuses for him. First you laughed at him and then you said he was an honest soul. But I'm going to put a stop to it! I'm going to show you who the boss is in this house. Barbara, go to your room! But as for you, Sir, you will get out of here and spare us any future visits. This is no place for handouts.'

"'Father,' said the girl, 'don't be harsh with him. He's already unhappy enough.'

"'That's precisely it,' the old man yelled: 'I don't want to be unhappy too. Now that, Sir,' he continued, pointing at the letter that Barbara had thrown on the counter earlier, 'that is a real man. He has brains in his head and money in his pocket. Cheats nobody, but doesn't let anybody cheat him either. That's the main thing with honesty.' I stammered that the loss of the security deposit wasn't certain yet. 'Ridiculous!' he cried, 'the secretary was no fool. He's a scoundrel, but he knew what he was doing. So, quick, get out of here; get; maybe you can still catch him!' So speaking, he laid the palm of his hand on my shoulder and was pushing me toward the door. I sidestepped him and turned toward the girl, who was leaning against the counter with her eyes fixed on the floor, her bosom heaving up and down. I wanted to go to her, but she angrily stomped on the floor. As I reached out with my hand, she halfway tensed hers as if she wanted to hit me again. So I left, and the old man locked the door behind me.

"I stumbled through the streets, out the city gate, and into the fields. At times I would get an attack of despair, but then hope would return. I remembered having accompanied the secretary to the Commerce Court for the deposit of the security bond. I had waited in the passageway there, and he had gone up alone. When he came back down, he said that everything was taken care of; the receipt would be sent to my house. The latter hadn't happened of course, but the possibility was still there. At the break of day I came back into the city. My first destination was to the secretary's residence. But the people laughed and asked me if I hadn't read the newspapers? The Commerce Court was only a few houses away. I had them check in their books, but neither his name nor mine appeared there. No trace of a payment.

So now my tragedy was certain. And it might have even gotten worse. Since there was a partnership involved, several of his creditors wanted to carry the suit over to me. But the courts didn't allow it. For that I give them my praise and gratitude! But it wouldn't have mattered much anyway.

"With all these calamities in mind, I must admit, the grocer and his daughter had faded completely into the background. But when things quieted down and I started to think about what might happen next, the memory of the last evening came back to me vividly. I completely understood the old man, self-serving as he was, but the girl! Sometimes the thought came to me that if I had been more circumspect with my inheritance and had been able to offer her a living, then maybe she would have even . . . but she wouldn't have been able to stand me." So saying, he dropped his hands apart and examined his whole sorry figure. "My politeness towards everyone always disgusted her too.

"That's how I spent days on end, thinking and pondering. One evening at twilight – it was the time I had usually spent in the store – I was sitting again, transporting my thoughts back to the familiar setting. I heard them talking, insulting me, in fact it appeared they were laughing at me. Then suddenly, there was a rustling at the door; it opened, and a woman came in. It was Barbara. I sat riveted to my chair as if I were looking at a ghost. She was pale, carrying a bundle under her arm. In the middle of the room she stopped, looked all around at the bare walls then down at the poor furnishings, and sighed deeply. Then she went to the chest of drawers on the side wall, unwrapped her package containing a few shirts and handkerchiefs – she had been doing my wash for the last little while – pulled out the drawer, clapped her hands together when she saw the scanty contents, but then immediately began arranging the clothing and putting away what she had brought. After that she stepped away from the chest a few steps and, with her eyes directed at me, she pointed to the open drawer and said, 'Five shirts and three handkerchiefs. That's how many I had, and that's how many I'm bringing back.' Then she slowly pushed the drawer shut, supported herself against the chest with her hand, and started to weep out loud. It almost seemed as if she had gotten ill, since she sat down on a chair next to the cabinet, buried her face in her towel, and I could hear from the gasping breaths she took that she was still sobbing. I had quietly approached her and took her hand, which she good-naturedly allowed. But when I moved my hand up her limp arm to her elbow to have her look at me, she quickly stood up, freed her hand, and said in a composed tone of voice: 'What good is all this? What's done is done. This is what you wanted; you've made both yourself and us unhappy – but certainly yourself most of all. Actually you don't deserve any sympathy' – at this, she got even more agitated – 'if you're so weak you can't even keep your own affairs in order, so gullible you trust everyone whether he's a scoundrel or an honest man. But still, I am sorry for you. I've come to say goodbye. Yes, you've got good reason to be shocked. But it's all your own doing. Now I have to go out among the ruffians, something I've been resisting for so long. But there's no way to avoid it. I've already had you take my hand, and so farewell now – for always.' I saw that tears were coming to her eyes again, but she angrily shook her head and started to leave. I seemed to have lead in my arms and legs. When she was at the door, she turned around one more time and said: 'Your clothes are in good shape now. See to it that nothing gets lost! Hard times are coming.' And with that she raised her hand, made the sign of the cross in the air and cried: 'God be with you, Jacob!' Then she added more gently, 'In all eternity, Amen!' and left.

"Only then did the use of my arms and legs return to me. I hurried after her, and as I stood on the landing, I called after her: 'Barbara!'

"I heard her stop on the staircase. But when I had gone down just one step, she called up from below, 'Stay there!' and went all the way down the rest of the stairs and out the front door.

"I've had some bad days since then, but none like that; even the next day was less severe. I really didn't even know how bad off I was, and so the next morning I sneaked around near the grocery store to see if I could find out what was going on. Since there was nothing to see, I finally took a glance sideways into the store and saw some unknown woman weighing goods and counting the change as she handed it out. I got up the courage to go in and asked if she had bought the store.

"'Not just yet,' she said.

"'And where might the owners be?'

"'Early this morning they started on their trip to Langenlebarn.'[20]

"'The daughter too?' I stammered.

"'Well, of course,' she answered, 'she's going to be married there.'

"The woman then may have told me everything that I found out subsequently from others. The butcher of the above-mentioned village – the same

---

[20] A town in Lower Austria, some miles from Vienna.

one I met at the time of my first visit to the store – had been making marriage proposals to the girl for a long time. She had always been able to evade them until finally, in the last few days – pressured by her father and despairing of any other alternative – she had consented. Father and daughter had begun their journey this very morning, and, even as we talked, Barbara was the butcher's wife. The saleslady may have told me all that, as I said, but I didn't hear it and stood motionless until customers came at last, shoving me to one side, and the woman gruffly asked if I wanted anything else, at which point I left.

"You can believe, honored Sir," he continued, "that I now felt myself to be the unhappiest of all people. And so it was in the first moment. But as I walked out of the store and, turning around, looked back at the small windows at which Barbara had undoubtedly often stood and looked out, a blissful feeling came over me. The fact that now she was free of all worry, a wife in her own house, someone who didn't need to carry worry and misery around with her as she would have if she had associated with a poor destitute man like me – all that spread across my breast like a balsamic salve, and I blessed her and her future paths.

"As things went more and more downhill with me, I decided to make my living with music, and as long as my remaining money lasted, I practiced and studied the works of the great masters – preferably of the older masters – which I had copied by hand. When the last penny was spent, I went about taking advantage of my skills, at first only in private social gatherings, the first occasion for which came at the invitation of my landlady. When the compositions I performed didn't find any resonance there, though, I positioned myself in the courtyards of houses, since among so many inhabitants there had to be some who could appreciate serious music. Then I finally took to the public walkways, where I actually had the satisfaction that some individuals stopped, listened, asked me questions, and continued on, not without some interest. The fact that they gave me money didn't shame me at all. For on the one hand that was precisely my goal, while on the other I realized that famous virtuosi – whose status I could not flatter myself with having attained – accepted honoraria for their accomplishments, and sometimes very ample ones. This is the way I have made my living, poorly but honestly, up to the present day.

"Years later, one more bit of happiness was to come my way. Barbara returned. Her husband had earned enough money to acquire a butcher business in one of the suburbs. She was the mother of two children, of which the oldest is named Jacob like me. My own professional activities and the memory of the olden days did not permit me to be intrusive, but finally I was invited into their house to give the oldest son violin lessons. He does have only a little talent and can only play on Sundays, since his father uses him in his business during the work week, but Barbara's song, which I've taught him, is already going quite well, and when we practice and make music, sometimes his mother sings along. She has changed a lot in all these years, has grown stout, and doesn't care much about music anymore, but it still sounds just as beautiful as it used to . . . ."

And with that the old man took his fiddle and started to play the song, playing on and on without taking any further notice of me. Finally I had enough, stood up, laid a few pieces of silver on the table next to him and left while the old man enthusiastically played on and on.

Soon after that I started on an extended trip from which I didn't return until the onset of winter. New images had pushed the old ones aside, and my fiddler had been pretty much forgotten. Only on the occasion of terrible ice jams breaking up the following spring and resultant flooding of the lower-lying suburbs did I remember him again. The area around Gärtnergasse had become a lake. There didn't seem to be any reason to worry for the old man's life, since he lived high up in the attic, while death had picked out all too many victims from among the ground-floor residents. But how great his need must have been, devoid of all help! As long as the flooding lasted, there was nothing to be done, though the authorities had dispensed food and assistance to isolated individuals by boat as possible. Contributions had been organized, collected, and had grown to unbelievable amounts. When the waters had receded and the streets had become passable again, I decided to contribute my own portion personally to the address that most concerned me.

The view of Leopoldstadt was gruesome. Wrecked boats and furniture in the streets, some ground floors still partly filled with water and floating goods. As I was getting away from the tumult and approached a back door that was slightly ajar, the door swung open to display a row of corpses in the corridor, obviously brought together and laid out for purposes of an official inquest. In fact, victims of the disaster could be seen inside their rooms here and there, still standing upright with their hands clutched at the window bars – there just weren't authorities or time enough to proceed with the legal confirmation of so many deaths. And so I walked on and on. Weeping and death knells came from all sides, mothers searching for lost children and lost children looking for their mothers. Finally I arrived at Gärtnergasse. Here, too, the black-bedecked retinue of a funeral procession had formed, but it seemed to be far from the house I was looking for. As I came closer, though, I did notice a connection of preparations and people passing back and forth between the funeral cortege and the gardener's residence. At the front door stood a sturdy-looking man, elderly but still robust. Dressed in tall boots, yellow *Lederhosen* and a long, flowing frock coat, he had the appearance of a country butcher. He gave orders, but in between he talked rather dispassionately with those standing around. I walked past him into the yard.

The old gardener's wife came towards me, recognized me at once, and welcomed me with a flow of tears. "You're paying your respects too?" she said. "Ah yes, our poor old man! Now he's making music with the angelic choirs, who could scarcely surpass him in saintliness. That honest soul was sitting up there in his room, safe and sound. But when the waters came and he heard the children screaming, he hurried downstairs and rescued and dragged and carried and brought them to safety until his breath was going like a blacksmith's bellows. In fact – since we couldn't pay attention to everything – when it turned out that my husband had left his tax books and a few guilders of paper money in the cupboard, the old man took a hatchet, waded back into the water that was up to his chest by then, broke into the cupboard and faithfully brought everything back to us. That was probably how he caught cold, and when there was no remedy for him right away, he started hallucinating and got worse and worse, though we were right there to do what we could and were suffering more than he was. For he kept on singing, you know, beating time and imagining he was giving lessons. When the waters receded some and we could send for the barber-surgeon and the priest, he suddenly sat bolt upright in bed, turned his head to one side as if listening to something exquisitely beautiful in the distance, smiled, sank back down and was dead. Go on up; he often spoke about you. The lady, the wife of the master butcher, is up there too. We wanted to have him buried at our expense, but she wouldn't hear of it."

She pushed me up the steep stairs to the room in the attic: the door was wide open and the room completely empty except for the coffin in the middle, already closed and awaiting the pallbearers. At the head of it sat a rather stout woman, well along in years, dressed in a bright calico skirt, but with a black scarf and a black ribbon in her bonnet. It almost seemed as if she could never have been beautiful. In front of her stood two adolescent children, a boy and a girl, to whom she was evidently giving instructions on how they were to behave during the funeral procession. Just as I entered, she pushed aside the arm of her son, who had been leaning rather clumsily on the coffin, and she carefully smoothed out the protruding edges of the shroud again. The gardener's wife led me on, but just then the trumpets began to blare down below, and simultaneously the voice of the butcher rose up from the street: "Barbara, it's time!"

The pallbearers appeared; I moved back to make room. The coffin was lifted up, taken down the stairs, and the procession started moving. In front were the school children with the cross and banner, the priest with his sexton. Directly behind the coffin came the two children of the butcher, followed by the couple. The man moved his lips incessantly as if in prayer, but was looking to the left and right as he did so. The woman earnestly read in her prayer book, but she had to look after the two children – once pushing them ahead, once holding them back – as it appeared that the proper comportment of the funeral procession was near and dear to her heart. But she always kept returning to her prayer book. In this manner the cortege proceeded to the graveyard. The grave lay open. The children threw the first few handfuls of dirt down on the lowered coffin. The man, standing there, did the same. The woman knelt down and held her prayer book close to her eyes. The grave diggers finished their business, and the procession, half disbanded, turned to leave. At the gate there was one little exchange of words as the woman evidently found one of the undertaker's charges to be too high. The mourners scattered in all directions. The old fiddler was buried.

A few days later – it was a Sunday – I went to the butcher's residence, driven by my psychological curiosity, on the pretext that I wanted to own the old man's fiddle as a keepsake. I found the family together, showing no trace of the recent distress. Still, the fiddle hung on the wall arranged in a certain symmetry, next to the mirror and opposite a crucifix. When I explained my reason for being there and offered a relatively high price, the man didn't appear opposed to making an advantageous profit. The woman jumped up from her chair, though, and said: "Why should we! The fiddle belongs to our Jacob, and we don't care about a few guilders more or less!" At that, she took the instrument down from the wall, examined it from all sides, blew the dust off it, and laid it in the drawer which – as if fearing a robbery – she furiously pushed shut and locked. Her face was turned away from me at the time, so I couldn't see what emotions were playing there. Since the maid entered with the soup just then, and the butcher, undisturbed by my visit, was loudly beginning to say grace, to which the children's shrill voices chimed in, I wished them all a good meal and went out the door. The last thing I saw was the woman. She had turned around, and tears were streaming down her cheeks.

"Friedrich Halm" was the pseudonym adopted by **Elegius Franz Joseph Reichsfreiherr von Münch-Bellinghausen (1806-1871)** in an effort to find a middle-class name to which his reading public could readily relate. Having descended from a long line of Austrian nobility, Halm was financially secure enough that he could spend his time in voluntary, unpaid positions, including stints as various commissioners and counselors, before becoming prefect of the Habsburg court library and simultaneously general director of both court theaters in Vienna.

The same concern for equality between the classes that motivated Halm's choice of pseudonyms is a dominant theme in his literary works. It is clearest in the play *King and Peasant* (1842), adapted from a Spanish comedy of Lope de Vega, where easy interchange between the classes seems desirable and possible, while in the drama that had first won him a lasting place on the Viennese stage, *Griseldis* (1837), a child of the working classes marries into the upper echelons of society. In the latter dramatic production, however, a sub-theme is developed that is also crucial for the plot of the novella presented here: in fighting his way up from the hard-scrabble existence of the streets, the working-class striver may develop antisocial and even dishonest habits that cannot remain hidden long and that may later drag him down.

Halm's prose is deeply imbued with the author's flair for drama. At the same time, it is innovative – traversing a path toward realism – and unparalleled for its day. The recurring novella motifs – calling forth grand emotional outbursts from the actors in a piece of fiction so inherently theatrical – are crime, sex, metaphysics, and fate. In *Marzipan-Lisa* (1854), there is a phantasmagorical blend of genres: we see romance, crime, mystery, horror and ghost stories all rolled up in one narrative. The result is as much dramatic as it is prosaic.

Psychological components in the novella predate the rise of the social sciences. Particularly in showing the reactions of young "Sensy" (nickname for "Crescentia"), the narrator opens up a wide range of emotions and complexes ranging from gullibility, betrayal, and guilt to schizophrenia and hallucinatory trauma – with occult sightings, catatonic states, and religious ecstasy thrown in for good measure. In the person of her father are found a believable mix of love and sternness, of steady if naive trust amalgamated with flashes of rash impetuosity, of paternal instincts conjoined with the bottom-line priorities of a businessman. Yes, and even the "bad guy" here remains consistent within his own character, attempting the same ploys and manipulations over and over.

The mystery of the story, i.e., the identity of the murderer, is not held in suspenseful abeyance until the very end of the story as in a traditional murder mystery, but rather the readers' first suspicions tend to be confirmed again and again. Therefore, the art of this novella is not in its exposition of "whodunnit" (hint: it wasn't the butler), or even in its character sketches, but in how the truth comes out – in the twists of plot, in the dramaturgical unfolding of narration, dispensing not only the judgment but also the gruesome justice – accepted by all as Divine retribution.

Marzipan-Lisa is a "framed tale," that is, the narrative world into which we are led at the beginning of the story – and which continues in altered form at the end of the story – becomes the frame for yet another earlier story, the story involving the title character, Marzipan-Lisa, as told by a visiting businessman, Herr Steidler. But that frame is raised and lowered a number of times – and in that sense it could be compared to Grillparzer's *Poor Fiddler,* where the old man becomes an intermittent second narrator inside the moving frame created by the main narrator. In Halm's novella, the relationships between the inner tale and the outer one constantly interweave on the stage, converging and diverging until the resolution of those scene shifts in the reader's mind becomes of tantamount importance.

There is another political drama alluded to as the flow of exposition guides us back and forth between Austria and Hungary in this tale. Written at a time of great debate on the merits or follies of a dual Austro-Hungarian monarchy – which was to become historical fact thirteen years later – contemporary readers would have read a great deal into the cross-cultural exchanges, including revelations of murder, that took place on the main road between the mountains of Austria and the metropolis of Budapest. Attention is drawn to this in the very first sentence when historical mention is made of a Hungarian rebellion against Austria's Habsburg dynasty.

Many thanks go to my colleague Kati Radics of the U.C.L.A. University Research Library for her assistance in deciphering the Hungarian references and allusions.

Marzipan-Lisa

Friedrich Halm

In the early decades of the eighteenth century, a short time after the signing of the Peace of Szathmár,[1] there lived a merchant by the name of Paul Horváth, wealthy and flourishing, in the Hungarian town of Veszprém.[2] He owned a large house outside the city gates with deep cellars and voluminous storage chambers that were nonetheless often scarcely enough to hold the mountains of balls, barrels and boxes they were designed to accommodate, since even though he primarily traded in linens obtained from Styria and Carinthia,[3] Horváth carried on an extensive business in wine and grains on the side. His efforts to get his business off the ground and the need to make favorable business connections had forced him, in his early years, to travel hither and yon to shows and trade fairs and had led him to Venice, to the German Empire and to Holland, so that the education of his only daughter Crescentia and the administration of his orphaned household was left for months at a time to old Margit, an aunt of his deceased wife. Later on, he found himself relieved of these strenuous trips: his reputation was now as solidly established as was his fortune, and buyers and sellers he had been forced to seek out before now knocked at his door. With the exception of a few days each year he was accustomed to spending at the trade show in

---

[1] This treaty, signed in 1711, signaled the end of Rákóczy Ferenc's war of Hungarian independence against the Habsburg dynasty of Austria.

[2] A city in western Hungary, just north of Lake Balaton.

[3] Two provinces of Austria whose names in German are "Steiermark" and "Kärnten" respectively.

Buda[4] during *Michaelmas*,[5] he was now able to carry out his business within the bounds of his own home, to see his daughter grow from a child to a promising young woman, and to practice with jovial relaxation the native Hungarian virtues of hospitality as impressively and as generously as his inclination and intelligence bid him: in those days, with the lack of satisfactory transportation and requisite lodgings, business people had to rely on their commercial colleagues to be hosts as well, and in the house of well-to-do Horváth, situated squarely on the road connecting Buda with Graz[6] and Városlöd,[7] there was no lack of frequent demand or of hospitable welcome.

One day, after Horváth had accompanied one of his guests on the road to Székesfehérvár[8] as far as Várpalota,[9] he was riding back towards his home in a one-horse shay, thinking about this and that. Careful and thoughtful as he was, he was allowing his pony to climb a small rise at a walk and bundling himself even tighter in his *bunda*,[10] since it was a raw fall evening and from the direction of Vörös-Berény[11] the wind, sharp and biting, was whipping off of Lake Balaton at him. Just then, at the intersection of the main road with one of the side paths, he became aware of a young person whose posture at first glance expressed deep exhaustion and despondency just as clearly as the cut of his worn and dusty clothing announced him as a foreigner to Hungary. He sat right at the edge of the path on a half-sunken curbstone; next to him lay a burl-handled walking stick, a small bundle, and his cap, while his long, pale-blond hair, tossed this way and that by the autumn wind, alternately revealed and then concealed the fine, pleasant features of his

---

[4] Twin city which, with Pest, forms Budapest.

[5] A religious festival held annually around September 29th.

[6] The capital city of Carinthia in Austria.

[7] A town about 12 miles west of Veszprém.

[8] The city where Hungarian kings were crowned in the Middle Ages, located about 25 miles east of Veszprém. Its name translates literally as "Presiding White Castle."

[9] A town 8 miles east of Veszprém.

[10] A traditional Hungarian folk mantle, usually an overcoat made from skins where the hairy side is turned to the inside and the smooth white side is turned out. The outside is frequently decorated with colorful lacework and appliéd patterns in colored leather. See also *Brigitta,* p. 57.

[11] That is, from the south.

pale, emaciated face, and his blue-gray eyes stared darkly in front of him as if in thoughtless defiance.

"Hey! Get up, young fellow!" yelled Horváth, reaching in his pocket and tossing a coin down to him.

The boy jumped to his feet at the sound of a voice: his first move was directed at escape, the second a hasty grab for his walking stick, but when he saw the coin he seemed to pull himself together again. He let the stick go and sank back down on the stone. "Too little to keep me alive and too much to keep me from dying!" he said and, with one kick, sent the coin flying into the dust of the street.

"Eszem adta!"[12] cried Horváth, holding tight to the reins and then adding angrily in German: "Are you a millionaire? Or is the Imperial coinage too crude for you to pick up? Do you want to answer me, drifter?"

The youth darkened and shot a wary, piercing look full of grim animosity at the speaker. Still, he seemed to have his reasons for holding back, for he bit his lip and replied with a constricted voice after a short pause: "I don't want any handouts! I want someplace to stay; I want to find work!"

"Work, indeed," cried Horváth, "with your fine, delicate hands! What kind of work can you do with those?"

The youth stood up straight and answered with a contemptuous smile and a visible feeling of intellectual superiority that there was more work to be done with a pen then with a wooden axe. He was trained, he said, in accounting and bookkeeping; he didn't know Hungarian, it was true, but spoke and wrote German, French and Latin and was capable of a number of other useful things.

Horváth listened to the confident words, nodding his head, and after pondering a bit, asked: what was his name, what had he done up to now, and did he have letters of reference?

The stranger hesitated for a while, but soon collected his wits and announced with a fluent tongue that his name was Franz Bauer, he was a native of Vienna, had assisted a lawyer there but left his employ to see something of the world. In Pécs[13] he had gotten very ill and some thief had robbed him of his letters of reference and the better part of his possessions; yesterday

---

[12] Hungarian: An expletive that originally had the colloquial sense of a compliment ("Very clever!").

[13] A city in southwestern Hungary, located near the Croatian border.

he had found his way across Lake Balaton and was now sitting there not knowing quite what to do with himself.

Horváth's encouraging head-nodding had changed to a concerned head-shaking several times during this report, but the stranger's pleasant exterior seemed to have corrupted the businessman's common sense. "Good," he said finally, "I'll give you shelter for tonight, and tomorrow if it turns out you're capable and willing to work, maybe we can find a place for you! Come on up here!" And with that he scooted over to one side of the seat to make room for him.

The young man thought about it a moment and, with skeptical wariness, examined the open and honest features of the merchant. Then he threw his bundle and burl-handled walking stick in the wicker basket attached to the back of the shay and swung up beside Horváth, who let his pony trot quickly down the other side of the slope to Veszprém.

The next morning, when Horváth tested the young man by laying out one of the many invoices that had, to his embarrassment, fallen into some disarray by the death of his bookkeeper a few weeks before, it soon became clear that Franz Bauer far exceeded the deceased not only in correctness of comprehension, skill, and insight, but also in depth of knowledge, so that Horváth hired the services of the young man on the spot to finish up the incomplete invoices and to help alleviate the backlogs that had arisen in correspondence and bookkeeping. Solving these problems could take roughly six weeks, but the eagerness with which Franz proved himself while fulfilling his new duties and the ease with which he routinely handled even the most complicated transactions – without ever compromising the content or accuracy of his work to the slightest degree – soon made him completely indispensable to his employer.

After only a month had passed, Horváth asked the newest member of the house staff to accept the position of his predecessor with all the attendant honors and benefits on a permanent basis, appearing so anxious for him to accept the offer that it would have been easy for the young man to gain even more favorable conditions and salary for himself by feigned reluctance. But Franz was too smart to risk losing any future favor and trust in exchange for some meager gain in the present. He accepted Horváth's offer humbly and gratefully as though it were an undeserved favor and declared himself highly fortunate to be able to be a permanent part of a business firm all of whose associates had accepted him with such friendly goodwill and had treated him so kindly.

Scribe Ferencz,[14] as he was now called after his promotion, had in fact become the favorite of all his business associates in a short time. In the very first days after arriving he had gradually exchanged the sullen wariness and defiant, suspicious manner he had shown at first for a gentle, long-suffering personality, for a quiet, modest friendliness, making impressive efforts to anticipate the wishes of others and to offer service without ever expecting any in return. He was able to win over the lady regent of the house, old Margit, by his unusually pious meekness, by his emphatic praise for the excellence of her housekeeping, but above all by the grateful willingness with which he allowed the inexhaustible plenitude of her medicinal remedies to be visited upon him during his frequently recurring eye disorders. He got the menservants of the house on his side partly by little gifts, partly by the enthusiasm with which he supported their requests for a vacation or a raise in front of their boss. He captivated the maidservants, though, by friendly greetings, modest acclaim for their charms, and by the melancholic tones of lamentation he was able to coax from his flute on lovely, moonlit nights as he leaned against the edge of the fountain. Sensy, the daughter of the house, was the one he approached last of all, but no less successfully.

The first impression Ferencz had made on the plain and simple seventeen-year-old girl was one of repulsion: she felt a sinister force when she was around him and was afraid of the glassy stare in his light-blue eyes. Her father's words of praise, however, the pleasing looks and refined manner of the young man soon erased this first impression. The accounts of the maidservants and of her great-aunt Margit about the depressed state and visible grief of the poor scribe gradually won him her sympathies, even as the richness of his knowledge, praised from all sides, piqued her envious admiration. Even with all of Horváth's wealth, the education that Sensy could receive in a rural Hungarian town in those days fell far below what the father as well as the daughter had hoped for: above all, her knowledge of the German language was extremely inadequate,[15] and Ferencz was able to use this fact to solidify his position from that angle as well. His offer to give her instruction in this language in his free time was accepted unequivocally by Horváth and with delight by Sensy; in fact, the latter insisted

---

[14] Hungarian equivalent of "Franz."

[15] A command of German as a language of commerce was vital during the many centuries that Hungary was ruled by the Habsburg emperors from Vienna.

on training her teacher in the elements of the Hungarian language in return. The reciprocal instruction began, and the two young people, who could just barely make themselves understood at first, continued it with such unusual success that after just a few months Sensy was able to confide to her great-aunt, under an oath of secrecy, that the fiancée of poor Ferencz had faithlessly deserted him and married another; that he had gone out into the big, wide world despairing about it; and only now had he gotten to the point again where he could listen to the voice of reason and accept comfort – a commentary delivered with such peculiar disquietude and frequent blushing that it would have left little doubt in a more cosmopolitan listener than old Margit as to the identity of the comforter and the ways and means of the comfort.

Meanwhile, the rapid rise of the scribe Ferencz in the favor of his associates had quietly awakened an enemy to the fortunate man, someone who gradually showed himself as one who threatened to force him out of the position he had victoriously assumed or at least to make his exploitation of it significantly more difficult. This enemy was Antal, the house butler. Whether it was because Ferencz had lavished too little attention his way or because Antal, a native of Máramaros[16] and a dyed-in-the-wool Hungarian, couldn't stand seeing the hated "Swabian"[17] entrusted with a position he himself had earlier proven himself incapable of assuming – in short, he spared no effort to trace every step the scribe made, and with the acuity of hate he was able to make observations which, when poisoned by suspicious assumptions and spread with the rhetoric of resentment, were at least capable of providing all sorts of embarrassment for his foe. Above all, Antal kept pointing out that the duplicate letters of reference to replace the ones stolen from the scribe in Pécs still hadn't arrived from Vienna. At the same time, he never stopped pointing to the curious fact that the acute attacks of head gout and eye disorders – from which the scribe suffered and which required him each time to cover his face with bandages and plasters of all kinds – almost always afflicted him on the precise days that business associates from Styria or Carinthia were visiting in the house; in fact, Antal claimed to have physical proof that Ferencz tossed aside Aunt Margit's ocular rinses,

---

[16] A region near the Carpathian Basin in Romania which was then a part of Hungary.

[17] A native of Swabia ("Schwaben" in German), an area of southwestern Germany now in the state of Baden-Württemberg. However, the term was often used by Eastern Europeans to designate any of the German-speaking peoples.

salves and herbal packs mostly unused, no matter how much he might extol their healing properties.

But Antal endeavored to make things uncomfortable for the envied favorite from another angle as well by expressing his astonishment very candidly, and indeed his indignation, that such an experienced, cosmopolitan man as Mr. Horváth would let his only daughter – and heir – associate for hours on end, in a language that was more or less unintelligible to the rest of the house, with someone picked up off the street, with a completely "unforeseen" man like the scribe. At least it was certain, Antal would further suggest, that Sensy's cheeks could compete with the loveliest scarlet linens in the warehouse of her father for colorful splendor after such rendezvous, while Ferencz, when he left his pupil, walked around as if he were about to become the next paladin[18] or even the King of Hungary himself. Antal would accompany such outbursts by frequently shaking his head and shrugging his shoulders regrettably, or by closing with some proverbs, such as: "You can't make a goat into a gardener," "The fattest bites are the easiest to swallow," and "When opportunity knocks, a thief answers." He repeated these and other idiomatic expressions so loudly and so long, everywhere he could, that they finally found their way to Horváth's ears. The latter, hurt beyond all bounds and irritated, however, squarely took the side of suspect Ferencz and loudly and publicly rejected any and all accusations that came his way as abominable slander. Ferencz had given proof of his unselfishness and honesty at present that was too striking for his employer to have been able to doubt his honesty in the past. It seemed just as irrational to the easy-going, good-hearted man – who seldom delved very deeply into the essence of things – to assume that his daughter could let herself get involved in a love affair with some total stranger who chanced her way.

Far from cutting off the possibility of such a continuing relationship by releasing the scribe, however, he was more concerned about giving the rumors spread by Antal the appearance of validity by doing so. At the same time, he worried that he might be depriving himself needlessly of a magnificent business assistant who would not be easy to replace. To preserve Sensy's reputation from slander, it appeared sufficient to him to prohibit the young people from continuing their reciprocal lessons, and so he interrupted the class period one day, directed the scribe to the place he belonged, i.e., back

---

[18] Paragon of chivalry, heroic champion.

to the ledgers in his office, forbade his daughter any further association with the flute-playing beggar, imposed eternal and absolute silence on Antal under threat of dismissal as the latter pled for mercy in deepest remorse, and everything was taken care of. The young people, who seemed completely devastated at first, adapted, even before it could be expected, to the limitations imposed on them and seemed, if not happy, at least resigned and calm. Antal mumbled and grumbled to himself, clenched his fists in his pockets, and bared his teeth in private, while Horváth, who heard no further suspicions and didn't notice anything improper from then on, let the things he thought he had now set aright take their course again, bit by bit, as they had before.

Two years had passed in this way. A beautiful autumn lay over the countryside, and in a few days the Michaelmas trade fair in Buda was slated to begin, the one Horváth was accustomed to visiting annually. Two freight-coaches of fine linens had already been sent ahead as usual, and the merchant was thinking of following after his goods a while later. It was noontime. Horváth had sent the scribe to the cloister at Bakony-Bél[19] to collect some cash, and he himself was rummaging through papers and textile samples when Antal, the butler, entered the office and stood humbly at the door, waiting to be addressed. Antal had some weeks before received an inheritance, not insignificant for his circumstances, and had as a consequence given notice to Mr. Horváth of his intentions to resign in order to open up a shop in his home province. His services had ended, the little cart to take him home was waiting out front, and now he had come to take leave of the man who for ten years had been unpredictable and gruff with him at times, but well-meaning and friendly for all that. Horváth had set his pen aside and had stepped up to the fellow – who was no longer exactly young but still bursting with strength and health. It was unmistakable – by a peculiar twitching in Antal's usually easy-to-read face and by the frantic way he was twirling his well-waxed mustache – that he was having trouble hiding his strong inner emotions.

Then, as Horváth laid a hand on his broad shoulder, thanked him amiably for the good services he had provided, for having proven honest and faithful for so many years, and voiced his regrets that in spite of all advice to the contrary, instead of waiting for better days in this house, he wanted to try standing on his own two feet in such a difficult time and to try his luck at

---

[19] In the Bakony Mountain region west of Veszprém.

business, great big tears started rolling down across Antal's brown cheeks. "Sir," he blurted out sobbing, "I know it might be my own misfortune by leaving, and certainly I will never have it any better elsewhere than I've had it here with you, but I have to go! God is punishing me: because I blabbered into the air at the wrong time, now when the time is right I mustn't say what has to be said, and I just can't watch it anymore, or my heart will break!"

"What is it you see then?" cried Horváth, who was beginning to be infected by the emotions of the young man, "and why do you have to keep it quiet?"

"I have to! I have to!" replied Antal, beating himself on the forehead with his mighty hand. "Because of my anger, I'll be selling my soul to the devil if even one more word about anyone in this house comes across my lips. There's only one thing I can do," he continued, clasping his hands together, "I beg you, I beg you, open up your eyes and see the way you're going! Get some helpful advice while there's still time! Think about why handsome Kis Sándor was too young and honest Barna László was too old to become your son-in-law! Think about it, take your heart in your hand... and God bless you!" and with that, sobbing, he kissed the gentleman's hand and the seam of his clothing and rushed out the door.

Horváth stood there, shaken and as if paralyzed with astonishment and some uncertain dread. When, after having come to his senses again, he rushed after Antal, the latter had long since hopped up on his cart, started the team moving by his voice and a crack of the whip, and was now flying towards his home province at a truly Hungarian breakneck pace, surrounded by swirls of dust.

Late on the evening of the same day, long after sunset, the scribe Ferencz, wrapped in his *szür*,[20] returned from Bakony-Bél with a heavy sack of money under his arm. Flames from the hearth shining through the kitchen window more brightly than usual and an unknown servant, whistling as he walked some visibly tired horses around in the yard so they could cool down slowly, soon made it clear to him that there was a guest in the house. He stood under the gateway indecisively for a while, but when he later heard the young

---

[20] A coat, similar to a *bunda* (see page 57), but long and sleeveless, originally made of cloth rather than skins.

man let out a merry "*Schnadahüpfl*"[21] as he showed the horses to their stalls, Ferencz stamped his foot with displeasure and quickly turned down a darkened passageway leading from the gate to the kitchen. The rattling and clanging of a mighty bundle of keys and the plodding patter of slippers announced the proximity of Aunt Margit, and he sought her out, greeting her humbly by kissing her hand and asking her to take the money sack to Mr. Horváth in his place and to tell the gentleman that his assignment had been carried out. Ferencz' head pains had started up again, he said: he was shivering and wanted to go to bed. "What? Where are you thinking of going, my boy?" replied the old lady. "You don't want to come to supper, and we have a visitor, Herr Steidler, the rich hammer dealer from Mürzhofen[22] who's on his way to the trade fair in Buda! And I'm supposed to take the money sack to our master and be scolded when I can't tell him what he wants to know? Going to bed? You ought to go to the supper table and pull yourself together as befits a young man, that's what you ought to do!"

To this and similar ideas Ferencz answered in a pitiful tone of voice that he was suffering today more than ever, he would rather put his hand on hot, glowing iron than move his jaw; at the same time, his eye was tearing up like a leaky bucket and every ray of light felt like a needle prick! The old lady said he should wash with her miracle solution, bandage up his head and put protective masks over his eyes, and it shouldn't be life-threatening. He should think what people would say and how unhappy his employer would be at his staying away from the supper table when guests were there! What's more, he had left around noon and Sensy would be sad if she didn't see him tonight! Whether this last consideration persuaded the young man or whether it was Mr. Horváth who decided it by appearing at the upper end of the staircase just then, accompanying his guest to supper – who called down, asking what was up and whether the scribe hadn't returned yet – in short, Ferencz replied to his call that he was back and would report to him right away. Then he hurried off to his room in order, as he whispered to Aunt Margit, to follow her medicinal prescriptions first.

---

[21] German: An encouragement to the horses, obviously spoken by a native Austrian rather than a Hungarian groom.

[22] A small town in Styria, north of Graz along the Mürz River.

The meal had already begun when Ferencz entered the room – with a cloth slung around his jaw and a mask over his eyes – and approached the master of the house, who was occupying the head of the table in a more serious and more contemplative attitude than he usually showed when receiving cherished guests. Horváth cast an annoyed glance at the scribe, took in his report by silently nodding his head, gestured for him to take his place at the foot of the table, then turned back to his guest while Sensy nodded to the latecomer with look of joy and of regret.

The table discussion proceeded for a long time with complaints about the unfavorable results of the harvest and with speculations about the influence of the same on the prices of goods at the upcoming trade fair, only then to turn to the weather conditions, which forecasted a rainy summer season followed by a protracted, bright, and beautiful autumn. This turn in the discussion gave the guest cause to come back to the terribly bad roads he had encountered from Steinamanger[23] until well past Sárvár,[24] and which had caused him at least two hours delay! "By the way," continued the very intelligent and only slightly long-winded man, "by the way, my horses would have gotten me here before sundown if I hadn't wasted so much time this morning with the poor sinner!"

"With what poor sinner?" asked Horváth, and Steidler, in order to satisfy the clamoring curiosity being voiced all around, next began to recount in his broad manner of narrative how an apprentice carpenter in Steinamanger had murdered his master two years before, but – having been able to shift all suspicion from himself – had later embarked on journeyman travels and made a good name for himself until, three weeks ago, driven by the never-resting, unbearable tortures of conscience, he had suddenly returned to Steinamanger to deliver himself up to the court as the murderer of his employer, whereupon this very morning, repentant and at peace with his God, he had – to the utmost moral uplift of a deeply shaken multitude – paid for his crime at the gallows with his life.

Steidler's account was not without effect on its listeners: proof of that was the deep silence with which it was received and which followed it. It was Horváth who first interrupted it. "Indeed," he said with an emphatic and emotion-filled voice, "God is able to find anyone, and no scheme,"

---

[23] In Styria, near the Hungarian border.

[24] In western Hungary, on the road to Veszprém.

he continued, casting a serious and searching eye on the young people, "no scheme yet is so hidden and gray, but what it will come to the light of day!"

The impression made by this rather sharply edged comment varied greatly: on Sensy's cheeks it called forth a dark blush. Ferencz, on the other hand, who was silently and indifferently playing with the bread crumbs on the table in front of him, didn't appear to hear it at all, while Herr Steidler shook his head thoughtfully and replied with these words: "Yes, that's what people say! But not everything comes to the light of day! I can tell you about such a case myself, about a horrendous murder that took place about two and a half years ago where not one trace of the murderer has been discovered since!"

"Is that so?" retorted Horváth, irritated because he thought he saw the scribe pursing his lips sarcastically, "You can't expect things to come easily! And can someone find out in an hour what was hidden for two and a half years? Even if humans can't get to him, God will be able to find his man, I still believe that! But please, let's hear the story you had in mind! Have another glass of Somlyóer,[25] esteemed Herr Steidler! You can trust the wine: it's from our own vineyards and from the best vintage. So now give us your murder mystery as best you can!"

While saying these words, Horváth had filled the glasses, and Steidler, after first protesting in vain that the case was not particularly suspenseful and was perhaps only of note to those who knew the persons involved, did succumb to the insistence of his friendly host and began his tale as follows:

"You have to understand," said Steidler, "that my business takes me more than once a year to Bruck,[26] a village situated on the confluence of the Mürz and the Mur, some miles from my home. Generally I take lodgings with the *Kreuzwirth*[27] there and, having been a regular guest for years, I've come to feel as well taken care of and provided for under his roof as I do in front of my own fireplace. One day, it may not have been quite three years ago, however, arriving toward evening, I find the house lit up from top to bottom, the corridors and staircases teeming with people and such a confusion of carriages bumping into each other in front of the inn that only with great

---

[25] A local Hungarian wine.

[26] Bruck an der Mur, a Styrian town on the Mur River.

[27] German: a noun best left untranslated; literally, the "Cross Host," or the owner of a food and lodging establishment known as the "Crucifix Inn."

effort could I make it to the entrance way. '*Kreuzwirth*,' I say, dismounting, 'today your place looks like Noah's Ark come to life. It's best I turn around and see what I can find at the brew house.'[28]

"He bows deeply, though, and begs my forgiveness: the guild of marksmen is holding its awards banquet tonight, to be followed by a dance. The room where I usually stay is serving as a banquet hall right now, but he always has room for me, he says. He would have a very nice room prepared for me in the house out back, if I wouldn't be offended by that, and there would be no lack of attention and concern for my comfort. What was I to do? I was already at the inn, and before I knew it I found myself being pushed up a back staircase to the promised room, which was in fact very comfortable and so secluded that I spent the night there in complete peace and tranquility, undisturbed by the stamping of the dancers and the pulsing of the music.

"I awoke to the full light of day, threw on my clothes and opened the window to breathe in some fresh air for a quarter of an hour, as is my custom in summer and winter, by sunshine or snow flurries. The window of my room opened out to a small alley that I'd never noticed, much less walked down, for as often as I had been coming to Bruck. Opposite me lay an antiquated, weather-blackened house with a high gable, and under the Gothic archway of the front door, to which a few steps arose, I saw two persons engaged in lively discussion whose intimacy, given the great difference in their ages and their class standings, aroused my curiosity. One of the two people, you see, a young man in an elegant blond bobtail wig, in a genteel brown linen suit and patterned silk stockings, was undoubtedly one of the dignitaries in town, while the woman who seemed to have accompanied him to the front door to see him off, looked like an ordinary middle-class woman in her dress and bearing. She was old and exceedingly ugly: her small, piercing eyes and the scornful smirk of her toothless mouth gave her yellow, wrinkled face a disgustingly malicious expression which the wild gray hair poking out from under her black winged bonnet was unable to soften. Her short and skinny body was covered by a somewhat worn dress of black Angora cloth and a short jacket of the same material decorated with faded satin ribbons. Her bony hands with their arthritically-deformed fingers protruded from the arm holes of the jacket like eagles' claws. She was wearing plain blue wool stockings as well, coarse shoes with tin buckles,

---

[28] Often the pubs or bars, in addition to the liquid refreshment downstairs, had rooms to rent upstairs.

a bright-yellow neck scarf and a fiery-colored ribbon on her bonnet: in short, all that was missing was a broom to make a complete . . . witch!'"

"Oh no, Blessed Trinity God!" groaned Aunt Margit, making the sign of the cross. Sensy threw her hands in front of her eyes, though, and cried out: "God protect us all: it's as if I can see her standing in front of me now, the ugly woman!"

"Just imagine my astonishment, honored maiden," Herr Steidler continued, "when I suddenly see the young, handsome man take the gaunt, crooked, and bony fingers of the old woman in his hand and kiss them with as much reverence and devotion as if she were an Imperial princess and the embodiment of beauty! Heavens alive, I say to myself, with what chain are these two people fettered to each other? And since just then the *Kreuzwirth* was entering my room with the steaming wine soup, my breakfast, I motioned him over to me and asked him who the two might be.

"'Oh, yeah,' he said, stepping up to the window, 'that's Marzipan-Lisa,' and since I curiously repeated, 'Marzipan-Lisa?' he informed me that the old woman was the widow of a rich gingerbread maker; that after his death, however, she had given up his business to take up a less sweet but by far more lucrative one: she lent money on mortgages, squeezed exorbitant interest out of her debtors, sold their houses and properties out from under them when they couldn't pay, and then if the poor people happened to curse at her callousness, she would say that as long as she had her money, everything else was marzipan to her,[29] to which expression could also be attributed her nickname. She was now nearly seventy years old, the *Kreuzwirth* told me, owned two houses in Bruck, three houses in Graz, as well as other pieces of land, vineyards, and money by the bushel basket but had no children or family, and nobody knew who would inherit all the wealth after her death.

"'And the young man there?' I asked after that, 'Who is he, and is he courting the old woman; does he intend to marry her?'

"Thereupon the *Kreuzwirth* laughed and said that fellow didn't want her, but only her money. He was the child of poor people and had worked his way up by industry and skill, but mainly by the favor of women whom he, as a handsome and cunning young man, knew how to exploit very well. As a result he was now the recorder in the magistrate's office and very popular among the city council and the people; only Herr Lamprechter, the head

---

[29] Probably a take-off on the German colloquial expression "It's sausage to me," meaning "I just don't care." Marzipan is a candy made of almond paste.

merchant at the marketplace, had it in for him since he was after Nani, his only daughter, who had already turned down three suitors for him, among them the city syndic.[30]

"After I repeated my question, though, about what the city recorder was looking for from the evil old lady, the *Kreuzwirth* said: 'Well, he's renting a room from her, and for as long as he's been in her house, he's been pampering and looking after the old woman, taking care of her business affairs, flattering her with words, and all that in hopes she will leave him a healthy hunk of money after she dies so he can marry Nani Lamprechter.' All this was supposed to be legal, the *Kreuzwirth* went on to say. In fact, the recorder even claimed to have set up a rough draft of a last will and testament at her request in which she declared him the only heir. The old woman, on the other hand, didn't want to talk about it; she would just smile maliciously when asked about it and say not everything that glitters is gold; there may still be birds in the bush, but they weren't in the hand; and even the hen sitting on her eggs doesn't try to count all her chickens before they're hatched ... plus more such sayings, so that nobody really knew which turns the plot would finally take! While this and other discussions were going on, the recorder had gone his way in the alley below, the old dragon had slipped back into her cave, and as for me . . . ."

Here the storyteller paused, for one of his listeners, in trying to get up quietly and move his chair back unnoticed, had caused more noise than would have been the case if he'd taken less precautions. It was the scribe Ferencz, who appeared quite confused at having drawn everyone's attention so exclusively to himself by this disturbance. Only at Horváth's repeated demand to know what was going on did he stammer his apologies: the bright candlelight at the spot he'd been sitting was hurting his sensitive eyes, and so he was thinking of moving back to the darker areas of the room. "Maybe you should just go to bed. Sick people don't belong here with the healthy ones!" was Horváth's harsh, rough answer. Ferencz, after thinking it over for a short while, replied with an uncertain voice that he didn't want to miss any of Herr Steidler's riveting tale and therefore, if it were permitted, perhaps

---

[30] The legal representative for the city in business transactions, an important local government official.

he could sit on the bench behind the stove.[31] "That's fine, just crawl behind the stove!" growled Mr. Horváth; but becoming aware right after of Sensy's turning pale and then blushing, of her concerned looks, of the poorly concealed uneasiness with which she followed the movements of the scribe, her father cried out, beating the table with his heavy fist so hard the bottles and glasses rattled: "Crucifix and damnation! Get moving, girl! Herr Steidler's glass is empty! Fill it up and offer him the cake plate again! Damn it, pay attention!" While Sensy recoiled and did as her father had bidden her, shaking, unaccustomed to such harsh scolding, the latter, hiding his aggravation behind a demeanor of joking, turned back to his guest and asked him to pick up the thread of narration again after this vexing interruption.

"Dear and honored friend," began Herr Steidler, "I told you right up front that there wasn't very much of note to the case I was going to recount to you. You didn't want to believe me, so now don't be surprised if instead of moving from the beginning of the story to a continuation of it which you expect and hope for, I leap straight to its conclusion! For you see, after I had become acquainted with Marzipan-Lisa and her renter in the way I've just described, I went about my business and returned to my home without hearing any more about those two or even thinking about them in the slightest. After another six weeks or so, I needed to make a business trip to Bruck again, and I used this opportunity to visit a hammer foundry scarcely a half hour away from Bruck. Once I'd arrived there, I wasn't allowed to leave again: I had to spend the night at my friend's place and it wasn't until fairly late the next morning that I continued on my journey.

"I knew that this was the day when the weekly market was held in Bruck, and I thought of taking advantage of this circumstance to make some necessary purchases. So I was more than a little astonished when I found all sorts of goods on display at the marketplace but neither sellers nor even buyers there, just a few children and old women to keep an eye on things. Arriving at the *Kreuzwirth's* Inn, I saw neither a doorman nor a waitress rush out to greet me, nor did the *Kreuzwirth* wave his green satin cap at me; on the other hand, I did notice a group of people by the corner of the house, increasing in numbers as more people arrived. This aroused my curiosity: I walked over to the crowd and had scarcely taken a few steps when I recognized

---

[31] A large tiled stove, designed to radiate heat in all directions in the days before forced-air heating. It would have been large enough that Ferencz could not be seen behind it.

the *Kreuzwirth*. He motioned to me and yelled: 'Over here, come on over here, Herr Steidler!'

"'*Kreuzwirth*,' I said when I'd finally gotten over to him, 'So many spectators standing around with their mouths wide open – has everyone gone crazy? Is there a fire or some other disaster?'

"Agitated and confused, though, paying no heed to my words, he snorted at me: 'Do you want to see her? I'll take you there if you want to see her!'

"'By the hammer and anvil of Zeus,' I cried, 'who or what is there to see?'

"'What there is to see?' was the response. 'It's Marzipan-Lisa, the one you asked about last time you were here. Just come with me! The syndic has just gone in, and the gentlemen from the city council!' And without giving me any further information, he just took me by the arm, yelled into the surging throng with a brusque voice: 'Make room! Coming through!' and pulled me into the alley, making room for me with his broad shoulders and clenched fists, the same alley I referred to earlier, which was now so crammed full with people of every age and description that there wouldn't have been room for even an apple to fall to earth.

"Finally we had reached the house, stumbled our way up the front steps, and forced our way down the dark corridor; past the steep, gloomy staircase; through several rooms on the ground floor into a small room with high, vaulted ceilings that was, as it turned out later, the bedroom of the old lady. The first thing to catch my eye there, tossed over a hat rack, was the bonnet with the fiery-colored ribbon; over the back of a chair hung the Angora cloth dress and its matching jacket. The owner of these clothes, however, lay on the floor not far from her bed, scantily covered; the thin, gray hair hung loosely around her wrinkled, bluish-black face and her parchment-like neck. Around her neck, pressed sharply into its puffy skin, was slung the bright yellow scarf with which the unfortunate woman had been strangled after a short, useless struggle: this was evidenced by her staring, bloodshot eyes, violently bulging from their sockets; her half-open mouth that seemed to be contorted into hideous, mocking laughter; and the arthritic hands that had obviously gone rigid in a vain attempt to loosen the strangling knot of the yellow scarf! It was a horrible sight!

"When I was finally able to tear my eyes away from the horrendous spectacle I had been staring at for so long, full of horror and indignation, I became aware of several eminent citizens of the city in one corner of the room, men I was acquainted with, assembled around a distinguished gentleman who was sitting at the opened desk of the murdered woman going through her papers and whom the *Kreuzwirth* identified for me as the city's syndic and one of those vying for the hand of Nani Lamprechter. The gentlemen, hardly paying any further heed to the corpse, were engaged in a quiet but exceedingly lively discussion from which, gradually getting louder, could be deduced from individual words that it had to do with the murdered lady's inheritance.

"This context induced me to ask what had become of the recorder – the renter and presumed heir of the dead woman and fortuitous rival of the syndic – and the *Kreuzwirth* was just informing me that the very same had been away for six days, commissioned with auctioning off some property in Laming[32] that had been forfeited due to bankruptcy, when an ever-increasing confusion of voices arose in the corridor. They appeared to be trying to turn someone away with angry warnings who was furiously pushing his way forward. At the same time, the boisterous shouting, 'I have to go in! Make room! I have to see her!' came closer and closer until at last the throng suddenly parted and a young man rushed into the room, great drops of sweat on his forehead. I recognized him right away as the recorder we had just been discussing. At the sight of the murdered woman, he fell back, trembling, wringing his hands and crying out over and over: 'Oh, woe! Oh, horror! Oh, miserable, wretched day!'

"Meanwhile the syndic, who had gotten up when the young man entered and had been appraising him from afar with scowling, almost hostile looks, had stepped up towards him and began to speak in slow and solemn tones, behind which, however, I thought I could hear his contempt and gloating coming through: 'Yes! Let him mourn the horrible end of his maternalistic lady-friend! Let him mourn and weep over her, as we mourn and weep over her, as soon all of Bruck will mourn and weep over this noble heart, this much misunderstood soul, this mother of the poor, this refuge for those in distress! Listen and take it to heart, my most beloved fellow citizens, for this often reviled and slandered woman, this lady persecuted with scorn and insults and dishonored with a derisive nickname, has heaped the fiery coals of hell upon your head by bequeathing exclusively to this town – by a totally admissible and legal will – her entire magnificent fortune, undiminished, for the erection of a municipal hospital, shelter and orphanage.'

---

[32] Valley named for a stream that flows into the Mürz River less than two miles from Bruck and that extends west-northwest from town.

"Whispers and murmurs of amazement moved like electricity through the crowd while the young man gaped silently and mindlessly at the speaker; but when here and there in the crowd a 'God bless her!' or a 'May she rest in peace!' was voiced, when the people – who had been apathetic at first, and more curious than deeply moved – suddenly threw themselves to their knees as one, overwhelmed with a feeling of gratitude, and began praying for their murdered benefactress, there erupted in his eye the flames of a most rancorous hatred that was transformed into an expression of insane rage as his gaze turned away and fell upon the corpse again. He ground his teeth, ripped at his hair with his hands, then let out a shriek that sounded half like a howl of pain, half like the laughter of desperation, staggered, rolled his eyes around in their sockets, and, in the next instant, fell down next to the corpse like a slab of timber!"

Herr Steidler, who had gotten unusually agitated in his attempts to make his listeners see what he had seen firsthand so long before, paused here to collect his wits and to organize his thoughts for continuing his tale, when suddenly from the stove – behind which hard breathing had been audible for some time – now came a hollow, fearful groaning like the last gasps of somebody choking to death. "Lord Jesus," whined Aunt Margit, "there's a ghost!" and buried her face in her apron; Horváth leaped up from his seat; but Sensy rushed toward the stove while shrieking fearfully: "In the name of God, what's happened?"

Even before she had reached the huge, green tile edifice, though, Ferencz came staggering out from behind it like someone whose knees had buckled and were failing him, frantically grasping onto the ledge and pulling himself forward. He was as white as a sheet; his chest was heaving and gasping for air; feverish shivers trembled through his body and made his teeth audibly chatter. He moaned that he was feeling deathly ill and couldn't breathe, but this would probably pass if he could just get to bed!

"Water, water!" yelled Sensy, "He's dying! Help!" and with that she rushed to him and supported his tottering weight. But no sooner had she touched him than she felt the heavy hand of her father on her shoulder, turning her around like a feather in the wind and twisting her away until she fell in a heap in one corner of the room.

"Is that proper?" yelled Horváth, whose anger has just been waiting for a spark to ignite it like a powder keg. "Is it the custom around here for virtuous young girls to throw their arms around any young man they want? God's tarnation! I'll teach you what's proper! . . . ." and with that he raised his hand. But he caught himself and motioned for Aunt Margit to come forward: "Help the lad to his room," he said, "and away with him! I'm tired of the whining and want my peace and quiet!" Margit obeyed and left with the semiconscious Ferencz, for whose revivification, of course, the scene just ended was not particularly well suited.

Scarcely had the door fallen shut behind the two when Horváth, who had been watching them leave with stern looks of displeasure, turned again to Sensy – who was sitting there pale and unmoving, and from whose eyelids great tears were dripping onto her hands as they were folded in her lap. "Go to your room," he said in a softer tone, "the story of our guest has gotten you worked up, and once the faucet starts to flow with you women, there's no more stopping it. Go now, and be smarter next time! And for all that, good night!"

Sensy repeated her father's last words in a flat tone and barely perceptibly, bowed quietly before the guest, and slowly left the room. Horváth's eyes followed her with the expression of painful regret and bitter hurt. The passionate concern that Sensy had shown for the scribe, on such an insignificant occasion as his feeling unwell, left no further doubt about the state of her heart, and in Horváth's own chest – which found itself deceived in its blind trust, injured in its pride, and forced by bitter necessity to hurt the heart it loved most – the most contradictory feelings waged a hard and painful battle against each other.

Finally remembering his guest, he gathered his wits and took his seat next to him again; but whether he thought it useless to try to deceive him about the significance of what had transpired or whether he felt incapable at that moment of concocting some other sort of acceptable explanation for it, he didn't mention what had occurred with a single syllable, contenting himself by asking his tablemate to finish the tale he had begun.

"Finish my tale?" asked Herr Steidler, who had been a silent but not totally dispassionate witness of the evening's events and who gladly grasped at the chance to take his host's mind off things. "Beloved friend, it's at an end, for what more there is to tell is scarcely worth talking about and tends toward unsubstantiated rumors and suppositions. The only thing that's certain is that Marzipan-Lisa was buried with mind-boggling splendor, that her last will and testament was completely valid, and that not a single penny of it went to her inheritance-coveting renter, the recorder, which also meant that any chance of his getting together with Nani Lamprechter turned to dust.

"The young man, who saw all his plots foiled and had insult added to his injury, as is often the case, ran around town disturbed and half crazy from that day on, until three weeks later he suddenly disappeared. His hat and his overcoat, found on the banks of the Mur River, support the idea that the poor devil drowned himself in despair. As for the murderer of Marzipan-Lisa, meticulous investigations haven't turned up a single clue. A former debtor of the murdered woman, someone whose house and property she had repossessed and who was seen in the vicinity of Bruck at the time of the murder, seemed suspicious and was arrested at the instigation of the recorder, but he had to be released since he was able to provide a solid alibi. Later on, and it was a short time after the recorder disappeared, the rumor was going around that he himself had been the one who, confidently hoping to inherit the old woman's fortune, had helped her along to her demise to get at her money and properties all the sooner and to marry his beloved. The story is going around that two employees at the brewery reported to the syndic that on the night of the murder, as they were returning home from a visit, traveling east, they had met the recorder – who at the time, as we've said, was stationed in Laming – hurriedly leaving town, and they had clearly recognized him even though he had jumped from the road into the bushes as they approached. Now even if the innkeeper in Laming claimed hard and fast that the recorder had gone to bed the night before as usual and had been awakened by him early the next morning, that doesn't preclude the possibility that the despicable murderer could have left the building by the still of night, done his loathsome deed and then returned again unnoticed. This hypothesis is also supported by the fact that the murderer must have known the house of Marzipan-Lisa very well, since there were no signs of forcible entry and the doors and windows had been left unscathed.

"Several people were also able to corroborate this bit of evidence with yet another by reporting that the syndic, around this same time, while putting Marzipan-Lisa's effects in order, found amongst her laundry a packet labeled "Legacy For My Renter." This packet had contained a dish cloth, a will in draft form prepared by the recorder for Marzipan-Lisa and a written communication from the latter in which she thanked the recorder for having prepared that draft for her, which she had finally used for her own intentions and toward her own ends. It had never occurred to her to name him as heir, she said; she had just held open that possibility so she could get a usable model for a will without too much cost to her. In fact, she would have remembered him in her will with a healthy chunk of capital as reward for his good services, if only her cat hadn't nibbled on the cake with which he had recently honored her – and died from it. She had her own ideas about that and thought accordingly that it would be plenty if she were to leave him the enclosed dish cloth with which . . . to wipe his filthy mouth.

"After reading these papers, the syndic, as the gossip mill had it, found himself in a great dilemma since these papers, in conjunction with the testimony of the brewery employees, did cast grave suspicions on the recorder. At length he decided to kill two birds with one stone, though: to avoid the unfavorable attention that pursuing a capital murder charge against a member of the magistrature would have brought with it, on the one hand, but, on the other, to make his winning over Nani Lamprechter all the more certain by appearing to display chivalrous generosity toward his rival. Thus it was that he proceeded to visit Nani, to lay the case out before her, and to persuade her that the man of her dreams, unless he could prove his innocence, would do very well to make himself scarce right away; at the same time the syndic had let her know in no uncertain terms the manner in which he hoped to see his gallant consideration towards her rewarded. In this way, people speculated, the recorder had gotten wind of the accusations, bolted from town, and the syndic had won the hand of his beloved. The last point, at any rate, was correct: Nani truly did marry the syndic. The rest of it is no doubt just idle talk with which evil-speaking mouths, uncharitably enough, continue to persecute the poor recorder even in death. The moral of the whole story is, you see, that the murderer of Marzipan-Lisa has still not been discovered and so God will have to find him, as you say, since we humans haven't been able to get at him."

This comment, thrown in by Herr Steidler on purpose to pull Horváth – lost in thought – back into the conversation, didn't get a response. Horváth didn't hear it: with his head cupped in his hand, he had fixed his gaze in front of him and let the words of his guest fly right past him unheeded. Only one thing concerned him: that Antal had been right, that he had let his child go to ruin because of his own foolish blindness; that he now had to make an end to it, and that perhaps it could already be too late.

The deep silence that had ensued after Steidler had completed his account finally tore Horváth away from his brooding; he snapped out of it with a start, and without any further preliminaries than complaining about the increasing sickliness of his scribe, he asked Herr Steidler if he could recommend a good bookkeeper for him. This question was answered by his loquacious guest, very precise when it came to business matters, in the form of another question about the qualifications he was looking for and the benefits he was prepared to grant. After clarification on these points, the guest promised that before three weeks had come and gone, he would send an elderly but still efficient man, one that would fill his needs. At that Herr Steidler, since he had to leave early the next morning, gave thanks for the friendly reception, rose from the table, and with the best wishes of his host for a quiet and restful night was accompanied to his room.

Sunrise came the next morning, and the first early light of dawn breaking into the room of the scribe Ferencz found him awake and half dressed, sitting on his jumbled bed as if he had gotten no rest or slumber all night. The mask for his eyes and the black silk cloth he had slung around his face the day before lay on the floor in the middle of the room where they had been thrown. The floor was littered with shredded papers; the cabinet and storage chest had been thrown wide open; pieces of clothing, laundry and other belongings lay partially strewn over tables and chairs here and there, partially heaped up next to the knapsack which sat half packed in one corner of the room. The scribe looked over at it uneasily, gloomily, as if considering whether he really ought to complete the task he had started. If the area surrounding the young man had – by these and other evidences – taken on a peculiar aura of discord and confusion, then the latter proved to be even more clearly stamped on all his features. His inwardly sagging posture – his head sunken deeply down to his chest, the sallow paleness of his cheeks – betrayed the utter exhaustion, while the heavy sighs that wrested loose from his constricted chest from time to time and the somber eyes flashing out from under fitfully twitching brows – eyes that first stared for minutes on end at the dying lantern flame and then jumped from object to object with skulking haste – testified to an inner turmoil, to a god-forsakenness of soul that only despair or guilt can call forth.

Suddenly he straightened up and listened. "Steps . . . weren't those steps? No, it was nothing!" He dried the sweat from his forehead, wiped the wild hair back that was covering it, and trudged uneasily back and forth in the room. "Why did I even listen to the urgings of old Margit," he mumbled to himself, "and why did I later insist on not leaving? Of course, I had to hear how much the old gossip knew, and who could guess that the stupid fever would catch up to me, and that like a school boy . . . ." He didn't complete the sentence, for now rapid footsteps were heard coming closer and closer outside, followed soon after by a rough knocking on the locked door. Ferencz stood still for a moment as if frozen, then, pulling himself together, he leapt to one corner of the room, tore his coat from the wall with shaking hands, spread it out over the open knapsack, and staggered back to the door to shove back the latch. The door opened, and Horváth stood at the threshold opposite Ferencz, who had turned as white as a sheet and was trying in vain to conceal his deathly turmoil behind a series of bows and honorific morning greetings.

As for Horváth, he hadn't spent the night any better than his scribe. He had gone to bed hurt in his pride, embittered by the lack of trust his daughter had shown him, and full of anger towards the disloyal servant who had repaid his kindnesses with ingratitude, but in the quiet of the night – which made him more and more clearly aware of his own contributory guilt to the confusion of the young people – gradually the flames of his anger subsided. Still, he made the firm resolve, come what may, to bring a relationship to an end that seemed to him as disgraceful as it was unnatural and totally impossible. This he would do immediately the next morning, as soon as Herr Steidler had left, and with all decisiveness. At the same time, he had such a thoroughly gentle and good-natured character, and it went so much against his inner nature to harm anybody purposely in any way – except in the first flashes of anger – that after Steidler's leaving it was scarcely with a heart any less heavy that he made his way to the scribe's room and the scribe saw him appear there.

"Have you recovered?" he asked, slowly stepping into the room and closing the door behind him. "Well, I'm happy to see that, because I have something to discuss with you, and it's good that you've gotten your wits together!" With these words he sat down on the chair Ferencz had pushed towards him, and he looked around the room as if embarrassed. "Yes, I do have something to discuss with you," he repeated in a brusque and even severe tone of voice, but something in his tone suggested he was forcing himself to appear more firm and resolved than he actually was. "I wanted to tell you that I'm riding over to Vásárhely[33] today to inspect the vineyards, and tomorrow," he continued after some hesitation, "tomorrow I'll be traveling on to Buda!" Here he paused again, but then, taking courage and blurting out what was unavoidable, he said, as he stood up and turned toward the table and away from the scribe: "And then I wanted to tell you that I have

---

[33] A generic name used for a number of townships throughout Hungary.

hired someone else for keeping my books, and that you have to leave my house today!"

Ferencz winced at these words like someone who's had lightning strike the ground right in front of him.

"Here's a letter of recommendation for you," Horváth continued, pulling a sheet of paper from his pocket and handing it to him with his back still turned, "plus here's the salary I owe you and some travel and food money besides!" With that, he tossed a roll of coins down on the table which burst open as it landed, scattering gold all over.

He remained silent as if waiting for a response, but when there was none he turned around, and one look at the scribe, standing there as if destroyed, was sufficient to disarm him. He walked up to Ferencz and said, patting him on the shoulder: "You are a good, skillful, and hard-working person. I don't like losing you and I've also recommended you highly in the letter as being faithful and hard-working; but you can see yourself that you can't stay. Tomorrow I'll be traveling to Buda, and so you have to be gone today, this very hour. Do you hear me?"

Ferencz mumbled a few unintelligible words while Horváth walked to the door, put his hand on the handle, but turned around one more time and said: "Just don't think for a minute that you can stick around in the area here and loiter around my house. I won't put up with it, and I have ways of making sure you're gone! You have to leave, right away and forever, absolutely! And so God be with you!" With these words he opened the door and left the room quickly, glad to have taken quick and decisive care of the awkward business.

For as long as the sound of Horváth's steps could be heard in the hallway and on the stairs, Ferencz retained the shattered demeanor that had served him so well in his employer's presence, but then he quickly straightened up from his bent position. His eyes, even as they were lifting up from their downcast mien, began sparkling with self-confidence. The pale and colorless face began glowing with joy, and an ugly sneer of malicious scorn began twitching on the still terror-blanched lips. "Not a thing, they don't know a single thing!" he cried, pacing back and forth in the room with quick, powerful steps, "It was just stupid self-torture that made me so crazy last night! But now everything is fine, even if he gave me my walking papers! A decision had to be made at some point, anyway, and this time I'm sure of it: Sensy is in my power!" The hoofbeats of the horse carrying Horváth to Vásárhely roused him from these and other thoughts; the time of Horváth's absence had to be used, and, now or never, he had to act quickly and decisively. Hastily dressing, he considered the paths he had to take, weighed the obstacles that could work against him, the means at his disposal to remove them, and, just as he had finally solidified his plan, he saw Sensy's slender profile moving through the courtyard towards the garden, where he immediately followed.

The features of the young man – still glowing with the jubilation of victory and confident gloating as he climbed the steps to the garden gate – had taken on the expression of deep pain and of laboriously recovered composure by the time he approached the young lady rushing towards him with the most touching devotion and asking him with tender concern about the state of his painful eyes that had caused her so much worry the day before. His answer was short, serious, measured: with a constricted voice – from the sound of which the ears of love could detect suppressed tears – he reported to her the cruel judgment that her father had declared and finished with tender words of farewell and passionate wishes for his beloved's future happiness, even if his own was destroyed forever and an early death would be the only goal he could look forward to from now on!

The effect that these words had to have on Sensy's enterprising and fiery soul had been carefully calculated. Overcome for a moment by horror and pain, she soon pulled herself together, took him in her arms and asked him if he doubted whether she couldn't promise him faithfulness, absolute faithfulness; if he thought she could break her word. Agitated and made even more emotional by the painful smile with which Ferencz replied to this question, she showered him with caresses and reproaches and swore to him she would throw herself down in front of her father that very day and would openly confess to all the world that she loved him, that she belonged to him, only him, and that no threats, force, even separation for years on end, would ever be able to alienate her heart from his!

Ferencz countered this overflowing of passion with the gloomy silence of hopeless pain, the hollow stillness of despair. Finally he asked what good their pleas would do? Did she think proud Horváth would decide on the spur of the moment to throw his daughter – the one bound to inherit his rich fortune – into the arms of a scribe picked up by the side of the road? Did she want to mourn her way through the best days of her life, the spring of her youth, in order to finally take his hand over the grave of her father, only after years of separation? No, they had to avoid all forms of self-deception here; there was only one way to fulfill the justified demands of their hearts in the face of arbitrary cruelness and to force her father into the happiness of his child, and this one way... he hesitated to say it; finally he did say it: this one way was... to flee her father's house!

Already robbed of her mother in the cradle, Sensy had at an early age – during the frequent and lengthy travels of her father and with the few attentions that old Margit was able to give to the fiery, vivacious sensibilities of the young girl – developed a strongness of will and a rare independence of spirit. Force and arbitrariness were odious to her; but as justified as she felt before heaven to seek and find happiness in her own right, she was just as fervently convinced that this must not occur at the expense of others, least of all at that of her father – rash and irascible at times, but who doted on her so lovingly.

It was a hard struggle that Ferencz had to wage until the duty of the daughter gave in to the passion of the woman, but finally he did win it. The flight was decided upon, and the best suited time to undertake it was set as the first night following Horváth's departure for Buda, because then they could hope to remain unpursued for at least the first few days. More difficult was answering the further question of where Ferencz should stay until that point. To keep himself hidden in the vicinity, given the suspicions already aroused in Horváth, seemed dangerous. The choice of a more distant hiding place, however, would place the success of the elopement plan in jeopardy, on the one hand, by the difficulty of communicating any changes or hindrances back and forth; on the other hand, Sensy had strongly resisted such a forceful break with her past and seemed so overwhelmed by the injustice of her decision and so troubled in her conscience that Ferencz recognized that only the continuing influence of his own presence and Sensy's acceptance of responsibility for his personal safety could serve as a sufficient counterweight to keep the doubting woman – who was nervously vacillating back and forth – bound to the barely committed plan.

In such a situation, gambles had to be taken to guarantee success, and so Ferencz declared that he couldn't part from Sensy, that he would have to remain there and keep himself hidden inside the house if their plan was to succeed. Sensy allowed herself to be persuaded that this was the correct idea, and a secure hiding spot was found after some short deliberations. A little room that Horváth had ordered to be built on the lowest level of his extensive cellars – in order to be able, with total ease, to oversee the delivery of his vineyards' production during the fall harvest and then to discuss the prices of different varieties with the wine consumers in a comfortable setting afterwards, tasting samples directly from the barrels – seemed all the more suited for this purpose since it was never used at this time of year and would only be set up for its designated annual usage after Horváth's return from the Buda trade fair. After the lovers had agreed on the choice of a secret lair and, in a few quick words, the manner in which Ferencz was to move into it, they went their separate ways to put their plan in motion before Horváth returned home.

Ferencz hurried back to his room, promptly packed up all his possessions, closed his knapsack, and went to the room of Frau Margit around noon to tell her what had happened and to take his leave from her. The goodly old woman completely lost her composure on hearing the news about the departure of her favorite, but he asked her, with the bearing of deepest pain, to say his last good-byes to the others in the house, since he couldn't bring himself to do so himself. Then he asked her for her blessing, and after he had received it and had asked her to keep his knapsack in safekeeping until he would ask for it to be sent, he tore himself from the arms of the sobbing old woman – who was half paralyzed with terror and worry – to make his way, as he put it, out in the wide, wide world. Before Frau Margit could think twice and accompany him, he had hurried down the stairs, convincing himself that all the house servants were assembled as usual at this hour for lunch by slipping by the kitchen and running out through the front door.

He took the road towards town; once past the corner of the house, he turned left again, ran past the garden wall until he reached the back door, which had been propped open. Stealing through it back into the house and sneaking past the back wall of the stables, he reached the timberyard. There Sensy was waiting for him at the cellar door with a basket filled with foodstuffs; she escorted him down the stairs into the small cellar room – which had been built of thickly-planked walls lined with brick at one corner of the cellar's bottommost level and in which the solicitude of love had already brought down bedding, candles, and whatever else could serve as conveniences for the voluntary captive. Here she left him with the promise she would bring news that night, when everything was quiet, about how things stood in the house. Ferencz, though, now certain of the imminent success of his plan of attack and full of the secure hope that he would someday take command of the house in whose loneliest corner he now had to conceal himself, refreshed himself with the food to be found in the basket and then stretched out on the bed prepared for him to make up for his lost night's sleep.

Horváth didn't return from Vásárhely until late afternoon; he didn't seem to notice Sensy's despondency and her tear-streaked eyes. He brushed off old Margit curtly and gruffly after she tried, in clumsy babblings, to bring up the topic of her favorite's departure, and then he went into town – claiming he had business to take care of – probably to start investigations into the whereabouts of Ferencz in case the latter was lurking about somewhere nearby. The results of his wanderings seemed to have satisfied him, since he proved to be gentler and more talkative once he had returned home. He didn't mention the scribe with a single breath, but he did announce at supper that the current year's crop of grapes was promising to be so prolific that he found himself a bit short on containers to hold the potential vintage and would be forced to use even some of the older, rather worn barrels. Since he had made an appointment for the cooper master and his apprentices to come the next day to repair the barrels as necessary, he wouldn't be able to embark on his journey to Buda until the day after next.

This bit of news was indeed a bitter side dish to the morsels that Sensy, shaking like a leaf, smuggled down to him in the cellar room in the middle of the night, for he saw not only his time in captivity extended because of it, but also his convenience and safety substantially impaired. It's true that the barrels to be reconstructed were located in the upper part of the cellar, but how easily might it occur to Horváth or one of the coopers to climb down to the lower level! Ferencz would be forced not only to confine himself strictly to the narrow space of the one room, while previously the entire lower cellar had been available to him, but also – at least during the time the coopers were at work – he would have to go without any candles or lanterns so that no glimmer of light escaping through a crack in the door might betray his presence. In fact, it even appeared necessary to lock the door to the room itself so that no unwanted person would open it on purpose or by chance. This could only be done from the outside, since – given the configuration of the room – no one had ever considered attaching a lock or bolt on the inside. No matter how bothersome and unpleasant all this may have been, it had to be patiently endured by Ferencz as something unavoidable, lest Sensy's disquietude and apprehension, which seemed to be increasing every second, reach the breaking point of total perplexity. In order to combat this danger, he did all he could to minimize the gravity of her news, to blunt her alarm with caresses, and – when she finally did turn to leave, half comforted – he jokingly asked her to lock her little bird up tight in his cage but to take good care of the keys and not to lose them, lest he be forced from voluntary captivity into a highly involuntary period of fasting.

Early next morning the cooper and his apprentices did, in fact, arrive at the topmost subterranean tier and soon sent mallet blows echoing through the cellar as they drove new hoops and bands onto the defective barrels. Horváth walked back and forth, oversaw the progress of the work, but couldn't help going out into the neighborhood from time to time to ask around and see if Ferencz had truly left once and for all. Neither he nor any of the coopers went anywhere near the lower cellar room all day, as they had plenty to do and were just concentrating on getting their jobs done. Ferencz had to learn from Sensy, on the other hand, when she carried food and drink down to him again around midnight, that whether on account of the coopers or because the sudden disappearance of the scribe without a trace left her father more uneasy than relieved, he had delayed his departure by one more day. Ferencz took the news of this additional delay with far less serenity and good temper than that with which he had submitted himself the day before to a forced entrapment in his cage.

While Sensy had gotten herself so upset and feverishly tense by the changing emotions of the previous day that precisely this crescendo of her inner life now gave her, despite all the inner exhaustion, the semblance of power and even peace of mind, exactly the opposite was happening to Ferencz: his strength of spirit was paralyzed and irretrievably broken as a consequence of the dark and lonely detention. Even the prospect of reaching his goal in the near future after long years of relentless striving, of possessing the long-desired means for luxuriating in a fullness of riches, seemed to have lost its magic for him and to have become incapable of suppressing the dark and ghostly figures that must have risen up before him by night in the soundproof stillness of that dark cellar room. Now he was the one – confused, fearful, and cowering at every sound – who had to be soothed and comforted by Sensy: he would have courageously withstood physical dangers, but he was unable to face the terrors of loneliness. As Sensy took her leave and again had to lock the door of the little room behind her, he held her back and behaved every bit as if he were being separated forever from light, air and life.

Finally, around noon on the third day, Horváth completed the preparations to embark on his long-planned trip. The horses had been harnessed to the coach, and Horváth, accompanied by Aunt Margit and his daughter, stepped from the house – in front of which all the house servants had assembled to see their master off. Horváth gave his final orders: he told the menservants to guard the house from any gypsies, beggars and other rabble and to keep the gates and doors tightly shut; he asked the maidservants to keep the home fires carefully burning, and after he had urged Margit to supervise the house staff and to oversee the jobs to be finished during his absence, particularly those of the coopers, he turned to his daughter. She threw herself into his arms, sobbing convulsively, torn to the depths of her soul by guilt and remorse, tortured by the awareness of deceiving her old, loving father so cruelly and of planning to leave him childless for such a long time, perhaps forever. So tenuous was her emotional state that it would only have taken a few sensitive and carefully placed words to lure the secret from her heavy-laden heart, from the daughter gone astray, and to thwart the plans of Ferencz forever.

An unlucky star was shining over Horváth, though, so that now he was about to enable by untimely sternness the thing he most wanted to avoid, even as he had earlier done so by foolish recklessness. He pulled the shaking girl aside and told her in a rough, harsh tone of voice that he would forgive and forget what had happened but wouldn't put up with any more vain excuses; he had given her hand to Herr Farkas, the rich grocery dealer in Pécs, and she was to be married before All Saints' Day.[34] With these words, the gravestone of defiance once again rolled across the depths of a soul that had been opening up in childlike trust: she wept but kept her silence.

As Horváth, accompanied by the best wishes of the house staff, rolled away, Sensy stumbled back into her room, tight-lipped and pale, to throw together in a bundle the few things she planned to take with her when she fled. Only with great difficulty did she succeed in carrying out this task, for the backlash of the overwhelming agitation and draining tumultuousness with which she had spent the last few days took their toll on her more and more perceptibly, marked by a sluggish unwinding of her emotions, by total exhaustion of her physical energies. Leaden heaviness came over her extremities: first shivering with cold and then burning up with fever, she was no longer able to hold up the weight of her head – hot and numb with pain as if clamped in an iron vice – and as exhausted and suffering as she was, she lay down on her bed to gather her strength with a refreshing nap.

There she lay, unconscious and still, her twitching hands folded across her breast and her life passing before her half-closed eyes like shadows

---

[34] November 1st.

in a long and colorfully convoluted parade of images. First the games of childhood smiled at her. Next she sat, a hard-working pupil, at Ferencz' side; she also saw Antal's face leering through the window at her just as before when Ferencz had hugged her for the first time and she had glowed with love. She heard Herr Steidler's voice telling about Marzipan-Lisa; she heard the groans of Ferencz, the threats and reprimands of her father; and then . . . then things went gloomy and dark before her eyes, as black as the night in which she was to turn her back on her father's house and as gloomy as the future towards which she was headed.

It must have been a number of hours that she lay there in half-slumber before the bells ringing from town announced midnight and domineeringly called her back to life, to reality. With the decisiveness of will that overcomes all exhaustion, she was able to get up from her bed, reach for her bundle, and – equipped with the shuttered lantern that had already accompanied her on her earlier nocturnal wanderings – she left her room. At the threshold she stood still and looked back into the peaceful, beloved room – in which, happily and free of cares, untouched by all the storms of life, she had blossomed from a child to a young woman – as if only now, when she had to leave it, did she realize what she was leaving behind! But Ferencz was waiting for her; she mustn't waste time!

She walked quietly down the hallway, illuminated only by the pale glow of a moon half covered by thick clouds. Coming to the door that led to her father's room, her steps faltered. It seemed to her as if it were opening, as if his tall, manly frame were stepping out from behind it to ask her what she was after, where she was going? But it was just the top of the linden tree out in the garden throwing its quivering shadows on the door, and she had to hurry: Ferencz was waiting.

She had rushed down the front stairs, and once she had come out into the courtyard the fresh autumn breezes fanned against her, refreshing and strengthening her. Carefully concealing the light from the lantern, she slipped towards the distant timberyard, pressing herself against the walls as she went. Finally having reached the cellar, her heart pounding, she opened the outside door with the keys she had brought along. When she was about to descend the first set of stairs, it seemed to her as if a glimmer of light were coming back at her from below, from where the steps turned down to the lower cellar level. Who could that be? It couldn't be coming from Ferencz, locked in his cellar room. Had some stranger locked himself in the cellar? She had to be careful now! Her knees were shaking, but courage and determination didn't leave her for an instant. She extinguished the light of the lantern so its flicker wouldn't betray her and pressed tight behind a beam to see what might happen. But nothing happened: everything stayed as still and hushed as before. After a while, she stuck her head out from behind the beam, listening: the light had disappeared, and only black darkness stared back at her. Had the appearance of light just been her own imagination, or was its source to be found down on the lower level? All at once, a type of anxiety came over her that she had never felt before: her pulse was racing, her teeth were chattering, but Ferencz was expecting her, and perhaps he was in danger.

This consideration outweighed all her worries, and she had quickly gone down about half the steps when suddenly – at the landing where the stairs turned down toward the lower level – a feeble gleam of light appeared, seeming to swirl around a female figure dressed in dark robes in the middle of the stairs who was waving her widespread arms at Sensy, threatening her and warning her to stay back. Rapid flight was the first reaction of the shaking, half-unconscious girl to this sight, and she rushed back up the stairs more quickly than she had come down. She stopped at the half-opened cellar door; she was ashamed of having fled, and, debating whether she should turn around again, she did turn back around – out of breath, her hand pressed against her irrhythmically shuddering heart – and no sooner had she realized, to her bewilderment and amazement, that the gleam of light was gone once more than it again started glistening up out of the floor right in front of her, and in its gray shimmer a woman rose up – staring back at her with angrily-burning, piercing eyes, her withered and wrinkled features contorted in a smirk – and while Sensy's eyes, as if hypnotized, were riveted on the fiery-colored ribbon of her winged bonnet and her bright yellow scarf, scrawny hands with deformed, clawlike fingers reached out of the black jacket and reached for her throat.

A sudden shock coursed through Sensy's soul like lightning! "Marzipan-Lisa!" she shrieked resoundingly, leaped from the cellar, slammed the door shut behind her, staggered heavily a few more steps into the courtyard and then, giving a hollow moan, collapsed in a stupor.

Two of the menservants – who had been at a bar until the wee hours and were trying to sneak back to their rooms by a circuitous route long after midnight – found her stretched out on the ground, as stiff as if she were lifeless, recognized her with unspeakable astonishment, and carried her into the main house. Frau Margit, soon awakened by the noise and by the hysterical weeping of the maidservants, rushed to her side and tried the entire barrage of her medications on the unconscious young woman, all without being able to awaken her from her deathlike catatonic state.

Even the arts of the doctor, who had been sent for in the meanwhile, proved unsuccessful for a long time, and only towards morning did the most meticulous efforts succeed in calling her forth from unconsciousness into half-consciousness, only to see her slide into hallucinations induced by a raging fever. The garbled nonsense syllables and first horrendous outbreak of maniacal fits were then soon followed by total exhaustion and vague, mumbled broodings – devoid of all rational thought – out of which the sick woman would only be jolted with gruesome twitching and frantic, fearful groaning when the hammering and pounding of the coopers reached her ear from the cellar. As a result, Margit soon ordered the coopers to stop their work completely and had the cellar shut up tight. When the doctor, shrugging his shoulders, declared about evening there could be no doubt that Sensy had been attacked by an extremely alarming and murderous nerve fever now loose in the area, a mounted messenger was sent to Mr. Horváth without delay to call him back as rapidly as possible to the sickbed of his only child.

When Horváth returned to Veszprém again on the fourth day after the outbreak of the disease, he found his sick daughter worse off rather than better, still lying unconscious in a catatonic state from which, however, she would regularly awaken around midnight in terrible distress, ask for the cellar keys, make motions to leave her bed, and could only be restrained at great effort until, suddenly collapsing with a loud shriek of terror, she sank back into her feverish half-slumber. This was all so taxing on her strength, and her appearance was deteriorating so drastically that the doctor couldn't avoid designating the condition of the sick woman as exceedingly serious, her recovery as highly doubtful.

Thus arrived the seventh night since the beginning of the illness. The patient had spent the night quieter than usual and was sweating profusely as she lay there. Kneeling behind the curtain surrounding the sickbed was Horváth, who in the pain of despair ascribed the affliction of his beloved child squarely and exclusively to his own unloving hardness of heart and prayed fervently for her recovery, while Frau Margit, exhausted by the exertions of six straight nights of vigilance at Sensy's bedside, had nodded off to sleep. It must have been about midnight when the sick woman threw her eyes wide open with a deep sigh and looked around, marveling and gradually starting to come to her senses. When she had laboriously gathered her thoughts, she tried to sit up, an attempt that totally failed, given her lack of strength, and had no further result than to waken Frau Margit, who jumped up and bent down over her, concerned.

How joyfully surprised was the good old woman when she saw the gaze of those beloved eyes, which had been a gloomy and glassy stare before, now looking into her own eyes peacefully and clearly, when the gentle exclamation came from Sensy's colorless lips: "My auntie, dear Aunt Margit!" Breaking out in a loud whoop of euphoria, she hugged her beloved patient, but the latter motioned for her to be quiet. "You need to do something for me, auntie," she whispered to her in agitated haste, "something very important! You need to go down into the cellar for me!"

"Oh no, dear God, now she's talking crazy again!" sighed Frau Margit.

"No, I'm not talking crazy"; answered Sensy, "I know what I'm saying, and I'm telling you, you need to finish what my sudden illness prevented me from doing yesterday. Ferencz is locked in the cellar room; you need to free him!"

"Yesterday! Oh, you poor woman!" stammered Frau Margit, wringing her hands in consternation.

In that instant the curtain was shoved aside, and Horváth rushed in from his hiding place, no less horrified than Frau Margit. "Merciful God, Ferencz in the cellar room!" he cried, and with that he tore the cellar keys from the wall, yelled for light, and hurried to the cellar with some servants he had quickly awakened.

It was a hideous sight that awaited them when they entered the cellar room. Its unfortunate occupant had tried to break through the walls at two different places, and even on the inside of the door were visible traces of the force that had been exerted in trying to get it open. Exhaustion appeared to have forced the desperate man to give up his fruitless efforts, for they found the corpse of unfortunate Ferencz swimming in his own blood, stretched out on the makeshift bed prepared by Sensy on which he had slit his wrists with a pocket knife – perhaps to quench the raging thirst with his own blood or perhaps to escape the torture of a slow and languishing starvation in this hunger chamber by a quick suicide – and had ended his days in despair and horror.

Sensy had been deeply shattered by the surprising appearance of her father at her bedside and by his involuntary learning of her secret, and it was only with utmost exertion that she was able to hold onto the consciousness to which she had just barely awakened. But then, as the thoughtless gossiping of one of the maidservants brought word to her of the hideous end of her lover, she gasped out a cry, went into horrible fits and convulsions, and soon the returning fever raged so high that the doctor gave up every hope and expected her death within the hour.

Fate had something else in store, however. Horváth – whether worry and shock had undermined his health or whether his stubborn watch at Sensy's bedside had poisoned it – strong and sturdy Horváth was the one, taken ill by his daughter's malady, who succumbed to it a few days later while the weak young lady, after months of infirmity, emerged victoriously from the struggle in which she had barely won back her life at the price of her youth and vitality. Branding herself the murderess of both her father and her lover, she spent the days of winter in a quiet, numb depression from which she was torn only at times by concern for Great-Aunt Margit, who now also, exhausted by excessive physical strain and the consuming emotional stress, began to sicken and visibly wilt.

With approaching spring, though, the desire awoke in Sensy's soul to apportion to the relatives of her beloved Ferencz some of the rich fortune she had hoped to share with him one day. In hopes of perhaps finding some clue to their unknown place of residence, she decided to open up the knapsack that the dearly departed had left behind in Aunt Margit's care. Nor were her expectations disappointed: in the knapsack were some papers that – though they bore the name "Anton Lenhart" – did appear to refer very clearly to Ferencz. One of the papers was a document written in a feminine hand whereby Anton Lenhart was advised, pursuant to an earlier oral discussion, not to waste any time in taking to the road to Croatia by way of Graz and Maribor,[35] since nobody would be following him there. A few words of farewell were appended to this advice along with the declaration that, because of what had happened, any further relationship between the letter writer and its recipient could no longer exist. She therefore asked him to send back her portrait, just as she was returning his herewith. The portrait accompanying the letter unmistakably showed the features of Ferencz, who had earlier gone by the name of Anton Lenhart, it seems, and who must have been staying in Styria. These facts convinced Sensy to send the papers she had found to Herr Steidler, the business associate of her father, and to ask him for

---

[35] A city in Slovenia, just across the border from Styria.

information about Anton Lenhart – though it was only with a shudder that she remembered the man who had originally stamped the horrible image of Marzipan-Lisa on her soul.

She received no answer for a long time, and the depression that had seized hold of her grew heavier and heavier, gloomier and gloomier. Her life – now spent only in prayer and self-castigation or at the sickbed of her Frau Margit, who was hurrying along towards her own imminent demise – seemed to her to grow more and more meaningless and more and more futile.

Finally, the long anticipated answer came from Herr Steidler. Retreating to her room, she opened the letter and hungrily skimmed its contents; but soon she began to shake so violently that the pages of the letter were fluttering back and forth in her hands, and her face went paler and more distraught the further she read. Finally she was done, and in a stream of bitter tears she threw herself on her knees to pray with passionate fervor to the Righteous Judge who had used her as the unwitting tool of His vengeance, who had tried her in the crucible and then saved her, who had guided her down dark passageways but ultimately into the light. Then she arose, threw the letter into the fire, along with the portrait of Ferencz that Herr Steidler had returned, and watched while the flames consumed them, crackling and popping. That same evening Frau Margit passed away in Sensy's arms, quietly and painlessly.

This death had loosed the final bonds of earthly inclination that chained the unhappy woman to life: she saw in this a sign that she should turn to God exclusively and forever. The next morning she bequeathed her entire huge fortune to the convent of Cistercian nuns in the valley of Veszprém, where she soon took on the veil herself to pass the rest of her days in prayer and repentance for her own sins and for the soul of the punished murderer whom no humans could reach but whom God had found.

The father of **Leopold Kompert** (1822-1886) was a wealthy wool dealer; his mother was the daughter of a rabbi. Born in Bohemia, he was educated early in the ways of Judaism and was then given humanist training – and an intimate look at Christian teachings and practices – at a school run by the Piarists.[1] Though he originally intended to study medicine, Kompert eventually quit his studies and ultimately changed the course of his life when his father's wool business failed. He eventually found his life's work as a journalist and writer. In addition, he was to serve as president of the education section for the Jewish community in Vienna, and as an educational advisor at the ministerial level in Lower Austria.

Kompert was not the first to write down tales of the Bohemian Jewish ghetto life he knew so well, but his collection of tales *From the Ghetto*, published in 1848, did raise this genre of prose to international prominence. The means of expression found in his ghetto tales reflect the unique situation of the Jewish people trying to exist, maintain a sense of identity, and thrive in *shtetls*[2] surrounded by a largely Gentile cultural environment. Thus, the plots of many of these tales display some aspects of Jewish-Christian relationships; in particular, the question of assimilation into the dominant culture is raised again and again.[3] The tale at hand, though, *Isaac's Glasses*, plays out entirely within the confines of the Jewish community in Bohemia.

Isaac's Glasses, the set of spectacles named in the title of this novella, are a metaphor for acuity of sight or for insight into one's own true self, but they also possess more of the material heft of actuality than would a mere metaphor, as you shall read. The problematic situation at the core of this framed tale is, to some degree, a generational one: an older, orthodox Jewish congregation is suddenly confronted with reformist mania that seems to them injurious to the traditional Hebrew worship and therefore little short of blasphemous. One elderly member of the congregation deals with local intolerance and arrogance in the outer tale by relating, through the inner tale, the lessons of wisdom he has learned in his own life.

---

[1] A Roman Catholic teaching order founded in Rome in the late sixteenth century.

[2] Yiddish: "little towns."

[3] Kompert, in much of his work, pleaded for cross-denominational marriages and Jewish assimilation into the mainstream as means for the empire to attain greatness. It may have been this tendency of his writing that later caused his prose to be suppressed, ignored, and finally forgotten.

With the ghetto tale, as Kompert popularized it and made it widely known at the time, the literature of German-speaking lands became more diversified and enriched. These texts are valuable in our own day as artifacts of a world that is now extinct: the traditional Jewish life of central and eastern Europe, a vibrant world that was cut short by a devastating Holocaust.

Isaac's Glasses

Leopold Kompert

Why does God allow the old people to die off and be buried in the ground with their lovely white hair? Why doesn't He spare them like he spares the tree that He permits to keep flourishing, blossoming and smelling so sweet even after the fierce fires of heaven have licked at its gnarled trunk? It may be that He calls the loftier and finer things back to Himself sooner for the very reason that they are lofty and fine – but, short-sighted as we are, with feelings that rise and fall from one day to the next, we can't comprehend why the laws of nature have set such a short time span to our "old folks." Floating after them like a dark shadow at sunset comes the saying of that Judge who rules invisibly over the heights and the depths: threescore and ten years![4] Or at the high end, fourscore! And their strength is not always "labour and sorrow!" In the midst of a full and lusty life they are felled: no tree in the forest is so gnarled as many of our old people, so brimming full of life from the hair on their head to the tips of their toes. Why does God allow the old people to die off?

I would really like to know that, more than I'd like to know a thousand other unnecessary things that basically bring me no joy. But you did bring me joy, you old folks from my childhood! It's because of you that I'd like to know these things. You were my favorites from the very beginning, and if one of you is called upon to report on me "up yonder," let him report that

---

[4] The allusion is to an Old Testament pronouncement of man's possible tenure on earth found in *Psalms* 90:10: "The days of our years are threescore years and ten; and if by reason of strength they be fourscore years, yet is their strength labour and sorrow; for it is soon cut off, and we fly away."

I never forgot to stand up whenever I saw his gray head. Especially Reb[5] Isaac Maier (on whom I wish the peace of the righteous) could tell how I loved him, and for the sake of that love may he forgive me over there in his other world for the story I'm audacious enough to tell about him right now.

To this day I'm unable to tell you why it was Reb Isaac Maier in particular that I had taken so fully into my heart as a child. He was the one I was devoted to above all others, even though my own grandfather and grandmother were still around; my eyes were riveted on his dignified countenance when he prayed, and if it so happened that I could enter the halls of the synagogue together with him, then certainly no one felt more blessed than I did. I loved him in that unconscious way that is always the mark of true love, since it's the only selfless one. I can't even remember if I ever received any sign of favor from Reb Maier other than the little colored banner that he gave me on the evening before the "Joyfest of the Torah,"[6] the banner he had delivered to my father's house with the words: "This is from Reb Isaac Maier!" But this banner I held up high and I prized it; no flag-bearer in bloody battle would have defended himself more gallantly than me if one of my enemies had dared to tear it from my hands. It came from Reb Isaac – and so the little banner wasn't thrown out with the trash after it had done its duty at the Joyfest; it wasn't torn up, but preserved as something sacred and invulnerable, like faith in a fairy-tale – and like the latter it was lost in the course of time!

Reb Isaac lived in the loveliest house on the whole street; he was generally considered a very rich man. The windows of his house sparkled as brightly as mirrors, but that's also how pure the old man seemed in the way he dressed and behaved. Around his neck he always wore a white scarf that festively glowed from afar; otherwise he wore only what others were wearing. There were no characteristics that set him radically apart from others: his gentle personality prevented it. On no occasion was he ever pushy, neither in the congregation nor in his social dealings. He went his way with the peace of a tranquil soul; only rarely did he deviate from that. It only happened when he had to settle arguments in the congregation, which were not long

---

[5] Yiddish: "Mister"; used as a title of respect.

[6] "*Simchath Torah*," the day of Torah joy or prayer joy. This marks the end of the annual cycle of Torah readings in the Jewish worship service.

in coming. Then, when he met with resistance and a spirit of contention, he could get quite passionate: his voice would start to quiver and his cheeks would turn a darker shade. "Won't any of you finally take off your glasses?" he would then usually cry out in a overly loud voice. It was strange what power dwelt in these few words; it was as if a magician had spoken his spell over stormy waves. As soon as the people heard those words about the eyeglasses, they quietly smiled to themselves and the argument then usually ended up favorably for all concerned.

Many smiled when Reb Isaac spoke the phrase about "the glasses" and even today many still smile when it comes unconsciously to their own lips. For Reb Isaac was not economical with it, using it on any occasion when he could conceivably make it apply; every time he did, though, it was like hitting the nail right on the head. Not once was its full effect lost by so much as a hair.

Reb Isaac had a good friend, the congregational singer Daniel Kremsier, who related to him much the way an Imperial Court Counselor did to his potentate. Daniel Kremsier had the weakness, not exactly rare among singers and musician folk, that he possessed a not insignificant passion for a good glass of wine. That was what he would find at the home of Reb Isaac every time he visited – the very same quality wine that he drank himself – and thus it was truly no wonder that the parched and thirsty throat of the singer appeared as a daily guest at the home of the rich man. In exchange, though, he showed gratitude, in his way, to the extent such a thirsty soul can show it. Daniel Kremsier came regularly as soon as the evening prayer was over and to Reb Isaac – who left his house very little – he gave a report about everything that was taking place in the congregation: from the new mother about to return to temple services next Sabbath for the first time since giving birth, to the slightest match being arranged on the street by any of the *shadkhanim*[7] under the veil of strictest secrecy. Daniel Kremsier was a living, breathing newspaper – with the sole exception that newspapers often lie while the congregational singer never lied. For that he had too thirsty a soul, as mentioned already, and, as we all know, anybody like that can only speak the truth.

And so it was through the conduit of this Daniel Kremsier that a lot of Reb Isaac's sayings and judgments, exactly as he had carefully delivered

---

[7] Hebrew: "Matchmakers," "marriage brokers."

them in confidential discussions with his newspaper reporter, became common knowledge. They all have to do with the "glasses," and it will soon be evident how much the entire sum of life experiences – the full flotsam, if you will, of what old Reb Isaac had been able to haul ashore from the storms and tempests of his existence – had been gathered together in these few words.

One time, after having adequately moistened his throat, Daniel Kremsier brought reports of an impending match on the street, an arrangement he thought to be ideal. The prospective groom had nothing and the bride had even less. But they were both incredibly attracted to each other, Daniel claimed, and even if a million in cash were stacked on the table in front of the groom, he still wouldn't turn his back on this girl.

"And you're serious about that, Daniel?" Reb Isaac asked with a certain mischievous smile that was becoming to the old man.

"What do you mean, Reb Isaac?" the congregational singer protested. "Isn't it a match better than all others when the one person doesn't have a thing, the other doesn't have a thing, either, and both of them have nothing to lose?"

"Daniel Kremsier, I see you've drunk one glass," Reb Isaac said with complete seriousness. "Pour yourself another glass and drink it down to lighten things up just a bit inside your head. Then you'll see what a totally foolish thing you've just said."

"How's that, Reb Isaac?" the singer asked, pretending to be puzzled, but he didn't have to be asked twice to follow the admonition of his potentate.

"How's that?" Reb Isaac mimicked him. "This is how it is: right now the groom still has his glasses on and is seeing everything double. The nose of his bride looks twice as lovely to him as it perhaps is in reality, and when she says something he thinks perhaps that even God Himself couldn't put it more eloquently. Let a year or two pass, though, Daniel! Let them be man and wife, children howling around them and such; then take a look, Daniel Kremsier, to see if he still has his glasses on."

The congregational singer was much too diplomatic as a newspaper reporter to endanger his own existence by contradicting. So he was content to grant approval to Reb Isaac's opinion by a peal of loud laughter and, at the same opportune moment, to fill his glass a third time.

Intelligent people can decide for themselves whether or not old Reb Isaac was right about his glasses. Let it be noted for the historical record of the street where that groom lived, however, that after just a few years he would have eagerly reached with both hands for the million he had hypothetically rejected earlier – if only somebody would have stacked it on the table for him.

A short time later the old, nearly ninety-year-old rabbi of the congregation died. For as long as he'd been alive, people had refrained from introducing any new improvements – or, as they're called in German, "reforms" – into the worship and the synagogue, all out of respect for the old man who had known most everyone on the street as children. The death of the old rabbi was the signal for embittered partisan battles; they raged back and forth undecided for quite some time until, finally, the victory fell to the younger members of the congregation. The younger ones had managed to install a "preacher" and with him a "regulated" worship service.[8] Most affected by these deep and thorough changes was Daniel Kremsier, the congregational singer, since they went straight to the heart of his livelihood. He wasn't to practice his lovely art of vocal embellishments anymore, no longer to present the wildly shrieking melodies of an ancient time to the ears of people who had become his own! Another age had come and with it a musical "cantor" who had been schooled in the choir of the magnificent Sulzer in Vienna.[9] Daniel Kremsier was released with full "pay"; he had become the victim of a struggle often called a "transitional phase" in our verbose era. This terrible "transition" thing rolled like a heavy wagon-wheel across the body of the poor congregational singer!

Sad and deeply disturbed, Daniel Kremsier came to visit his old friend one evening.

"What's happened to you, Daniel?" the latter cried out to him, horrified. "You look like you've been fasting forty-eight hours straight!"

"Can you tell just by looking at me?" the congregational singer asked with a melancholy mien, examining his own spindly-thin body with a kind of self-satisfaction. "Is it any wonder I look like this? I ask you, Reb Isaac: Wouldn't it just break your heart if you'd sung before God and man for

---

[8] A worship service developed by Jewish reformers at the beginning of the nineteenth century that included preaching and singing in the German language at the same time that Hebrew prayers were shortened. Simultaneously, "regulated" (*i.e.*, composed) music was introduced (see footnote 9). One of the goals was to raise the level of worship to something closer to Christian worship services.

[9] Solomon Sulzer (1804-1890) was the innovator of modern ("regulated" or composed) synagogue singing by a "cantor." Previously, more spontaneous and impromptu vocalizations punctuated by ululations had been the practice.

thirty years, and then an interloper dropped in out of the blue who couldn't even read Hebrew very well and snatched the bread out of your mouth?"

"He didn't exactly snatch it away from you, Daniel," noted Reb Isaac quietly, "And I think the congregation won't leave you begging. You have your bread, Daniel."

"Well, what good is my bread," cried the deposed congregational singer in a pitiful voice, "if I can't sing anymore? Isn't my heart supposed to be broken when someone like that sings with his new choir in the same synagogue that's known me for more than thirty years?"

"So that's what eating at you, Daniel?" asked Reb Isaac again with his quiet smile. "Daniel Kremsier, don't be a fool in your old age: maybe you need to take your own glasses off."

"How's that, Reb Isaac?" asked the retired singer, totally baffled.

"Fill your glass first, Daniel," said Reb Isaac bluntly, "and then I'll tell you how it is."

In spite of his grief, the pitiful victim of a transitional age didn't have to be asked twice. With obvious haste he reached for the glass, and his countenance, etched with grief, began to take on a rosy sheen.

"Daniel Kremsier," said Reb Isaac, having noted with satisfaction the change that had come over his companion, "Daniel, you know I'm not one of those who take their Jewishness lightly. I've known you for thirty years, Daniel, and my heart has always been uplifted by your songs and your improvising. When I heard you with your voice control on *Yom Kippur*,[10] bellowing out so powerfully that the whole synagogue shook, my heart was filled with joy. I've always sensed it: you know what you want from God. But what can you do if a new age has grown different ears? For me you shout and sing well enough. But what can you do if the recent world has put on its glasses?"

"There you go with your glasses again, Reb Isaac!" said the congregational singer with a hint of annoyance in his voice.

"Try to help yourself out, Daniel, by looking at things differently," said the old man, unmoved. "I can only give you one bit of advice: Take your own glasses off, and you'll see you don't fit into the present world."

Daniel Kremsier sadly shook his head; he had to agree with the advice of the old man when it came to the difficulties always besetting victims

---

[10] "Day of Atonement," the highest Jewish holiday, marking the end of ten days of fasting and repentance in an effort to reach a reconciliation with God.

of a new age. And up to this very day, in fact, the deposed singer is still chewing on the mercy bread of the congregation and has taken his glasses off just as Reb Isaac advised him.

The way things went for the congregational singer Daniel Kremsier was the same way they went for many others whom Reb Isaac approached with his "glasses." Not everyone laughed at them: they tore into many of the people's souls like a sharp arrow. Even the new preacher couldn't avoid them. Flushed with eagerness in his new job, the young man had taken the axe to a number of local things and cast them into the fire even though they hadn't died yet and, on closer inspection, were showing even greater promise in their next life.

"Mark my words, Daniel," Reb Isaac once said to the deposed singer, "Mark my words: the preacher will be taking his glasses off soon, too!"

"But unfortunately," complained Daniel, who still had a bitter taste in his mouth despite all the wine, "unfortunately he still has them on. Do we have to wait until there are no more Jewish children on this street? Then he'll put them away for sure."

"No harm done, Daniel, no harm," Reb Isaac countered. "We won't be running out of Jewish children all that quickly, but soon enough the preacher will stop running things down. He still has his glasses on, too, and so he thinks he sees every jot and black tittle[11] in our sacred religion twice as large as it really is. He's just the opposite of that groom! The groom saw too much beauty in his bride and our preacher sees too much blackness. The one has already pulled off his glasses; the other will, too. And the longer it takes, Daniel, the better. For the quicker someone jumps to conclusions and the more firmly he's convinced that he's right about things, that just means that his return to reason will be all the more thorough. Just don't force people! Wait until their own introspection takes over. I'd be willing to bet you a million, Daniel, that both of us will still be around to see the preacher take his glasses off."

As well as Daniel Kremsier understood the glasses-language of his friend, frankly, this time it was too much for him. He still felt his honor too deeply wounded by the wanton and sacrilegious attack of that interloper's choir for him to rise so easily to Reb Isaac's philosophical attitude. Nevertheless, he was clever enough not to raise objections; Reb Isaac had some of

---

[11] "Jot" and "tittle" are two tiny orthographic symbols used to make distinctions in written Hebrew.

the stubbornness of intelligent people who won't let a dust particle of contradiction waft up against a principle of life once it's been tested. Perhaps this was part of the reason why Daniel Kremsier circulated the opinions of his friend about the new preacher even more widely than Reb Isaac would have wished.

So it was that these opinions reached the ear of the new preacher, who had a strong reaction to them. The young man had to admit that they weren't new, on the one hand, but they did contain the type of truth he had least expected to come from the mouth of an old man. Glowing with enthusiasm for the ways he considered better, he thought that inside every old man in the congregation was lurking an enemy trying to destroy his freshly sown seeds. Just as every eager zealot proceeds from a position of intolerance towards whatever opposes him, likewise the young preacher had forgotten to be tolerant. Now from the mouth of one of the oldest men in the congregation he was hearing advice to use patience and consideration on himself, the preacher. He felt somewhat shamed by it; at the same time, though, his soul was burning with anger that someone would dare question his views and refer to them as temporary. In his first flash of rage, he wanted to lash out from the pulpit and had already gotten his text together to do just that. But an inexplicably loud voice inside him, fortunately, kept him from taking this ill-advised step. His shame had the upper hand. He decided to seek out the old man, whom he had only gotten to know superficially; and it was more than mere curiosity that was motivating him.

One Sabbath after preaching, the young preacher showed up unexpectedly at Reb Isaac's door. The old man was greatly touched by the honor of this visit: something akin to friendly sunlight flew across his face. It was easy to see he felt flattered at having been selected. This is a trait we notice among elderly people when they are sought out by the young.

"Reb Isaac," began the preacher after his first introductory words and after the old man himself had shoved a chair over to him, "Do you know why I've come to see you?"

"What am I supposed to do, guess that?" Reb Isaac replied with a smile. "I'm not a prophet, you know!"

"And yet, Reb Isaac," the preacher raised his voice with a slight touch of scorn, "you've prophesied that I'll be changing my ways shortly."

"You already know about my glasses too, do you then, Preacher?" said Reb Isaac, totally relaxed and not looking the least bit startled.

"So you think I'm a hypocrite, do you?" the young man blurted somewhat excitedly, "someone who thinks one way but acts another?"

Reb Isaac laid his hand on the preacher's arm as if to calm him. "You haven't put your glasses down yet, Preacher." he retorted with his disarmingly gentle smile.

"What do you mean by that, Reb Isaac?"

"Look here, Preacher," said the old man with his unshakable smile, "If you were the hypocrite and fortune-seeker that you say I say you are, then there's something you wouldn't have forgotten to do when you entered this room."

"There's something I forgot?" the young preacher cried out excitedly.

"There on the doorpost," said Reb Isaac, stretching out his finger, "hangs a *mezuzah*[12] like you'll find in any good Jewish home. For our enterings and our leavings should be with God. You forgot to kiss the *mezuzah*."

A brilliant crimson shot across the otherwise pale face of the young man.

Reb Isaac noticed this sign of inner shame, and regret started welling up in his gentle heart right away.

"I didn't mean to cause you any pain, Preacher," he said, and touched his arm all the more cordially.

"I thank you, Reb Isaac," cried the young man, grasping the elderly gentleman's hand, "I thank you for teaching me what you just have. I won't forget it."

Reb Isaac didn't know exactly what he was feeling. He looked into the reddened face of the young man a long while. Perhaps what flashed through his otherwise so gentle soul at this moment were pangs of distrust. A young man in the fullest and best years of his life was standing in front of him – yet with an attitude that seemed to say he'd been insulted. The old man said in a soft voice:

"For heaven's sake, Preacher, don't say anything more. It's not good when the one chosen to preach God's word is quick to admit his failings. That's not good. What's the common man supposed to do then? He's forced

---

[12] A container attached to door frames as a sign of Jewish faith, containing the passages of Deuteronomy 6:4-9 and 11:13-21 and the word *Shaddai*, a name of the Almighty.

to see what the children of Israel saw on Moses as he came down from Mount Sinai."

"Do you mean the holy wrath as he caught sight of the golden calf?" the young preacher exclaimed, totally flustered.

"No, Preacher," replied the old man gently, "I mean the shining halo God placed around Moses's head as he was carrying down the stone tablets."

"Reb Isaac, what a man you are!" exclaimed the preacher, totally charmed, grasping his hand anew and looking into his delicate countenance, bright-eyed.

"Don't praise me too much!" begged Reb Isaac with touching modesty. "I really don't deserve it."

"Just tell me, Reb Isaac," said the preacher, still caught up in his enthusiasm, "Just tell me where you came up with this veritable treasure trove of practical wisdom you've acquired? You're not only intelligent; you're also a connoisseur of humans and can see their inner workings. You've gazed deeply into my own soul. Who taught you how to do that? From books I doubt you've learned that much!"

Reb Isaac was silent a considerable while, but on his countenance was clearly etched the joy of hearing his praises from the mouth of the young man.

"No, I haven't learned very much, dear Preacher, not even as much as what you've probably forgotten twenty years ago. But I was able to set my glasses aside fairly early."

"I think I understand you, Reb Isaac," exclaimed the preacher animatedly. "You went through the real-life school of hard knocks at an early age, and, from the bitter bumps and bruises you received, you learned to judge life itself and to reduce its phenomena down to their true measure. In this strict school your eyes were sharpened, and that, Reb Isaac, is what you call 'taking your glasses off.'"

"It's easy to see and hear," said Reb Isaac, grinning, "that you're a preacher. You know your stuff and you understand it well. Why, someone could get the idea that you've just been talking about some passage in the Bible that others might have overlooked, but in which you were able to find beautiful and sublime truths! But don't get that idea about me, Preacher. I actually did take my glasses off."

"How's that?" asked the young man, more than a little confused.

"Or to put it more precisely," Reb Isaac immediately added, "I did take off some actual glasses."

The preacher stared at the speaker with a look as if he were convinced the latter were talking nonsense.

"So you really don't know anything about my glasses?" asked Reb Isaac, having noticed the preacher's astonishment.

"Not a word," the young man assured him.

"Then I'm truly happy from the bottom of my soul that you're the one to whom I can retell the story about my glasses. Here on this street every little child knows it. You'll be able to see from it, Preacher, that I didn't mean to cause you any pain at all with my glasses."

"Reb Isaac!" exclaimed the preacher with an accusatory tone.

"Fine, fine," said the old man, "decide for yourself when I'm done. But will you have enough patience to listen to a talkative old man that long?"

"For days on end I could listen to you!" exclaimed the preacher enthusiastically.

Reb Isaac smiled slightly and began: "I was the only child of very rich parents. Since you weren't born in our congregation, there's no way for you to know what kind of a man my father was. Just imagine one thing. When people spoke of Reb Anschel Maier, they imagined someone like Baron Rothschild[13] would be today. His name was known in all of Bohemia and Moravia,[14] indeed even in Vienna, and if anyone received a promissory note that had my father's signature on it, then he was certain to remark that it was as good as cash. By saying that I'm just trying to show what kind of a man he was.

"My mother was born over in the German Reich;[15] my father got acquainted with her at the Frankfurt Fair,[16] where he went twice a year. She was a remarkably sophisticated and unique woman: she wrote both in German

---

[13] Of the preeminent Rothschild family of European bankers and philanthropists, Baron Lionel Nathan de Rothschild, 1808-1879, was the most prominent in Kompert's day. Two years before this tale was written, Lionel had become the first Jewish member of British Parliament.

[14] Two former Austro-Hungarian provinces comprising the present-day Czech Republic.

[15] That is to say, within the empire of German states that were later to be united under the leadership of Bismarck.

[16] One of the two traditional sites for large commercial fairs in Germany, the other being Leipzig.

and Yiddish and in ways a man scarcely could – which is saying quite a lot for that time. It was also said of her that she could read French books and that she played the piano. That was seen as a miracle in those days. But people can be so mean! The magnificent education was my mother's misfortune. Because of it she was yelled at, to her face, and no woman in the congregation was so bold as to get involved in a friendship with her. The people always thought they had to talk French with her; and since no one knew that language, the effect was that they didn't speak with her at all. Because of it my mother never felt at home on this street; she always thought of herself as an outsider!

"Only to my father and me was she no outsider; she showed us what she was made of and what lay hidden in her. As an only child, I was the apple of her eye. The Living God knows where a mother like that finds all the love and tenderness for her child. A mother will think of what no one else considers; what's not a worry to anyone else concerns her and makes her heart heavy. I'm willing to bet it wasn't Amram, the father of Moses, who had that good idea about the princess,[17] but his mother instead. How would a man come up with something like that? Of my own mother it could have been said just as easily: God chose her specifically to be a mother and me to be her son!

"Outsider though she was on the street, she had no desire – by the time I was ten or twelve years old – to leave her house even for an hour. Only in the early morning and in the evening when I had to go to synagogue did I leave her side; other than that, I wasn't out of her sight for a minute. My father was nearly always on business trips; he could only worry about me a little. Nor was anyone surprised that it was my mother who gave me my first schooling: from her I learned reading, writing and arithmetic, and even the Bible training came from no one else but her.

"As if it were yesterday I still remember when my father brought something back from the Leipzig Fair, something wrapped in gray paper. I wanted to reach for it and open it up, but my father yelled at me as if I'd dipped my hand in molten iron.

"'Why did you bring it home for me, Father,' I wept, 'if I can't even touch it?'

---

[17] The stratagem of allowing Moses to be discovered in the bulrushes by the daughter of the Egyptian Pharaoh and thus to be adopted – rather than being slain as had been commanded of all newborn Hebrew males.

"'Wait until nighttime,' my father said uneasily, hiding the gray package in a safe spot. I cried and moaned, but Mother comforted me. When night had come, my father went and got the package from its hiding place after making certain that all the doors and windows were securely shut and locked. The gray covering was taken off: inside were five books that Father laid down in front of me.

"'Why, those are the *chumesh!*'[18] I cried, almost disappointed.

"'Shhh . . . Be quiet, for heaven's sake, if you don't want me to take the books away," my father yells very nervously, and at my mother's pleadings that's what I had to promise. From the *chumesh* she taught me. Only long years later was I able to comprehend the precautions and fear of my father. If someone had found that *chumesh* in our possession, the Living God knows what would have happened to us! This had been the *German* translation by Moses Mendelssohn from Dessau![19]

"When I'd reached my thirteenth year I was supposed to travel abroad to learn a trade. That was the custom at the time; after the *bar mitzvah*[20] a boy had to leave the area. Now, of course, things are very different: in today's world some would still like to have a wet-nurse around for their thirteen-year-old children. My good mother didn't want to allow it for a long time, but finally my father insisted on it. I went to Prague to work with the great businessman Abraham Taussig, who at the time had a grocery shop on *Meiselgasse*[21] next to the synagogue. I stayed with him for four full years as an apprentice and never made it back to visit my parents during all that time.

"I was supposed to wean myself, my father said. Fine! I weaned myself, learned what there was to learn, but when the four years were up and a letter arrives saying I should come home now, I admit I was extremely happy.

---

[18] The five books of Moses, or *Pentateuch*, the first five books of Hebrew Scripture.

[19] At the time, the original Hebrew was the only acceptable form of the Holy Scriptures. Moses Mendelssohn (1729-1786) was a Jewish-German philosopher and translator who is credited with having aided Jewish assimilation into German culture.

[20] Attainment of full Jewish religious maturity celebrated at age 13.

[21] German: "Meisel Street."

In the meantime a great change had come over me. I had left home as a short little imp and was returning, having shot up as tall as a vine of hops.[22]

"'What will the people on our street have to say to me?' was always my foremost thought. Now I don't know how it happened, but one day before leaving I'm walking down *Zeltnergasse*,[23] wanting to look the city over one more time. And then, without really thinking about anything in particular, I stop right in front of an optician's shop. After taking a look at the various things laid out in the window for a while, suddenly the thought comes to me: 'How would it be if I were to show up at my parents' house with glasses like that over my eyes? With glasses like that I'd look several years older at least. Why, people wouldn't recognize me at all.'

"So without thinking it over any more than that, I enter the shop and buy the first pair of glasses I happen to come across.

"As long as I was still in Prague, I didn't dare put them on, since people knew me there. But no sooner had I seated myself in the coach than I quickly tried them on. The strange and unusual sensation of wearing something on my nose and in front of my eyes was such that I would have gladly tossed those glasses out on the street a hundred times during the first few hours. But what kept holding me back was the thought that people wouldn't recognize me and I'd look much older. And so again and again I took the glasses out of their case and put them on. Strange what a person can do if he wants to badly enough! By the time I was two hours from home I didn't even notice the glasses anymore; they seemed to be a part of my nose. That made me even happier than if I'd brought a million home with me. As I'm riding past the Lord's House,[24] which is on *Pragerstrasse*[25] as you know, who should be walking towards me there? Naphtali Kremsier, the father of our former congregational singer Daniel, out selling rabbit skins door to door. He looks into the coach in which I'm slowly riding past and cries out right away: 'God be with you, Isaac; are you back again already?'

"In that first moment I think I'm going to die from shock! The very first person to see me recognizes me! Somebody else might have torn the glasses

---

[22] The hops plant (*humulus lupulus*) can grow as much as eighteen inches in one day.

[23] German: "Tent-maker Street."

[24] That is, the synagogue.

[25] German: "Prague Street," *i.e.*, the main street to and from Prague.

off his nose and broken them in a thousand pieces. Not me, though – I kept them.

"'You're not supposed to recognize me!' I cried out in my anger.

"I'll never forget how I was greeted by my good mother. Even today I can feel her warm tears, the way they were spilling down my cheeks, and she wouldn't let me out of her arms for minutes and minutes! I can still feel it as an old boy; it tears into my heart like a knife wound when I think back to that hour. Because do you know what thought came to me under the flow of my mother's tears, while she was laughing and crying all at once? I was upset that my parents had recognized me so easily, that they hadn't said a word about the way I looked, about my glasses! Isn't that something worth beating my chest over, worth regretting even today?

"It wasn't until fifteen minutes later, sitting across from my parents with my mother's eyes constantly on me, not able to get their fill of her son, that my much more composed father said: 'You know, Yettl, I think our Isaac has changed a little bit; there's something strange about his face but I'm not quite able to put my finger on it.'

"I turned as red as a girl put on show by her matchmaker. Then finally, my mother got up, frightened by the words of my father, and looked in my face for a long time.

"'I don't think he's changed,' she says after that, 'He looks just the way he always has.'

"Then my father takes an even sharper look at me, and all at once he breaks out in laughter that shakes the whole house.

"'Yettl,' he calls, gasping for breath, 'Would you have thought our boy would bring back something like that from Prague?'

"'What are you talking about?' she replies, turning pale.

"'Don't you see the two lanterns our Isaac has in front of his eyes?'

"At that my mother gives a little cry and rushes over to me.

"'Did something happen to your eyes?' she says, trembling as if I had truly come home half-blind. I couldn't speak: the words got stuck in my throat, so I could only shake my head. What more can I say? My father kept laughing, but Mother got more and more concerned from minute to minute, because the more I shook my head the more she thought there really was something wrong with my eyes. So then, in the face of all the coaxing and shaming, I finally use the despicable lie: famous Doctor Jonas Jeitteles in Prague had examined my eyes once and told me I had to wear glasses!

"After four years abroad, the first thing I do in front of my good parents is to lie to them! From this moment on my father held back his laughter, of course, but what hurt me the most was my mother, who, remarkably sensitive as women are, didn't believe me. She didn't let it show, though, and not until we were alone did she tell me as much and brought the whole truth out of me by pleading and flattering. But I gave her a real struggle. My good mother! Instead of insisting that I get rid of the glasses, if only because I'd lied about them, she agreed I should keep them. She wanted to spare me the shame and laughter of my father!

"I did keep the glasses; I thought that now I truly had a right to them. And when I went walking down our street the next day and many people actually didn't recognize me right away and followed me with their confused eyes, I felt a joy in my soul no different than if the emperor in Vienna had appointed me to the uppermost rung of feudal lords. Many people laughed at me, for it was highly unusual in those days to see an eighteen-year-old adolescent wearing glasses, and then something else happened that was totally foreign to my nature: I became bold and arrogant because of it. There were certain people who, I knew, couldn't stand the sight of my glasses, and it was in their company that I most loved to be seen. Finally it got to the point that people put up with my glasses. Whoever holds out the longest on this earth, you see, has won some sort of victory.

"The loveliest thing about it was that with all the foolishness about the glasses my head for business had gone totally useless. I didn't show any skill for it at all, and only later did I realize that the glasses were actually responsible for it. My father often complained: "I have no idea what our boy actually learned in Prague. What good does it do us that he's wearing glasses on his nose? When he's supposed to see something, he can't see a single thing!'

"My good mother made excuses for me whenever she could, but I often saw my father extremely annoyed. In spite of it all I came to love my glasses more and more; you can fall in love with an inanimate object just as easily as something with flesh and bone, and I have to say: I was in love.

"Once my father came home from a business trip in the middle of the week, even though this usually occurred on a Friday. His face was pale and his eyes deeply sunken. My mother let out a loud cry when she saw him: she suspected something bad right away. Yet he wouldn't answer any of the questions she asked him; he locked himself away in his study, and through the keyhole we could see he was writing something. Towards evening he called Mother in: after a terribly long hour she came back out with teary eyes, her face pale as death. She wouldn't tell me what was going on, either, and all I could conclude was that something horrible must have happened. That same night Father left again, not saying where. For a full ten days he was gone; he came back on Friday. But his appearance was just as sad as the first time, and when Mother asked him what he'd managed to get done, he shook his head. We had a Sabbath like I wouldn't wish on my own worst enemy. And all this time I had no idea what was going on.

"After the evening meal on Sabbath my father said to me all at once: 'Isaac, I have something to discuss with you. Come into my study.'

"Trembling and frightened, I followed him. 'Isaac,' my father said to me when we were alone in his study, 'you've probably thought up till now that I'm a rich man.'

"'Aren't you?' I asked, scared to death.

"'No,'" my father responded with a broken voice, 'I am worse than poor. I can't even pay my debts.'

"All I could do was exclaim a '*Shmah Yisrael*';[26] my senses were reeling. Father was very sympathetic with me.

"'Can you help it,' he asked, 'if you have no head for business?'

"Only then did his words pierce all the way to my heart: I began to weep out loud. Father told me that he'd been noticing a reversal in his business for a few years but he'd kept it from my mother and myself since it seemed to him my glasses were more important to me than the business, and, having noticed that, he'd been keeping it all to himself. But things were going so badly now that everything was getting out of hand and he couldn't keep it to himself any longer. All this I heard from the mouth of my father and had to tell myself: 'This is going to change my life!' I started to pay for my sins at that point, but I hadn't recognized yet that they *were* sins.

"'So you think my glasses are responsible for this misfortune?' I asked time and again.

"'Yes,' Father said, 'since you're not able to understand what I'm telling you on account of your glasses.'

"Then I kept quiet, for when someone thinks he's been unjustly attacked, his heart clamps tightly shut. Father went on to tell me, though, how things were with him. The bankruptcy proceedings were as good as finished. In

---

[26] Hebrew: "Listen, Oh Israel." A central prayer of the Judaic faith begins with these words, and they are also used as a phrase of lamentation.

the ten days he'd been away, Father had crisscrossed half of Bohemia, seeking out creditors to make things right with them. Most of them had come to an agreement with him, but a single one, the one to whom we owed the most, Reb Joel Bischoff in Kolín,[27] had roundly rejected all his offers. He treated Father like a thief when he came to him for a settlement and threatened to send him to jail if he didn't get all his money back, right down to the last penny. To my father he'd said something like that!

"'And isn't there anything we can do?' I asked him at last.

"'Not a thing,' he answered sadly, "Joel Bischoff is too tough; he has a heart like a hunk of scrap iron.'

"'Maybe you could send me to talk to him!' I say suddenly, as if I'd received an inspiration from God.

"'You!' my father exclaims with a scornful laugh, 'You and your glasses!'

"I don't know what gave me the power to ignore the scorn at that moment. But I say again: 'Send me, Father. Just send me.'

"He started up about the glasses again and again, though; the Living God knows how I put up with it. Finally, after I get back to asking him to send me, he says: 'For all I care, go ahead, Isaac, go! You won't be able to do anything anyway. But just let me tell you: it's important you take your glasses off.'

"Very early the next morning I left for Kolín, eager to carry out my special mission. Mother cried when I said goodbye, but Father – half sad, half laughing – saw me off with these words: 'It's good that we have lovely weather so at least you'll have a nice trip. You know you won't be able to work anything out. I wasn't able to, so why do you think you can?'

"I kept the glasses on, of course. As I think back on it, it must have been in defiance to the insults I'd taken from my father. That was my attitude as I left.

"Back then it took almost two days to get to Kolín, a distance we cover now in less than a day. So I had plenty of time to think about how I wanted to talk things over with Reb Joel Bischoff. Strangely enough, not even the slightest fear came over me. I often said to myself: 'Is Joel Bischoff a cabinet minister or the emperor himself that I shouldn't be allowed to talk to him?' and 'Am I not the son of Reb Anschel Maier?' And so I vowed not to put up with anything from this man; he had to realize I wasn't some little kid

---

[27] A town approximately 30 miles east of Prague.

anymore, and if he wanted to give it to me then I could give it right back to him. It was with these and similar deliberations that I arrived in Kolín; it was exactly noon. Having made up my mind and not wanting to put things off, I had someone show me where Reb Joel Bischoff's house was, and I went directly there without eating or drinking anything first. The house is not far from the inn where the coach let me off. As I was standing in front of it, my heart started to pound intensely; only then did it really occur to me how much difference it would make if my visit were not successful. That thought just lasted a fleeting moment, though, as I reminded myself I was Anschel Maier's son and adjusted my glasses.

"'Is Reb Joel Bischoff at home?' I very boldly ask a girl that I meet in the corridor.

"'Yes,' she said, 'Go on in; he's alone in his study.' That didn't seem right to me, for I would rather have spoken with Reb Joel Bischoff in front of the whole world to prove to him who I was and where he fit into things. Since this wasn't going to be, however, I knock courageously on the door and step inside.

"In the first instant I didn't notice a living thing in the room. All at once I hear a thin voice from one corner saying: 'Welcome to you.' I look over to where the voice was coming from and catch sight of a little old man wearing a velvet skullcap on his head, sitting in front of a large, magnificent desk, occupying himself with counting money.

"'Have I found the residence of Reb Joel Bischoff?' I ask, full of courage.

"'Yes, you have,' exclaims the thin voice of Reb Joel, and he doesn't even turn towards me but keeps on counting his money. After a while he asks: 'Who are you? And what do you want?'[28]

"This familiar form of "you" upset me a great deal. What right does Joel Bischoff have to use that tone on me when he doesn't even know me? And so I answer back with supreme boldness: "I'm Reb Anschel Maier's son, and I've come to speak with you.'

"'Did you bring some money with you?' Reb Joel Bischoff asks in his sarcastic voice.

"'No!' I answered back.

"Then Reb Joel shoves back the chair he's sitting on – with an energy I wouldn't have imagined inside such a little gnome – and he leaps up to

---

[28] In these questions, Joel Bischoff uses the German word "*Du*," the familiar form of "you" usually reserved for children, pets, or those one knows very well.

confront me. Now I saw him face to face for the first time: though he was short and thin, he did have a face like a wolf; a pair of eyes were flashing out from under his bushy eyebrows like a cat in the night, eyes truly worth being frightened at. With these eyes, short Joel Bischoff looks me over from head to foot as if he wanted to examine me inside and out like a sack of wool and then says in his falsetto voice: 'So you didn't bring any money with you, boy?'

"'No,' I answer again, not as bold as before, 'but my father wants to straighten things out with you.'

"At that, the short little gnome gets fiery, his face turns red, and his eyes actually seem to be spitting out green poison at me. Then he lets loose: 'And your father sent *you* to straighten things out with me, with Joel Bischoff? You, an arrogant kid with glasses on his nose, is who the scrounger sends to me, thinking he can work something out? Did he think I'm a scrounger like he is? Someone who ought to come begging to me on his knees sends me a kid still wet behind the ears with a pair of glasses on his nose? Now make sure you get out of my sight; and go tell your father there's not the slightest chance of a settlement! I'll see him in jail, and you can quote Joel Bischoff, who's never broken his word.'

"God Alive knows how I escaped from the room and that ferocious wolf: I don't even know today how I did it. But I was so filled with a fear of Joel Bischoff's eyes, I was shaking and trembling so much, that I was already out the door and onto the sidewalk before I could even think about making any kind of reply. And even as I was standing out there on the street, fear of that horrible Joel continued to haunt me. I ran as far as my feet could carry me; I didn't stop until I got to the inn where I'd rented a room. But God Alive! What a state I was in! Beaten and broken from the great insult I'd just experienced; shamed and humiliated like a dog who's been chased off with a stick: that was my condition. I ran to my room, still thinking I could hear the voice of Reb Joel behind me. Once I got there, I threw myself down on the bed lengthwise and buried my face in the pillow. At that point, the pain of the insult I'd suffered cried out inside me, and my tears flowed unchecked. I wished I were someplace where no human eye could ever see me again, and I cursed my life. To treat me like that! Me, Anschel Maier's son! Oh, what if my good mother had found out what happened to me this past hour! My tears were flowing faster and faster; I was convinced my life would ebb out with them. But they did somehow come to a stop, just as always happens when the heart gets too excited. But in their place now came a different feeling: I wanted to have my revenge on Joel Bischoff. I leaped to my feet, and God would have had to protect him, that hard-hearted human, if he'd been in the room with me in that instant. Once I even threw the door open and wanted to rush back over to Joel Bischoff's house.

"But that's all that came of it. I didn't make it any further than the door, and, if you want the honest truth, I was just plain afraid of him!

"Then I threw myself on the bed again and cried and moaned and cursed the day I was born. Now and then I leaped up again and made a fist at Joel Bischoff. That's the way things went for half the night, until, towards midnight, I fell into a deep sleep from the sheer efforts of weeping and wailing. I can't tell you how long I slept, but all at once I seemed to be hearing my father's voice right next to me, and he was saying: 'You see, Isaac, we have your glasses to thank for all this. Joel Bischoff won't listen to reason and I have to go to jail, and whose fault is it if not yours and your glasses?'

"I woke up with a cry that I can still hear to this day; my body was ice-cold, that's how much the horror had gripped me. I had heard the voice of my father so clearly, so distinctly, that even after I was awake and in full command of my senses again, I still couldn't believe it had been a dream. But it had just been my own voice, the voice of my own soul speaking to itself during my sleep. I wasn't able to fall back asleep again. The words of my father, which were actually my own, kept echoing in my ears. So I really was the one responsible: me and my glasses! That gradually became clearer and clearer to me, and a light went on in my head. And the more clearly I thought about the whole foolishness with the glasses, the more depressed I got. It's a miracle my hair didn't turn gray overnight. But I can guarantee you I turned twenty years older, at least, in that one night.

"In the solitude of this despair, unseen by any eye but our Sacred Lord in heaven, I awakened to a new life. I felt a strange power coursing into my head, working its way up, stumbling and bumping its way from my heart to my head. Then I grew quieter. Something curious had taken place within me. A humility had come over me like nothing I had ever known. Joel Bischoff had been right to treat me like that. What did I think I was doing, the young, inexperienced character, approaching him with such arrogance? Trying to talk him into something with glasses on my nose, telling him he ought to accept my father's offer? All pride and foolishness had left me; any trace of insult towards me had vanished. 'Joel Bischoff just treated me the way I deserved,' I kept yelling to myself. And I wasn't the offended and injured party: he was! Then I asked myself: 'What can I do now?' and like the voice of God, the answer resounded within me: 'Repent and go ask Joel Bischoff for his forgiveness!'

"'Yes, apologize!' Once the thought had come to me, it wouldn't let me loose again. The only thing left for me to do, it appeared, was to go to Joel Bischoff and beg him, the offended party, for his forgiveness. That's how far I'd come! And like a drowning man grasping for a straw, I clung to this idea as the only means of making things right. At the same time a joy came over me as if I were on my way towards something particularly pleasant. I could hardly wait for morning, for I was bound and determined to apologize to Joel Bischoff.

"As if newly awakened, I turned to God at dawn, just as the day had broken. Never since have I prayed as I did then. Every word of our sacred tongue seemed especially important to me and perfectly designed for my situation. Meanwhile the day had fully arrived, and I finished with my prayers. No longer was I about to throw the door open; no longer was I looking for any revenge. Very composed and slowly, like a man who's exhausted, I walked through the streets. My glasses? I had left them behind in the room!

"'Is Reb Joel Bischoff home?' I asked again. He had just returned from the synagogue, and they showed me the door to his study. There he was, just like yesterday, sitting at the desk with his back turned to me, counting money.

"'Good morning, Reb Joel,' I say almost inaudibly. He doesn't even turn around, but only exclaims with his falsetto voice: 'Good morning to you, too.'

"What I could possibly say next was a total mystery to me at that moment. I only know that I stood there and couldn't coax a single word out of my throat: it seemed to be sewn shut. After a good while, Joel calls out, without turning around: 'Who are you and what do you want?'

"'It's me, Reb Joel,' I say, and a river of tears floods out of my eyes. At that, Joel Bischoff turns around and yells: 'Aren't you Anschel Maier's son?'

"I couldn't answer for all the heavy weeping, but he jumps up, just like the day before, and leaps at me as if he wanted to cause me pain.

"'What do you want from me again?' he yells, 'Didn't I show you the door yesterday?'

"But now he can't get a word out, either; all at once he pauses, as if his voice had failed him, and he looks at me with his piercing eyes again. He claps his hands together and cries out, completely shocked: 'Young fellow, are you really Anschel Maier's son? For God's sake, just look at you! Did you spend the night in a grave?'

"The Living God knows what came over Joel Bischoff at that moment, but he was a changed man. I could only sob; whenever I tried to talk, I almost choked with convulsions.

"'Are you sick, my boy?' he asked then, taking me by the hand.

"Finally, with great exertion, it all comes tumbling out: 'Forgive me, Reb Joel!' and scarcely had I said these words, Joel Bischoff jumps back away from me and stares at me. His eyes weren't flashing so much anymore; something particularly gentle was looking out from inside them.

"'Are you really Anschel Maier's son, the same one that visited me yesterday? I don't even recognize you anymore! And you took those glasses off, too!'

"Joel Bischoff could scarcely speak, either: he had to turn away. After a good while he turns back around, and a completely different person was standing in front of me. Joel Bischoff had tears in his eyes. Then he takes me by the hand again: 'Young fellow,' he said softly, 'I want you to see that I'm not the hard-hearted person you probably think I am, the one you cursed. I can see by looking at you that you've had a mighty change of heart. Yesterday, when you entered my room with your arrogant attitude and those glasses on your nose, I was furious at you, and even if you'd been an angel from heaven, you couldn't have gotten anything out of me. But today I don't recognize you anymore. You've humbled yourself, dear boy, and taken your glasses off! In return you're going to see what Joel Bischoff can do! Tell your father: not only will I accept any financial arrangement he proposes, but tell him that Joel Bischoff places his entire fortune at his disposal as a resource to help him get back on his feet – and if he asks you why Joel Bischoff changed his mind so quickly, then you tell him it was because you took those glasses off . . . .'

"What more can I tell you?

"How I arrived back home? What my father had to say to that? That's the kind of thing you had to be there to appreciate. To make a long story short, Joel Bischoff kept his word faithfully to the letter, my father got back on his feet, and I became a capable businessman. You know my good wife, may God keep her long at my side. She is that girl who first showed me the door to Reb Joel's study. She is the daughter of Reb Joel Bischoff, may he rest in peace!

"All that was possible because I took my glasses off. I still own those glasses, but I haven't used them again since that horrible night. That's where my little saying comes from. I hope now you'll understand it, Preacher!'"

Deeply moved, the young man shook old Reb Isaac's hand.

"I give you my word, Reb Isaac," he said gently, "I won't forget this story about your glasses."

Leopold von Sacher-Masoch (1836-1895) was born in L'vov[1] as an Austrian subject in the province of Galicia,[2] but he didn't begin learning the German language until the age of twelve, when his family moved to Prague. He studied in Prague and Graz, fought in the Austro-Italian War of 1859, and taught as a professor of history in L'vov for a short while. It was his intimate acquaintance with the ethnic groups of Galicia that permitted him early in his life to write of the often problematic interplay between the Austrians, Russians, Ukrainians, Poles, Ruthenians[3] and Jews of the area. Though not Jewish himself, Sacher-Masoch devoted a number of early writings to tales of the Galician Jews.

Sacher-Masoch is best known today for the novels and novellas he wrote – many of them published only after his death – whose main theme was the sexual perversion that came to be called "masochism" after him. The male heroes of such prose works welcomed the ill treatment and physical pain that their dominating female lovers inflicted on them. The characters of ***Don Juan of Kolomyya***[4] (1866) exhibit some of this tendency.[5]

What is even more striking about *Don Juan of Kolomyya*, though, making it in at least one way a precursor to literary naturalism – which didn't arrive until the end of the century – is its almost total reliance on dialogue, allowing the narrator very little say. In fact, the dialogue between hero and narrator

---

[1] A large city in western Ukraine (German: *Lemberg*) with strong historical ties to Poland; it was under Austrian administration at the time of Sacher-Masoch's birth.

[2] After being partitioned from Poland in 1772, Galicia became a crown land of Austria, located in what is now southern Poland and part of western Ukraine. This "Galicia" is not to be confused with the region in Spain of the same name.

[3] Both Ukrainians and the Ruthenian subgroup concentrated in and around eastern Slovakia and western Ukraine were referred to as the "Little Russians" in contrast to the greater mass of Russians to their northeast.

[4] Kolomyya (German: Kolomea) was an administrative capital and political district in Galicia located approximately 270 miles southwest of Kiev, Ukraine; 120 miles east of Slovakia and Hungary; 60 miles north of the present Romanian border; 100 miles south of L'vov; and, as we shall see in the tale itself, within a short horse ride of the Carpathian mountain range.

[5] One such example is found on page 245, where the wife of the hero takes the whip off its peg on the wall to punish a male servant, who in turn rejoices at the prospect of his punishment.

becomes essentially a first-person monologue of self-justification and braggadocio in the words of the titular hero.

The dialogue style of presentation is visually obscured somewhat by the use of numerous and short paragraphs – with paragraph changes even when the speaker and topic remain the same – and by the total absence of quotation marks. Sacher-Masoch's style is retained in this English translation and will require the reader in many passages to deduce the end of narration and the beginning of dialogue by linguistic and contextual cues.

Thematically ambivalent views of women are presented: at times women are shown as conniving, grasping, and self-centered (not unlike the hero himself); at other times they are antagonists and combatants in what is portrayed as the inevitable tragedy of unhappy marriages. In the end they seem lifted to objects of religious devotion that call for mystic worship of their divinity through the sacrament of sex. In any case – and despite protestations by the hero about women's equality and narrative inklings of their humanity – they are objectified here.

The ebb and flow of dialogue in this novella allow the reader's opinion of the title character *Don Juan of Kolomyya* to fluctuate between assessments of a gracious gentleman and champion of women's rights, a brilliant moral philosopher, and a self-deceiving buffoon.

Don Juan of Kolomyya

Leopold von Sacher-Masoch

We drove out from the district capital, Kolomyya, into the countryside. It was evening and a Friday. The Pole says Friday is a great way to start the weekend, but my German coachman, a colonist from Mariahilf,[6] claimed Friday was an unlucky day, being the day on which Our Lord died on the cross and started Christianity.

This time the German was right, for a half hour from Kolomyya we were stopped by peasant guards.[7]

Stop! – Your pass!

We stopped. But the pass! – My papers were in order, but who thought of my Swabian?[8] He sat on his coachman's seat as if the pass were something still to be invented, cracked his whip once, and stuffed some fresh tinder into his short pipe. He could be a conspirator, of course. His face, impudently at ease, challenged the Russian peasants. He didn't have a pass; that was true. Now they shrugged their shoulders; that was true all right.

A conspirator, they said.

But my friends, please reconsider! – All to no avail.

A conspirator!

---

[6] A district of Vienna, at the time a village outside the city walls. Thus the coachman is not German in the sense of coming from what is now Germany, but rather an Austrian whose language was German.

[7] Due to suspicions that Polish loyalists were conspiring to reintegrate Galicia into Poland, local peasants sporadically set up paramilitary checkpoints in efforts to locate and root out Polish spies and infiltrators.

[8] The term "Swabian" was often used by Eastern European peoples to mean any of the German tribes. (See also page 164, footnote 17).

My Swabian scoots about nervously on his seat and fruitlessly butchers the Russian language. All to no avail. The peasant guards know their duty. Who dares to offer them a banknote as a bribe? Not I. So we're gathered together in a clump and marched a few hundred steps to the nearest inn.

From afar there seemed to be something flashing in front of it from time to time. It was the upright, clenched scythe of a farmer keeping guard in front of the door, and directly over the chimney of the inn stood the moon and looked down on the farmer and his scythe. It peered through the small window of the inn, casting in its light like silver coins and filling the mud puddles in front of the building with silver, just to tease the greedy Jew. I mean the innkeeper, who met us at the threshold and expressed his heartfelt joy at his distinguished guests by breaking out into some sort of monotone cry of lament.[9]

He waddled up and down like a duck, kissed a dirty spot on my right sleeve and on the left as well – for symmetry's sake – and cursed the peasants at the same time for having arrested such a gentleman, such a – he wasn't able to find a more descriptive term for me – such a gentleman, such a black and yellow[10] gentleman through and through, a gentleman whose face was thoroughly black and yellow itself and whose soul was black and yellow. He would swear that on the Torah[11] and chided and carried on as if they had done him the gravest injustice.

Meanwhile I left my Swabian with the horses – where the peasants were guarding him – and escaped with my black and yellow soul into the inn proper, where I stretched it out on the wooden bench that ran clear around the large stove.

I was soon bored, for my friend Moshku[12] had plenty to do pouring out brandy and news for his guests, only seldom hopping like a flea past

---

[9] The narrator is perhaps referring to the type of celebratory ululations common to peoples of the Middle East. The mocking narrative tone reflects stereotypes that flourished in nineteenth-century Europe with regard to the Jews. (See also *Tambi*, page 446, footnote 10.)

[10] The colors of the Galician flag to which it was proper to give allegiance just then, in contrast to the red and white of Poland.

[11] The Hebrew five books of Moses, the Pentateuch of the Old Testament.

[12] The name of the innkeeper.

the wide bar and over to me, where he sucked in his cheeks and tried to carry on an educated conversation about politics and literature.

That's all I needed. I was bored and looked around the inn. Its basic tone was verdigris.[13]

The sparsely fed petroleum lamp filled the inn with a greenish light. Green mold on the walls; the great quadrangular stove was varnished with verdigris; green moss grew from the field stone parquet flooring of Israel.[14] Green sediment in the schnaps glasses; actual verdigris on the small brass jugs from which the peasants were drinking as they walked up to the bar and plunked down their copper coins. A green vegetation was covering the cheese that Moshku put down in front of me, and his wife sat behind the oven in her yellow robe with its large verdigris flowers and rocked her pale green child. Verdigris in the careworn face of the Jew; verdigris around his small, fidgety eyes, around his thin, energetic nose flap, in the sour corners of his sneering, twisted mouth.

There are faces that take on verdigris with time; there are such, and my Jew had just such a face.

The bar was between me and his guests. They all sat around a long, narrow table, mostly farmers from the surrounding area. They conversed softly and put their shaggy, depressed green heads together. One of them looked to me like a choir singer. He did most of the talking, had a large tobacco tin from which, for the sake of proper respect, he alone took the snuff as he read to the people from a half-moldy, green Russian newspaper.

It was all quiet, serious, dignified, and the peasant guards outside were singing a melancholy song whose tones seemed to be coming from the far distance. Like ghosts, they floated around the inn and lamented and appeared not to dare enter in among the living, whispering humans. The melancholy flowed in through all the cracks as mold, moonlight and song.

Even my boredom turned toward melancholy, that melancholy so peculiar to the Ruthenians, toward a manly surrender to the feeling of necessity. And my boredom was as necessary as sleep and death.

---

[13] The greenish tone that copper, brass or bronze surfaces take on after having been exposed to oxygen for long periods of time.

[14] Since there was no nation of Israel when this story was written, the word "Israel" as used in this novella refers to the House of Israel, specifically the tribe of Judah, i.e., the Jewish people.

In his green newspaper, the choir singer had just gotten to the dead, the passed away, the stock market report, the railway schedules, when suddenly outside was heard a confused jumble of cracking whips, the clattering of horses' hooves, people's voices.

Things grew quiet again.

Then a strange voice was heard mixing in with those of the peasant guards. It was a laughing, male voice; there was music in it, but a frolicking, bold, cocky music that wasn't the least bit afraid of the people in the inn. It came closer and closer until a strange man stepped through the door.

I stood up, but I only saw his tall, narrow silhouette, since he stepped back the other way into the room, still speaking to the farmers in a jovial tone.

But friends, do me a favor and recognize me! Am I an emissary? Look at me! Does the national government ride along the Imperial Highway with four horses and no pass? Does the national government go around with a pipe in its mouth, like me? Brothers! Do me the favor of being clever!

Now a few peasant heads came into view and just as many hands rubbing these peasant heads under their chins, which meant as much as: That favor we're not going to grant you, brother.

So, you won't? Well, show me the mercy of being reasonable.

It won't work.

What am I, a Pole? Do you want my parents to turn over in their Russian grave at the churchyard in Czernelica?[15] Didn't my ancestors stand together with Bogdan Khmelnicky,[16] the Cossack, against Poland? In how many battles? At Pilavc, at Corsun, at Batov, at the yellow waters; they were with him at the siege of Zbaraz, where the Poles were left lying, standing, or sitting as they pleased – but do me the favor of letting me travel on.

It won't work.

Not even if my ancestor was with Cossack Leader Dorochenko[17] at the Siege of L'vov? Back then, I tell you, the heads of the Polish nobility were worth less than pears, but – drink to your health and let me go.

---

[15] A village not far from Kolomyya.

[16] Sinovy Bogdan Michailovich Khmelnicky (1595-1657) was historically the most significant Cossack leader of western Ukraine. Some of his victories were at the places listed in the rest of the paragraph.

[17] Pyotr Dorochenko (1627-1698), Ukrainian Cossack successor to Khmelnicky.

It won't work.
It won't work! – Really won't?
Really won't.
Well then, fine, here's to your health! – The stranger surrendered in a manly way to the necessity, without complaint. He stepped over to my area, his face still turned away from me, nodded to the renewed duck-waddlings of the Jew, and sat down at the bar with his back to me.

The Jew's wife listened, looked at him, laid the sleeping child on the stove and stepped up to the bar.

She was beautiful when Moshku took her home with him, I'd bet on it. Now everything is so strangely severe in her face. Pain, disgrace, kicks, whippings have long gnawed at the countenance of her people until they took on this fervent-flaccid, melancholy-mocking, humble-vengeful expression. She hunched her tall back; her delicate, clear hands played with the brandy glass; her eyes were fixed on the stranger. A fervent, hungry soul escaped from these large, black, passionate eyes, a vampire from the grave of a decayed human nature, and flowed into the handsome countenance of the stranger.

It really was a handsome countenance; it bent over across the bar to her like the moon, but tossed genuine silver coins on the bar and asked for a bottle of wine.

Go outside! the Jew said to his wife.

She hunched over even lower and went away with her eyes closed, like someone walking in her sleep; Moshku whispered across the table to me, though: He is a dangerous person, a dangerous person! – and shook his small, careful head with its thick little curls at the temple.[18]

That made the stranger aware of me.

He turned around quickly, saw me, stood up, pulled the round sheep-wool cap from his head and excused himself in the most gracious manner. We greeted each other. Russian courtesy has become so incorporated in language and custom that an individual is no longer capable of surpassing its fondly flattering mannerisms of speech. But in fact we greeted each other even more amiably than is customary.

After each of us had characterized himself as the most miserable of servants and had fallen at the other's feet countless times, the dangerous

---

[18] Orthodox Jews wear the hair in twisted curls at the temples, an area they believe is not to be cut or shaved.

man sat down across from me and asked for permission to fill his pipe. The farmers were smoking, the diack[19] was smoking, at long last the stove itself was smoking, but he asked, and I gave permission out of pity. So he filled his long Turkish water pipe.[20]

These peasants! he said cheerfully. But why me! Tell me, would you take me for a Pole at one hundred paces?

Certainly not.

Well, you see clearly, dear brother, he added in gushing gratitude, but try talking to those there. He pulled a flint from his pocket, laid a small piece of tinder on it, and beat on it with his knife.

All right, but the Jew calls you a dangerous person.

Yes, he does! He looked in front of him on the table and smiled. My Moshku means – dangerous for women. Did you see how he sent his wife away? It catches flame so easily.

The tinder caught fire, too. He laid it in the pipe and soon blanketed us in thick, blue clouds. He had modestly lowered his eyes and was smiling in a pleasant way.

I had time to observe him.

He was obviously the owner of an estate – for he was very well dressed, his tobacco pouch richly embroidered, his manner elegant – from the vicinity or at least from the area around Kolomyya – for the Jew knew him; a Russian, that's what he had said right away, and was also not talkative enough to be mistaken for a Pole. This was a man who could please the women.

He had nothing of that crude power, of that raw clumsiness that other peoples consider to be manliness; he was completely noble, slender, and handsome, but his elastic energy, his inexhaustible tenacity spoke from every movement he made. The brown, smooth hair, the somewhat curly, well trimmed beard cast their full shadow over a weather-bronzed but well formed face.

He wasn't so very young anymore but had happy, blue eyes like a boy. Indestructible, kind philanthropy lay gently in this dark countenance, dark in so many lines that life had deeply carved.

---

[19] Russian, Ukrainian: Choir singer.

[20] A pipe apparatus in which the smoke circulates through water and is cooled by it before reaching the mouth.

He stood up and paced across the room a few times. With his wide pants tucked into his puckered boots, his body girded about with a colored waistband under the broad, open jacket, and the fur hat on his head, he looked like one of those old, rich, brave boyars[21] that sat in counsel with Vladimir[22] and Yaroslav,[23] who went into battle with Igor[24] and Roman.[25]

For the women he could be dangerous; that I can believe, and as he walked up and down smiling, it was even a pleasure for me to look at him. The Jew's wife did come back with the bottle of wine, set it on the table and then retreated behind the stove to squat down, her eyes fixed unwaveringly on him. My boyar came back, looked at the bottle and seemed to be waiting for something.

A bottle of Tokay,[26] he said cheerfully, is still the best substitute for the hot blood of a woman.

He rubbed his chest with the palm of his hand; the impression it made on me was that his heart was aflame.

So of course you were on your way –

I was afraid of being indelicate, but he completed the sentence enthusiastically: to a rendezvous? I certainly was! – He closed his eyes, puffed thick clouds of smoke from the pipe and nodded with his head. A rendezvous! And let me tell you, what a rendezvous! Oh, I am fortunate when it comes to women, let me tell you, extremely fortunate. May God forgive me the sin! Be so gracious as to believe me.

I'm happy to believe you.

Well, look. This just verifies what the proverb says: What you won't tell your best friend and you won't tell your wife, you'll tell to a stranger

---

[21] Noble class of liegemen in Russia before the time of Peter the Great (1672-1725). The *boyars* were both warriors and administrative advisers.

[22] Vladimir (d. 1216), Prince of Polochk, who fought against Lithuania and the Teutonic Order of Knights.

[23] Yaroslav Osmomyssl (1152-1187), Prince of Galicia who was mentioned with high praises in *The Lay of Igor* (see the next footnote).

[24] Igor Svatoslavich (1151-1202), Prince of Novgorod-Sibirsk. His campaign against the Asiatic nomads is the object of celebration in *The Lay of Igor*.

[25] Roman Mstislavich, (d. 1205), Prince of Wollyenia and Galicia.

[26] An aromatic Hungarian wine made from Furmint grapes, named after a district in northeastern Hungary.

you meet on the road. Open up the bottle, Moshku, let's have two glasses – and you'll have pity, drink some Tokay with me and listen to my love adventures, love adventures as valuable and rare as an autograph from Goliath the Philistine;[27] and the pieces of silver for which Judas Iscariot sold our Lord[28] aren't even that rare. Take my word for it, I've already seen so many in the churches of Galicia and Russia that he actually didn't make such a bad deal.[29]

The innkeeper hopped up, expelled his flatulence a couple of times, pulled a corkscrew from his pocket, knocked off the sealing-wax, took the bottle between his skinny legs, and, with terrible facial contortions, pulled out the cork. Then he blew into the bottle superfluously and poured the yellow Tokay into the two cleanest glasses tolerated in Israel. The stranger lifted his glass towards me: To your health!

He meant it sincerely, for he emptied the large glass with one draft. He was no drinker: he had tasted the wine too little for that, hadn't rolled it around on the tongue, hadn't let it trickle through his gums.

The Jew looked at him and spoke meekly: It is an honor that Herr Benefactor dropping in once again to see me.[30] And how good looking; still right on mark! Moshku tried to imitate the stance of a lion while making this observation, and it appeared essential for him to spread his emaciated arms out wide, like broken handles on a vase from Pompeii, and to stomp his feet up and down as if he were on a treadmill.

Well, and how are the Frau Benefactor and the dear children?

Fine! Fine! My boyar poured himself a second glass and drank it down, but all this he did with his eyes cast down, as if ashamed. And he meekly looked over, long after the Jew had left, and was crimson all over. For a long time he was quiet, just smoked, poured me another glass of wine; finally he said very quietly: I must look quite ridiculous to you. You're thinking, no doubt, the old jackass has a wife and children at home and wants to regale

---

[27] The Old Testament giant slain by David.

[28] Cf. Matthew 26: 14-15.

[29] The allusion here is that pieces of silver, allegedly from Judas' betrayal payment, were displayed as religious artifacts in such abundance in Russia and Galicia that their total far exceeded the original sum.

[30] Part of the characterization of the Jewish innkeeper is his poor command of language; see a similar stereotype for the Jewish storekeeper in *Tambi*, page 446, footnote 10.

no doubt, the old jackass has a wife and children at home and wants to regale me with tales of his romances, his dates, and his love letters. I beg you, don't say it: I know it myself. But look, on the one hand it's a pleasant task to entertain a stranger, and I thought – then again – pardon me for saying so – it's really very peculiar. We meet, and maybe we'll never see each other again. So I could have the attitude: what does it matter what he thinks of me? But that's not the way it is. At least that's not the way I think. Of course, I don't want to paint too rosy a picture of myself: a seducer like me acts only half out of lust and half out of vanity. If nobody knew anything about my adventures, I would be the unhappiest man on earth; and so I tell everyone about them, and they all envy me, but today I've made myself look ridiculous.

I made some objection or other.

Don't even try: it does indeed look ridiculous, since you don't know my story. Everyone around here knows what happened to me, but you don't know. And then a man gets so ridiculously vain when women are attracted to him, ridiculously vain; he wants every person to think a certain way about him and gives his money to the beggars on the street and his stories to strangers in the inns.

Oh! It is ridiculous. But now I have to tell you the entire story. Do me the favor of listening to me. I don't know why, but I trust you.

Well, fine. And besides, what else could we do right now? We don't have any cards! – And so I'd like to – but no – and yet – keep in mind – a good bird doesn't dirty his own nest. That's what every peasant around here says. But I'm not a good bird; I am a flighty bird, a playful songbird! Another bottle of Tokay, Moshku! – I'd like to tell you my story.

He cupped his head in his hands and meditated. It was quiet. Once again the dreadful song of the peasant guards started up, first sounding like a death dirge from far off in the distance, then up close and *pianissimo* as if the soul of this strange man were floating on its despairing, heartbreakingly sweet melodies.

So you are married?

Yes.

Happily?

He laughed. His laughter had the peculiar ring of innocence, like the laughter of a child, but it made me shudder; I don't know why.

Happily? he said. What shall I tell you? Do me the favor of thinking about what that means: happiness! – Are you a farmer?

No.

But you do understand something about agriculture? Certainly. Now look, happiness is not, if I may put it this way, a village or a piece of land that belongs to you, but rather a lease. I hope you understand what I'm saying: it's like a lease. Whoever wants to establish himself there for eternity, whoever lets the land go fallow by the book, or even spreads manure, or tends the forest, or plants new trees, or builds a road – he held his head as if in despair – Lord of Hosts! – he acts as if he had to babysit his children. The idea is to produce something this very year or even for today, not for tomorrow. The idea is to deplete the soil, chop down the forest, trample the meadows, let grass grow over the pathways, the barns, and if everything is ruined in the end and the shed is about to collapse any hour – great! And the granary, too – all the better! Or even the house itself – that's the best! The best! He has enjoyed himself then, he is in total jubilation! – There you have your happiness! Jolly! Jolly!

The new bottle of Tokay was uncorked, and he poured the wine quickly and with enthusiasm.

What is happiness? he cried. The breath I take. Here – look here! – He breathed into the air. – There you have it! Look! Look at it! – He pointed with his finger. – Where is it now? – One moment, one second on your clock, one movement of the second hand – gone! The song the guards are singing! Listen to the last note crescendo, the way it rises up and flies away – and then just floats in the air. People think it will never go away. It carries us away, away – further – there – there – now the night has swallowed it up – forever – that is happiness.

We were both silent for some time.

Finally he said, quite cheerfully: Pardon me, may I ask you why all marriages are unhappy, or at least most of them? Can you disagree with me there?

Me? No, not at all!

So, you see, it's a fact! But any person who just accepts the way things are without thinking about them or trying to do anything about them is a weak person in every respect. – I mean, you do have to put up with what's necessary, with given circumstances, or with what's natural, like winter or night or death. But is it absolutely necessary that marriages have to be unhappy? Is there – I think you know what I mean – some necessity, some rule, or, if I might put it this way: some law of nature?

The man asked with the vigor of a scholar discussing his subject. He was obviously certain of himself, and when he looked at me, it wasn't with seriousness in the least, but with the a most charming curiosity.

What is it that makes most marriages unhappy? he repeated. Do you understand me, brother?

I said something or other that you'd usually say.

He interrupted me, pardoned himself, and kept talking.

Pardon me, but that's what you've taken from the German books;[31] that's not the way things really are. You like to read them, no doubt – so do I; but they give you such strange ideas, such phrases – I think you know what I mean. – And so I, too, could say: my wife just wasn't woman enough for me, or she didn't understand me, and how terrible it is when you're not understood; I've got to be myself, I just need to be accepted for who I am; I've got to have my own thoughts and express my own feelings; and I'm so disappointed not to find a woman who understands me, but I'll keep on looking – phrases like that, you know – but those are all lies, all lies! My friend, have you noticed that everybody is a liar? There are just two types, and that's the way you can differentiate people: there are those who lie to others; those are the materialists you read about in the books; and then the idealists, as the Germans call them – who lie to themselves.

I must admit, the man began to interest me more and more.

He drank another glass of Tokay and was in full flow. His eyes were swimming, his tongue was swimming, and his words just flowed.

Well, sir, what makes a marriage unhappy? he said and laid his hands on my shoulders as if he wanted to embrace me. – Think about it, sir – *the children.*

I was astounded.

But, dear friend, I said, look at this Jew, how miserably he lives and his wife, too – wouldn't they run away from each other like dogs if it weren't for the children and their love for the children?

He nodded eagerly with his head and lifted the palms of the hands towards me as if he wanted to bless me.

So it is, so it is, brother! That's precisely it, that alone – that's it; that's it! Just listen to my story.

---

[31] This refers to 19th-century psychology or self-help books from German-language publishers.

When I was a boy, what can I tell you – such a clumsy oaf! I was afraid of women. When I was on my horse, I was a real man, and I took my gun and rode across the fields into the forest, into the mountains – I won't tell you any hunting stories – but, to make a long story short, when I came across a bear, I let him come up real close and I just said: Beat it, brother! – Then he stood up on his hind legs so I could feel his breath, and I shot him right in the white spot, in his chest. But when I saw a woman, I avoided her. If she talked to me, I turned red, stuttered – such an oaf, you know. I still thought a woman just had longer hair than us and wore dresses, and that was all. Such an oaf! You know how it is around here. Not even the servants talk about these things; you grow up; you've almost grown a beard, and you don't know why your heart starts thumping when you see a woman like that. Such an oaf! I tell you.

Then I thought I had discovered America or at least some new planet, when I finally found out – Fine! Then I fell in love all of a sudden. I don't even know myself how I did it – but I'm boring you, no doubt?

No, please go on –

Good! I fell in love. At the time my father, may he rest in peace, had an idea, an idea of sponsoring a dance for us, my sister and me. A short Frenchman came with his violin, and then the estate owners from all around here came with their sons and daughters. It was a happy party of neighbors. Everybody knew each other and was in high spirits; but I was shaking from head to toe. The short Frenchman doesn't think about things but just puts couples together any old way, grabs me by the sleeve, also grabs a neighbor girl, a child, I tell you. She was still stumbling over her dress and had blonde pigtails down her back.

So there we stood, and she held my hand – for I – I was as good as dead; so we're dancing, but I don't look at her at all; our hands are burning as we hold them! Then at last, we hear: Messieurs![32] You step in front of your lady, click your heels together, let your head fall to your chest as if it's been chopped off; you bend your arm, take her by the fingertips and kiss her hand. The blood shot to my head. She made a curtsy, and when I lifted my head, she was all red and had eyes – such eyes!

He closed his own eyes and leaned back.

---

[32] French: "Gentlemen." This was the call for the gentlemen to give the final bow to their partners.

Bravo, Messieurs! – I was saved. From then on I didn't dance with her anymore.

She was the daughter of a neighbor. Beautiful! – What can I tell you – Beautiful! So elegant, I'd like you to know. – Every week there was a dance class. I didn't even talk to her, but when she danced the Cossack, her arm delicately bent, my eyes were just riveted on her; and if she looked at me, I would whistle, I suppose, and turn on my heel. The other young gentlemen licked her fingers like sugar, sprained their ankles and wrists to pick up her handkerchief for her, but she would throw her pigtails back and look at me.

When she drove home, I was a hero if I lit the stairs for her and stood below in wait. She would wrap herself up snugly, pull down her veil, nod affably to all until jealousy ate at my stomach; and when the carriage bells could be heard in the distance, I was still standing there, holding the candle crooked in my hand, the wax dripping on the ground. Such an oaf, I tell you.

Then the dance classes were over, and I didn't see her for a long time.

I would wake up at night with tears on my pillow without knowing why; I would learn love poems by heart and recite them incessantly, all to my hat rack; I would dare to improvise songs on my guitar, singing and playing until our old hunting dog would crawl out from under the stove, lift his nose to heaven, and howl.

Then in spring I got the idea of going on a hunt. I wander around in the mountains, lie down inside a ravine, and the twigs break as I'm lying there, and down through the underbrush comes a large bear, slowly, very slowly. – I stay completely still, and it is still in the forest – and a crow flies over me and caws. – Then a nameless fear comes over me; I make the sign of the cross and don't even breath, and as soon as he's gone I run as fast as my legs can carry me.

Then there was the annual fair – pardon me, probably everything I'm telling you is hopelessly mixed up – so I go to the fair, and when I get there, she's there, too. Right! I'm forgetting to tell you what her name is: – Nicolaya Senkov. The walk she had now was like a princess, and her pigtails weren't hanging down any longer but lying on her head like a golden hoop, and her walk was so free and easy; she swayed back and forth, and the pleats in her dress rustled so pleasantly – you could have fallen in love with the rustling alone. – There's noise all around at the fair; the peasants are tromping along in their heavy boots, the Jews are shooting through the crowd – the yelling and whining and laughing crowd – and young boys are whistling on the little wooden whistles they've bought. But she saw me right away. So I take courage, look around and think: Wait a minute! I can give her the sun! That will make her happy! What more can I give her? – Pardon me, it was a sun made out of gingerbread, frosted a magnificent gold, I tell you. I noticed her from far off, and she had such an astonished face, like our priest when he's asked to bury someone for free. So, good, I have courage like the devil this time, I go, throw down my twenty – it was my only one – and buy the sun; then I take big strides and catch my girl right by one of her pleats – which is actually quite improper, but that's how you are when you're in love, totally improper! – catch her and present the sun to her, and what do you think, what does my Nicolaya do?

She thanks you, no doubt?

Thanks me? – She – She laughs in my face; her father laughs, too; her mother laughs; her sisters and cousins laugh; all the Senkovs laugh! I feel the same way as when I was at the ravine there, when the bear is coming down so slowly. I'd like to run, but I'm ashamed. – The Senkovs, though, keep on laughing. – They're rich people, and we were, too – we had our means. – Then I put both my hands in my pockets and say: That's not kind of you, *Pana*[33] Nicolaya, to laugh at me. My father gave me nothing for the fair but the twenty that I threw down for you, like a prince when he takes his twenty villages and casts them down at your feet – so have a little mercy. – I couldn't say anything more – my tears started flowing. Such a total oaf, I tell you. But *Pana* Nicolaya takes my sun with both hands to her breast and looks at me. Her eyes were so large, so wide – the whole world didn't seem that wide to me – and so deep! They sort of drew you in, and she begged me; with her eyes she begged me; her lips were twitching so.

Then I cry aloud: Oh! What an oaf I am, *Pana* Nicolaya! The sun is what I would like to rip down from heaven, God's true, bright sun, and lay it at your feet; just laugh at me, laugh. – At that point, a Polish count drives through. Six horses he has out in front of his *britshka*;[34] he's sitting up on his seat with a whip, just flying along, I tell you, right through the fairgrounds. Such craziness! Driving so fast there. There's some yelling, a Jew tumbles to the ground, the Senkovs start running; only Nicolaya stands there paralyzed,

---

[33] Russian: "gentlewoman" or "lady on a landed estate."

[34] Russian: a light, open coach.

just raises her hands towards the horses, I put mine around her, lift her up and carry her away, Nicolaya's hands around my neck. Everyone's screaming, but I prefer to dance with her in my arms – then the count is past us with his *britshka* – the girl is out of my arms – in an instant, I tell you! – that Polack! Driving so fast here.

But I'm telling you all this just the way I lived it; I need to make it short. No! No! Just continue as you are. – I stretched out on my bench. He filled a new pipe.

It doesn't matter anyway, he said; after all, we're both being held under arrest, so you might as well hear the story all the way to the end.

The Polish count had separated us from her brave family. The Senkovs were scattered to the four winds. Do you think I was looking for them? *Pana* Nicolaya took my arm, very gently, and I guide her to her people, that is to say, I keep looking all around to see them from afar off, so I can scoot us down a different row of fair booths in time. I lift my head proudly like a Cossack, and we chat. What do we see right away? A woman is sitting there, selling water jugs. *Pana* Nicolaya claims the ceramic jugs are better for water and I say the wooden ones, just to have something to talk about; she praises the French books and I the German ones; she the dogs and I the cats, and I only contradicted to hear her speak, so charming! And when she got angry – this voice! – like music, I tell you!

Finally the Senkovs had me surrounded like wild game, there was no more escape; we ran right into Father Senkov's arms. He wanted to drive home right away. Good! I had gathered my courage now, literally yelled at the coachman and told him where to bring the coach. I lift Madame Senkov in the coach first, then push Father Senkov, who's climbing in, from behind – you know – all so I could get down on one knee, allow Nicolaya to put her foot on the other and jump up to her seat. Then come the sisters and cousins, I kiss another half dozen hands, the coachman whips the horses, and they're off.

It's really – you'll pardon me – if only I could – such a bad habit – to tell it like this. But I'd rather continue; otherwise I'll delay the whole thing even more. After all, we *are* under arrest.

So back to the fair!

I had sold my soul there, sold myself just the way I was. I went around like an animal that's lost its master. I was completely lost.

The next day I rode out to the Senkovs' village and was received well. Nicolaya was more serious than usual, let her little head hang a bit. I got sad, too, looked at her and thought: Why are you like that? I am yours, your possession, your creature, do with me as you will, I'm yours, just go ahead and laugh! – I didn't have a single thought that she could wish for anything more.

I now rode out to the Senkovs often.

Once I said to Nicolaya: Permit me to stop lying to you.

She looked at me, astonished.

You're lying?

I tell you I'm your servant, my soul belongs to you, that I fall at your feet and kiss the ground you walk on, but I'm not and I don't. Permit me to stop lying to you.

Believe me, I – I stopped lying that very hour.

After some time, our old Cossack said this to the servants: Our young master has gotten religious now, has found his proper place on his knees. – Well! So, now I have to tell you about a dog.

The Senkovs' village was closer to the mountains than ours was. – They had numerous sheep out on the open meadows, towards the deep forest. The camp was surrounded by a sturdy fence. The shepherds made fires every night, had armored the tips of their sticks with iron, even had an old full-muzzled shotgun once used for duck hunting, and a few wolfhounds. All because it was close to the mountains, and the wolves and bears ran around there like chickens, were numerous, and reproduced like Jews.

There was one black wolfhound.

They called him Coal.

He was black as coal, too, and his eyes sparkled like pieces of coal.

He was the friend of my – pardon me – what am I saying there . . . .

He blushed a bit and lowered his eyes.

So Coal was the friend of *Pana* Nicolaya. When she was still just a toddler lying in the warm sand, Coal came up to her – himself just a pup – and licked her with his tongue, all over her face, and the child put her little finger between his big teeth and laughed, and the dog laughed, too.

Then they both grew up. Coal became large and strong as a bear. Nicolaya wasn't able to keep up so quickly, but they kept loving each other. And when Coal came to be with the sheep – not that he was assigned there by anyone. Let me tell you that. He was so generous by nature, he always had to have something to protect. For miles around there was no animal like him.

If he tore apart a dog, it was only because that dog had bitten another one. The wolf avoided him, and the bear stayed away when he kept watch. So it occurred to Coal to protect the sheep. Those were such poor and anxious animals, just right for Coal. So he came to them and from then on only made visits in his master's house; and when he came back, the lambs rushed up around him and greeted him, and he licked right and left with his red tongue, as if he wanted to say: Okay, okay! I know, I know! – Nicolaya came to visit the herd now, as a result, and they both took it very seriously. If the child didn't make it sometimes, then the dog would pout, and once, instead of running back to the estate, he ran into the forest where he amused himself by seducing the wolf's mate.

He was a majestic animal. When Nicolaya came, he would drive all the little lambs toward her. She sat on his back, and he would carry her so lightly; what do I mean lightly – proudly! He knew what he was carrying.

When I got to know Coal, he was already old, had bad teeth, a lame leg, slept often, and it would happen that now and then a lamb would be lost.

About this time, those in the region spoke much about a bear, a gigantic bear, I tell you, that was even sighted at the Senkovs once.

I thought immediately of the bear in my ravine and was a little ashamed.

Once I ride over to the Senkovs; peasants are running right across in front of me, running toward the herd – a tumult – I spur my horse on; from far off I hear: The bear! The bear! – Fear creeps into me, I race over, leap from my horse; a lot of countryfolk are standing there – Nicolaya is lying on the ground sobbing, the wolfhound in her arms. The people are standing around and just whispering.

The bear had been there, the big bear, and taken a lamb. The shepherds, the dogs don't move, just howl for all they're worth, the girl shrieks, Coal is ashamed and jumps over the fence with his lame leg, straight towards the bear.

His teeth are blunt. He attacks the bear, the bear attacks him – the shepherds run out with their shotgun, the bear flees, the lamb is saved. Coal drags himself just a few steps, though, and falls, like a hero, I tell you. – Nicolaya throws herself over him, hugs the wolfhound to her breast. Her tears flow onto his head, he looks up at her, takes one more breath of air – it's all over.

I feel as if I had committed a murder. Let him be, *Pana* Nicolaya, I say; but she lifts her eyes full of tears to me and says: You are a hard person, Demetrius – that is my name, you see. – Me, a hard person! Just think!

I give my horse to the shepherds, take a long knife, sharpen it, take the old gun, unload it, load it again myself. One more handful of powder and lead shot into my sack, and off I go – into the mountains.

I knew he would come down through the ravine.

The bear?

Right. I was waiting for him. I took up my position in the ravine; there was no thought of avoiding him. The walls fell right off there, steep, stone hard. Up on top were the trees, but not one of them lowered its roots down far enough that I could reach it with my hands and swing up.

He can't avoid me – and he won't turn around either – and neither will I!

So I stand there and wait for him.

Were you ever lonely? – Do you know what it means to wait for someone? – But here I stood in the lonely back woods, and it was a bear I was waiting for.

Strange precautions, the foolish intelligence you have when you're excited. I put my ramrod into the muzzle one more time to make sure the bullet was solidly planted.

I don't know how long I waited.

It was lonely, infinitely lonely.

Then the brush up above me in the ravine started rustling step by step, like the heavy boots of a peasant. Now he roars to himself.

There he is.

He sees me and holds still.

I step forward one more step and cock – want to cock? – want to cock the gun. I reach around, can't find – the firing pin is missing.

I just make the sign of the cross, throw off my coat, wrap it around my left arm. – The bear's already coming at me.

Beat it, brother! I cry. But he doesn't listen to me, doesn't look at me, either.

Stop, brother, I'll teach you some Russian.

I turn my gun around and beat him over the nose with it as hard as I can. He roars, stands up; I stick my left arm in his teeth, the knife in his heart, he puts his claws around me.

The blood gushes over me like a wave – the world fades away.

He sat there a while, holding his head in his hand, silent.

Then he beat his palm lightly on the table and said, smiling: Now I really have told you such a hunting story. But you should have seen his claws. Permit me to open my shirt.

He pulled it open and showed me a scar like the white handprint of a colossus on each side of his chest.

He had my undivided attention.

The glasses were empty. I motioned to Moshku to bring us a new bottle.

That's how the peasants found me, the boyar continued, but let's forget about that. I lay in a fever at the Senkovs' house for a long time. When I came to my senses during the daytime, they would be sitting around me, my people as well, as if around a dying man, but Father Senkov would say: Well, it looks pretty good, and Nicolaya would laugh. Once I woke up during the night and I look around. Only one lone lamp is burning. Nicolaya is down on her knees and praying.

Enough of that! It's all past; only now and then it comes back to me in a dream. Enough! You can see I didn't die.

Now Father Senkov came to visit us on his *britshka* and my father returned the visits, both of them usually with their wives. The old people whispered, and if I came into the room, Senkov smiled, winked his eye, and offered me a pinch of snuff.

Nicolaya – loved me! From the bottom of her heart! Believe me. For I believed it at least, and also – the old folks believed it.

So then she became my wife.

My father turned over the agricultural concern to me. Senkov gave his daughter an entire village.

The marriage was in Czernelica. Everyone was drunk, I tell you; my father danced the Cossack with Madame Senkov.

The next evening – they were all still trying to put their joints back together – like the dead on the Day of Judgment, and not succeeding – I harnessed up six horses in front of my coach myself, all white as doves. The shimmering, long-haired pelt of my dead bear lay spread out across the seat, his claws hanging down with their gilded nails on either side, the great head with its sparkling, lifelike eyes lying at our feet. My people, peasants, Cossacks on horseback, torches, fires in their hands; I lift up my wife, her red ermine fur on her shoulders, and carry her into the coach. My people cheer; she sits like a princess wrapped in the bearskin, her small feet on his large head. My people on horses around us – and so I take the lady of the manor to her house.

It's also such a great stupidity that you read about in the German books, all about the heavenly bliss of love and then the idolatry surrounding a virgin. As Schiller[35] himself said in –

Oh, I beg you, you're not going to quote me something from Herr von Schiller? Have pity on me!

Just one passage, you know –

Pardon me –

> With the belt and with the veil,
> The lovely madness tears in two![36]

I declaimed mercilessly.

Well, he's right about that, Herr von Schiller is, said the country nobleman; a lovely madness is what it is. It would be something if a virgin were the crown of creation and love were the lovely, stupid feeling that you feel for a girl like that. For me as well, the madness tore in two.

Only when she was my wife did I finally have the full courage to love her, and she me. My love and her love grew up together like twins.

As *Pana* Nicolaya, I kissed her hands; as my wife, I kissed her feet and bit into them so often that she would shriek and kick me in the face.

Now I came to understand why people kneel down and worship a woman with her child, but they also made a virgin out of her,[37] those domesticated animals of our Lord God.

You see, a girl is a slave in her own house. Many fathers consider a daughter to be just one of their possessions. But a woman! – She can leave me at any moment. Am I right or not? She chooses, just as I choose. And then people say: You beautiful little child! Such a butter-colored duckling is supposed to be my equal? Do me a favor and think that one over.

Love between a woman and a man is marriage. I mean marriage the way nature performs it.

---

[35] Friedrich von Schiller (1759-1805), a major author of German Classicism along with Goethe (footnote 38).

[36] From Schiller's poem, *Song of the Bell* [*Lied von der Glocke*], written in 1799.

[37] This alludes to the Madonna and Child imagery, i.e., the Virgin Mary holding the infant Jesus.

So what do you have?

Take the trouble to look at this life a bit. A strange text –
He listened to the song of the peasant guards for a moment.
And the melody, too.

Now the Germans have their *Faust*,[38] you know, and even the English have a book like it.[39] – Every peasant here knows about it. It's like a premonition of life that comes over him.

What makes our people so melancholy?

The steppe.[40]

It pours out like the ocean and waves about in the wind like the ocean. The sky sinks into it – as into the ocean – It silently surrounds man like infinity, as strangely as nature itself. He wants to talk to it and get an answer from it. Like a cry of pain, the song wrests its way loose from his breast and dies unanswered like a sigh.

He feels so peculiar. Isn't he a part of it? Didn't it create him? Is it just his master? – Did *he* leave *it*? Did *it* reject *him*?

It gives man no answer.

Out of his grave grows a tree. Sparrows squawk on the branches. – Is that some sort of answer?

He watches the ants, the way they move along through the warm sand and back in long caravans, loaded down with eggs; that's what his world is – a swarming across the narrowest of spaces, a restless agitation for – nothing. He feels abandoned; he could almost forget at any moment that he's even alive.

Then it's through the woman that nature speaks to him: You are my child. You are as afraid of me as you are of death, but I'm here just like you. Kiss me! I love you, come on! Work with me on the puzzle of life that has you so frightened. Come on! I love you!

He was silent for a while, then he continued.

---

[38] *Faust*, the play by Johann Wolfgang von Goethe (1749-1832), often considered the finest piece of literature by Germany's greatest author. The first lines of the prologue speak about struggling to make sense of life – to no avail.

[39] *Dr. Faustus* (1588) by Christopher Marlowe (1564-1593).

[40] The wide and seemingly endless plain that begins in Hungary and sweeps far into Russia. See also *Brigitta*, page 48.

Nicolaya and I, how happy we were! When our parents came to visit, or the neighbors, you should have seen the way she commandeered the house, and everyone obeyed her. The servants bowed and bobbed like ducks in the water when she so much as looked at them. Once my young Cossack drops a dozen plates. Carrying them right up to his chin – drops them all. My wife takes the whip from its peg on the wall. Well now – if the lady of the manor whips him, he says, he'd be happy to break a dozen plates every day – do you understand?

And both start to laugh.

The neighbors came, too.

Formerly, they had only come to visit me at holiday time, to eat venison[41] at Easter for instance. But now they tried to make up for it. They all came, I tell you.

There was a retired Lieutenant Mack. He knew Schiller by heart, but otherwise he was a good person. The only unfortunate thing about him was that he liked to drink. You know, he wasn't the type to get drunk and slip under the sofa. What do you think he did? He would station himself in the middle of the room, the short, fat, ruddy codger, declaring war on the dragon; and when he was sober – just imagine – he would tell us the details of every one of the French wars. Tell me yourself, what can you do with someone like that?

Then came Baron Shebicki. You don't know him? – Actually the name of his father was Shebig, Solomon Shebig; he was a Jew, ran around buying and selling with his money bag, became a contractor to the public treasury, bought an estate and called himself Shebigstein. Somebody's called Lichtenstein, he said, so why shouldn't I call myself Shebigstein? And his son became a baron and now calls himself Raphael Shebicki. He laughs at you no matter what! If you say to him: Pay me the honor of visiting me – he laughs in a certain way, and if you say to him: If you please, there is the door; now get out! – he laughs in exactly the same way. And the first thing he can think of for every lovely woman is to bring her some clothes from Brody[42] and

---

[41] There is an untranslatable play on words at this point in the original, *"ein Geweihtes,"* which at that time meant both "something consecrated" and "something antlered."

[42] A town in western Ukraine a few miles east of L'vov and 250 miles west of Kiev.

a shawl from Paris; he only drinks water, goes to the steam bath daily, wears a large golden chain on his red velvet vest, and always makes the sign of the cross before the soup and after the dessert.

Then there's the nobleman Dombosky, a tall Pole with bloodshot eyes, a sadly drooping mustache, and empty pockets, who's always collecting for the poor emigrants and who impulsively hugs and tenderly kisses anyone he sees for the second time; when he's had one glass too many, he sheds tears beyond number, sings *Poland's Cause Is Not Yet Lost,* and wraps his arms around everyone to map out the entire Polish conspiracy. When he's finally happy, he bellows out a "*Vivat*;[43] let's love one another!" and drinks from the women's dirty shoes.

Father Maziek, such a righteous country priest; he found consolation for everything, for birth, death and marriage. Mostly, though, he praised those who blissfully pass away in the arms of the Lord. Even the Church itself had bestowed distinction on them as well, he claimed, by the symbol of a loftier fee for service. Whenever he wanted to punctuate a claim, he always said "Purgatory!" just as someone else would say "By God" or "On my word of honor."

Then the scholarly Thaddeus Katernoya, who had been working on his doctorate for eleven years, and just think, in the field of philosophy, no less. The lord of a manor, Leon Bodoshkan, a true friend, and other jolly noblemen.

Jolly! Jolly as a swarm of bees, but they had respect for Nicolaya.

The women came to visit as well. Good lady friends who gossip, smile sweetly, make a vow a minute, and then – well, we know about that. So this was how we lived with our neighbors, and I was proud of my wife when they drank from her shoes and directed grand speeches at her: she looked at every one of them the same, as if to say, Why do you even bother? – We did prefer to be alone, too.

So many agricultural fields, you know! We had our worries and our joys. She accepted her own full responsibility. We want to rule ourselves, she said, and not be ruled by our government functionaries. There was one functionary, Mandatary Cradulinsky, an old Pole; a person of some consequence, I tell you! – He never had a hair on his head or a calculation correct. Then Forester Freidel, a German, as you can see from his name. He was

---

[43] Latin: "Long life!"

small, had small eyes, large translucent ears and a large translucent greyhound.⁴⁴

My wife held their horses for them! You know, I truly believe she would have taken the whip to them if they hadn't driven precisely the way she wanted.

And, on the other hand, the peasants. Whenever we walked through the fields. Praised be Jesus Christ! – In eternity, Amen! – So happy, I tell you. At the harvest festival they just streamed into our courtyard, the harvest workers, the country folk. My wife stood on the stairs, and they laid the harvest wreath at her feet. They rejoiced, sang, and danced; she took a glass of brandy: To your health! – and drank it down.

Her feet, I tell you; they literally kissed her feet.

She would ride with me. I held my hand out for her; she would put her foot on it and be in the saddle as quickly as that. On horseback she had a Cossack cap; the golden tassel danced on her neck, and the horse would blow its nostrils wide open and whinny when she patted it next to its mane.

And then she learned how to handle the rifle. I had a small one I had used to shoot sparrows when I was little. She threw it across her shoulder, went out into the meadows with me and shot quail. Terrific, I tell you! Terrific! – Once a vulture flies out of the forest, takes my chickens from me, even steals Nicolaya's black hen with the white tuft. I'll watch for him. Just you wait!

Back I come from digging potatoes with just a switch in my hand.

There he is.

He's still shrieking and flying around the courtyard. All I can do is curse! – Then a shot rings out. The vulture flaps his wings in the air one last time and falls to earth.

Who shot him?

My wife. He won't be taking any more of my hens, she says, and nails him to the barn door.

The salesman comes, unpacks all his wares with a great hue and cry. All real, all new, all cheap. – Oh my, does she know how to bargain!

The Jew just sighs each time. A stern woman! he says, but kisses her elbow.

I ride into town.

---

⁴⁴ The German term for greyhound (*Windhund*) also has a figurative meaning of "scatterbrain."

The wife of the *starost*[45] is walking around in a blue dress with little white ribbon butterflies. Must be the latest fashion! So I buy a blue dress with little white ribbon butterflies. My Nicolaya turns red.

Once I ride to Brody, bring back velvet in all the colors of the rainbow, bolts of silk, furs, what furs they were! All dyed black. Her heart skips a beat, I tell you.

I'll tell you; was she ever dressed!

She had a *kazabaika*,[46] sap green, magnificently sap green, with gray Siberian squirrel – the Empress of Russia doesn't have any finer – squirrel rimming it as wide as your hand. And completely lined with silver-gray fur, so soft, I tell you.

On long evenings she would lie on the divan, her arms folded under her head, and I would read to her.

The fire is crackling, the samovar[47] is whistling, the cricket chirping, the woodworm tapping, the mouse nibbling, for the white cat is lying out on the front rug, playing with threads.

I read her all the novels. In the district capital, you know, there was a public library, and then the neighbors – this one has this book and that one has another.

She lies there with her eyes closed, me in the recliner, and we just devour the books like that.

Often we don't fall asleep for a long time, discussing whether the hero of the story will get his lady or not. When it comes to stories of noble and magnanimous characters, my Nicolaya can turn dark red with anger all the way down to her little earlobes. Then she rears up a little, braces herself with her hand, and says to me, as if I'm the one who wrote it: She really shouldn't do that, do you hear me!? – and is nearly in tears.

The women, you know, they are particularly magnanimous in the novels. At the point where the beloved is in danger, they're ready to go out and sacrifice themselves, just imagine! They're ready to sell their souls to the devil. And then there's one scene where a woman sacrifices the man in order to save her child. A stupid story, I tell you: *The Power of Maternal Love*

---

[45] Village elder with the functions of a mayor.

[46] Decorative article of women's clothing, something like a *mantilla*.

[47] A metal urn used in Eastern Europe to heat water for making tea.

is the name of the book, I think. A stupid story, but my Nicolaya gets all agitated and won't look at any book for weeks.

Often she jumps up, shuts the book in my face, and sticks out her tongue. Then we run around like children! I hide behind the doors, jump out and scare her.

Or she plays full-length fairy tale games with me.

Goes into her room: When I come back, you're my slave. Then she dresses herself up like a sultana, wraps a shawl around her hips, another around her head like a turban. With my Czerkassy[48] dagger in her belt, completely covered in a white veil; that's the way she comes out. A wife! – A goddess of a wife.

When she slept, I could just watch her for hours on end, the way she breathed – and if she sighed, my heart ached as if I had done her the gravest wrong, and a fear came over me that she were no longer mine, she had died. And if I called out her name, then she sat up, looked me square in the eyes, and laughed.

But it was the sultana that she did best. She never left her role. If I said: But Nicolaya! – and made a joke, then she would just raise her eyebrows and drill her eyes into me until I nearly felt like I was lashed to the stake. Are you crazy, slave? – Really, there was nothing to be done! I was her slave, and she commanded me like a sultana.

So we lived like a pair of swallows, sat together and twittered.

A sweet hope[49] heightened our joy.

And yet, how anxious I was for my wife. I often swept the hair off her forehead a certain way, and tears came to my eyes. She understood me, took me in her arms, and wept.

But it came unexpectedly, just like good fortune.

I went to Kolomyya for the doctor, and just as I enter, she holds the child out to me.

The grandparents absolutely gushed with joy, the servants – they yelled and laughed and they all got drunk, and the stork out on top of the barn pensively held one leg up.

There were things to think about, to worry about, and every difficult hour just bound us together all the stronger.

---

[48] A city on the Dnieper River southeast of Kiev that was an important Ukrainian Cossack stronghold.

[49] Within this context, the phrase refers to the news that Nicolaya was pregnant.

But that's *not* the way things remained.

His voice had gotten infinitely gentle and quiet; it sort of trembled in the air, just as quiet as the thin vapor from his pipe.

It couldn't stay like that – I beg you – and then – this way and that – you understand. There's some kind of rule. – I mean, it's just nature. I've often thought about it; what do you think?

I had a friend – Leon Bodoshkan. He read too much and got ill over it. He often said to me –

But why tell you about it; I can show you –

He pulled a few yellowed strips of paper from his breast pocket.

He wrote a lot, too. Was so unknown, but he knew so much – he peered inside everything as if it were all mountain water. He opened up people like clocks and looked inside to see if everything was alright. Said right away what was the matter. He understood you; when cats talked together, for example, he laughed and told you right away what it was they wanted. He would take a flower, cut it open and show you how it lives, how it nourishes itself.

He liked to talk about women.

Women and philosophy ruined him, you know.

Often he wrote something down, and later, when he went walking in the forest, he'd throw it all away. Paper made him nervous.

But I usually forget that.

He said that whoever can put his love down on a piece of paper isn't really in love.

He could read big, fat books in pigskin, everything about Nestor[50] – but he would run away from a love letter.

Like this, for example.

With that, he laid the dirtiest strip of paper on the table.

No, that's a bill. He put it away again. Here it is.

He coughed and then read:

What is our life? – Suffering, doubts, fear, despair. Do you know where you come from? Who you are? Where you're going?

And to have no power over nature, and to get no answer to this poor, desperate question! Suicide is, in the final analysis, the entire sum of our wisdom.

---

[50] In mythology, an old and wise counselor to the Greeks at Troy.

But nature has given us a suffering even more terrible than life – love! People call it joy, lust!

My friend would always laugh bitterly at these words. – Look at the wolf, he told me, when he's looking for a mate; the way he stumbles through the underbrush, his mouth watering – he doesn't even howl anymore, he just whimpers; and his love, is that pleasurable? – It's a struggle, a struggle as if for life itself, blood running down his neck.

My God! Doesn't a man clamor to throw himself at a woman the same way as he does at the enemy? Doesn't he feel infinitely subjected to a merciless enemy?

Doesn't he lay his proud head at the feet of a woman and beg: Kick me, kick me with your foot; I'll be your slave, your indentured servant, but come on, save me!

Yes, love is suffering, the pleasure – salvation! – But then it's a power that one thing exerts over the other; it's a contest to subject yourself to the other. Love is slavery, and you become a slave when you fall in love. You feel mistreated by your wife, you just wallow in the lust of her despotism and cruelty.

We kiss the foot that kicks us.

I'm frightened by the woman I love. I shake when she suddenly walks through the room and her clothes rustle; a movement that surprises me is terrifying.

You'd like to unite for eternity, for this world and another to come; you'd like to just flow into each other. You take your soul and dive into a foreign soul; you climb down into foreign, hostile nature and receive its baptism. It is ridiculous, completely ridiculous, that you weren't always together. You shake every moment at the prospect of losing each other. You're terrified when the other closes her eye, when she changes her voice. You'd like to become one total being; you'd like to tear all characteristics, ideas, relics of a life from your personality just in order to meld completely with the other. You relinquish yourself – like a thing – like a material. Make of me what you are!

As in suicide, you throw yourself into another nature until your own rebels.

Then comes a shudder at realizing you're completely losing yourself.

You feel a sort of hatred against the other's power. You think yourself dead. You want to revolt against the tyranny of the alien life and find your way back to your own self.

That is the resurrection of nature!

He pulled out a second scrap of paper.

Man has his work, his plans, his enterprises, his ideas!

They float around him on doves' wings; they lift him up on wings of eagles. They won't let him fall.

But the woman?

She cries for help: I don't want to die! She doesn't want to, but there's no help!

Then she carries his image under her heart, feels it grow and move – it's alive! – there – there now, she's finally holding it in her arms. She lifts it up. –

How does she feel now?

Is she dreaming? The child speaks to her: I am you and you live in me. Just look at me! – I'll save you.

She holds the child at her breast and is saved.

Now she takes care of her own self, the self she'd despised and rejected, in the form of the child, sees it growing on her lap and surrenders herself to it and devotes herself completely to it.

With that he put together the scraps of his friend's thoughts and tucked them back into his breast pocket. Then he patted them one more time with his palm and buttoned his jacket shut.

That's the way it was with me, too, he said, very much like that. Of course, I can't explain it like Leon Bodoshkan, you know, but I want to tell you about it all the same. What do you think?

Of course, brother.

So it was the same way with me. Exactly the same, exactly the same! Believe me, exactly the same!

I wanted to encourage my friend and said in a cold-blooded way: Usually they call the child a pawn of love.

My country nobleman reflected for a moment and looked for all the world as if I had mortally insulted him. A pawn of love? he cried. Yes, indeed, a pawn of love!

Anyway, I make my way home. With agricultural fields like that, where there's so much work! I come home tired as a hunting dog, take my wife in my arms, kiss her; her hand wipes the cares from my brow. I rub myself against her like a cat, she laughs – but then the pawn of love starts crying – the whole story is over. You can start back at the prologue if you like. It's over, I tell you.

The entire morning you storm around with the mandatary, with the bookkeeper, with the forester.

You sit down for the noon meal, right – no sooner have you tied on your napkin – I do tie it on, all according to the old style – and my pawn of love is crying because it doesn't want to take its food from the servant girl. My little wife stands up, feeds the child. But the child demands a hunk of meat and weeps and wails – on into the next room, and I am able to eat alone and whistle myself a little tune as well, if I like, for example:

> Here sits the cat
> Upon the fence
> And from thence
> Meows. You see my song
> Is not too long?

So then you leave – to go on a duck hunt.
All day up to your knees in water.
You look forward to coming home.

Well, fine! You come home, kiss little hickeys on your wife's cheeks, neck, bosom. You take her in your arms – then the pawn of love starts crying.

Your wife jumps up, walks back and forth rocking the child in her arms. Lullaby! Lullaby! You hear it half the night and sleep – alone. Lullaby! Lullaby!

Then comes a year like no other.

Everyone has a strange feeling; something's in the air. Everybody senses it, but nobody can put his finger on it.

You see foreign faces. The Polish manor lords riding this way and that. One buys a horse, the next one powder. At night you see a strip of fire in the sky. The peasants stand together in front of the inn and say: That's war, or cholera, or revolution!

It comes over you like a deep worry. You sense at once that you have a fatherland, that your border stakes are deeply sunk in Slavic, German, and other soil. What do the Polacks want? you think and you look out for the eagle in front of the district offices and look out for your own barn. You go around your house at night to see if anyone has set fire to it.

You want to talk about all this.

With whom? – With your wife. Ha! Ha! Ha! The pawn of love is howling right then because a fly is sitting on its nose.

The horizon is colored fire-red. A peasant rides past you, crying out "Revolution!" into your yard and spurring his skinny horse on.

In the village the storm bells are ringing.

One farmer straightens his scythe; two more come by with thrashing flails over their shoulders.

Others come into the courtyard.

Master! Let's take precautions – the Poles are coming! I load my pistols, have my saber sharpened.

My wife, give me a ribbon on my cap,[51] a scrap, for all I care! – Ha! Ha! Ha! Do you think so? – Leave me alone! she says. My child is crying, the noise is going to kill him! Ride into the village and tell them to stop that infernal bell-ringing right away! Get out of here! – Aha! That's different; I'll have the storm bells ringing in all the villages; let the brat howl, you know – the land is in danger!

Finally she's with me for once. We're sitting on the divan; I have my arm around her. She's listening to make sure the child doesn't stir. What did you say? she asks after a while. Nothing! I say, Nothing! But my heart aches, I guarantee you!

Where is your *kazabaika*, Nicolaya? – Oh, don't you remember, it's back at the house, with our child! – Yes, of course! You just comb your hair quickly, put on the first dress you find. Who would dress up just for around the house? Of course! – Often I don't recognize your beautiful face anymore. But the child – you understand. – If I put on my makeup, my child doesn't recognize me. You can see that, can't you? Of course, I see everything clearly, everything! – But when guests are there, you know, then the child can cry!

She runs in for a moment, comes back out and pours the tea, laughs and chats; what won't we do for our guests?

Aha! There's that sap-green *kazabaika* again, trimmed with Siberian squirrel. I have to dress up for the guests. – Don't you see!

After a long time I'm going on a bear hunt.

My wife is rocking the child, and when I kiss her, she says: Get out! You'll wake the child! – So what do I do? I leave.

My gamekeeper had seen the bear – but now I've nearly gone and told you another hunting story. To make a long story short, we were in danger, the gamekeeper and I. A peasant runs home ahead of us.

---

[51] Yellow and black, to serve as identification for the local, partisan cause.

A tumult in the house, I tell you, as we arrive home – my wife has her arms around me for the longest time.

She brings me my child.

The blood, you know, is running down my head. – The child starts crying. – Get out!

He shrugs his shoulders disgustedly.

It wasn't worth talking about, the little bit of blood and the tears of the poor little child, but – the danger was past for me, too – women are very practical. – Fine, I wash off the blood. The gamekeeper, an old soldier, binds me up. But what do you think now, the pawn of love cries again at the sight of the white bandages. Get out of here, get! Our child will go into convulsions, leave. – Of course, what else can you do? You throw yourself on your bed and lie there, alone, just like before you ever knew your wife.

To hell with the pawn of love! – God forgive me the sin.

He made the sign of the cross, spit defiantly and continued.

The bearskin I spread out for my wife, in front of the bed. What do you think? She gives a scream. Take that skin out of here; it reminds me of my child's fears. Just think: that was her concern, not my blood, not the danger! Oh, the women are so practical, cursedly practical!

Permit me to ask, I said, have you told your wife –

Pardon, he interrupted me almost violently, his nostrils flaring. I told her – oh! Do you know what her response was?

Fine, what about the children then?

Think about it; she would have been able – you're a slave to a woman like that. Do you want to be unfaithful to her right away? – No. – Or a monk? You don't want that either. What choice do you have but to let yourself be kicked around!

Oh, there was a time with my child, when I – understand me correctly – oh, such a scene.

I'm smoking my pipe early in the morning, a long Turkish one like this, with a porous cord cover. The child starts crying right after I light it.

I let him cry. My wife is already getting agitated. Well, give it to him then – she means the piece of amber – but I hold out the red, glowing pipe to him.

He takes hold of it and cries and howls.

Jesus, Mary, the poor child! As for me, I wish my wife good entertainment, go out into the fields with my gun, nearly laughing myself silly while she stays behind with the crying child and his burned fingers.

Back then my disposition had changed – Well, what am I saying? When things are already going a certain way! You do what you can. But – I'd ask you to ponder that on your own.

As an example, have you ever had a clock suddenly stop? A grandfather clock? Why, certainly! But are you impatient?

Sometimes.

Fine, so you're impatient. You want the clock to start up again, right now. So you give the pendulum a little push. Okay, now it's going. But for how long? – Now it's stopped again. – And once again. It's stopped. Well, you get impatient. Just give the whole thing a kick. Fine – now it's stopped for good.

That's the way things go when you try to set your heart straight, exactly the way it goes.

In the beginning, you understand, brother, I only wanted to take my mind off things.

The hussars[52] were camped all around.

So I became acquainted with the officers. Those were some people! Banay, for example, did you know him?

No.

Or Baron Pát? Didn't know him either. But you must have known Nemethy with his pointed handlebar mustache?

One time we'd ride out to see one, next time the other.

They came to my house almost daily. Then we'd smoke, drink our *chai*;[53] someone would tell a story; finally we'd play some cards.

We went on hunts together a lot, too. That's when I learned to shoot snipe.[54]

My wife couldn't help but notice. Came to me, sat down, was quiet, finally a string of accusations. I just say: my love, what's here for me at home? – By the way, your child is crying. – The next time, my Nicolaya comes outside in her sap-green *kazabaika* with silver-gray squirrel fur, a proud hairdo; sits down right in the midst of the hussars.

---

[52] Members of the Hungarian light cavalry.

[53] Milky Russian tea, originally from India.

[54] Long-billed game birds found in marshy areas of Eurasia.

I laugh; she wants to make me jealous; she turns this way and that, chatting and cooing. She doesn't cast a glance my way. As for my hussars, you know – first of all, they were deeply honorable in what they didn't say, for none of them wanted to start anything – why should they? – Death or at least the danger of becoming a cripple – for what purpose? If you don't love a woman to the extent that it doesn't matter, one way or the other.

But they do tease me. What do you have to say to that, brother, your wife is inviting us to woo her? – Just woo for all you're worth. Am I right?

About that time another man came to our house, though – who – you wouldn't know him.

I couldn't stand him right off. So blond, you know, very white; a manor lord. Had his hair singed by his chamber servants every day, read *Igor*[55] out loud, and Pushkin;[56] he acted the whole thing out at the same time, a real comedian, I tell you.

So him – I didn't like him; but my wife liked him.

His voice had grown hoarse. The more passionate he got, the more suppressed his tone became; it sounded squeezed and strangled from deep inside his chest.

But that'll come later.

It was a time for merrymaking back then.

In winter all the manor owners from the region came with their wives. There was dancing, masquerade balls, sleigh rides, everything, everything!

My wife was in high spirits, too.

Then came a second child the next summer. Also a boy. Both of them boys. That's what really started to change our relationship.

I told Nicolaya once – I was sitting on her bed, covering her up as she was tossing and turning: I beg you, have mercy on me, take a wet nurse for the child. – She just shook her head. What can I do? Tears come to my eyes, and I leave again. It was all useless.

Nicolaya spent almost another whole year just looking after the child. We seldom talked.

---

[55] *The Lay of Igor*: see page 230, footnote 24.

[56] Alexander Sergeyevich Pushkin (1799-1837), a famous Russian poet, short-story writer and playwright.

So then came what I wanted to tell you about earlier, before I started to ramble on about details: my wife began to get bored with me. She couldn't stop yawning, and her eyes would go blank. It became obvious we were ready to quarrel at a moment's notice. She always had to be right.

If I showed some favoritism to any of the servants, he or she was given walking papers right away. A scene, of course. Or if I remark that the blue scarf has seen better days. Right! The very next Sunday the lady of the manor is wearing it to church.

And always in front of strangers, that's so unpleasant. You don't want to call your wife wrong about anything, and yet – you're still a man. And when she always takes sides with others. I'm always wrong and the other person is right. What do you have to say about that?

After he had spit contemptuously to one side, he went on:

Or even – after I introduce someone to her – Dear Nicolaya, don't do that to me, please, have mercy. Right, she's silent the next time. – And you, dear lady, what you do have to say to that? – I say whatever my husband says. Oh, Tataric[57] wickedness!

She has to force herself, you see, to ever agree with me. When I think about it, I don't understand how I'm still alive.

Suddenly I lost a great sum of money. We played with high stakes, you know, and I was unlucky, of course – in the card game. One time I lost all my cash, my horses, a coach.

Now he cordially laughed about it.

Fine. I took myself to task and said: I've done a bad thing. Retreated from society in an honorable manner. Friends and neighbors stayed away.

Only *he* came.

I didn't worry much about it, you know. I began to take charge of the fields and crops myself at that time, had some success with it, and when you see something growing under your care that you've sown yourself, it has an attraction of sorts; and in the final analysis, agriculture is also a game of chance. You make your plans as you do with card games; you have to know how to change strategies any second, depending on the circumstances, and chance also plays its role. Thunderstorms, hail, frost, drought, disease, locusts.

---

[57] Referring to a group of originally nomadic Turkic peoples, the Tatars, enemies of the Cossacks.

When I come home for tea, fill my pipe, it occurs to me that the horse needs new horseshoes nailed on, or that I need to check in the fruit orchard to see which is stronger: the orchardkeeper or my brandy. I take my cap, leave again, and it doesn't even occur to me anymore that my wife is there tending the children.

We've already talked about it: this is a marriage just like all the others. Even Father Maziek came to visit with great anointing! His face, his hair just glistened; and even on his coat collar. The anointing even extended to his boots and elbows. He glistened like a cherub, lifted up his yellow cane above me like a shepherd's staff and his voice even a little higher. But, Father, what if we don't love each other anymore, my wife and I? – Aha! Purgatory! That's it for sure! – and laughed until his reverend belly and his anointed cheeks were jiggling. Aha! Purgatory! That is Christian marriage for sure.

But Father, Herr Benefactor, should we be living like that? It just isn't working.

Aha! Purgatory! Of course it isn't working. Why else would you need the church around? Do you, honorable wayward friend, know what Christianity is?

In any case, if you take carnal delight in a woman without loving her – what will people say? – the lecher! – In a Christian marriage, it's taken for granted.

In any case, if you pay a woman like that or give her something, a scarf or something else, everyone will spit at her. The prostitute there is selling herself. – In a Christian marriage, my wayward friend, it's taken for granted.

And of what does the righteous female Christian marriage partner speak? Of the lusts of the flesh, do you imagine? Purgatory! She speaks of the gift her groom will give her on the morning after the wedding night and of how her righteous Christian marriage partner clothes and feeds her. Am I right?

Love? – Here's what it comes down to: look after your wife, feed your children. *Basta!*[58] That's what a Christian marriage is. Purgatory! That's my opinion.

---

[58] Italian: "enough," "that's all."

Do you marry for love, I ask you, or for the blessing of the priest? Well? If you were to marry for love, you wouldn't even need the blessing of the priest. *Ergo!*[59] That's what I think. – Thus spake the priest.

It gets lonelier and lonelier for me at home, I feel driven out. Now I stay at the field during harvest, sit down below the sheaves stacked against each other, as in a tent, and listen to the people as they sing. I go into the forest when wood is being cut and shoot a little squirrel. No marketplace in the whole district that I wouldn't visit. I often even ride to L'vov, especially during the time of grain contracts. Stay away from home for weeks.

It's finally clear that we – you know – in short, that we are in precisely such a Christian marriage. My neighbor, though, just can't see that. He thinks you should be able to let your heart burn a little each day, just as he does his hair; he sits a full half day with my wife, particularly when I'm not home. Whenever I go to the annual fair or just on a hunt – he's there right away.

Isn't my friend – he was accustomed to calling me that, so let's stick with it – isn't my friend home? – No! – Oh, I'm very sorry. – Now take note – the weasel – and he sits down and reads Pushkin aloud. In conversation then: But he's really never at home. Hmmm! – Never! – Just shakes his head, and my wife, oh God, you know how it is – she laments at the woes he introduces; such allusions, and he keeps shaking his head and sucking air through his nose sympathetically. Speaks in general about men so instructively and entertainingly, you know, but won't go so far as to spit with true contempt while doing so, but just coughs a bit into his hanky.

In front of me, don't you know, he makes a big scene that I'm neglecting my wife, and what a wife! A beautiful wife, a wife that has such spirit, pure spirit, and an intelligent woman who reads Pushkin like a prayer book.

That's easy for you to say. You see her at the *samovar*, friend, in her squirrel fur and lively as a baby squirrel, while I – ah, well! Let's leave it at that.

So she lets him read all of her books, gets strange ideas from them, and sighs whenever my name comes up.

And what's actually going on? What have we done to each other? – We don't understand each other, she says word-for-word from a German book, you know, word-for-word, I tell you; that's where these ideas come from.

---

[59] Latin: "therefore."

One night I come home from legal matters in Dobromil,[60] you know. My wife is sitting on the divan, one foot up and holding her leg with her hands, lost in thought. My friend had been there, too. – My wife has on her squirrel fur, and then – I smell him. For a moment I have an impulse to get angry, but I let it go. My wife looks so delightful that I kiss her hands and stroke the fur on her jacket. All at once she looks at me, such a look – so alien; all I can do is stand there gaping.

It can't go on like this, she said very suddenly. Her voice was totally hoarse. Then she forced herself to speak up. – What's the matter with you, anyway? – The only time I see you anymore is late at night, she yells; even a mistress needs to be courted, and – I – I – I want some love! – Love? So I don't love you? – No! – Gets on her horse and races off.

I look for her all night, all the next day.

When I get back that evening, her bed has been moved into the children's room, and I have to sleep alone.

I should have put my foot down; that much is true – but – I was too proud for that, since I thought everything would take care of itself – but these wives of ours! You know, there was a government official in the district offices, a German. His wife allowed some riding teacher to write love letters to her. What do you have here, my love? Takes the letter out of her hand, reads it, and starts beating his wife right away. Keeps on beating her, what can I tell you? – Beats her long enough for her to start loving him again. Now that was a happy marriage.

But me! – I was a slave. If only I'd put my foot down right away. But now it's all water under the bridge.

From then on we just said: Good morning and: Good night. That was it. Good night. Those were some nights. I should have been canonized every day.

Then I began to go on hunts again.

I was in the forest for days at a time.

There was a gamekeeper at that time whose name was Irena Volk, a strange person. He loved every living thing. He would tremble so much whenever he came across an animal, but he would kill every one nevertheless.

Then he would hold it in his hands, look at it and say in such a sad voice: Now he's well! Now he's well!

---

[60] Located west of L'vov near the present Polish border.

He considered life to be some sort of misfortune. I don't know, a strange person. But I'll tell you more about him another time. – I would put a piece of bread and cheese in my *torba*,[61] fill my hunting flask with brandy and be off.

Then we'd set up camp at the edge of the forest. Irena would go out into the fields, dig up potatoes, make a fire and roast them in the coals. You eat whatever you can find.

When you're roaming through the quiet, dark forest at the higher elevations; coming face to face with the wolf, the bear; seeing the eagle sit on its nest; breathing in the moist, heavy, cool forest air on which some acrid aroma is floating; using a felled tree as a dinner table; sleeping in a mountain cave; bathing in the blackness of a lake that has no bottom, no waves, and whose smooth, coal-black surface swallows up the rays of the sun as easily as it does the light of the moon – at that point you don't have feelings anymore; your feelings become cravings – you eat when you're hungry and make love when the impulse comes.

The sun goes down. Irena is out searching for mushrooms.

A peasant woman is sitting on the ground.

The faded blue skirt isn't long enough to cover her small, dusty feet; the filthy blouse is falling halfway down her shoulders.

Around her is the aroma of thyme; she's propping her head up with both hands, her elbows resting on her knees, and she's staring in front of her. A firefly has landed in her dark hair, which is flowing uncombed from a red head scarf down her back.

From the side, her face is almost a dark silhouette against the red evening sky, sharp, as if cut from a pattern. Her nose is animated, graceful, like the beak of a bird of prey; and when I call to her, she lets out a shriek like an Alpine vulture, her eyes darting up at me, the gaze floating for an instant like flames of naphtha[62] across her eyes.

Her shriek echoes onward – the steep rock wall returns it, the dense forest once again, once again the distant mountains. –

I am almost terrified of the woman.

She bends down and plucks thyme and tugs the red head scarf down over her crimson-flooded face.

---

[61] Polish and Ukrainian: "hunting pouch."

[62] A liquid petroleum, natural gas, or coal tar mixture used as a fuel.

What's wrong? I ask.

She doesn't answer, but pours out melancholic chanting tones into the air like tears.

What's the matter with you? I say. Do you have some pain, some sadness? – She's silent. – Well, what's your story? She looks me in the face, laughs and lets long lashes fall across her eyes like dark veils.

Well, what do you want? – A sheepskin, she says quietly. – I laugh. Wait, I'll bring you one from the fair. She hides her face. – But that would have a bad smell. So how about a tanned sheepskin! You know what, I'd rather give you a *sukmana*;[63] what do you think, trimmed with rabbit, with black – or with white, milk-white rabbit fur.

She looked at me, astonished but not quite serious, pursed her brows, and her lips quivered and danced around her large, white teeth. Then the movement flowed slowly from the corners of her mouth across her cheeks, and a roguish laughter suddenly contorted her whole face.

Well, what are you laughing at?

Nothing.

So tell me, you do want the *sukmana* – don't you? – How would that be with rabbit, with milk-white rabbit fur?

Suddenly she stand ups, straightens her skirt. No! she says. If you want to give me one, then it needs to be silver fur.

Silver fur, what do you mean?

I mean the kind that the rich ladies wear.

I looked at her.

Selfishness lay on her face, as sunny as innocence. It kissed her soul and her desires as unthinkingly as it kisses an icon of the saints – it was totally without principles or ideas! Or anything else! She had the morals of a hawk and obeyed the law of the forest. She had no more Christianity in her than does a young kitten that might happen to scratch its claw across your nose.

I really did bring her the *sukmana* from L'vov, and, you'll laugh at me now – I fell in love with the woman.

That was such a love story; you won't find its equal anywhere.

When she heard the first shot from my gun – she was there.

Now I combed her hair with my fingers and washed her feet in the forest brook, but she splashed water in my face.

---

[63] Polish, Ukrainian: a long, wide-bottomed peasant coat made of cloth.

Her teasing had some cruelty to it. She tortured me with her deepest humility in a way the arrogance of a lady never could.

But have mercy on me. Sir! Noble Sir! What can I do with you? And it got to the point where she could do with me whatever she wanted.

We were both quiet for some time.

The peasants, the choir singer had left the inn. The Jew had tied on his phylacteries[64] and fallen asleep. He was singing quietly through his nose in his dreams while keeping time by nodding his head.

His wife was sitting at the bar. Her head had slipped down inside her hands; she had put her two pinkies between her teeth; her sleepy eyes were half closed, but her eyes were still riveted on the stranger.

The latter put his pipe away, took a deep breath.

Shall I tell you about how things were with my wife? – You'll forgive me if I do. My wife was in poor health for some time. I stayed around the house, reading. One time she went through the room and quietly said: Good night. I stood up, but she was already gone again – her door was shut and locked. That was the end of it.

About that time I had a legal case against the administrators of the Ossnovian estate.[65] Before I team up the court and take a lawyer as my coachman, thought I, perhaps I should team up my horses and ride over there myself. Whom do I find? A divorced woman living solely on her estate because the big, wide world disgusts her, a modern female philosopher.

She called herself Satana and was a most delightful little devil. She just about jumped at every word I said and had eyes that seemed cut from a jack o'lantern with candles flickering inside.

I lost the case, of course, but in return I won her heart, her kisses.

I still loved my wife.

My wife, meanwhile, was burning up with love and hate for me. Her heart was like one of those flowers that only blossom in the dark; now it bubbled over with wild tenderness. She was inventive in the ways she revealed that she wanted to hide her emotions from me. One day she laid in front

---

[64] Prayer straps (Hebrew: *tefillin*) with leather containers that hold written excerpts from the Torah. Orthodox Jewish males tie these to the left arm (across from the heart) and to the forehead as a symbolic reminder to serve God with mind, heart and hand.

[65] Ossnovian was apparently the name of the estate owner.

of me a letter that the Cossack of my lover had brought, and burst out laughing – but her laughter broke off right in the middle, so it was almost ugly.

From an overabundance of love I turned away from her, and she sighed for revenge at her passionate, unrequited love.

When she left the house, it was always in haste. She would scream in the middle of her dreams at night; she would beat the servants, the children.

All at once she changed.

She seemed accepting, at peace. Her eyes rested on me, so curiously satisfied, and yet there was a wince of pain in her proud laughter.

My gamekeeper came.

The manor lord doesn't go into the forest anymore. I know of a fox on the other side of the moss gully and there are also some big, fat snipe – which I really enjoyed hunting – and her – she's waiting at the rock. Show some mercy to the poor woman.

I take my gun and go with him as far as the last fence in town.

At that point some nameless fear comes over me; I leave my gamekeeper and run nearly all the way home.

I'm almost ashamed – walk quietly on my tiptoes – then I hear –

He wiped the hair off his forehead several times.

How can I tell this! – I tear open the door, and my wife is lying there – Perhaps I'm interrupting, I say and close the door again.

What should I do?

That's the way things are here in Galicia. The German treats his wife like an inferior, of course, but we deal with her on an equal footing, like one monarch with another.

We don't think: I can do what I want; my wife has to put up with it. Here the husband doesn't have any special privileges; we have just one standard for husband and wife.

If you sweet-talk every barmaid, then you have to tolerate your wife being whispered sweet nothings by all the men.

If you're lying in the arms of some other woman, then hold your tongue if your wife is in the embrace of another man.

So, then, did I have a right?

No, I had no right.

So I stepped back and paced to and fro in front of my wife's door.

I actually didn't feel anything at all; it was all motionless, quiet, totally quiet.

I kept saying to myself: Haven't I done the same thing? I have no right; I have no right.

Now he comes out.

I say: My friend, I didn't want to disturb you, but don't you know that this is my house? He was shaking; even his voice was shaking. Do with me as you please, he said.

What should I do with you? – But do you have some concept of honor? – I suppose we'll have to exchange a few bullets. I lit the way down the stairs for him. Then I rode over to Leon Bodshkan; I asked him to be my second.

He smiled dimly. This is actually stupidity, he said, but by tomorrow morning everything should be all right – do me the kindness of reading these pieces of paper tonight. With that he gave me these papers. You see, and I've been carrying them around with me ever since. What a peculiar person he was!

And so I read them.

Why, really?

I challenged my wife's lover to a duel, but actually it had no meaning.

I was wrong; I knew it, but the sense of honor – well, you know. Still, it all had no meaning.

I knew he wouldn't hit me. At fifteen paces he couldn't tell a haystack from a sparrow – and me – well, I shoot quite well.

I could take my revenge. I could kill him; nobody would have said a word – but I had no right and shot right past him. Because I was just as guilty, as I've said, as he or my wife was.

At the time I thought about a separation from my wife. But what about the children?! That's it. That's what welds us together in pairs for eternity and drives us into the storm winds, just like the damned in Dante's *Inferno*.[66]

So then we stayed together.

He never came to my house again, but they did see each other at one of her lady friends' houses; there are such good souls in the world, and I went back to shooting my snipe again.

I now began to view women as a type of wild game, the hunt for which is more difficult but is also more rewarding.

---

[66] Perhaps the most famous poetic depiction of hell, as created in the *Divine Comedy* by the greatest of all Italian authors, Dante Alighieri (1265-1321).

Do you know how to shoot snipe? – You don't? – First of all you need to know how the snipe flies.

It flies up, makes three stunt maneuvers to confuse you: Zig to the left! Zag to the right! Then straight ahead.

That's the moment. If I wait for it, the snipe is mine.

Similar thing with women.

If you press the trigger right away – it's all over. But once you get into the right rhythm, you can get any of them.

At home, everything was peaceful.

The children were already running around the place, and just think – now I loved them. I loved them because my wife loved them.

Often I thought, our love has come alive and is running around and playing and laughing – and this brought out strange feelings in me.

But then it came over me again like evil. I demanded that the children love me more than their mother, that I was the only one they should love.

I took them to the fireplace, let them ride on my knee, told them fairy tales, sang songs to them that the common folk sing, told them stories like a hunter would tell them. And that was truly odd. You see, I had gotten – certainly – you know – I had gotten one more child; it was the child of another man. A girl; you wouldn't believe how much she looked like my wife, the perfect likeness.

They usually say that a girl looks like her father and sons look like their mother. But that's not my experience. The one son looks like his grandfather; the other one I don't know where to place him; maybe my wife got him from some novel. Neither of my sons has any of their mother in them, but the – other child, the girl, certainly does.

Could it be because she was only thinking of herself and her revenge at the time?

Anyway, this child is the one that's devoted to me with such love, even though she knew I detested her at first.

When I told stories, she quietly asked for permission to listen and sat down on a little stool off in the dark corner, listening with her eyes sparkling.

I often yelled at her until she shook. When I left the house, she stood in the distance and watched me go. When I returned, she would run out to meet me and then seem terrified of herself. One time her older brother said: The bear will probably kill father. – At that, she leaped up with her eyes full of big tears.

It seemed to me as if this were my wife, the one who felt so anxiously drawn to me, who begged my forgiveness and cried for me.

Once I said to the child: Come on over here. Then she turned crimson red and ran away.

Slowly we became best friends.

Neither of my boys was like me.

Would you like to go fox hunting? Sure, says the boy, if only the gun wouldn't make such a loud bang.

When I told my story about the bear: Well now, he came towards me. What do you think I did? The boy says: you ran away. But the girl just laughs.

Often she took a wolfskin and scared the two of them until they hid under their mother's skirts. Don't you recognize your own sister? – Mother, they said, she must really be a wolf; the way her eyes glitter makes her look like one, and she howls like she enjoys it.

When I was away from home, the child would wander restlessly all around the house. If only father doesn't get killed. – How could he get killed? – Oh, I know about the Wallachians,[67] the dark people; they're like wild animals. Or if the bear –

Father will shoot him right in his white chest spot, my son says very knowledgeably. – What if he doesn't hit it! – Oh, he'll hit it all right.

When the girl gets bigger, she throws herself on the ground in a tantrum and rolls around and cries.

So finally I took her along.

I had the small rifle – my wife had shot with it – I bought her a hunting pouch, took her along.

The girl had courage, let me tell you, courage like a man. No, not like any man! How should I explain it to you?

As we were making our way through the undergrowth, I say: Well, now, what if things go wrong? – She just laughed. – I'm here with you. She was only afraid for me.

At home she was feverish with fear, but face to face with the wolf, she was composed, as if facing a hen, I tell you. And how we understood each other. I almost didn't need to say a thing. She understood the look in my eye, every feature, every movement.

And yet we liked to talk so much.

---

[67] The ethnic group that settled between the southern Carpathians and the Danube River in Romania.

When the wild game lay there, Irena kneeling beside it, cleaning it, we sat together, and for us the world was a picture book I was showing my child – and yet she wasn't really my child! But yet she really was my child, and I loved her.

My wife also loved the child passionately, all the more passionately as the girl became more and more devoted to me.

When I took the child along, she would kneel down, kiss her, and say softly: Stay with me. But the girl shook her head. I laughed, and far from home, in the deep forest, I still remembered and was glad that the child was with me while her mother was almost perishing from fear back home.

If my wife gave the girl something to sew, she just pretended to work on it for a while, suddenly put the handwork away and ran off – to clean my gun.

Or my wife told her something. The child looked at me and wouldn't move.

Once my wife screams out: He's not your father. Then you're not my mother, the child says calmly. She turns pale, holds her tongue from then on, and just cries from time to time. Such nonsense! Who's going to go around shedding tears? The world is so funny!

He plunged the last glass of Tokay down his gullet.

Funny! – Who is it that says – who – who – who is it – he rubbed his forehead – oh yes, it's Karamzin,[68] the great Karamzin – he's actually a Great Russian[69] – but that doesn't matter – the great Karamzin! – How is it he puts it again? Don't you know?

He rooted at his hair, as if trying to dig something from out of his head. Right! Right!

> All the wisdom of my lifetime
> Has for me one truth amassed:
> Love is mortal! Vain and empty
> Is the hope that love will last.
> Changing with the latest fashions,
> People laugh if you are true;

---

[68] Nikolai Mikhailovich Karamzin (1766-1826), a writer who helped to refine the Russian literary language and who introduced themes of social protest.

[69] A member of the main ethnic group of Russia, a pun that compares Karamzin to the "Little Russians" (Ukrainians or Ruthenians; see page 222, footnote 3).

> If you change, then you discover
> Jealousy surrounding you.
> So avoid the trap of Hymen;[70]
> Let no thoughts of marriage brew!
> But be loving and deceptive,
> So deceit can't work on you!

That's how it is:

> Let no thoughts of marriage brew!
> But be loving and deceptive,
> So deceit can't work on you!

Now, at any rate, I could tell you about my adventures.

Adventures, adventures, I tell you. Adventures like – where shall I begin?

Right now, for example, I'm having an affair with a young woman. Oh, is she in love, and how! A lady, a true lady.

But my head hurts a bit. –

I have another lover now. She's the wife of a burglar. Her husband was hanged, and as for herself – what do I know? What do I care? – She can't even read. We don't talk much, either, but make love – like wolves.

And how is your relationship with your wife now? I asked, after he had been quiet for a long while.

Well – we're civil to each other, he answered. Sometimes, when I – when I think – of that time – then – then – I get a headache – headache. – But now we're jolly, jolly, jolly!

He threw the wine bottle against the wall, terrifying the Jew out of his sleep and making him tear the phylactery off over his nose.

So, now I'm doing fine, he said, unbuttoning his coat, fine, jolly!

Such is life. When we're like this – then we're doing fine. Jolly, jolly!

He stood in the middle of the inn, his arms bent at a rakish angle, and began to dance the Cossack while singing the innocently-wild, bacchantic-melancholy melodies himself.

First he was squatting on the floor, throwing his feet around like they were something superfluous, then he was leaping up to the ceiling and turning around in the air.

---

[70] In Greek mythology, the god of marriage.

Next he was standing still, crossing his arms across his chest and swaying his head around so sadly. Then he grabbed it with his hand as if to tear it off and gave a screech of joy, the same way an eagle rejoices as it flies into the sun.

I stood and watched him; and the more I observed the more I understood the conflict within this friendly personality who could easily handle the wolf and the bear, but for whom the enigmas of human nature, that eternal sphinx with the intelligent head and the animal's body, remained unresolved.

Suddenly the door was thrown open, and an old, dignified peasant in a brown *zierak*,[71] with long white hair, mustache and clever eyes stepped into the room.

It was Simion Ostrov, the judge.

A melancholy smile glided across his pale face when he spotted us.

Gentlemen! How long have you been here? he said good-naturedly. For a long time, no doubt. Well, I can't help it.

So we can leave? asked the boyar.

Certainly, said Simion, the judge.

Of course, it's really too late now, the other man continued, I mean for myself – but perhaps not for you. God be with you; stay healthy.

Jokingly he stroked the Jew's wife on her chin; the red blood flooded into her face.

He started to leave and turned around one last time. He shook my hand.

Oh, well! he exclaimed. Water gets back together with water, and people with people.

I stood on the threshold as he drove off.

He waved one last time. Then he was gone.

I turned to the Jew.

Oh, he's a funny person, the latter whined, a dangerous person; they call him *Don Juan of Kolomyya*.

---

[71] Polish: An overcoat made of coarse cloth.

Karl Emil Franzos (1848-1904) was born in the town of Chortkov[1] in the province of Galicia[2] during the revolutionary year of 1848. The son of an assimilated, liberal-minded Jewish doctor, he grew up in the city of Chernovtsy[3] in the district of Podolia.[4] He left home at a relatively young age to study law in Vienna and Graz; finding no employment in the legal realm, he turned to journalism and to writing.

One of the main themes in his writing is the proposed betterment of a downtrodden eastern European culture – including the "decadence" of landed nobility and the "superstitions" of his own fellow Jews – by the spread of German culture and customs. Related to that is another common theme, assimilation and understanding between the Jewish and the Germanic peoples, a goal which he despaired of in his later years.

Franzos's background in both secular and Jewish ecclesiastical legal issues assisted him in writing **The Higher Law**. The collection in which this story first appeared, *The Jews of Barnow*, was based on ghetto life in his native Chortkov and was dedicated to Ludwig Kompert, who had been a particularly strong influence on him. In the foreword, he discussed his literary considerations:

"... I wanted to write novellas and struggled to give them poetic value. But precisely for this purpose it seemed necessary that I focus on a life-style intimately familiar to me. Such was the case with the Jews of Podolia, and this offered me the unique added charm of some subject matter that no one else had fictionalized before me.

"So it was above all as a writer that I went into the Podolian ghetto, and the main thing I strove for in these novellas was an artistic sense. But I didn't try to force it at the cost of truth. Nowhere in the service of beauty have I falsified facts or circumstances, and I believe I've depicted this adventurous and exotic way of life in all its details precisely as it appeared to me.

---

[1] Now in Western Ukraine, Chortkov is situated approximately 60 miles north of Chernovtsy (or Czernowitz, as described in footnote 3 below).

[2] This former Austro-Hungarian province extends over a vast area that now comprises parts of southern Poland, eastern Slovakia and western Ukraine. See also footnote 2 on page 222.

[3] A town in western Ukraine roughly 100 miles south-southeast of L'vov and just a few miles from Kolomyya, the backdrop for Sacher-Masoch's novella.

[4] The author's native district in Galicia, surrounding the city of Chernovtsy, in which the town of Chortkov is also situated.

If the anthropologist was supported by the novella author in my first published book[5], then here the novella writer could not have gotten by without the aid of the anthropologist...."[6]

Franzos goes on to say that if his audience – which consists of "the reader of the Western World" – will "trust [his] love of truth and read the stories as a whole ... [the reader is] assured at least of an orientation into that way of life."[7]

The author coined a controversial phrase that was to be used and misused from then on: "Every country has the Jews that it deserves."[8] But he went on to explain what he meant by that: "... it's not the fault of the Polish Jews that they're on a different cultural level than their fellow believers in England, Germany and France. At least certainly not their fault alone ... I'm not depicting the Polish Jews any better or any worse than they are, but exactly as they are. These novellas are not written to mock the Jews of the East any more than they are to glorify them...."[9]

Focusing more finely than upon images of an entire race of people, though, *The Higher Law* makes individuals and individual archetypes come to life in a tale where the main characters are forced to seek happiness and even peace of mind by making their own rules and exploring justification by a "higher law." The narrative tone ranges from outer comic humor to inner tragedy. In the person of Nathan Silberstein we meet a personality with traits of selfless devotion and an almost Messianic feel for atonement. Carrying tolerance to a fault, he seems a somewhat distorted version of the great literary model of Jewish tolerance, another Nathan, Lessing's *Nathan the Wise*.[10]

---

[5] *Aus Halb-Asien : Culturbilder....* [*Quasi-Asia: Cultural Vignettes of Eastern Europe*]. (Leipzig : Duncker & Humblot, 1876).

[6] Karl Emil Franzos, *Die Juden von Barnow* [*The Jews of Barnow*] (Stuttgart & Leipzig: Eduard Hallberger), 1877, pp. vii-viii. The translations are mine.

[7] *The Jews of Barnow*, pp. viii-ix.

[8] *The Jews of Barnow*, p. ix: *"Jedes Land hat die Juden, die es verdient."*

[9] *The Jews of Barnow*, pp. ix-x.

[10] *Nathan der Weise*, the master drama of the German playwright Gotthold Ephraim Lessing (1729-1781).

The Higher Law

Karl Emil Franzos

In the swampy lowlands along the river, surrounding the weather-beaten old synagogue, is – as you already know – the Jewish quarter. For as long back as anyone can remember, only one of these people has dared to build his house right in the middle of the Christians. That was Moses Freudenthal, the richest man in the congregation: his large, white, single-story house lies right on the main road into town and looks defiantly across at the monastery of the Dominicans[11] across the way. But there was no lucky star over this man and over this house. You are well aware of that, and of how lovely Esther's life ended.[12] Now Moses has been dead for a long time, too, and the house belongs to the miracle rabbi of Sadagóra[13] to whom he bequeathed it, just as a pious Christian would bequeath his worldly goods to the monastery.

The rabbi spends very little on the house's upkeep, even though all it ever cost him were a few spoken blessings. But it still looks very stately all the same, almost the same as during Moses's lifetime. Over the front door hangs an oval-shaped metallic sign on which is painted a black eagle

---

[11] A Roman Catholic mendicant religious order founded in Spain by Saint Dominic (1170-1221).

[12] The tragic fate of Esther, daughter of Moses Freudenthal, was depicted in *The Shylock of Barnow*, another tale – also written in the year 1873 – from the same collection, *The Jews of Barnow*.

[13] "Miracle rabbis" were those leaders and scholars of the Jewish faith who believed in miraculous manifestations of God's mercy. "Sadagóra" is a fictitious name which means, in Ukrainian, "Orchard Hill."

against a yellow background, and encircling it is the inscription "Royal and Imperial District Court." For Ruthenian[14] thieves, Polish confidence men, and Jewish usurers are now interrogated at the very place that Moses Freudenthal and his daughter once lived. That's on the ground floor on the right side; on the left side, though, you'll still find the store that Moses ran; only now the sign has a different name on it: "Nathan Silberstein's Grocery Gooods and wine Shop." The "w" in "wine" is left uncapitalized and there's one "o" too many in "Goods," but that's just the fault of Janko, who painted the sign.

Under the new owner almost nothing has changed on the second floor; there, as in Moses's day, the district physician and the district judge live in rented apartments. The only change is that the district judge is now a different one, no longer the jaundiced, skinny Herr Hippolyte Lozinsky, but rather someone who's not like him in any way. The eternal targets of Herr Lozinsky's wrath were the Jews – rich and poor alike – not their hearts, but their wallets. And whatever he could extort from the rich Jews he would feed to the poor Christians: the noblemen, the bureaucrats, the lieutenants. His wife Casimira, from the high-born noble house "von Cybulsky," which directly translates as "from onion," outshone all other women five miles around by three splendid qualities of heart: by the highest debts, the most glittering outfits, and the wildest dance fever. And her horniness piled up on the head of her cuckolded husband so high that people wondered how he could still pull his top hat down over his jaundiced, skinny head.

But now all that has changed.

Herr von Negrusz doesn't extort anything from the Jews and doesn't squander any gratuities on the Christians. He just lives for his job and his family, two darling little boys and his lovely young wife. This woman is beautiful, very beautiful. Her figure slender and yet buxom; supple and yet proud as royalty; her countenance pale, noble, sharply etched; her eyes dark and wistful and deep, as deep as the ocean. But the most remarkable thing about all this beauty is the color of her skin – a faint and gentle yellowish white – you could call it amber-white – on which the pink of health lies like a soft breath. Her figure, her look, her countenance – they are all

---

[14] A Slavic group (see p. 222, footnote 3) that was concentrated in and around eastern Slovakia and western Ukraine.

reminiscent of Sulamith and Suleika,[15] of the sweet magic of Oriental beauty. But the wife of the district judge wears a crucifix around her neck and on her calling card is the name: "Christina von Negrusz."

It's actually quite puzzling and strange, but this woman is able to interact with the rest of the people around here with just these cards alone. She doesn't receive any visits, she doesn't make any . . . a barrier between her and the honorable upper crust of Barnow has been set up that neither party oversteps.

If a married official is transferred to Barnow, then he is painstakingly instructed by his colleagues: he borrows the old coach from old Herr von Volansky and drives up in front of the large white house with his better half at his side. Then he sends both calling cards up to the second floor and receives the reply: regrettably the Herr District Judge is indisposed and his gracious wife is not feeling well. And one week later Herr von Negrusz comes driving up with his wife in front of the residence of the new colleague in the very same coach, and then the same comedy is played out with the roles reversed, and with that all further contact is broken off. Such is the custom that has finally become law.

And then one thing more. Frau Christina never goes out alone; she only leaves the house a few times a week at the side of her spouse. All the rest of the people in the little town promenade in the new aristocrat's park, the park surrounding the castle of Countess Jadviga Bortynska, who, people say, broke the bank in Monaco a short while back. But the district judge and his wife regularly go walking in the lonely, badly maintained grounds which surround the old castle on the other side of the river. The direct path there leads through the Jewish quarter. But this socially shy couple avoids it. They go all the way around town in a semicircle. You could get the impression that they do that to avoid the dust and smells of the Jewish street. But no! – Once, when a storm surprised them, they made the long detour back in the pouring rain just the same.

Why? Herr von Negrusz looks everyone straight in the eye and doesn't avoid meeting a soul when he's alone. What type of spell is it, then, that keeps his beautiful wife separate from the rest of humanity?

You need only ask the news announcer of Barnow and surrounding territory, the pretty and voluptuous Frau Emilia, the wife of the new actuary. He's been in town for ten years, but he's still called the "new" actuary in

---

[15] Legendary heroines from apocryphal Hebrew lore.

contrast to his colleague, who's already been in Barnow for twenty years. Well, Frau Emilia will show you a calling card and then add this commentary: "I ask you; how can you associate with a woman like that? Just look at the card itself... Why didn't she have her family origins printed on it? – Because it would look pretty bad for her: 'Christina von Negrusz, née Bilkes, divorced Silberstein.' Her actual given name is Hannah, you see, and Nathan Bilkes who lives in the tiny shack by the synagogue is her father, and another Nathan, Nathan Silberstein, was her first husband. You know, this Negrusz person is someone who pushes things to the extreme. First he wanted to marry the daughter of a millionaire, an Armenian baron, and when they wouldn't put up with that, of course, he suddenly got very modest and fell in love with that reasonably attractively Jewish woman and bought her from her husband...."

"Bought her?" you'll ask astonished. "For money... for cash money?"

"Naturally . . . for what else?" the announcer will assure you. "And that surprises you? Seriously? I tell you... for a Jew like that, everything's for sale, even his own wife. They even tell how much it cost Negrusz: one thousand guilders. And by the way, if you don't want to believe me, then ask anybody in town, or better yet, go ask Silberstein himself ... He's a wine merchant, and even if he travels around the rest of the year, he always here during the high holidays. He'll confirm it for you: 'I let the district judge have her without an argument.' – So ... then I ask you: can you associate with a woman like that?"

Voluptuous Emilia is right... she's right about everything. Frau Christina did earlier have the name Hannah, first Hannah Bilkes, then Hannah Silberstein. And the wine merchant did truly let the district judge have her without an argument. And she's also right that it's impossible for her – Emilia – to associate with a woman like that. But with respect to the purchase price, she's very wrong indeed.

The price of purchase was not a one-thousand note, but rather a human heart . . . .

*

The old synagogue is a gray, weathered building that was built in far-off ages, probably during the Middle Ages. The peasants call it the "Jewish Castle," because once the Jews hid and barricaded themselves in it when a certain Prince Czartorysky wanted to rob and murder them. He wanted to do this for two reasons: in the first place, it was hunting season right then, but there weren't many fox or wild boar out in the meadows; and in the second place, he needed money. But the Jews sheltered their goods and their blood behind the walls and iron doorbolts of the synagogue and held out long enough to be liberated when the vassals of the Jagellonian[16] king rushed to their defense from the nearby Fortress Jagiellnica. At that time the walls were strong and the iron bolts were solid; now there's nothing more to be seen of the bolts and the walls have half crumbled, half sunk into the ground. As if to indicate the former significance of this house of God and of refuge, though, the pitiful houses and huts of the Jewish quarter squeeze up intimately close to it on three sides.

On the fourth side, the nearby river, the sluggishly creeping River Seret, has only left room for two houses, a large new house which is painted with yellow oil-based paint – a rarity in this region – and a dirty, ramshackle hut that clings dismally to the riverbank. It's almost as if the yellow house were forcing its shabby neighbor over into the river, so precariously do the musty walls of the hut tilt towards the dark, slow waters. In the yellow house lived the rich wine merchant Manasseh Silberstein at one time with his son Nathan, and in the little shack lived Nathan Bilkes, who still lives there today, a poor man – a very poor man.

Nathan was a "village walker" for as long as his strength held out, and now, a weak and lonely old man, he lives from his hard-earned pennies and, when those aren't sufficient, from the support of the congregation. He became weak and old at an early age – like everyone in his trade, for it is an exceedingly hard, exceedingly strenuous trade.

A "village walker," in the language of his fellow believers, is the man who supplies the peasants in the surrounding villages with their needs, earning his daily bread in the process. Early in the morning on Sundays he leaves town, his back stooped over with a gigantic pack of wares. Inside is contained everything that a Ruthenian peasant's heart could long for, except for the one thing such a heart longs for the most: the "village walker" doesn't sell schnapps. But other than that, he truly sells everything: straw hats, leather belts, boots, pocket knives for the boys, flowers, bows, pieces of coral, love potions, dress material, spindles for the girls, canvas, suet, dishes, icons

---

[16] Members of a Polish dynasty that ruled from the 14th to the 16th centuries.

of the saints, magic paraphernalia, wax candles, needle and thread for the house, prayer books, old pants and caftans, new *teffilim*[17] and *mezuzahs*[18] for his fellow believers living off by themselves, snuff tobacco, calendars, newspapers of the past week, fine materials and embroideries for the clerical and noble courts, liqueurs, playing cards, smuggled cigars and other items for the cavalry officers, in short, everything... everything! So it is he moves from village to village and house to house all week long, year in, year out, again and again, despite cold of winter and heat of summer. He knows everyone and everyone knows him. If they need him, they permit him to darken their threshold; if they don't need a thing, they chase him off, and, if he's still persistent, they sic their dogs on him. The peasant and the nobleman, the cadet and the chaplain all test out their jokes on him or, if they're not intellectually minded right then, their whips and spurs. But he doesn't tire of raising his hoarse voice from early morning to late evening, of haggling and conniving wherever he can. If there's no cash in the house, then he's happy to be paid with furs, or with grain, or with chickens and ducks, or with eggs. On Friday afternoons, though, he would return to town and be a human being for one day, only to become a "village walker" again.

Nathan Bilkes was just such a village walker, and that describes his life: other than that, there's nothing much to say about him. His father had picked out a girl for him... she became his good, honest wife, bore him two children, and died young. The children, though, a boy and a girl, grew up splendidly in the dark and moldy hut – just like lovely flowers thrive at times in rubble and filth. But, as their father mourns: "they died from their beauty and strength." For him, the two are dead and buried. The son had to become a soldier because he was so ideally suited to it and because Nathan couldn't come up with the fifty guilders that the draft board demanded to make him exempt. Or at least their broker, Bear Blitzer, claimed it would take fifty guilders. But the fifty guilders just weren't there. – So the boy was sent off to the country of Italy; and then came the war, and after the

---

[17] Hebrew: "phylacteries"; prayer straps holding leather containers with written excerpts from the Torah. Orthodox Jewish males tie these to the left arm (across from the heart) and to the forehead as symbolic reminders to serve God with mind, heart, and hand.

[18] Containers attached to door frames as a sign of Jewish faith, containing the passages of Deuteronomy 6:4-9 and 11:13-21 and the word *Shaddai*, a name of the Almighty.

Battle of Magenta[19] his name was on the list of official "missing in action." But, oh vey! His old father missed him in a totally different manner. He waited and waited, but his son never came back. And his daughter is dead now, too. "My Hannah," he'll gladly tell you, "was an honest Jewish woman . . . but that Frau Christina up there, that goy,[20] I don't know her at all."

The village walker couldn't have foreseen that his child would cause him such bitter pain. His Hannah was as lovely as she was obedient, as demure as she was diligent. Not only her father loved her: she was well thought of by everyone.

People in general rejoiced for her when old Manasseh Silberstein sought her hand in marriage in behalf of his only son Nathan. That was a great and unexpected stroke of good fortune. For the class barriers are otherwise tightly drawn for these people; the rich only associate with the rich, the poor with the poor. That's also the most normal thing in the world for a people who have been granted the earning of money as their only trade and the possession of money as their only joy for century after century. The poor village walker could scarcely believe it at first . . . old Manasseh was rich indeed, so rich . . . he owned a large grocery store and ran a very lucrative wine business with Hungary and Moldavia. It was the finest testimony to the honor of the poor village walker's daughter when their neighbor's choice fell to her. For Nathan Silberstein was without blemish as well; he was an honest, sober, intelligent young man, healthy and handsome, who knew his way around in the Talmud[21] just as well as he did in business affairs. And because he didn't want to become a scholar, but rather a merchant, his father had hired a tutor to teach him proper German. Nathan had learned to read and write, and then he worked his way through *Correspondence Practice for Everyone* and *The Book of General Austrian Civil Statutes*. For the record – and in his father's eyes – these two books comprised his German library. In truth, though, hidden among the large and mighty Hebrew folios in his bookcase was one more little German booklet. On Saturday afternoons, when he went walking with the others in the Countess's park,

---

[19] A town about 20 miles west of Milan, the site of the Battle of Magenta in 1859 where the Italians, in their struggle for independence, won a decisive victory over the Austrians. The color of a purple-red dye was named in honor of this battle.

[20] Hebrew: "gentile."

[21] The book of Jewish law and tradition.

he tucked the booklet in his pocket, moved away from everyone else, and read it at a quiet and secret spot where the leaves were quietly fluttering around him. As he read, he felt something quietly fluttering inside him, too, something he never felt on weekdays. On the spine of the little booklet was printed in gold lettering: *Schiller's Poetry*.[22]

When his father told him that he had chosen a bride for him and who it was, then . . . then this something inside him didn't move at all. He said obediently: "As you wish, father!" and turned a bit paler than usual maybe for a moment. And, just as indifferently, the bride-to-be submitted to the will of her father, only she turned a bit redder in the process. And then the engagement was celebrated and, two months later, the marriage. In the meantime, Nathan made presents to his fiancée of lovely pearls and expensive jewelry, and the poor girl gave him a prayer shawl on which she had embroidered artfully with gold and silver threads. Also during this period they spoke with each other several times – about very trivial things – but didn't talk about themselves and their future together. Even about the past there was no cordial word to be found: though they'd grown up in the same neighborhood, they had no common memories.

With great pomp and expense, the marriage was celebrated . . . the wine flowed in streams . . . entire mountains of meat and baked goods were annihilated . . . the best musicians and the best entertainers amused the guests . . . then the young newlyweds moved into the large, stately household which Manasseh had set up for his son across from the Dominicans. They had a great deal of work; they had to take great pains with it all day long, and they lived quietly and at peace with one another. They were both good, honest souls, and since they had scarcely dreamed ahead about the days of their marriage or painted themselves a picture of heavenly joy, there wasn't a thing to disappoint them, either. Tradition bound them together, as did the work they had in common, the reciprocal respect and hence the reciprocal faithfulness. Thus everything went along on a quiet, time-honored track, and when Hannah bore her husband a child after a year had elapsed, he even felt that mysterious something moving inside him again that had been silent for so long. The child died after a few weeks, but the great sadness only brought the couple closer to each other. Then they had to bury good old Manasseh, and so the guidance of the entire, extensive business fell

---

[22] Friedrich Schiller (1759-1805), along with Goethe one of the two major authors of German Classicism.

on their shoulders alone. Nathan had to travel a lot now, but Hannah became the most loyal administrator of the large household. She learned to read and write German in order to help her husband in his business and, with touching prudence, looked after all his personal needs. He also held her in high esteem and dressed her charming body in the heaviest silk fabrics and the most massive gold jewelry from the shops of L'vov[23] and Chernovtsy.[24] They were satisfied with each other, probably even happy.

Probably even happy ... what was lacking for their happiness?! They didn't love each other. But what did they know about love? They knew – even before they got married – that it was a fashion among the Christians. Why should a Jewish child have to go along with Christian fashions?

They were happy ... and the house that was their marriage stood proudly and solidly, built upon a foundation of respect and labor and daily habit ... until the storms of passion came rushing in and shook the house to the ground as if it were a house of cards and took them under its merciless spell and expelled them into struggle and pain! ....

*

The town of Barnow is very small, a deserted, dreary little burg in a godforsaken corner of the earth, and the great stream of life and culture scarcely casts an atom of attention its way, but ... Barnow does have an exclusive "Clubhouse." Of course, it does look modest enough ... it's out in the back, behind Nathan's store, a small room with two tables and several chairs. It's what Nathan had furnished for his regular customers. Here the bureaucrats and other luminaries of Barnow drink their morning half-liter of wine while talking politics, and, when their wives permit it, they talk politics here in the evening as well while drinking their evening half-liter of wine. His Nobleness Florian von Bolvinsky, an estate owner without an estate, who doesn't have a wife, drinks his morning, mid-morning, noon, afternoon, evening and nighttime half-liter of wine here and only interrupts the regimen now and then to take a walk, declare his love to a cook, borrow

---

[23] A large city in western Ukraine (German: *Lemberg*), formerly a Polish possession; it was under Austrian administration at the time of this story.

[24] See footnote 3, p. 272.

money from a Jew, or carry out some other important business. The former district judge, Herr Hippolyte Lozinsky, was a regular guest here as well, and one accomplishment of this small room was that at least it made the nose in his jaundiced, skinny face turn red. But just as it was becoming a shining ruby through sustained efforts, the hearty man died... to the considerable joy of the district but to the inexpressible grief of his exceedingly numerous creditors. Frau Casimira retired to the lands of the 'von Cybulsky' family, a small, debt-ridden feudal estate near Ternopol,[25] and the new district judge, Herr Julko von Negrusz, moved into the second floor of the white house. He also took the place of the dearly departed in the "Clubhouse," though without using it as frequently or as substantially as the latter, of course.

Herr von Negrusz was a young man, approximately in his early thirties. He was regarded as an excellent jurist right from the beginning, and soon as a good person as well. A district judge in Podolia[26] is a demigod and can become the curse or the blessing of his district. Herr von Negrusz only used his power for good. As far as his external appearance is concerned, there's not really that much to tell: he was a slender man; and quiet, brown eyes were placed in a face that couldn't be called either handsome or ugly. The three somewhat greenish, exceedingly grown-up daughters of the Herr Tax Office Superintendent claimed he was a barbarian and totally unreceptive to feminine charms. In fact, he didn't enjoy the company of ladies very much.

So then Herr von Negrusz became a regular guest in the small wine locale, as mentioned. He would spend a half hour there each day, as a rule, and read the newspaper before he went up to his apartment for the noon meal, which his old housekeeper prepared for him. And since the access was so inconvenient and dirty through the courtyard, he, like most of the guests, would go through the store where the lovely wife of the merchant was always tending the business herself. But he contented himself with greeting her silently as he passed, and never spoke or joked with her like the other older gentlemen or young officers were accustomed to doing. He didn't do this for any special reason, but simply because superfluous laughing and joking were foreign to his nature. He may also have thought that the attentions the others expended towards her were bothersome enough for

---

[25] A town in West Ukraine, roughly 80 miles east of L'vov and 90 miles north of Chernovtsy.

[26] See footnote 4, p. 272.

the lady anyway. There he was wrong, though . . . Hannah was very even-tempered in that regard and accepted all of it just as she did the other unpleasantries associated with being in the shop, as, for example, the drafty air when the door was opened. This woman had a remarkably assured manner of keeping every advance, even if only in words, away from her. Usually she made good-natured replies to the older gentlemen when they talked to her, but the officers only received very meager and often quite strange retorts. She could turn scornful and jovial to the point of exuberance when they talked to her of love. This feeling was not only puzzling to her, because she didn't know it ... it had gradually gotten extremely odd and contemptible. So whoever told her between the first and second half-liter, "I love you!" was just laughed at publicly and despised in secret; but whoever tried to grab her around the hips at the same time . . . just ask the little lieutenant Albert Sturm – that revolting, importunate, malicious creature – why his right cheek was redder and more swollen than his left one for a full week once . . . .

She needed no defense either in word or in deed with regard to the district judge. The two of them didn't even speak one word with each other for the first three months. And since this was something conspicuous in such a small town where everyone associates with everyone else, and twice as conspicuous since they were also residents in the same building, Hannah spoke with her husband about it once – on the spur of the moment and very casually. Nathan had been engaged in an animated discussion with the district judge and with His Nobleness, Herr Florian von Bolvinsky, for a long time out in front of the store; then Negrusz had gone up to his office while Florian entered the store with the storekeeper in order to attend to the task – as a special one-time exception – of putting away a digestive constitutional half-liter between the noon half-liter and the afternoon half-liter. "Nathan," said his wife, "it's kind of a strange thing with the district judge. Is he that proud? He's never spoken a word with me."

"It isn't pride," replied Nathan; "on the contrary, he's the best, most helpful person on earth. But he *is* a man of few words ... who knows why? Perhaps he's unhappy."

"Ho, ho," roared His Nobleness, "What a vain wife you have, *Pany*[27] Nathan. We've all been courting her for all we're worth, but she still doesn't

---

[27]Ukrainian: equivalent of German *"Herr," i.e.,* "Mister" or "Master" in English.

have enough. Now she catches a glimpse of this young Herr Julko . . . Ho, ho, ho! But all her efforts are a waste of time, ho, ho! He's already in love, deeply in love . . . yes, he is! That's God's punishment!"

The lovely wife listened patiently to the old wine barrel . . . she was already used to his joking. "Not everybody has such a jolly nature as you," she replied. "This man seems to me too serious and too hard-working to fall in love!"

Herr Florian stood with his hands on his hips and blurted out his whinnying, comical laugh for what must have been minutes. "Ho, ho, ho!" he coughed, "I have to beg your pardon . . . ho, ho, ho . . . have you ever heard anything like that? . . . ho, ho, ho! . . . as if only dumb people could fall in love, ho, ho, ho! . . . me, for example; am I dumb? Sure . . . and . . . *Pany* Nathan, don't be jealous, but I'm in love with your wife. But because of it I do have to tell you, as your punishment . . . ho, ho, ho! . . . that with von Negrusz all your efforts are a waste of time. He's already taken . . . ho, ho, ho! . . . taken and gone; he loves a dead woman, ho, ho, ho!"

"Nonsense," mumbled the woman, annoyed, as His Nobleness staggered towards the "Clubhouse," accompanied by Nathan. But she couldn't get it out of her head. Late that evening, as she was sitting next to her husband in the living room, helping him write the business correspondence since he had to leave on a trip very early the next morning, she suddenly asked: "What did Bolvinsky mean today about the dead woman that the district judge is supposed to be in love with?"

"What do I know?" replied Nathan. "People talk here and there. They say he was in love with a girl, and when she died he decided to stay single. Maybe it's true. Christians get wrapped up in all kinds of nonsense when it comes to love."

"Okay, I see," his wife replied, staring thoughtfully into the flame of the gaslight. But then she took her pen in hand and finished writing the letter to Moses Rosenzweig in Chernovtsy, ordering a barrel of herrings and five hundred kilograms of sugar.

*

Something strange happened the next day.

Herr Florian von Bolvinsky is not merely a fat man, he is also a good man. And because he has never wronged anybody, he also isn't afraid of anybody – except for his housekeeper, though he has never wronged her, either. A good man, but he has one big failing: he tells everything that he's been able to find out, and then he adds more to it. The latter comes partly from his natural imagination, partly from his abundant wine-drinking. And so the district judge learned the following morning, when he happened to be alone with Herr Florian in the "Clubhouse," how Frau Hannah had, under a stream of seething tears, opened up her heart to His Nobleness the day before and had revealed the insane love in her heart for Herr von Negrusz and how it was nearly driving her to suicide that her superhuman beloved, the man of her dreams, wouldn't even give her the time of day, indeed, wouldn't even waste a last word on her before she died. And Herr Florian didn't relate this gripping story as briefly and to the point as it is reported here, but with juicy embellishments in every detail, interrupting himself countless times by "Ho, ho, ho" and "Do you know what I mean?"

These interruptions were necessary so His Nobleness could catch his breath. For the district judge was not the one to interrupt him. He sat there, mute and serious as always, and only at times did a slight, sarcastic smile cross his lips. This smile was very unpleasant for Herr Florian, and whenever he saw it he got a little embarrassed and tried to hide this embarrassment with doubly juicy embellishments. "And what do you have to say about that?" he finally asked, taking a deep breath.

"What do I have to say about that?" said the district judge, "Nothing ... I just admire your poetic talent: Mickiewicz[28] is a bungler compared to you!"

"How's that? What's that? ... Ho, ho! Why, I think you don't believe me! Oh, respected Herr von Negrusz, respected Herr Benefactor, how do I deserve this? Have you ever caught me in a lie? And by the same token ... why would I even bother? No ... on my word of honor! It's the truth, the holy truth. On my word of honor! I assure you ... I had sympathy for the woman ... She's totally head over heels ... totally head over heels in

---

[28] Adam Mickiewicz (1798-1855), a Polish poet known for long epics and narratives.

love with you. I've never seen anything like it; me, me, the one who – ho, ho! Do you know what I mean? – me, who knows women. Head over heels ... head over heels ... and now I ask you: what should I tell her? Nathan is off on a trip ... do you know what I mean? ... He'll be gone for three weeks ... ho, ho! The woman ...."

"Herr von Bolvinsky," the district judge interrupted him, reassembling the newspaper he'd been glancing at now and then, and straightening up to his full height: "Whatever it is you – the Catholic nobleman – want to say to the spouse of Silberstein – the Jew – while he's gone is something I'll have to leave to you. But for my part, I have something to tell *you*. If I didn't know that the entire novel you've just narrated to me is a fiction from the first word to the last ...."

"Herr von Negrusz ...."

"I'll repeat the phrase: 'a fiction from the first word to the last.' If you had approached me in truth as the broker for adultery, I wouldn't be putting up with your company anymore from this hour on. But you were just poking fun in your way, which is not my way, of course. I can't be a party to joking about the honor of such respectable people as this married Jewish couple. And therefore I most seriously beseech you not to keep the jest going and, if you feel inclined to do so at the expense of others, then seek out some other unwilling accomplice than me ...."

Herr Florian is beside himself. In the first place, this strange person here doesn't believe him and is spoiling a delightful joke. But that alone wouldn't be so bad. Herr Florian is certifiably tolerant on this point: there are other people who don't believe a word he says. This man goes so far, though, as to take the whole thing seriously, almost like it's a tragedy! He's belittling His Nobleness as if he were a little school boy. That's one thing he can't tolerate ... that goes against his sense of honor. Compromise is impossible here as well. And so he pulls himself up to his full height, puts his hands on his hips, and declares in the tone of voice he usually reserves for the pushiest of his creditors: "Whom do you think you're speaking with? Do you hear me? ... whom are you speaking with, I ask you? Let me tell you ... you're speaking with me, Florian von Bolvinsky. How about some respect ... I have to ask for proper respect! Have I ever heard such a thing?! A liar, a procurer of women, me ... ho, ho! So ... give me a little respect, do you hear me? Stay virtuous if you like, but what I said is true. This Hannah is very much in love, totally reckless ...."

"Silence!"

The word comes whooshing through the air like an arrow, and its sharp point slices the impressive speech in two. His Nobleness looks towards the door and lets the hands on his hips fall to his side as quick as lightning. He turns very pale. But a bright crimson is rising in the district judge's face.

"Silence!" commands the lovely woman once more and stretches her hand out domineeringly towards the fat, quaking coward. Having drawn herself up to her full height, she stands there in the opened doorway, deathly pale but royally proud and royally beautiful . . . .

His Nobleness sank his head down and let his lower lip droop like a sheep before the storm. The woman closes the door behind her and steps up to the two gentlemen. "You were . . . spying . . . on us," stammers the old sinner and makes an attempt to smile.

"I wasn't spying," replies Frau Hannah very pointedly. "As God is my witness . . . I'm not in the habit of listening in to what the gentlemen have to say to each other out here; it's no business of mine. But I was just getting some spices in the back of the store, next to the door here, and I couldn't help hearing every word. That was bitter enough for me, and even more bitter is . . ." A hot blush flames across her forehead and her cheeks . . . "Even more bitter for me is that I'm the one who has to speak in this matter. But my Nathan isn't home right now. And so I have to tell you to your face, Herr Bolvinsky, that you're a totally rotten liar. All I did yesterday was ask my husband if . . . if Herr District Judge is proud – since he doesn't talk to me and all the rest of the other gentlemen do. I didn't mean anything . . . anything bad by it. And so, Herr Bolvinsky . . . shame on you . . ."

Herr Bolvinsky does as he's commanded: he's ashamed. His lower lip is hanging down very low and he can't lift his eyes from the floor. But Herr von Negrusz looks right at the woman and can't take his eyes off her. Perhaps it's not good for him that he's taking such a close look at this proud, living beauty; for him, who's only "in love with a dead woman . . . ."

"Herr District Judge," Frau Hannah continues but stops short right after these first words, and then, when she starts speaking again, the blush flames across her face again even hotter, "Herr District Judge deserves our thanks for having looked after us so well, my Nathan and me. And even if Herr District Judge doesn't want to speak with me, I will speak with him and tell him: You are a good and honest man, and the people are right when they praise you; and I thank you . . . ."

Now the district judge can't find a word of reply, either, just like Herr Florian, and almost like the latter, he now casts his gaze on the floor too.

Next he reaches for his hat and makes a mute but very, very respectful bow to the woman and goes up to his apartment.

His old housekeeper, who loves him too, just like everyone else, is inconsolable today. He generally has a good appetite, but today he scarcely touches his meal, and almost as many of his favorite dish, the cheese *piroshki*,[29] are cleared off the table for leftovers as were brought there in the first place. And besides that, he has such a strange look in his eye, so very different than usual . . . .

*

And the days came and went, and, quietly and unobtrusively they forged between two good and pure souls a bond that was sinful and criminal before God and man.

To all outward appearances, that strange scene in the small wine locale had resulted in no consequences at all. At the most it meant that Herr Florian von Bolvinsky drank his afternoon, evening, and nighttime half-liter within his own four walls – with twice the quantity, of course, in an attempt to forget the insult he had suffered so undeservedly. But the very next morning he showed up for the early morning half-liter at his usual place again and even took his normal route there once again . . . through the store and past the wife of the storekeeper. Herr von Negrusz also showed up at the noon hour as punctually as ever. Well, now, that was not so much of a surprise. But it was almost inexplicable that even in the behavior of the two towards Hannah apparently not a thing had changed. Herr von Bolvinsky continued to favor her with his usual jokes and flattering speeches, and when she gave absolutely nothing in response, he said at most: "Ho, ho! How proud! But I'm still in love with you, ho, ho!" And Herr von Negrusz continued to pass by her with a mute greeting.

Why?!

When someone wants to deceive himself, it's usually successful. "I won't do it," he told himself, "so as not to give the old blabbermouth the opportunity for barbed comments or new accusations." But at the same time he sensed very acutely that it wasn't the real reason. And at times he was

---

[29] Small baked pastries – dumplings or turnovers – with various fillings, popular fare in Slavic countries.

even so childish as to be angry with the lovely woman for causing his honest heart to be untrue to itself. What was the real reason though? Not the "shyness" which voluptuous Emilia had proclaimed about him because once, after a very meaningful handshake on her part, he had stopped offering her his hand when they met. Nor was it his lack of "receptivity to feminine charms" about which the three greenish graces of Herr Tax Office Superintendent had complained. He was not shy, since a hardworking and gifted man doesn't act that way towards anyone, and as for his lack of "receptivity" ... oh, my! The image of that woman, twice as lovely in her anger and embarrassment, had made a deeper impression on him than he liked. But ... the wretched behavior of that nobleman had put him in such a unique relationship to the woman – who had formerly been nothing but a stranger to him – that now, in order to find the right words and the right tone for associating with her, he would have to act casual about things. And "casual" is not precisely what he was feeling, even though he swore to himself up and down that it was. And no matter how often he told himself: "I won't talk to her so that some malicious old woman dressed in a man's work jacket, pants and boots won't have anything to gossip about again ... and as far as that goes ... what do I have to discuss with her, anyway; or is it even necessary for me to talk to her?!" But he did sense that he was just lying to himself and that it was unfitting for him not to talk. And as week after week went by, and it grew more and more impossible for him to correct his mistake, this silent passing-by became all the more awkward for him each day, and yet ... he couldn't stop it! And for the life of him, he would have been happy to know what she had to say about it. . . .

What did she say about it?!

To others she didn't say a thing, nothing at all; not even to Nathan did she speak a word about it. Before that scene she would have been able to report to him about it very quietly, even in the presence of someone else, but now she just couldn't anymore. She even kept the heroic deed of Herr von Bolvinsky silent when Nathan finally returned home from his business travels after an absence of over a month. "Why should he have to get angry about it?" she excused herself, but in truth she sensed that she was only avoiding it in order not to have to mention the district judge at the same time. An inexplicable timidity kept her from it. Precisely because she had to think of him and his behavior so much, that was precisely why she couldn't talk about it. And she thought so much about it, and from so many different angles ... almost every day something new. "It's not at all nice of him that he won't send even one word my way, especially now that we do know each other." Or: "Does this arrogant Christian seriously think I'm in love with him, and is he just trying to prove to me that I don't mean a thing to him? That's not necessary; he doesn't mean a thing to me, either." But then right away again: "He is such a good man! The way he's looked out for me! The only reason he's not talking to me, I'm sure, is to take away all cause for further lies from this fat, ugly Bolvinsky." But her most frequent thought was: "That story about the dead woman must be true! He loves her so much that he doesn't even want to speak with a woman who's alive. He doesn't even speak with the wife of the district actuary. How can someone love a woman that's dead? What is love anyway? . . . ."

The power that rules over all our lives often utilizes peculiar means. In this case it brought two people close to each other by not having them speak to one another.

They didn't speak and saw each other daily and kept on not speaking for three long months. Summer was coming to an end: the first yellow leaves in the monastery garden were falling to the ground, the time of the wine harvest was approaching, and Nathan was embarking on his long annual journey to the wine countries, to Hungary and Moldavia. He was to return on the Sabbath before the high holidays.[30] "Stay healthy and see to it that we're able to make a good wine vinegar from the new wine that's gone bad!" . . . Those were his parting words. Then, as usual, he took his wife quietly and tenderly in his arms and kissed her on her forehead. He had no idea that she was resting in his arms for the last time.

*

It was a day in September, a lovely, clear, sunny autumn day. Frau Hannah was in the store, weighing out coffee and sugar for her customers; Herr von Bolvinsky and Herr Tax Office Superintendent were sitting in the "Clubhouse," talking about liberalism. Everything as usual. And, as usual, Herr von Negrusz entered the store, too. He silently lifted his hat, she greeted him back with a silent nod, and then he tried to pass through. But he couldn't, since a large barrel of herrings was standing right in the middle of the aisle.

---

[30] Jewish New Year and Day of Atonement. See footnote 35, page 294.

"You'll have to come around this way," the woman said and pointed to the route leading behind the counter.

"I thank you," he said quietly and went on past her. But then he stopped. "You're rearranging things here?" he asked as a way of saying at least something.

"Yes . . . for autumn . . . since the fruit will be arriving."

"This will be a productive fall . . . ."

"Yes . . . particularly the apples . . . ."

"The wine too, they say. Where is Herr Nathan now?"

"By now he's probably in Hegyvallja.[31] I don't know exactly . . . he seldom has time to write when he's traveling . . . but he's probably in the Tokay[32] region by now." And then the pride of the merchant's wife won out over her reticence, and she added: "Since this spring all the Potockis and Czartoryskys[33] have been our customers. And so we have to offer only genuine Tokay wine, of course. We're also able to get everything directly from the Rhine[34] now."

"Is that right, is that so? . . . Well, my congratulations." With that he went on into the "Clubhouse." That was their first conversation. Herr Florian von Bolvinsky himself wouldn't have been able to claim, even after the thirtieth half-liter, that it was a dialogue of love. But the ice had been broken, and after this conversation there followed a series of similar conversations. They talked about the weather, about business, about the minor daily occurrences. And strangely enough, while they had felt very self-conscious during the time of silence and were, after all, only capable of thinking of one another with a blush, the self-consciousness dissolved during these quiet and friendly conversations until they felt more at ease in each other's company. At that point the two must have been standing at a crossroads: these simple, quiet discussions would either completely make an end to the peculiar relationship the two had entered into by virtue of that scene and their silence; or else from this association . . . that relationship would start to develop all the more,

---

[31] A small town in northeastern Hungary; see the next footnote.

[32] A district in northeastern Hungary that surrounds the town of Tokay, after which is named the famous aromatic wine made from Furmint grapes.

[33] Two of the historically most revered families of nobility in western Galicia (now Poland).

[34] Wine from the Rhine Valley region in Germany.

growing deeper and more dangerous than before, since it was now perceptibly rooted in their reciprocal acquaintance and no longer in some dream world. They had no idea that they were standing at that crossroads; and as they gradually became better and better acquainted and spoke longer and longer with each other and enjoyed being together more and more, they also had no idea that they had now chosen and taken a path that had to lead, under the present circumstances, to pain and self-denial or else deeply down to shame....

They had no idea. Otherwise how could they have so casually discussed things that could lead them so easily to a passionate phrase, a rash eruption of the heart?! She told him once, for example, what Herr von Bolvinsky had said about that passion of his for a dead woman. She talked almost jokingly about it, but she regretted it very much when she saw how his face darkened at the mere mention. "Have I hurt you?" she asked, concerned.

"No, no!" he replied. "I certainly ought to talk to you about it, now that others have done so. There's nothing about it that I have to hide." And at that he told her the story of his heart, a simple, sad, everyday story. As a student he had loved a girl that he was tutoring, the daughter of distinguished noble parents. The young baroness had reciprocated his love, but the world had been mightier than their hearts: she was promised to somebody else and died after a short marriage.

The Jewish wife listened to this story like a miracle tale; there was something in it that she hadn't understood at all a few months before and that she still didn't clearly understand. Perhaps she summed that up in the question that she asked him after a long pause: "And . . . and you still love her?"

"She's dead," he replied, "and I no longer love her with the same love I felt for her when she was alive. But her memory will stay with me and will be cherished and vivid until I die. I'll never forget her."

The woman stared ahead pensively for a long while. "Love must be something wonderful," she whispered to herself. He didn't respond; perhaps he hadn't understood her quiet words ....

Weeks passed. The high holidays were approaching closer and closer. Nathan was supposed to return . . . The two talked about him frequently, very frequently, and praised his industry, his honesty, his good and righteous heart. That was strange . . . again and again they ended up talking about him. Perhaps they instinctively sensed that it was necessary to strengthen each other in their respect for this man. For this respect was the very barrier between them and, at the same time, the last refuge to which their feelings of honor and justice were clutching.

And so the Friday before the Jewish New Year[35] arrived, the day of Nathan's return. The decisive word between the two of them had still not been spoken. Then coincidence brought this word to their lips, and they recognized – with infinite bliss and infinite grief in their hearts – the chasm looming up before them.

*

That was on a dreary, wet October day. It had been stormy all night; the rain had fallen incessantly over the desolate countryside and over the gloomy town. Then the autumn winds had whipped it away and were now chasing after individual clouds and moaning through the crooked streets and throwing the last red and quivering leaves off the poplar trees of the monks across the way and down into the mud. It was a sad, sad day; and the heart of anyone depressed by worry or loneliness had to feel twice as anxious today.

Frau Hannah sat alone in the store; today there were no customers to be seen. She watched the wind play its game with the leaves. She didn't have any specific concerns or else none that she was perceiving clearly, and yet her heart was heavy, so heavy . . . .

Then Rosel Juster came into the shop, a poor girl, but lovely and ample of figure. She was making large purchases of sugar and almonds and raisins and all kinds of spices.

"Is this for the pastry goods at your engagement party?" Frau Hannah asked in a friendly tone. "I've heard about it and wish you all the happiness. They say he's a good man."

"I thank you," the girl replied, "the engagement party is on Tuesday, and the marriage will be very soon, the second Sabbath after that. That's on account of his small children . . . he's a widower . . . ."

"You'll certainly have a lot of work on your hands?"

---

[35] *Rosh Hashanah*, the high holiday of the Jewish New Year that begins ten days of penance leading up to *Yom Kippur*, the "Day of Atonement."

"Oh my! If only it were just the work alone! But his sister is living in the house, too. And then . . . he is an old man. But what good does it do to talk about it? . . . ."

"So this isn't something you want for yourself?"

Rosel looked up at her, surprised. Then she answered grimly: "Since when am I asked around here what I want?! I'm a poor girl and he'll take me and provide for me . . . that's all there is to it." She shrugged her shoulders, wiped her hand across her eyes, and quickly added: "I'll also be needing thirty grams of ginger."

Frau Hannah said nothing more but weighed out the order. Her hand was shaking, though, when she tied up the bags; and she picked up the wrong weights a few times and had to reweigh everything.

"It seems to me you're not feeling well," said Rosel as she left. "You look so pale . . . ."

"I'm tired," the woman answered and sank down on a chair. When the door had closed behind the customer, she put her hands on her face and sat there for a long time, such a long, long time. There were wild and chaotic voices struggling and crying out inside her . . . "Since when have they ever asked me what I wanted around here? . . . I was a poor girl and he took me and he's provided for me . . . my God; that's all there is to it, that's all!"

She kept her eyes pinched shut, but in that moment she still saw clearly, more clearly than ever before . . . oh! . . . everything was terribly clear. Her whole life lay in front of her, and this life was a big lie . . . "Everything belongs to him . . . my body and my soul . . . not because it's what I want . . . not even because he wants it . . . no! . . . because our fathers thought it wise . . . and now when I feel like I'm a person who has a will and a heart . . . now that I love someone else, now I'll stay miserable, or otherwise I'll have to . . . ."

She didn't think this thought through to it's conclusion . . . her senses were starting to reel. Infinite pity for herself overcame her, and burning hot tears gushed from her eyes. She didn't think about where she was; she didn't think about the fact that the man she loved – and whose presence she now feared the most because of it – would have to be entering the shop any moment. She only thought of it when the noon bells of the Dominicans rang out, and she tried to pull herself together.

But it was too late. There he was, already standing at the open door.

And now something peculiar occurred between the two of them. They hadn't spoken of their love till now; it may well be that they hadn't even known about it. But as he walked towards her and took her hands and looked in her eyes, those large blue, tear-swollen eyes that were riveted on his features with such an indescribably charming expression . . . at that point he guessed all her thoughts, her struggle, her pain, her love. And as he squeezed her hands and then stroked the hair from her forehead, quietly and tenderly as with a sick child, he knew that his heart belonged to her and that she could depend on him until death. Then he let loose of her hands and stepped back.

"We will have to suffer a lot," he said, as if their love were a matter of course as was their fight for a life together. "But I will be unshakable, and so will you. I have a lot to tell you. But this is not the right place, and this evening . . ." he stopped short and then continued with a firm voice, "this evening your husband will be coming back, and I don't want to encourage you to arrange a secret meeting behind his back. So I will write and tell you what I recommend."

He squeezed her hand one more time, then he went to the "Clubhouse."

The woman got up, sent the apprentice – who had been outside up till now, polishing the silver- and brassware for the holidays – into the store to look after things, and stayed in the kitchen herself to prepare for the Sabbath and to receive her husband. She did everything as efficiently as normal yet in a different way than usual. "Is your head hurting you, Ma'am?" her maid asked her when she suddenly stood still and pressed her palms to the sides of her head as if she had to return to her senses. She had confused and tangled feelings, and yet, on the other hand, she felt like rejoicing. And thus did the day pass.

Towards evening the office courier brought her a letter. "From the district court for your husband," he said, but when she took it from its envelope, a letter for her was inside. She didn't open it; she was afraid of what it might contain.

Twilight was breaking; the lights were lit and she spoke the lovely ancient blessing on them that is the duty of the woman of the house. That light and peace might dwell within the house, that God's mercy might keep all worry, all adversity, all disgrace away from them. . . There are only a very few prescribed words and she knew them very well, yet today they came to her lips only hesitantly and haltingly. Oh! Was she still worthy to pray to God, herself, a Jewish wife who was carrying with her the letter of her . . . Christian lover?! . . . .

Mortally exhausted, she sank down on a chair and groaned aloud with the bitter struggle going on in her soul. Then she pulled out the letter and looked at it. It was sealed. Seals must not be broken on the Sabbath. "That's not the greatest of my sins," she said in a dazed voice and broke it regardless. She read. He wrote about how he loved her, how he would have to die without her or go crazy. "Become a Christian, become my wife . . . the sin against your husband is not as great as the sin against both of us if you don't. I know that you love me . . . now just assure me of your decision to go with me. All the rest is my worry."

She crumpled the letter up in a ball and threw it across the room, but then she picked it up again and smoothed it out and read it again. Then she let her hands drop to the table, her fingers intertwined in desperation, tears flowed in streams across her cheeks, and she stammered while sobbing: "My Lord and God, help me, enlighten me! Don't let me be like Esther Freudenthal;[36] don't let me end my life in disgrace and contempt! . . . My Lord and God, don't forsake me. I've been an honest woman up till now . . . my husband is good . . . I can't be an adultress . . . but I do love him . . . I can't live without him . . . he's a decent man . . . but even if he were as bad as that Husar[37] that made Esther so unhappy . . . my Lord and my God! I'm going crazy . . . help me, help me! . . . ."

And as she was crying out like this from the depths of her tortured soul, she didn't hear the door open and the footsteps of a man coming up behind her. Then a hand touched her shoulder . . . she gave a jump . . . her husband stood before her.

"God be with us," he exclaimed merrily, "finally I've made it back. The storm last night made the streets . . . ." He looked at her, he stopped short . . . "Hannah," he cried out, frightened, "just look at you . . . Hannah, what's the matter with you?"

She gave no answer. Then his eye fell on the letter. He reached out for it . . . she quietly let him take it. He read the top heading and turned deathly pale. "To you . . . and just like that!" Then he quickly browsed the first few lines and rapidly looked down for the signature. "That fellow," he mumbled, "He's not the one I would have expected it from." Then he read on. His eyes nearly bulged out of their sockets, the hand holding the letter started

---

[36] See footnote 12, page 274.

[37] "Husar" was a type of Hungarian cavalry officer.

to shake, a look at the man showed how much he was suffering. "What?" he cried out at one point with a hoarse and horrified voice, "What? . . . is that true?" . . .

He didn't add any details. She glided down to the floor and held him around his knees. He finished reading the letter. Then he threw it on the table and bent down to her. "Get up," he commanded, "sit on the chair!"

She obeyed.

"Just one thing," he said and stepped in front of her, "I just want to know one thing . . . the Christian writes that you love him, too . . . he's lying, isn't he?! . . . Hannah, the Christian is lying?! . . . ."

She bowed her head down low, very low. "Kill me," she said gently but firmly, "kill me if I deserve it, but . . . he was writing nothing but the truth."

Nathan gave a wild jump. There was a terrible devastation in his otherwise so gentle, peaceful features. "The truth?" he hissed. "And you dare to stay in my house, you adultress?!"

She set herself up to her full height. She was horribly pale, her eyes were flashing. "Nathan!" she exclaimed, "I swear to you by my dead mother, today was the first time he touched my hand!"

He gave out a shrill laugh. "And if I believe you, what good does that do?! Are we supposed to divide you up, the body for me, the soul for him?! Isn't your soul entrusted to me as well? And if your body was all you could give me, why did you take me as your husband?"

She stepped up closer to him and let her hands – which she had been raising up beseechingly – drop down limply at her side. There was something eerie in the look of her eyes and it was an eerie sound as she said gently, but with a vaguely threatening tone: "Nathan, don't be too hard. My body is commanded by my will, and I will protect your rights! But over my soul I have no power. Husband of mine! Don't force me into extreme measures . . . I'm suffering terribly enough as it is. Why did I become your wife then, you ask? Oh! . . . have you ever asked me about what it was I wanted?"

The question must have hit him hard, very hard. He looked at her, took a step backwards, and kept his peace. Then there was a long silence between the two. She had thrown herself down on the couch after those words, emotionally broken, and was burying her head in the pillows; he was walking back and forth restlessly. Then he stopped right in front of her and said gently: "Go now . . . we'll talk about this tomorrow . . . ."

She staggered from the room.

He locked the door and began to walk back and forth in the room again. An old servant lady came and knocked on the door . . . she was bringing him his evening meal. He turned her away. She left mumbling, and he heard her say to the cook: "That cries out to God, the confusion we've got in the house right now. The man of the house locks himself in the living room and the woman in the bedroom. And neither of them wants to eat a thing."

The bright crimson of shame rose in the man's cheeks. "The servants have already noticed it," he said, "soon everyone else on earth will know about it. Oh, our old Jutta is right: that does cry out to God, the confusion that's come over my house! And only God can help, God alone; I don't know any way out of it."

He threw himself down on the couch, closed his eyes and reviewed everything that had happened. It forced him up again . . . he couldn't rest while such wild storms were raging inside him.

"Only God can help?" he asked himself and walked back and forth again without pause in the lonely, light-filled room. "That was a foolish statement. God isn't always duty-bound to do a miracle for us. What can God do? He can make him die or me. Is that a solution?"

He pressed his burning forehead to the windowpanes and stared out into the wild, rainy night. "I've owned a treasure," he said softly, "I've owned it and not suspected it was a treasure until someone else came around who knew better. Maybe it serves me . . . serves me right . . . .

"Right?" he then cried out wildly. "No, no! Isn't she my wife? Didn't she pledge her faithfulness to me? Mine . . . she's mine, my property. And whoever steals her from me is a cowardly thief! . . . .

"A cowardly thief . . . him! . . . he's otherwise such a good man, honest and hardworking. I've never expected anything bad from him. So it's her, just her. She's the wicked one. But was she ever really mine, my property?! Is a woman a thing I can own like a piece of jewelry or a house? Doesn't she have her own free will? And did we actually ask her what it was she wanted back then?

"Back then a crime was committed," he suddenly shrieked. "What's happening now is the just retribution for that crime.

"I wasn't guilty back then. She wasn't either. And then we lived on, pure and spotless, for long years. Now the disgrace has come back upon our heads anyway, the retribution for the crime. Who will take on the burden of atonement?"

He stepped up to the table. "Can I let her have a divorce? My heart will hurt a great deal . . . but I'm not asking about my heart. I'm not asking about myself; but can I do that to God and the Law?! Should I turn a Jewish child, my wife, away from my house for her to go and woo the Christian or even become a Christian herself?! Should I permit such disgrace to come on our name, on the name of our God?!"

He raised himself up to his full height and stretched forth his right hand as if swearing an oath to heaven: "And even if it breaks my heart and hers . . . upon Your Name no disgrace shall come, not upon Your Name, my Lord and God."

Then he suddenly let his hand drop straight down and he pondered some more. "Hasn't disgrace already come upon Your Name?" he hissed softly. "Hasn't she stretched forth her hands over these lights of my house and pleaded to You with the image of that Christian in her heart? Isn't that a terrible sacrilege too? And can it be Your will that such sacrilege is to go on even longer, our whole life long? Can You desire that, my Lord and God?!"

Then he took his head in his hands and gave a deep sigh of woe. "I can't find a way out of it," he groaned. "Help me, my God! You have made known Your will to us through Your priests and scribes. I will consult with the Law."

He stepped to the bookcase, opened it, and pulled out one of the magnificent folios. Behind it, a small, thin booklet tumbled down. He paid no heed to it; he carried the folio to the table, opened it up and began to read in it.

He read very slowly and at various passages. Then he shook his head and violently closed the book and stood up. He laid his clenched fist on the cover. "The Law is not sufficient," he said glumly, "the Law knows nothing of my case. 'She shall be stoned,' says the older Law, and the Law of the *talmudim*[38] says: 'Kill her if you can by the laws of the land in which you dwell. If you cannot, then she shall be expelled from the house of her husband and shall return to the home of her father, and the latter shall punish and discipline her as he pleases. She shall be without honor or justice, excluded from all inheritance and all benefices of her relatives. Her name shall not be named . . . .'

---

[38] Interpreters of the Talmud, the Book of Laws.

"The Law doesn't fit!" he repeated. "She's not an abject sinner; she's preserved my rights to the degree it was in her powers. Her body was mine . . . she kept it pure for me. Her heart . . . I've never desired her heart! The Law doesn't fit. But who can point me the way to a higher law?!"

He sighed deeply and shoved the folio back in its place. As he was trying to close the door of the bookcase, though, he was unable to do so . . . since a little booklet had gotten stuck there. He bent over and picked it up. It was strangely moving as he recognized that German booklet as the one which he had secretly read so often and so much in his youth. That booklet which he had never completely understood, but which he had enjoyed reaching for again and again because his heart was so oddly moved whenever he read in it . . . the booklet with the poems of Friedrich Schiller which he hadn't seen for a number of years and which happened to fall into his hands right now in this stormy and depressing hour . . . .

He sat down at the table and opened it up and began to read. The days of his youth opened up to him again, and he remembered how he'd read this passage under the large oaks and that one secretly in the basement while supervising his father's workers. But now the contents of the booklet itself began to come to life again and . . . strangely enough! . . . he hadn't learned anything new since that time, at most the varieties of wines, and yet he now understood much more of these poems than he had back then. And what he did understand gripped him in an odd way because it was so very different than what he had generally heard and read and thought, so very different. Whether better, whether worse; he didn't brood about that, but since his heart was moving more quietly now and the convulsions of his soul were relaxing, it certainly must not have been anything bad . . . .

He stood up and walked back and forth in that Sabbath-blessed room and whispered the words of the book to himself. It was very quiet around him; only the many candles softly rustled, and from time to time an individual raindrop struck against the window . . . .

*

The long, long autumn night was coming to an end. The rain had stopped; the last clouds were still scudding along through the dreary gray skies, shredded by the wind. The ruby sunrise was beginning to glimmer in the east, throwing its transfiguring glow across the sad, autumnal plain.

The red light of morning was also forcing its way into the living room of Nathan Silberstein. It found him still awake. But he wasn't walking back and forth any longer, he wasn't whispering any longer: mute and silent, he was standing at the window with his countenance turned to the east. And the ruby sunrise cast light and shadows around this pale, weary countenance that was now peacefully gentle and clear again. It was the gentleness and clarity of a solid and good decision. Since he was still holding his head bowed toward the east and his eyes were looking out as if transfigured, he must have been praying. But not with his lips.

He may have stood there like that for a long time, for hours. He had a lot on his mind and in his heart, no doubt, that he was expressing to God in that quiet morning hour.

Then the other residents of the house awoke. Among the butlers and maids there arose a whispering... they knew that something had transpired during the night, even if they were unclear about what it was. Then Hannah came out of the bedroom, pale, with sleep-deprived eyes puffy and red from crying. She walked past Nathan with her head down.

He addressed her. "Hannah," he said in gentle and quiet tones, "I've made my decision. I hope it'll be the best thing for you and... and for him! And as for me, our God is a merciful God... he won't forsake me."

The last part of it he said very quietly; she could scarcely understand it. A deep crimson blush shot into her face, but she said nothing. Then she went out, and after a while she brought him his breakfast.

And then both of them went to the synagogue together, and whoever saw them walking together like that had no idea of what was going on inside them.

There are perhaps no two people who have ever prayed to God the way Nathan and his wife did on that Sabbath morning. Their souls were lying in the dust and pleading to be strengthened and uplifted.

"Praise God... there's nothing wrong," said old Jutta to the other maids as the couple came back home from the synagogue so peacefully and ate their noon meal together. But after the meal, Nathan said to Hannah: "What has to be done is best done quickly. Be of good cheer... I will go to him and speak with him. Within an hour everything will be clear to you."

Then he went up to the second floor, to the apartment of the district judge. Herr von Negrusz was sitting at his desk right then and turned quite pale when he saw the husband of his beloved enter. He feared an awkward scene, no doubt. But Nathan stayed calm; and after a polite greeting, he

The Higher Law 303

said: "Herr District Judge, you know why I've come to see you, for I see you've turned pale. This letter I'm holding in my hand you wrote to my wife. I'd like to give you an answer to it. But first, just one more question: Why did you do it? Isn't the commandment, 'Thou shalt not covet thy neighbor's wife' written for you as well?"

The district judge looked him calmly in the eye. "Yes!" he answered, "It is a sin. But I love your wife. That's all . . . I can't think of anything more to excuse myself."

Nathan nodded. "I'm glad that you're answering me so honestly. The answer is quite sufficient, too, and I can't think of anything to counter it with. And now I'd like to respond to your letter. My wife loves you, too. Therefore, she can no longer remain as my wife, and I shall allow the divorce to take place. She will be free . . . but what then, Herr District Judge?"

"Then I will marry her," the former rejoiced, "so help me God!"

Nathan looked him calmly and squarely in the eye. "Good!" he said. "I don't doubt that you want that. For you are a good man. But you are a government official, a Christian, from nobility. She is a simple Jewish woman. You are educated, Hannah isn't. So you also have some things to take into consideration. Perhaps you'll allow yourself to be swayed by your considerations and end up just plunging the woman into disgrace and misfortune. That's something I need to prevent, since Hannah was my wife, and in the instant that this thing with you becomes public knowledge, her father and the entire congregation will turn from her and she will be totally abandoned. And then I shall have to be responsible for Hannah, because I . . . well, that's none of your business. And so I'm going to tell you one thing, very brief, very clear: If you don't marry Hannah, then I shall kill you, so help me God! You are the Herr District Judge, I'm just a Jew. You have a hundred means of making me powerless. But I shall keep my word nonetheless!"

The district judge had turned white as a sheet and raised his hand as if to give a solemn oath. But Nathan arose and interrupted him gruffly: "Don't swear an oath! Just keep your word so I don't need to keep mine. In the next few days the divorce will be final. If you wish Hannah to stay longer in my house, I have nothing against that for a few weeks. But to repeat myself: If Hannah is not your wife in two months, then you're a dead man. Farewell!"

Then he went home and said to his wife: "Tomorrow we'll go speak to the rabbi and declare that we have an irreconcilable aversion to each other. That's the only grounds on which he can divorce us right away. The Christian has promised to marry you. If he wasn't serious about it earlier, he certainly is now...."

"Nathan!" she cried and kneeled down at his feet and covered his hand with kisses and tears. "Nathan! What a good person you are!"

"No!" he said. "It is no particular goodness on my part, it's just my duty. I'm atoning for some guilt that is not my own. They matched us up and didn't ask if we liked each other. That was a sin and it's come back to punish us. For I love you now, even if I've only recognized that since yesterday; you don't love me, though, but someone else. Should I keep you away from your happiness? Every person has a right to be happy. So I'd rather atone now for the old mistake, that first one. That's how the matters stand . . . you see . . . it's not at all any goodness on my part. There's just one thing that weighs heavily on my soul: you're turning your back on our faith and I'm abetting you. But I've begged God so much for forgiveness that I hope he *will* forgive me. He sees my heart; he knows there's nothing else I can do . . . ."[39]

There's not much more to report.

After a few days Nathan had effected the divorce, and a few weeks later Hannah became the wife of the district judge. No event for years and years had caused such a gigantic uproar in the area as this. Innumerable curses, envy, and resentment followed the couple, and even their well-wishers shook their heads at the peculiar bond.

You know that the curses proved powerless and the fears ungrounded. You know that Hannah, that Frau Christina von Negrusz, lives as a happy wife and mother in the same house at the threshold of which Esther Freudenthal had to die because she loved a Christian. This time love proved stronger than religious differences. It proved itself almost miraculous. For it not only wiped away all the hindrances, but, in spite of all opposing circumstances, in spite of the different backgrounds of the two marriage partners, it also made their matrimonial bond lovely, peaceful and strong. It was a true love,

---

[39] The last phrase in the German original here: "... *ich kann nicht anders*" is the same phrase that Martin Luther is said to have uttered as he began the Protestant Reformation.

you see, and such a love is miraculous and omnipotent – just like God, who bestows it on chosen souls.

Only one shadow hovers over Christina's happiness. It's not the fact that Frau Emilia scarcely dignifies her with a greeting and that the three daughters of the Tax Office Superintendent, who have gotten very old and very green in the course of time, turn their backs on her when they chance to meet. It's also not the brazen and intimate smile with which Herr von Bolvinsky whispers to her every time their paths cross: "I was the first to point it out, ho, ho!" It is truly a shadow in her light-filled life. That shadow is the anger of her father, which will probably only come to an end when the lonely, bitter old man finally shuts his eyes for eternal slumber.

Nathan has tried to take this worry from her heart as well, but he hasn't succeeded. He doesn't give up hope, of course, and visits the old man every time he returns to Barnow.

This only happens a few times in the year and always for a short time. A cousin of his keeps the shop in town for him; he himself is almost always on trips that take him very far away, to Italy and to the south of France. He's no longer a small merchant, but now the premier wine wholesaler in the country.

He's remained unmarried. Once people were saying that he'd gotten engaged to a beautiful and rich girl from Chernovtsy. But nothing came of it. Why? Only one soul on earth knows that: Frau Christina.

It was the only time that they'd talked with each other since she had left his house. For Nathan speaks with the district judge frequently and easily, and the two little boys – when he's at home – are in the store almost more than they are upstairs with their mother, but he has avoided any contact with Christina. Just once by chance, when people were spreading that rumor, did a meeting come about. Both boys were sitting with Nathan on the wooden bench in the corridor, rejoicing at the lovely presents that he'd brought them. So they'd been away quite a while, and their mother herself came down to find them. They ran to her, shouting with glee, showed her their new things, and took her over to see the merchant.

And so now, after a long time, these two people were standing across from one another again.

"I thank you, Herr Silberstein," she began hesitantly, but then she corrected herself right away and repeated: "I thank you, Nathan . . . how good you are to the children!"

"They are such charming boys," he replied in a forced voice. "I'm glad, very glad, that things are going so well for you, Hannah."

"Yes, they are," she replied, "I'm very happy. And . . . you?"

"Thanks for your concern," he said. "Business is going well."

"But then," she said, "I recently heard something else that pleased me a lot . . . about Chernovtsy."

"Oh . . . there's nothing to that," he said dismissively.

"Why not?" she asked. "They say she's a lovely and decent girl."

He looked at her; then he cast his eyes to the ground and a bright crimson blush flooded across his manly face. "I just couldn't bring myself to do it," he said quietly.

Since that time many more years have passed, and Nathan is now the richest man in the region. Everyone wonders why he works so tirelessly, this man who doesn't have anyone else to provide for. But Nathan generally answers such questions by responding that he *does* know who it is he's working for . . . .

Ada Christen, pseudonym for Christiane von Breden, née Christiane Frederik[1] (1839-1901) has been a forgotten writer for over a century now. In the 1860s and 1870s, though, she created quite a storm of controversy in Viennese literary circles by the realistic candor with which, in her transparently autobiographical poetry and prose, she portrayed the life of a lower-class woman. One of her central themes was survival by sinning, an admission that seemed a slap in the face to traditionally held ideals of womanhood. Christen was forced at an early age to earn her own way in life after her father, a well-to-do merchant in Vienna, was imprisoned for his participation in the revolutions of 1848 and then died soon thereafter. Her mother, living in an apartment complex entitled "The Blue Goose," made a sparse living by sewing gloves. Ada herself, in what was in essence a bordello-like existence, had been a nominal actress with traveling German comedy troupes from age 15 on, but she also performed on the stages of Vienna and St. Pölten. Compounding the disputes surrounding her writings were her very unfashionable undertones of weary despair and resignation. She did have help with her writing career. Theodor Storm, the German poet and prose artist, corresponded with her for years and was a poetic mentor. In 1868, the established writer Ferdinand von Saar helped her to publish her confessional *Songs of a Lost Woman*, a poetry collection that anticipated the stories to follow, focusing on social misery and her own hardships. *Sketches From Life* appeared in 1876, a prose collection that revealed the true aim of her literature: not to glamorize immorality, but to highlight the spiritual suffering of a broken inner life.

Cathy's Feather Hat takes place in the abovementioned "Blue Goose" apartment complex, a trivial real-life niche of poverty that has come to take its place in Austrian fiction. As in biographical reality, the mother in the story gets by with sewing gloves in a rented room, and we must presume that the young narrator relates other details and relationships from Christen's early years as well. Even in a milieu of despair, as this particular tale relates, small glories such as a feather hat may serve to give some form of escape, if not hope.

---

[1] The author's name has been rendered in various spellings, perhaps reflecting laxer orthographic conventions in the 19th century. At times her given name appears in certain reference works as "Christine," while at times her family name is "Frederik" or "Friderik." The name used above shows the form that's found most often.

The quotes and descriptions from the narrator's childhood often come across in breathless and naive run-on sentences. There is a sense of innocence to her perspective that makes the poverty and other misfortunes of the house appear all the more poignant. Perhaps the best example of the naive narrative voice is when, without understanding the connection to a pregnancy out of wedlock, she describes Cathy going away to visit a peasant lady in the woods, drinking goat's milk, and coming back pale and skinny. This is not an omniscient narrator: rather, we as readers seem to know more than what the child is telling us.

Though the tale might superficially resemble that of Cinderella with what seems a fairy-tale ending, there are differences both in content and in form. The depiction of social milieu doesn't change, and the Prince Charming is still very much just a day laborer at the construction site (and a stranger in a strange land, an Englishman in Austria). There is no black-and-white delineation of good and evil: the characters, even for this shortest of stories, are sketched out as somewhat complex, and they display mixed motivations.

Despite her deficient education and other obvious disadvantages, Christen succeeded in rising above her past while supplying frank narrative views of her suffering and of the social climate surrounding it. The courage to lay out her festering sores to the reader must be admired; at the same time, it is understandable that many readers were not interested in seeing them. A poet and publisher of the day, Ludwig August Frankl, said of her prose: "It is a ray of light reflected in a mud-puddle, but still it is a ray of light."[2] Ferdinand Kürnberger, another Viennese writer who had risen from similar surroundings, couldn't bring himself to decide whether she was a talent or a disaster. It's highly possible, he said, that she was both in the same lifetime and that there was a necessary connection between the two.[3]

---

[2] As quoted in Hans Heinz Hahnl, *Vergessene Literaten* (Vienna: Österreichischer Bundesverlag, 1984), p. 88. The English translation is mine.

[3] Ibid.

Cathy's Feather Hat

Ada Christen

Poor people buy their firewood from the construction site. It isn't delivered to their front door by wagon; rather, the children go on site with old scarves and gather together as many wood scraps as they can carry, pay a few pennies for them, then carry the bundles home on their backs.

All day long on large construction sites, as a consequence, there is no lack of the children of the poor, and often it comes to blows there. At times the carpenters, the foreman, often the master contractor himself take swings at them, but for the most part the children themselves are the ones who beat up on each other. That's the way it was when I was a child myself, and no doubt it's still that way today.

Rain or shine, from the first day of spring until the frosts of autumn, I had to go out to the site and carry home the next day's supply of wood, or even a little more for good measure, since a bushel of wood scraps was always piled at the back wall of the pitch-black kitchen. One bushel every day: that became a supply pile that reached up to the ceiling and would see us through many days of winter.

"Isn't good for anything else, that thing, Christa," said old Herr Fox, in whose tiny little rented room[4] my mother, I, my sister Maria and my little brother lived.

---

[4] The German word here is *Kammer*, a small room adjoining the *Stube* (main room or family room). For ease in differentiating between the rooms, this will be referred to as the "rented room" or "our room" in the narrative that follows.

"Isn't good for anything else, the thing . . . this thing . . . ," Herr Fox would growl three or four times, chewing on a horrendous plug of tobacco, his face turning dark red as he rolled up freshly sewn gloves with a wooden dowel over a large, smooth table until they were as tight and fine as the French glove maker, our "Boss," sold them. My mother and Maria sat at the window of our room, Cathy sat in the family room,[5] but they all sewed from early morning until late at night while I squatted under the high, wide table that was my home play area, dozed and daydreamed or had to sew buttons on the finished gloves. Now and then the scraggly white head of old Herr Fox cruised down to my level, looked at me fiercely, and growled his: "Isn't good for anything else, this thing!"

At that time I had just turned seven, was starting to shoot up taller, was skinny, sunburned, had coarse, straw-colored hair, and was always happy and hungry. I would trade my largest scrap of wood for the biggest piece of bread that one of the children brought to the construction site, and I still didn't have near enough until supper, which was our only meal besides some bread for breakfast.

My mother didn't know I was engaged in such entrepreneurial trading; she was upset enough already at the many bumps and bruises I brought home or at the rips in my skirt.

My mother was a very sensitive woman who was always looking for something to cry about. Every day she moaned and cried about our misery and about all the illnesses and deaths in the neighborhood, and if by chance nothing were amiss, she would borrow a newspaper and cry about all the misfortunes in it. As for me, with no worries except that there be sunshine and large scraps of wood at the construction site tomorrow, I was always supposed to cry along with her . . . .

Whenever she was beyond comfort, sobbing about my ripped skirt and asking me again and again, "How did you manage to do that?" I was never able to explain that the boys weren't always totally willing to give me their bread for my wood, and that it would come to some very strange duels then, all the more bitter since they were fought without a sound and as unobtrusively as possible. Crawling around on the ground while collecting wood scraps

---

[5] The word here is *Stube*, the family room, an area used for many purposes from dining to working. See the previous footnote. This will be referred to as the "family room" in the rest of the story (though the concept of "family" is misleading here).

– under some workbench where the workman above us kept on sawing and hammering – we would grab each other by the head, kick each other in the legs, strike a blow wherever we could, and try to grab any old piece of the enemy's clothing as a sign of victory. Sometimes during these combative diversions we tumbled in too close to the carpenters; then there'd be a quick kick, and all of us would be banished from the site. Then we would stand just outside our Paradise Lost, as it were, looking through the slats in the fences surrounding the open, rectangular construction site and begging pitifully for reentry. But at that point it was always too late . . . .

We knew what awaited us back home; that would be coming soon enough anyway, so we went out to play in the fields and procrastinated until it was our usual time to go home. The later it got, the more melancholy was our mood; the closer we came to our residences, the more gentle and considerate we mutually became – those who had scuffled with each other the worst walked hand in hand, touchingly reconciled – and by the time we said our whispered good-byes at the front doors of houses, fluttering shreds of clothing were the only evidence that we had tried to settle differing opinions in our own manner that day.

Returning on such evenings without a bundle, I always pushed my way slowly through the front door, knocked barely perceptibly at the kitchen door, and was in luck if Cathy opened the door. Cathy had been at the construction site, too, years ago, so she knew what went on there.

"Cathy, I don't have anything today," I whispered to her almost before the door was open.

"Just be quiet; your mother is back in your room. . . ." she would answer quietly.

I whooshed through the kitchen to the family room, my soul ecstatic.

"So it's you! Are you back already? Don't you look neat and tidy again!" blustered old Herr Fox, whom I had to pass whenever I wanted to go to our room. Once I was inside, my mother didn't ask about much, and I would get involved with my sleepy little brother.

But sometimes, when she opened the door herself and saw me standing in front of the door without any wood scraps! . . . .

She was a child of rich people and had only become so poor after my father's death, and since she had never had to go to a construction site in her childhood, I could never fully make the business habits of my colleagues clear to her . . . I never thought much of her beatings, since she had a small and weak hand, but she wept and complained unceasingly that we would all have to freeze to death in uttermost misery next winter; and she said it with so little hope and so convincingly that I would ask her, wringing my hands and fearing for my own death, when the next winter was actually going to begin . . . .

On such turbulent evenings I even believed it when old Herr Fox would push open the door and yell into our room: "Of all the worthless children stealing the dear Lord's time down here on earth, this thing is the very most worthless of all!" Then he'd shift the tobacco around in his mouth to and fro, give a hefty pull on his loose suspenders, and slam the door shut again, still shaking his fist at me.

With inexpressible repulsion at my own worthlessness and with a thin slab of buttered bread – which my mother always gave me in a more affectionate mood afterwards – I'd crawl next to my brother on the sack of straw and would generally fall asleep right away.

But all my troubles at the construction site ended immediately when I found a powerful benefactor there. "The Englishman" is what the others called a tall, broad-shouldered workman who walked around with his legs far apart, wearing a forest of hair in his face, and always working on the largest rafters. The others said he had formerly spent all his time on a ship and had sailed all around the world; now he wanted to live on solid land for once and learn our language. It may well have been true, for he spoke German only with great difficulty and often sang strange and foreign songs that sounded so funny that everyone laughed, especially when he danced in place and kicked his feet in the air . . . He was tall enough that he could see over the heads of the next tallest workers, and there were muscles as thick as your thumb on his brown arms, which I thought at the time were ropes.

I didn't really feel confident going near him in the beginning, until one time the children said, "Look, he's a giant!"

Then I snuck up cautiously, wanting to see the giant up close; I inconspicuously busied myself with his wood scraps at first, and when he paid me no heed, I gazed over at him. As I was standing in the sun like that and blinking up at him, a wasp flew right in his face; I didn't think about how short I was or how he tall he was, but, startled, I just swung as high as I could in the air with a protective hand. He laughed out loud, slapped himself on both thighs with his hands, squatted down to me on the ground, balancing himself on his heels, looked me straight in the eye and said, "You little monkey!"

Then both of us laughed, I don't know why.

Suddenly the wasp zoomed back, though, and, wasting no time, landed right on his nose . . . . Without thinking, I took a hefty swing at it, and it fell down dead. The Englishman first looked at me, stunned, put his hand up to feel his nose, and then lifted me up by the creases of my skirt, tossed me through the air a little, and set me down on the ground again next to his workbench.

Laughing, he kicked some wood scraps together with his feet and pointed to them: "Here, take those!"

Meanwhile it had become noon, and the other workmen left the site. The Englishman sat down on a block of wood, though, took bread and meat from his blue linen sack, asked me to go fill up the jug with water, and then he began eating. I sat down quietly at his side and started looking up into the bright sky just like he was doing.

Large, shimmering-blue flies were hovering in the air above us, only shifting around in the air when a short breath of wind came at them . . . Above the fields something intangible . . . something invisible was pulsating and glittering; pigeons were circling far above us, their wings glowing like pure silver. It was very quiet round about; only at the far back of the site were a few workmen still busy with their axes: rhythmic chopping was the only sound. When we heard hollow sounds all striking at the same time, they had dropped their axes, too, and soon passed us, waving, as they went out through the fields . . . .

The sunshine lay hot like a clear golden veil over the unshaded site, the freshly chopped wood gave off a strong smell, and from many of the stripped tree trunks oozed heavy, pure yellow resin. The Englishman lay down under the only shade tree that was there, stretched out his long legs, and motioned to me.

"What's your name?"

"Christa."

"I see . . ." he yawned, put his arms under his head, pushed his wide straw hat over his face, and lay so still for a while that I thought he had fallen asleep, and I didn't dare move a muscle.

"Do you want a piece of meat, Christa?"

Now I acted a little coy, knitted my hands together under my apron, hunched up one shoulder after the other, alternately stuck out my left and then my right hip, and stared straight across at the linen sack . . . I know exactly how I did this, since it took me a lot of effort later to get out of the habit of posing with those pretty gestures. Some say I still keep doing the shoulder part of it, especially when I want to look elegant. But I got the piece of meat anyway, in spite of my strange behavior, and my benefactor gave me a large piece of bread to go with it as well.

"For whom is it that you gather the wood scraps?" he asked me suddenly from beneath his straw hat.

"For my mother and Maria," I carefully explained, "old Herr Fox says I'm not good for anything else, the thing, me!"

"You?"

"Yes!... But even old Herr Fox will be warming himself next to our stove next winter again when I've brought enough scraps of wood so we don't freeze to death."

Unclear ideas were dancing around in my mind about the horrible sort of death that my mother knew how to describe so ominously, and I became very depressed.

"Where's your home, Christa?"

"Down there at the Blue Goose, where Cathy is always sitting at the family room window."

"Down there?" he asked, and kicked his foot in the direction indicated.

"Yes, yes, there!"

The Englishman quickly sat up straight, pushed his hat back, and rubbed his eyes.

"The classy girl who wears thick braids on top of her head, is that Cathy?"

"Yes, that's her, because my Maria wears her hair in pigtails down the back, and my mother always wears a bonnet."

"So who is this old Herr Fox? How did you end up living with those people?" And as he asked this, he held me by my skirt as if I were trying to run away.

"Herr Fox is Cathy's grandfather, and we live in his place and sew gloves, and Cathy does too, but he swears at us all the time because my mother still owes him something for the rented room ... oh well, we just don't have any money. My mother cries every day and sometimes Cathy does too, because she's a good person and also she has ...."

It was a great struggle I fought within myself now, gasping for air, as I came to the fateful "she has ..." and was about to betray a proud secret. He seemed to me to be the worthiest person, though, the only one who knew how to appreciate the rare value of this information ... I first looked carefully around the construction site to be certain no one else was there, then I mustered up my courage, took the black-haired Englishman's large head in both my hands, and mumbled in his ear: "Cathy has a feather hat! . . . ."

Then I took a few steps back, watched the man and waited; I thought he would take his hat off in front of me right away, the way he did in front of the master contractor, but he didn't do that. First his face started twitching as if he wanted to laugh . . . then he gave me a look of disbelief, opened his mouth dubiously, and said, "Ohh . . . .?!"

I understood the questioning look and the hesitant "Ohh . . ." and just nodded solemnly: "Yes! . . . ."

Next he grabbed me by my skirt again with his long arm until it started to tear, pulled me to him and whispered, "A real feather hat?"

"Yes! . . . and she has something else that's secret in the same box: she doesn't show it to anybody at all, not even me," I whispered even more quietly than he had.

"Wait a minute, Christa!" he exclaimed suddenly, took a tube out of his linen sack, pulled it farther and farther apart, looked through it, then held it up to one of my eyes while holding the other one shut, fiddled around with it a while longer, and finally said, "Look! . . . ."

I looked through it and – whoosh – in that very instant I was sitting in terror on the ground . . . for the Blue Goose was standing right in front of me, and there was Cathy sitting at the window of the family room, so close it seemed like I could touch her.

"Is that Cathy Fox?" asked the workman when I had pulled myself back together again.

"It certainly is," I stammered, apprehensively watching the tube get smaller and smaller in his hand.

"And she has a feather . . . ." he just pointed at his head.

"Yes," I said defiantly, for Cathy's feather hat was my only point of pride.

It may have been two years ago, once when she and I were at home all alone, that she pulled the black velvet hat with the gushing white feather from its box, looked at it terribly sadly, and told me that I was to tell no one what a lovely hat she had; to my dismay, though, she very soon locked it away in her closet again. Sometimes before I had seen elegant ladies riding around wearing hats just like it, so now – on certain pensive evenings under the table of old Herr Fox – I would convince myself that Cathy was secretly a lady of nobility, perhaps like some enchanted princess whose story she had told me herself. From this time on I always saw her with completely different eyes: soon all I could think of was that hat . . . and gradually I transferred this feather-hat dignity and secret nobility unto myself, and if earlier I had cried for my mother when the boys up on the hill beat on me, now I always yelled, "I'm going to tell Cathy; she's really something. She's got a fe . . .," each time swallowing the rest no matter how incensed I got. So the Englishman was the first one to whom I'd entrusted this valuable secret, and in return he was now shaking my arms and yelling, "Where did she get the hat?"

Where? . . . As if I'd ever thought about it. So I told him everything I knew . . . I told him that Cathy had once gone into the woods for six weeks to stay with a peasant woman who had goats. She had to drink goat milk there, said my mother and all the people in the Blue Goose. But old Herr Fox said at the time that Cathy could never darken his doorway again and my mother should hang a millstone around my neck and throw me in the depths of the sea, because I was a girl and would someday get in the same situation as Cathy . . . But when Cathy came back she was very pale and skinny, and I was afraid when she fell on her knees in front of the old man, but he spat on the ground in front of her and then slapped her on the cheek . . . She got even paler, threw her hands over her head, and cowered in a corner. Once, much later, she took the hat out of the box, then the beautiful dress she had bought from my mother, then the fine scarf she had inherited from her deceased grandmother, looked at it all, wept bitterly, and locked it all away again: before that she had put all her secret things in the box and never taken them out.

That's the story I knew at the time and that came out even more tangled than it does now; The Englishman listened to me, sometimes nodding his head . . . then he grabbed me tight by my shoulders and said with a twinkle in his eye: "Come on, let's go visit your poor Cath' together . . . ."

Was that ever a walk home! – Whenever I planted my feet against a wall and refused to go on, he lifted me up in the air, and when – in spite of my innermost indignation – I asked him not to say anything about the feather hat, he laughed in a way that made my blood run cold.

Howling aloud, red in the face, and with my skirt twisted, I arrived back home. He opened the door and pushed me into the family room ahead of him where Cathy was sitting at the window, not looking around. Only after I had crawled under the table did she look up to see the Englishman standing awkwardly next to her.

She asked what he wanted.

Wasn't there a room for rent here? Christa had said something like that, but of course he didn't understand German too well, he boldly lied. I made a fist under the table and yelled out: "It's our room! My mother's already paid for it!"

He laughed again and just pointed threateningly at his hat... This gesture deeply shook me: I stayed quiet, humiliated and shaking. He talked with Cathy quite a bit longer, but he did keep my secret....

From that day on he would walk past the window every evening and every morning and usually spoke a few words with Cathy; it was to me he gave the best wood scraps at the whole site, and gradually he started showing up in the family room every evening as well. Old Herr Fox must have liked him all right, because in his early years he had been a sailor himself, and the two of them talked about the seven seas so much that all I played under the table anymore was ship games. Whenever the Englishman was talking with Cathy, though, I would spy on them, because I thought sometime he would say it after all, the thing about the feather hat.

And sure enough, one evening when he was sitting alone next to Cathy, and she was telling him about the struggles of her childhood, as she often did, he took her by both hands and asked out loud: "Cathy, who gave you the feather hat?....."

I lay down flat against the floor under the table – Cathy wasn't going to have an easy time pulling me out from under there, I thought, and closed my eyes. For a while it was very quiet in the room... and when I finally looked up again, she had the hat in her hand already, and was struggling to say:

"I bought the hat for myself; and the reason is, I wanted to meet him in elegant style since he had become an officer in the meantime... my sweetheart... the one I loved more than my grandfather and... even myself ... and wanted to marry him when he came back, but he didn't come back, didn't... ever... come... back. Somebody shot him dead... Here's the newspaper where it tells about it... here's his picture and his letters... and here... here... is the... baptismal certificate and death certificate ...of... of our little child.... So now you know it all, Sir, and now you'll never tell me, of course, that you want to marry me."

Cathy wept softly to herself, and I cried out loud from under my table, since I felt so sorry for her. With one quick pull, the Englishman had ripped off all the buttons from his jacket, then he took a few steps through the family room and quickly returned to Cathy, who was taking dainty, colorfully ribboned baby clothes out of the box and looking at it . . . He stopped in front of her, wiped his forehead once and then again, and kept looking down at her thick, black braids as if waiting for her to say another word; but she kept quiet, even though her hands were shaking . . . Then he bent down to her, pushed a few little wisps of hair from her temples, stroked her face with both hands and then let them glide over her shoulders and arms; after that he took her fingers, counted them, examined her hands with the utmost attention, one after the other, clapped Cathy's palms together and gently let them fall back into her lap, all the while smiling like a young boy . . . Probably because she didn't want to look up at all, he tweaked and tugged at her short wisps of hair again, took her by the chin and lifted her brunette head to his chest; he gently dabbed at her moist cheek with one finger, suddenly threw the baby clothes and the papers back in the box, put the lid on it and pounded on it with his hand when it wouldn't shut right away.

Slowly Cathy lifted her eyes up to him, but he just kissed her on her sad eyes, stood up tall, and said in the same tone that old Herr Fox used on Sunday before going to church: "All right! . . . ."[6]

Everything was all right now, too, and Cathy turned out to be a happy wife, though she never wore any feather hats. My mother had an excellent opportunity to cry a whole lot, and old Herr Fox chewed a pack of the finest tobacco on the day of Cathy's marriage. For my part, I got a new skirt, made from one of my mother's old coats, a pair of shiny leather shoes from the Englishman, and Herr Fox said in a friendly way, "This is one day you don't need to go to the construction site, good-for-nothing Christa."

He didn't live to see the day when "the thing" was good for anything but carrying home scraps of wood.

---

[6] These two words, "All right!" are quoted in English in the original German-language story.

Marie von Ebner-Eschenbach, née Marie von Dubsky (1830-1916)[1] was born at Castle Zdislavitz[2] in Moravia[3] to a noble family with a long ancestral line. Her childhood was spent literally shuttling back and forth semi-annually between the Moravian countryside and the city of Vienna, hence between the Slavic and Germanic worlds, between the worlds of rural gentry and urban enticements. After early encouragement from Franz Grillparzer and a literary beginning that focused on efforts to compose drama, she went on to become the recognized *grande dame* of Austrian letters in the late nineteenth century, particularly for her prose. In 1900 she was the first woman to receive an honorary doctorate from the University of Vienna.

The Gemperlein Barons was written in 1879, and its fictional setting, Castle Vlastovitz, is reminiscent of the writer's own upbringing as a baroness in Castle Zdislavitz. Though many of Ebner-Eschenbach's other prose works deal with tensions between castle-dwelling nobility and the common village folk – a tension apparently eased in her own life by frequent and easy movement between the classes – this novella concentrates more on criticism of the nobility (and of male arrogance) via an emblematic set of two barons who are also brothers.

The Gemperlein[4] brothers are emblematic in that they represent two ideological poles of the former Austro-Hungarian Empire: the royalists and the revolutionaries (or to put it another way: the conservatives and the radicals). The struggle between the two and, at the same time, their heartfelt attachment to one another, are depicted with rich and warm humor. At no point does the feeling come across that one or the other is given the narrative upper hand; rather, both appear foolish in their excesses, of which the greatest excess is their habit of living in fantasy worlds.

The most pronounced of the brothers' fantasies are those relating to women. Assuming themselves to be splendid matrimonial candidates, having already relegated themselves in their own minds to the status of respected patriarchs, Frederick and Ludwig do not choose actual human beings for

---

[1] Remarkably, her years of birth and of death are exactly the same as those of the last great Habsburg emperor, Franz Joseph I.

[2] Czech: "a well-situated manor."

[3] A former Austrian province now located in the eastern Czech Republic.

[4] The name 'Gemperlein' had, in the early sixteenth century, a rare colloquial usage meaning "frisky little pony."

their wives, but rather delude themselves into concocting distorted images of women, images that in the end can be dismissed as easily as typographical errors or verbal misunderstandings. This cavalier and dismissive attitude of male anti-heroes toward women seems to be no mere fictional accident; it is consistent and unremitting throughout the novella. By contrast, the one true and wise visionary portrayed in the tale is not only a woman but one from the lower classes, the wife of the Gemperleins' steward.

Ebner-Eschenbach's early training and experience as a dramatist have left their mark in this novella. The emphasis is on histrionic and farcical journeys of human interaction as introduced, sketched out, complicated, and eventually resolved in dialogue. Even when wagons, trees, sheep, goats, and sway-back horses enter into the narrative picture, they do so as objects of spoken dialogue, inner monologue, or – in one highly comedic scene – as stage props for a vehicular accident, a literal fall from grace that illustrates the buffoonery and mock-heroic posturing of brothers Frederick and Ludwig. The two siblings exit the stage as tragicomic characters whose mannerisms fit somewhere between the quixotic and the neurotic, somewhere along a comic viaduct leading from intrinsic delusion to inevitable ruin – comical only to those, perhaps, who are observing from a safe and objective distance.

The Gemperlein Barons

Marie von Ebner-Eschenbach

1

The lineage of the Gemperlein family is a noble and ancient one; its destinies are intimately tied to those of its fatherland. Many times it blossomed gloriously; many times it declined into misfortune and poverty. Members of the house itself bore the greatest responsibility for the rapid changes to which its star was subject. Not once did Mother Nature create a patient Gemperlein, nary a one who felt justified to lay aside his warrior title. This strong family trait was common to them all. There are no greater contrasts, on the other hand, than the ways in which the various Gemperlein generations related to one another when it came to political convictions. Some spent their lives actively devoted to their ancestral rulers, sword in hand, sealing that devotion with their blood until the last drop had been spattered, while others became champions of revolt and died as heroes for their cause, as enemies of despots, wildly contemptuous of all forms of subjugation.

The loyalist Gemperleins, as reward for their energetic services, were called to positions of honor and respect and were deeded with sizable land holdings while the rebellious ones, as punishment for their no less energetic opposition, were banished in disgrace and forfeited their land holdings. Thus it came about that this family line could not rejoice from time immemorial in an ancestral realm to be passed down from one generation to the next.

At the end of the eighteenth century there was a Baron Peter von Gemperlein who served the state as a civil servant, the first of his warrior house to do so, and who in the evening of his life came to own a handsome stretch of land in one of the most fruitful regions of Austria. There, well stricken in years, he closed out his existence at peace with God and with the world. He left behind two sons, Barons Frederick and Ludwig.

The Gemperlein nature, which had been disavowed in the father, appeared to have remembered itself in these last two offspring. Once again it brought forth both family types – the feudal and the radical Gemperlein – but this occurred, as never before, in the very same generation. Frederick, the older, following his inclinations, was educated in the crafts of weaponry at the military academy in Wiener Neustadt.[5] Ludwig entered the university in Göttingen at age eighteen and returned home at twenty-two with a superb dueling scar on his face and the ideal of an international republic in his heart.

The brothers needed exactly fifteen years of hard-pitched battles, fought with might and boldness, to realize that there was nothing for them to do in the world, that Frederick's time was past and Ludwig's time had not yet come.

The former laid down his sword, tired of serving a monarch who wanted to live in harmony with his people; the latter turned away grumbling from his people, who willingly and cheerfully put their necks under the yoke of authority.

At this same time, Frederick and Ludwig moved onto their property, Vlastovitz,[6] and dedicated themselves with love and enthusiasm to its agricultural care.

Even if they were as different from one another as night and day, the barons did come together in one salient point: in the inexpressible devotion they developed, bit by bit, for their country manor.

No doting father ever spoke the name of his only daughter in more dulcet tones than did *they* speak the name "Vlastovitz." Vlastovitz was to them the quintessence of all that was good and beautiful. For Vlastovitz there was no sacrifice too great, no praise exhaustive enough. "My Vlastovitz," said each of them, and each would have been angry at the other if he hadn't said it that way.

Soon after their arrival the brothers decided to divide their father's estate into two equal halves. The castle with its annexes was to remain in Frederick's possession, who in return was to take on the responsibility of

---

[5] Literally "Viennese New City," a town located on the rail line between Vienna and the Semmering Pass, site of the Theresian Military Academy from 1752 to 1918.

[6] Czech: "native manor" or "manor of our fathers," also linguistically related to "patriotism" and "ownership."

having a log cabin built in the midst of Ludwig's acreage where the latter proposed to live and die at the head of the family he intended to found.

The division was discussed heatedly over and over, but to actually carry it out, that was another matter. First they planned one thing. Then they were able to decide something else, but as for actually carrying it out, they put it off from year to year. Which piece of ground, which foot, which clod of the beloved soil should one of the brothers willingly relinquish? The border line that would have separated mine and yours from each other and would have split the estate – unique and complete as a whole – into two incomplete halves, would have gone straight through the midst of each of their hearts. Nevertheless, the boundary between Upper and Lower Vlastovitz had long been entered in the registry file, the blueprints for Ludwig's log cabin were safely in the archive, and once it came to pass . . . but we don't want to get ahead of ourselves in narrating the inevitable catastrophe in this true family history.

The life that the barons led in the countryside was an extremely predictable one. Early in the morning they would both leave the castle and ride off together, to the fields in summer and to the forest in winter. Yet it occurred very rarely that they returned home together. Usually Frederick would come riding slowly back down the row of chestnut trees from the north first, his cheeks flushed and his eyes blazing. His former personal servant and current employee Anton Schmidt generally received the order: "Bring breakfast!" with the angry-sounding addendum: "Just for me!"

Anton would go to the kitchen door, wait a while, and then suddenly call to the women at the stove: "Breakfast for the gentlemen!"

That was the moment when Ludwig would fly into the courtyard through the gate from the south on his foaming, sweaty horse. His narrow, finely featured face was as gold as a grain of wheat on the festival of Peter and Paul,[7] his scholarly brow heavily clouded. With an imperious attitude he would enter the dining room. There sat Frederick, much too engrossed in the *Royal and Imperial Exclusive Viennese Newspaper* to be able to notice the appearance of his brother. The latter would immediately open up the *Augsburg General News* and hold it up in front of him with his left hand while pouring tea in his cup with his right. Serious reading went on, breakfast was eaten hastily, and then the Turkish pipes were smoked with great enthusi-

---

[7] June 29th.

asm. Both barons would sit across from each other on their stiff-backed chairs, their newspapers in front of their faces, wreathed from head to foot in heavy clouds of smoke from which, from time to time, a curse, an angry outcry could be heard as the precursor of the approaching storm.

All at once there would be a cry: "Oh those fools!," and a newspaper would fly under the table. The political debate was underway. Usually it took a stormy course and ended after about a quarter hour's time with the words "The hell with you!" issuing forth from both sides.

But there were also days in which Ludwig's particularly incensed mood would introduce some variety into the procedure. He made diatribes so personally poisonous and insulting that his brother refused to answer them. Frederick's open and otherwise friendly face then took on a grim expression, a trace of irreconcilable rage planted itself around his mouth; every hair of his mustache seemed to bristle. He stood up, took his hat, called for his brown short-haired hunting dog, and quietly left the room. His broad back, his mighty shoulders were somewhat stooped as if carrying a heavy load.

Ludwig took note of it, though he only gave him a quick glance, mumbled a few unintelligible words, and finished reading his newspaper with all the attention any person can expend who has pretty much lost control of his thoughts. Soon, though, he got up and began walking back and forth in the room with loud steps. His countenance turned darker and darker. Chewing on his lower lip, he threw his head back and straightened his slender figure more and more boldly, defiantly.

What was he asking for other than some peace and quiet? Here he had hoped to get his share of it. Yes, indeed, pure peace, pure quiet. In order to find *that* you shouldn't have to withdraw into the desert, you shouldn't have to sequester yourself in some soul-numbing isolation. On the other hand, what if that's not the way things are? What if Seneca[8] turns out to be right? If life means waging war and absolutely has to be fought, then it should be on a worthier battleground! Then it should be in a world where fate has properly blessed – or cursed – man with unusual stamina and with unusual gifts of the mind and soul.

Ludwig went slowly down the steps. His shaggy, ever morose Doberman followed after him, yapping.

---

[8] Lucius Annaeus Seneca (ca. 4 B.C. - 65 A.D.), a Roman author who coined the phrase: "What fools these mortals be!"

Under the entry gate the baron stood still and looked at the region again. The verdant hills that pulled the horizon in close with their gentle, wavy lines, weren't they advising: "Don't set your goals too wide! What we enclose is a world in itself, a quiet one, granted, but it is yours . . . Try to be content within our shelter!"

On one of the ridges rising from the lowlands lay the inviting farm complex which housed the pride of the Vlastovitz estate, the elite of the Negretti[9] flock. It had the appearance of a castle full of style and polish in the midst of stately poplars. The gently descending hillside next to it, barren land until thirty years earlier, was now transformed into a fruit orchard. Thanks to their loving father who had planted it! Not for himself, for he was never to rest in its shade, never to enjoy its fruits. It was for his sons, whom he thought about so often and whom he saw so seldom; for his sons, who were chasing their ambitious goals far removed from him and who were looking for lasting goods, lasting happiness – how futile! – out in the inconstant world . . . .

Now the pear trees were at the peak of their production, the apple and plum trees were spreading their heavily-laden branches in a wide circle about them, and the delicately slender cherry trees . . . how much fruit they had borne in the last few years! As large as nuts and as juicy as grapes. Indeed, it wasn't just children who loved the taste of the cherries of Vlastovitz!

And the fields round about . . . an ocean of green in spring, of gold in summer, but in the autumn a truly ecstatic sight for the agronomist: new promise after the richest fulfillment . . . Ah, yes, the soil of Vlastovitz! Turned, harrowed, plowed, as fine as the most meticulously tended bed in a flower garden, as aromatic as Spanish tobacco made from Havana leaves . . . you could use this soil for snuff!

Ludwig's gaze feasted on all these glories; the wrinkles in his brow and the churning tides inside him smoothed out. One more short struggle, one more attempt to hold on to the anger and the indignation threatening to dissolve away, and then it was over and done: "Where's my brother?" he would ask the first person he met and would make quick use of the information received.

At two o'clock the gentlemen came back from the fields, quarreling, of course, but still together, and sat down to eat. In the afternoons they dedi-

---

[9] An strain of sheep that dates back to antiquity.

cated themselves to training their dogs and horses, embarking on a reconnoiter of the estate or a portion of it, and discussing the next day's work with their steward, Herr Kurzmichel. The close of each day involved an extremely serious argument about religious, political, or social questions, carried out with the greatest of bitterness. Very agitated, each swearing undying opposition to the other, the brothers would go to bed.

By and large, with the exception of those variations brought about by the particular season of the year, the hunts, or the social calls in the vicinity, this was the life-style of the Barons von Gemperlein.

To a casual observer, such a life may not have appeared especially attractive, but anyone looking more closely would have to admit that it also had its pleasant aspects. The most pleasant was the high regard in which the brothers were held in the area. Even if there was a good deal of fear mixed in with this regard, that took nothing away from its value. It was difficult to decide which of the two noblemen was sterner with his servants. They demanded a lot, but never unjustly; they were often relentlessly harsh, but they honored the humanity in the lowliest person, even in the irretrievably lost.

"Because I'm on a higher plane than the poor devil, my neighbor, and must respect the inner protégé in him," said Frederick. "Because I am his equal," said Ludwig, "and recognize my own features even in his distorted image."

"You rascal!" Frederick would yell at the unrepentant sinner, "Don't you know what the law demands of you? Can't you hear what the priest is preaching? Just you wait; the police will catch up with you, and when you get to the other side . . . you're well on your way to hell, for sure!"

Ludwig's admonitions on the other hand went like this: "When will you finally learn to discipline yourselves? When will you get tired, you idiots, of paying people to watch over you, lock you up, and sometimes even hang you? Govern yourselves, you fools, so you can save yourselves all the money the government is costing you now."

Such vivid ideas didn't keep from having their effect, and the barons ascribed a much greater effect to them than they actually had. The brothers, despite many past disappointments, generally elevated their innermost desires to the status of high probability. In this way they enjoyed much good fortune that never came their way: they savored it in their thoughts and likely had much more vivid enjoyment by doing so than if it had actually befallen them. The rich imagination with which nature had endowed them developed much more profusely than would have been possible in the vortex of daily tumult, and it gave them an abundance of pure joy that is only ridiculed and rejected by those who are incapable of creating the same for themselves.

The more uniformly human life flows, as is well known, the more rapidly it seems to vanish, and before the brothers knew it the day came that Frederick was able to say: "I wonder if there has ever been a thinking person who hasn't made the observation that time actually flies very rapidly."

"Quite the contrary;" replied Ludwig, "this truth has been expressed so often that there's absolutely no reason not to say it one more time."

"Would we believe it if we didn't know it?" Frederick continued, "It's now been exactly ten years since we moved to Vlastovitz."

Ludwig swiped at the tips of his dusty boots with his riding whip, then he crossed his arms and stared out with melancholy into the green fields . . . that is to say, into the yellow fields, since it was autumn and they were sitting in front of a golden ash.

"Ten years," he mumbled, "ah yes, ah yes . . . ten full years. If I had married back then, back when I had such a good chance, when I was so loved . . . ."

"When you were loved," repeated Frederick, forcing himself to keep a serious face.

". . . then I could be the father of nine children by now."

"Or eighteen, if your wife had brought forth twins every time, or even far more, since apple blossoms seem to come to earth in bushel baskets!" said Frederick and laughed.

Ludwig gave him a look from the side. "There is nothing dumber," he said dismissively, "than a dumb laugh."

"There is nothing more ridiculous than a man who dreams by the light of day and hallucinates without benefit of a fever," cried Frederick. "Forget all your *ifs*, *ands* and *maybes*, all your delusions and fantasies! You're compulsively obsessed! Why don't you finally get back to what's real and actual!"

Now Ludwig broke into loud laughter. Wringing his hands, he lifted them, and his eyes, accusingly to heaven. "What's real!? What's actual!?" he shrieked. "Oh God, this man is talking about such things . . . this man who was in love with a typographical error for three years!" Angry and ashamed, Frederick hung his head and chewed on his mustache. Suddenly he exploded: "And you . . . don't you know . . . ?"

A fateful word rested on the tip of his tongue, but he didn't say it; he just growled quietly to himself: "Damn it all anyway!"

2

In the first year after having settled in Vlastovitz, the brothers had already decided to marry and had even chosen their future wives as well. Frederick decided in favor of the Duchess Josepha, daughter of the Nobly Born Sir Karl, Imperial Duke von Einzelnow-Kvalnov and of the Nobly Born Lady Elisabeth, Imperial Duchess von Einzelnow-Kvalnov, née Baroness von Czernahlava, Lady of the Stellar Cross Order. Ludwig, who had long settled in his own mind that he would rather remain in the dreaded ranks of bachelorhood than to marry an aristocrat, decided to make Lina Appleblossom, daughter of a merchant in the nearby town, his wife and the mother of a great host of free-thinking Gemperleins.

The claim could not be made that the acquaintance which the brothers had made with their chosen ladies was of a very intimate variety. Frederick had met his bride in the *Genealogical Handbook of Noble Houses*[10] and knew only a little about her, but what little he knew, he knew with certainty. She lived in Silesia on the 1100-yoke[11] estate of her father, was twenty-three years old, had five brothers of which the oldest was thirteen, and was devoted to the Catholic faith.

Her family connections, both from the paternal as well as the maternal side, were exceedingly respectable. She was not a member of the highest rank of nobility, it was true, but was from a good hereditary strain whose antiquity conceded nothing to that of the Gemperleins. It was no minor influence on Frederick's choice that Josepha had only brothers and no sisters: thus, the man who carried her across the threshold would not be in danger of seeing his domestic bliss threatened by sisters-in-law who might be sentenced to celibacy. In short, of all the daughters of the land entered on the pages of the pocketbook of nobility, not a one was as suited for Frederick as was Josepha Einzelnow.

He followed the life of his selected bride with loving attention through three yearly editions of the almanac and hardened his resolve more and more to travel to Silesia someday and to introduce himself to the Count of Einzel-

---

[10] This annual genealogical guide to families of nobility, published in Gotha, was also known as the *Gotha Almanac* or simply "the almanac," as it is called numerous times later in the novella.

[11] A "yoke" was a land measurement comprising the amount of land a yoke of oxen could plow in one day.

now as a suitor for the hand of the Countess Josepha, imbued only with the most honorable of intentions.

Ludwig, meanwhile, not only knew Miss Lina face-to-face, but he had gone so far as to talk to her once when she had come to Vlastovitz to visit her aunt, the wife of Steward Kurzmichel.[12]

"How's it going?" he asked the lovely young creature he had seen busily embroidering in the garden.

Lina Appleblossom arose from the bench on which she had been sitting, made a short, resolute curtsy, the curtsy of a true middle-class girl – which expressed purest self-consciousness with the most charming awkwardness – and answered: "Just fine, thanks."

She could tell how that pleased him because of a fiery look in his blue eyes, and her brown eyes lowered.

A pause . . . "Now what should I say to her? . . . My heavens! Now what should I say to her?" thought the baron and finally said: "That comes from the good country air!"

"Oh, I do just fine in the city as well!" replied the young thing with a cheerful smile.

The memory of this discussion preoccupied the baron quite often and quite pleasantly: he gave himself over to its contemplation without reserve, and his imagination adorned the modest experience with the most delightful of additional details. The greetings of the sweet young unsullied woman, her smile, her blushing took on a daily-increasing significance ever more flattering for him.

One day – it was on a Sunday when the Kurzmichel couple had dined at the castle – Ludwig suddenly turned to the steward's wife with the words: "An absolutely charming girl, your niece! A lovely, captivating girl!"

Frau Kurzmichel had just been listening to the deliberations of Frederick and her husband about the imminent sheep-shearing with that knowledgeable interest in serious matters which she credited above all for her reputation as a prodigiously bright woman. It took her a few moments to turn her train of thoughts in the new direction called for by Ludwig's comment out of the blue. As soon as she succeeded in doing so, however, an expression of gracious goodwill spread across her large, dignified face. She shook her head in hearty assent, setting in motion her hair curls – indivisibly affixed

---

[12] The name in German, perhaps ironically, has connotations of plainness and perhaps even of a simpleton.

with her Sunday bonnet – and said: "A good child! Well brought up, domesticated . . . I must admit it."

Coming from this lady, this bastion of decency, the praise was of inestimable value as a morality credential.

Ludwig merely said: "I see, I see," but he rubbed his hands together in the sort of frenetic state that for him signified extreme contentment, true rapture of bliss.

One evening a few months later, he reported to his brother that it was his very determined, unshakable will – a will not to be vanquished by any considerations, any resistance, any obstacle, that is to say, not by anything on earth – to marry Lina Appleblossom.

When he said this name, Frederick shot a look at him laden with indignation and wild scorn, yet he lowered his gaze again immediately to the book lying in front of him. It was *Arch-Traitor Judas*, his favorite book. With his elbows propped on the table and his fists clenched at his temples, he went back to his reading with passionate attentiveness. Ludwig had also laid his arms on the table, but they were folded; he arched his back like a cat and stared at his brother fiercely and directly. The latter's face grew redder and redder, the wrinkles on his brow compressed more and more threateningly, but all he would do was read and be silent.

Now Ludwig emitted a loud "Ha ha!," leaned back and began to whistle.

"Stop the whistling!" Frederick yelled ferociously, but without lifting his eyes.

"Stop the yelling!" answered Ludwig, in a voice much too loud, and then quickly ranted on: "What do you have against my marriage? It's all the same to me, of course, but I'd like to know!"

Frederick shoved the book away. "I have . . . nothing against your marriage!" he said, "Marry whom you want, a day laborer for all I care! But the thing is . . ." His face took on an expression of cold cruelty; he sliced at the air between himself and his brother with a solemn movement of his raised hand, "The thing is: To each his own! There are steps in life . . . Yours are taking you downward, mine . . . are taking me upward . . . ."

"What?" Ludwig interrupted him with provoking sarcasm. "What do we have in life? . . . Steps?"

Frederick wouldn't let himself be intimidated; he continued in the magisterial tone of voice he knew how to adopt at crucial times: "My wife here . . . yours over there. I won't put up with bad company. My Josepha will never darken the threshold of anybody born an Appleblossom."

"I hope not!" cried Ludwig. "Keeping company with an arrogant aristocrat? No, thanks. My wife shouldn't even have to suspect the existence of foolish women who think they're something special just because their ancestors can be counted!"

"Why can they do that?" Frederick broke in. "Because their ancestors made a name for themselves, didn't disappear back into the crowd ... that's why they can be counted."

"Coincidence!" responded the younger Baron von Gemperlein, "A coincidence that they were able to make a name for themselves: benevolence of circumstances that allowed the memory of their honorable or worthless deeds to live on in the people ... There are deeds enough – read your history! – There are enough world-shaking events whose originators no one can name ... What happens to the descendants of these men? Can you swear that your Anton Schmidt does not descend from the singer of the finest German hymn to the gods, or from one of the electoral kings of the Goths? Can you swear on that?" he asked and looked piercingly at this brother. The latter, just a little unsettled, shrugged his shoulders and said: "Ridiculous!"

"Ridiculous? I'll tell you what's ridiculous. It's ridiculous to accept honors earned by someone else. It's more than ridiculous: it's low and cheap to cash in on the efforts of strangers!"

"Strangers? Are my ancestors strangers to me?"

"Leave your ancestors in peace! Are you going to always stake your claim to the most valuable thing there is, the respect of other human beings, by trying to excavate it from the most revolting thing there is, death and decay? ... Yuck! That disgusts me!" Ludwig shook with repulsion and then added more quietly, in an almost pleading tone of voice: "Won't you ever realize that nothing can be said in favor of the institution of nobility except what Prosecuting Attorney Séguier[13] – read your history! – had to say in favor of other abuses: that their long practice makes them honorable ... or what the Bollandists[14] had to say in favor of thievery – read the *Acta Sanctorum* all the way through to the forty-fourth volume . . . ."

"To the which and what volume?" shrieked Frederick, incensed at this lame-brained cheekiness.

---

[13] Pierre Séguier (1588-1672) was a lawyer who rose to prominence at the French National Court.

[14] The Bollandists Society, named after the seventeenth-century hagiographer John Bollandus, published the *Acta Sanctorum* (Latin: *Lives of the Saints*).

His brother smiled contemptuously and asked: "Do you know the price you pay for your ancestor worship? It's called self respect . . . The person I am, how I act if my name, my rank, my possessions are taken from me, that's where I have value: that's the only thing I'll count on as my right. All the rest I despise as the gift of blind, senseless coincidence!"

Both had jumped up; the older brother came at the younger one and grabbed him by the shoulders: "Whose gift are these shoulders then, to whom do you credit this chest, this build of yours that makes you taller by head and shoulders than the average man? And that an honest heart is beating in your chest and that ideas can inhabit your head – crazy ones, of course but still ideas . . . To whom do you give credit for all that? Do you have it from coincidence, or do you have it from your ancestors?"

"I have it from nature!"

"Yes, indeed, from your Gemperlein nature," retorted Frederick triumphantly.

"The circling of your thoughts," Ludwig said after a short pause, "has no greater circumference than that of a guinea fowl. One solid point is there, and you keep turning around and around it like that beast on a desert plain . . . ."

"Guinea fowl? Beast?" bellowed Frederick, "For once you could stop with your zoological comparisons."

"The solid point, from which any jackass," Ludwig let his voice repose on this word to show how little respect he had for the admonition just received, "from which any jackass can turn the rational world upside down, is called prejudice."

"Ludwig! Ludwig!" at this point his brother interrupted him, "With my hands raised I implore you: don't get started with prejudice . . . prejudice!" he repeated and laid an indescribable – you could almost say tender – emphasis on the word: "That's what the ill-mannered calls politeness, the egotist calls self-denial, the scoundrel calls virtue, the atheist calls faith in God, an unruly child calls respecting his parents! Take prejudice from the earth, and you take away duty!"

"Hey, that's enough," said Ludwig in a domineering voice. "Reasoning proves nothing to you; we'll have to show you some facts." He threw his head back, his view prophetically scanning far into the distant future while his voice took on a sublime confidence. "*My children* will teach you what it means to be raised with respect for what is respectable, but . . . without prejudice."

"Your children! Keep your children away from me!" Frederick screamed and struggled about in the air with desperate haste as if trying to ward off small, prejudice-free Gemperleins flying at him in thick swarms from all sides, "They're not permitted to cross my threshold! I forbid them to enter my house!"

Deeply injured in his somewhat premature paternal pride, Ludwig turned away.

"Children without prejudices!" Frederick continued, incensed, "God save us from such monsters!"

"You don't need to call on God; you're already saved," his brother replied with icy coldness. "This much is self-evident, by the way . . . I will never knock on the door from which my wife and children were turned away. Our paths are separating. Where are the keys to the archive?"

He brought back the map of Vlastovitz, spread it out on the table, and along the boundary line, which was already sadly disfiguring the lovely sheet, he began to shadow in both sides so crudely that the line now looked like a tall, impenetrable mountain range snaking its way precipitously through the mirror-smooth plains, through the flowering fields and meadows. Frederick watched him sadly and angrily.

"There!" Ludwig growled each time he dipped the pen in the ink again, "That comes between us. That's you there . . . this is me here. Community values are good in heaven, but sadly, sadly, not down on this earth . . . Today's human beings just aren't ready for it yet! . . . ."

Ludwig was not able to make a final decision about the location where his log cabin was to be constructed as quickly as the plots of land had been divided up and long since carried out on paper: for every spot he decided on, Frederick had a valid objection worth considering. Ludwig finally lost the little bit of patience that was left for him to lose. "Now I've had it! This is where it's going to be!" he cried, and pulling out the pen in angry haste, he marked the place where his future home was to arise. Oh no! Like a black tear, a great ink spot fell on the map of Vlastovitz. Upon the lovely map, the exquisite work of a top-notch engineer, drawn at the behest of their dearly departed father with true monkish devotion . . . Frederick winced from head to toe, and Ludwig mumbled: "Hundred-thousand-million double blazes! This damned pen!" . . . .

That evening, Herr Steward Kurzmichel was just about set to climb aboard the marital camp, on which his wife had already taken refuge, when his plans were disturbed by a loud knocking at the outside door. Fast steps down the wooden stairs, rapidly exchanged words . . . Frau Kurzmichel was sitting upright in her bed by now . . . husband and wife looked at each other: he the image of consternation, she the image of vigilance. Next comes a knock at their bedroom door: "Herr Steward," cries the maid, "You need to go . . . to the castle . . . right away!"

"For heaven's sake . . . is it on fire?" groaned Herr Kurzmichel and rushed for the door. But his wife fortuitously stepped in front of him: "Kurzmichel . . . you're surely not going to . . . you're still . . . in your night shirt . . . ."

"True, true!" replied Herr Kurzmichel with chattering teeth, hurried back to the night stand, put on his glasses for any eventuality, and made frenzied attempts to put his snuff box away in the pocket that wasn't there.

"Take it easy, Kurzmichel! . . . In any situation in life, just take it easy!" advised Frau Steward and now was the one to call out through the closed door: "Is it on fire?" "No, it's not on fire," responded Anton's harsh voice from the other side. "But Herr Steward is supposed to come to the castle right away!"

Frau Kurzmichel helped her spouse into his clothes: "What's going on? What's going on?" her husband asked one time after the other, and the large *Frau* answered, agitated on the inside but as peaceful as a good conscience on the outside, "What do you think's going on? Your flannel jacket, Kurzmichel! . . . Who can accuse us of anything? What can happen to us? I think we can hold our ground! No, no . . . without a flannel jacket you can't go out into the night!"

A quarter hour passed. Frau Steward had boiled water for tea in the meantime and filled the hot-water bottle. Above all else Herr Steward, when he returned, just wanted to go to bed. The tea his wife forced on him burned his gums and the hot-water bottle burned the soles of his feet. He complained about that a little. But his better half, knowledgeable at healing, instructed him: "That's just your cold making its way out; that won't hurt you . . . And now tell me: what's going on at the castle?"

"Orders, my dear wife, urgent orders to be strictly carried out to assist in the construction beginning at the crack of dawn tomorrow on Baron Ludwig's . . . ."

"Log cabin!" Frau Steward finished the sentence with ironic sarcasm.

Her husband looked at her full of astonishment: "Where did you come up with that idea?" he said.

The answer he received was a very remarkable one. It went as follows: "The temptation would truly be great, if respect didn't forbid it, to call the barons in spite of all their excellent qualities, which I admire, a little . . . how shall I put it nicely . . ." Frau Steward paused before opening her narrow lips again for the memorable words: "Mark my words, Kurzmichel! Mark my words after ten years if you're still alive, which I hope God will grant: The log cabin will never be built! . . . Good night, my husband; lay down your head and sleep. Tomorrow I won't bother waking you!"

You have to admit, this rare woman provided proof at that very hour – proof shining brilliantly through the darkness of the ages – of her discernment, her notable foresight, and her knowledge of the human heart.

3

It is a sure bet that battles fought with such investments of spirit, tenacity and temperament as those undertaken by the Barons von Gemperlein gradually become ends in themselves, while the original reason for them loses more and more meaning in the eyes of the valiant warriors. If Frederick had been truly honest, he would have admitted that he'd have given a hundred Josephas for a Ludwig converted to proper class distinctions. Ludwig did admit to himself, on the other hand, that it would be sweeter to hear "You're right" a single time from his brother than to hear "I love you" from his Lina.

Only in very wretched hours, when they absolutely despaired in each other, would the brothers gird up their loins to make important decisions. So it happened that Frederick had his luggage packed one day, having set the next morning as the time of departure for his trip to Silesia, while Ludwig was casting about for ways in which he could best inform Frau Kurzmichel of his feelings for her niece. But . . . in the midst of these preparations, a sign from heaven came down in the form of a book delivery from Vienna. The shipment contained, among others things, the latest edition of the *Gotha Almanac* with the news that Frau Countess Lady Einzelnow had passed away at Castle Kvalnov on the third of August of the present year.

Frederick was deeply shattered by the painful loss that Josepha had suffered, and Ludwig, though he had no cause to love his sister-in-law, did not withhold from her his own sympathies in this tragic moment either.

"*Ah! Ça ah ça!*[15] My poor Josepha!" repeated Frederick six times, one after the other, while energetically snapping his fingers. "I feel so sorry for my Josepha. She's the one who will be hardest hit by this cause for mourning. On whom will the entire weight of the housekeeping rest now? Who will now be her father's support? Who will take the place of mother to her younger brothers? Nobody else but her . . . my poor Josepha!"

He gave himself silently over to his thoughts for a while and then said with dignified resignation: "To disturb her while she's carrying out such holy duties, to present myself before her with selfish motives at this moment, that would be nothing more and nothing less than boorishness! . . . Anton, unpack my things!" he commanded his butler who at that very moment was in the next room trying to close up the suitcases.

Ludwig had immersed himself in studying the almanac and suddenly called out: "Tell me now, where did your Josepha disappear to? I can't find her anymore. All I can find is a 'Joseph,' first lieutenant in the 12th Regiment of Dragoons."[16]

"Sure, you and your *Gotha Almanac*!" said Frederick and took the volume out of his brother's hand with an attitude of know-it-all jauntiness.

He browsed around in the relevant place; he read; he scanned; he downright hypnotized each word with his stare, but . . . he wasn't able to find his Josepha either. She had disappeared without a trace.

"What's going on . . . what is the meaning of this?" he asked in profound dismay and finally answered himself: "It can only be a typographical error!"

He began his investigation afresh: "The 'a' is missing here . . . it's supposed to say 'Josepha,' not 'Joseph.' The title of first lieutenant, *etc.*, belongs down in the next line with my brother-in-law Johann; during the typesetting it must have accidently slipped down there . . . ."

"This brother-in-law of yours," Ludwig replied, "is only sixteen years old, and you think he's already a first lieutenant? That would be a curious thing indeed . . . Even with all the patronage the young fellow may enjoy, it would be curious indeed . . . There was of course – read your history! – a nine-year-old bishop of Valencia in the sixteenth century . . . ."

"Don't believe all the rumors you hear!" mumbled Frederick angrily.

---

[15] French: Oh me, oh my!

[16] Note: *Dragoner*, the German word for "dragoon," has a secondary colloquial meaning of "masterful female."

"Still," Ludwig continued, "I consider a sixteen-year-old first lieutenant in our day and age to be an absolute impossibility."

They began arguing.

Frederick wasn't really in top form, though. He let many of Ludwig's boldest claims pass by unchallenged and responded to one of his brother's most reckless conclusions by saying: "It's a typographical error. It would be nice to let the editors know about that."

That very evening before going to bed, he wrote the following letter:

> Honored Editors of the *Genealogical Handbook of Noble Houses*!
>
> The undersigned, for years an admirer and reader of your almanac, allows himself the freedom of notifying you of a painfully sense-altering typographical error that has slipped onto page 237 of this year's volume, whereby in place of the line formerly occupied by Duchess Josepha now stands a first lieutenant in the 12th Regiment of Dragoons, who obviously does not belong there, of which you would be so good as to convince yourselves by referring to the last three yearly editions and sending me an urgently requested explanation by return mail.
>
> With best regards, *etc.*

After a few days, he received the "requested explanation." It read as follows:

> Honored Baron!
>
> No typographical error, but rather a correction. *Herr* Duke von Einzelnow (who appears to lend regard to our publication only sporadically) only now, on the occasion of informing us of the tragic passing of his wife, was able to point out the regrettable error that slipped into three annual editions of our handbook. From our side we would ask you to refer to the earlier editions of the almanac in which *Herr* Count Joseph is entered as cadet, lieutenant, and so forth.
>
> Thanking you for your concern, we take this opportunity to ask you to keep us punctually informed of each and every change that occurs in your noble house, and remain sincerely, *etc.*

The brothers were sitting at breakfast when the fateful lines arrived. Long after having read them, Frederick held them in front of him and looked at them like a farmer at his hail-damaged crop or an artist at his life's work destroyed. Ludwig, watching him with impatient consternation, finally took the sheet from his brother's trembling, unresisting hands, glanced through it, and broke out in peals of laughter. But suddenly he stopped, gave a cough, and began to busy himself by reading the *Augsburg General News*.

Frederick had put down his pipe, crossed his arms in front of him, and lowered his eyes. Great beads of sweat clung to his forehead, standing out ultra-white against his otherwise suntanned face. Ludwig threw glances of concern toward him, cleared his throat more and more aggressively, threw the newspaper on the floor and screamed like a madman: "That's the way you are! Something like this could only happen to you! Among the millions of people on earth, only you! . . . If I wanted to be a fool and look for my bride in the *Gotha Almanac*, then at least I would do it thoroughly, trace her back all the way to her source, back to her very first origins, get to know her great-great-grandparents before they were even born! But you! . . . What you do you can only do gallantly, that is to say – read your history! – superficially, recklessly, in a word: stupidly . . . with thoughtlessness and ignorance . . . yeah, that's it! That's your downfall, you and your whole illogical class!"

Now Frederick rose up roaring like a wounded lion. His spell of silence was broken, and he regathered his strength in the battle that next ensued.

The collapse of Frederick's air castles naturally postponed the construction of Ludwig's snug house. How could one of the brothers think of building a cozy hearth at a moment when the other was standing before the ruins of his patrilineal bliss? Ludwig delayed his conversation with Frau Kurzmichel until a more favorable time. In three months, in six, when the wound in Frederick's heart had scarred over, only then would he vigorously pursue his own amorous destiny.

But . . . only too often do people think they can decide their own fate when it has long been decided for them. Such was the lesson Ludwig was to learn by the following Sunday.

Frau Kurzmichel appeared for dinner in stunning fashion. She had ornamented herself with the most notable pieces from her wardrobe: with her brown silk dress, the wedding present her husband had given her, and with the yellow shawl that came from the estate of the deceased Frau Baroness, mother of the two barons. The Frau Steward would wear the brown dress on every festive occasion but the yellow shawl only when she was in particularly high spirits. This was the case today. From the anticipation in her mien, it was clear that in spite of all the freshness and originality that peppered her conversation as usual, she was saving up the best for last, just like the final bouquet of bursts at the end of a fireworks show.

It was over coffee, when a general lull had descended, that she lifted her voice and said: "May I allow myself the honor, Your Baronial Excellencies, of making an announcement that has to do with someone of a lower social class, to be sure, and somewhat distant, but yet known to Your Baronial Excellencies: someone who some time ago enjoyed the hospitality of glorious Vlastovitz?"

"Who do you mean?" asked Frederick.

"You mean your niece Lina Appleblossom," said Ludwig with the clairvoyant instinct of love. Frau Kurzmichel bowed in agreement: "My niece indeed... no longer Appleblossom however, but Klemper, since three days ago she married Herr Notary Klemper in K.[17]

Ludwig recoiled in horror, and Frederick cried: "What the devil! *Who did she marry?* That old sourpuss?"

"Sourpuss?" corrected the steward's wife, "Sourpuss is a rather strong expression, Herr Baron; I would scarcely dare to use it. The Herr Notary does have many... eccentricities, but he is a very good man, Herr Baron, and is well-to-do...."

"So that's why," Frederick broke in derisively.

"That's not why, Herr Baron... out of love...."

"Out of love?" shrieked Ludwig.

"Out of love," repeated Frau Kurzmichel, "for her penniless parents and her nine homeless brothers and sisters. She was able to bring three of them into her new home right away. That was her condition; otherwise she would have probably said no; since, dear God, if she had been able to follow her own heart... things would have come out quite differently... another ... a very different object...." Frau Kurzmichel was moved; her usual reserve left her, and she closed, carried away with concern and emotion: "I shouldn't actually... it isn't right, but now that the sacrifice has been made, all done, the gates of marriage have swung shut behind her... she left her heart, Herr Baron... right here."

---

[17] K. = a locality beginning with the letter K.

"How? Where? In Vlastovitz?" said Frederick, bewildered, and Ludwig got up and left the room.

"But dear wife," said Herr Steward, "such personal matters are of no interest whatsoever for . . . ."

"Frau Kurzmichel," Frederick interrupted, having become quite serious, "I wish to speak with you alone for a moment."

Frau Kurzmichel blushed, and her husband, discreet and tactful as ever, removed himself immediately.

For some time a deep silence reigned in the room. Frederick rubbed his forehead and eyes, he pulled unmercifully at his mustache, and finally began: "Can you tell me . . . well?"

"At your command, Herr Baron," said Frau Kurzmichel.

"Well now," he avoided her eyes, "tell me . . . don't be afraid: who is this object of her affections, you know, the one your niece . . . ."

"Herr Baron, this question . . . ." stuttered Frau Kurzmichel, totally shocked at the quizzical importance that Lina Appleblossom's matters of the heart seemed to hold for the barons.

After another pause, Frederick said with an unusually gentle voice: "I *beg* of you, don't be afraid; trust me with it, Frau Kurzmichel . . . Who is the object . . . you know . . . ."

"Herr Baron, you spoke of trust," replied Frau Kurzmichel, stooped her shoulders forward a bit, and laid her hands in her lap as if completely helpless and giving up all resistance . . . "If you speak of trust, Herr Baron, then it's settled; I can only answer, quite simply and to the point: It is the official scribe . . . ."

"Not my . . . ." the baron had nearly blurted it all out in the first throes of his astonishment, "Well now, look here, the official scribe; so it's the official scribe, you say!?"

He was in a strange mood. Actually joyful, but no one can imagine a darker shade of joy. He took a deep breath, as if liberated from a heavy load, and at the same time threw a glance full of painful tenderness toward the door from which Ludwig had just retreated.

"Frau Kurzmichel," he asked, "would you do me a favor?"

"Oh, Herr Baron, whatever may be within the power of an honest woman . . . ."

"I would not be turning to a dishonest one," Frederick broke in, pulled his chair closer to hers, and gave her a look that was indescribably gracious and good-hearted. "The favor I ask is this: If my brother should ask you,

'To whom did Fräulein Lina lose her heart?' then answer him: 'That is a secret' and . . . Frau Kurzmichel, you would rather die than reveal it to him. Will you swear to that for me, Frau Kurzmichel?"

"I promise you," said the large woman, lifting her head as she spoke like a soldier unafraid to die though bullets were whizzing all around her head: "My word is my pledge, Herr Baron."

"The reason I ask this of you," he added, "is something – please don't be angry with me – that I will have to keep to myself now and forever."

The steward's wife responded simply and nobly: "Herr Baron, I don't need to know the reason."

With admiration unfeigned, Frederick shook her hand: "I believe you; you are a good woman!" he cried, getting up from his chair. "I've always said there is a certain something about you . . . something of antiquity, Frau Kurzmichel, something Roman."

Frau Kurzmichel made a bow and left the room; infinite feelings were surging in her bosom.

Frederick went out to the lane behind the castle, where his brother – bare-headed, gesticulating wildly, storming up and down – received him with the words: "It's all gone now! And whose fault is it? . . . Yours! It was for you I gave up my happiness, mine and the happiness of the girl who loved me so deeply . . . ."

"That loved you . . . oh yes, yes," repeated Frederick and thought to himself: "The poor fool!"

4

The neighbor with whom the barons were most involved was Her Excellency, Frau Chancellor von Siebert, Lady von Perkovitz.

This noblewoman had been running a wise regimen on her estate, bequeathed by her dearly departed husband, for nearly a half century. Widowed at a very young age, she retained independence for herself and faithfulness to the memory of her "little master." She never again left the residence where she had lived a few years with him and didn't remarry again, either, though there hadn't been a dearth of opportunities.

Perkovitz[18] formed the eastern boundary of the baronial Gemperlein estate and drove an old shed and three fields like so many wedges into the borderlands of Vlastovitz. A most unpleasant boundary line! The type of boundary that makes irritations between neighbors unavoidable from time to time. A misplaced stake, a crooked furrow can give even the greatest peacemakers cause for disputes and rivalry. The thing is, that was precisely what lent more than a little interest to this involvement, by giving it a spicy edge. Her Excellency was a cheerful old lady of seventy years, as sociable as Madame de Tencin,[19] with whom Ludwig loved to compare her. She was afraid of nothing so much as boredom, measured people's value by the degree of attention they paid her, and demanded that everyone most eagerly recognize her uncommon intellect. On the other hand she put up with unpretentious company, unlike her famous example, could appreciate a practical joke, and didn't concern herself in the least about the frustration of those at whose expense it was played. She didn't care much at all for being considerate of others and still shared the old-fashioned view that a "good person" was just a polite euphemism for "dimwit."

In the eyes of Frau von Siebert, who had become accustomed to a reputation as the oracle of the region, even in questions of agronomy, the young Gemperleins were talented amateurs. She laughed at the barons' rapturous passion for their Vlastovitz but was basically very favorably disposed toward the feuding brothers. Not rarely did it occur that Frederick and Ludwig would show up at Perkovitz angrily quarreling with each other, kiss Her Excellency's hand, give their greetings to Fräulein Ruthenstrauch, the lady's social companion, and to Herr Scheber, her secretary, continue arguing for another hour, jump up enraged, take their leave all around, and ride off arguing.

Her Excellency, who had been adding fuel to the fire the whole time by first agreeing with Friedrick and then with Ludwig: "Now *you're* right about that! . . . And now again *you're* right on that point!" held her sides for laughter afterwards.

---

[18] Czech: "protruding manor" or "manor that juts."

[19] Madame Alexandrine Guérin de Tencin, instigator and proprietress of a famous literary salon in Paris.

Herr Scheber twiddled his thumbs, tried to straighten the wig that always sat crooked on his cucumber-shaped head, but in doing so only made it more crooked, sweated a great deal, took a pinch of tobacco and sighed: "Oh my, that is just so ridic . . . .!"

The limpid blue eyes of Fräulein Ruthenstrauch expressed helpless indignation; her pale lips said in a quaking voice: "I really thought they were going to tear each other to pieces; my face turned every possible shade of red . . . ."

"Don't flatter yourself!" cried Her Excellency. "The interesting pallor of your cheeks didn't suffer the slightest deviation the whole time."

With an inner delight in the distraught countenances of her underlings, she continued: "What weak stomachs you have, you two! . . . The ruckus did me good. For once we were able to hear what the human voice is capable of. A discussion like that clears the air: I feel as refreshed as after a thunderstorm!"

On the day the brothers made the discovery that they had been inhabiting Vlastovitz for ten years, they paid a visit to Her Excellency. The gathering had, as usual, assembled in the *salle à terrain*.[20] In the right corner of the sofa that was stationed in front of the round table sat Lady von Perkovitz; Frederick and Ludwig had taken their positions in two armchairs. Fräulein Ruthenstrauch was unwrapping silk in the window bay; Secretary Scheber had planted himself on the edge of a thin-legged stool at a respectful distance from the high-born nobility in a posture that took the golden mean between hovering and sitting. He stole glances at the barons from time to time and asked himself: "What's it going to be today?"

But there was going to be nothing. The brothers were in a gentle, melancholy mood. The observation about the rapid flight of time which Frederick had made just a short time before had left a strong impression in his own soul and in Ludwig's.

Both had suddenly become aware of their lost youth, of their misplaced happiness, and felt strangely moved.

Her old Excellency swung her little Eris-torch[21] about in vain; the sparks that otherwise would have fallen into a virtual powder keg now fell into wet grass, as it were.

---

[20] French: sitting room on the ground floor.

[21] Eris was the Greek goddess of disharmony and argument.

"Does Your Excellency know," said Frederick, "how long we've been living in Vlastovitz now? . . . It's been ten years! Yes, for ten years we've enjoyed the honor of being your neighbors!"

"Only ten years?" she replied. "I would have thought that ours was already a thirty-years' war."

"Really? . . ." Frederick counseled with himself whether this was flattery or just the opposite. "Look here, Your Excellency! . . . I made the comment to my brother just a short time ago that time actually quite quickly . . . that I found, that actually . . . time, oh the time . . . ."

He didn't know what he was saying anymore; he just put the words out like a robot and went completely mute before finding his way to the end of the sentence.

But even if his voice betrayed him, his eyes spoke a language all the more eloquent. Translated into words, they would have been: "Oh, how beautiful! . . . Oh, for the gracious goodness of heaven, how devilishly beautiful! . . . I can't imagine anything more beautiful!"

The eyes of all those present followed the direction of his enraptured gaze. At the door leading to the guest rooms stood a tall, feminine figure. No longer in her first blossom, but, as truly as a man's heart opened at seeing her, in her most beautiful one. She was wearing a simple white dress; her luxurious chestnut-brown hair, braided into thick pigtails, encircled her nobly formed head. In her hand she held a straw hat, gloves, and a parasol, and Frederick thought he had never seen such uniquely tasteful and even winningly attractive items in his life as the petite black straw hat, Swedish gloves, and parasol of unbleached silk.

"This is the way I had imagined Josepha," he thought. Ludwig was thinking: "Not even my Lina can compare with her," and both were thinking: "No dream can be sweeter! But she has the advantage that she won't turn to dust when I wake up, that I could see her with open eyes, yes, and even speak with her."

When Her Excellency introduced her to the barons and then said to the latter: "My niece Siebert," she bowed, smiled, and assured them in the most charming manner that she was "very pleased."

She sat down by her aunt on the sofa, in the left corner next to Frederick's armchair.

The older baron immediately began a lively discussion with the lovely guest of the castle while the younger one fell pensively silent and the noblewoman observed with exceptional wonderment.

The impression that this enchanting creature's appearance made on him was all the more overwhelming since it caught him in a moment of innermost vulnerability; in a moment of depression, of regret . . . in a word: of *weakness*!

But there are also coincidences in life so curious that you would have to take them to be strokes of fate, even if you were as wise as Kant[22] and as enlightened as Voltaire.[23] I would like to see the one who, in the hour he's mourning the loss of a good opportunity, would find one a hundred times better and not cry out: "Fatum! Fatum!"[24]

As for Ludwig, he thought he heard a voice calling to him: "There you have it again, your happiness . . . which you thought was lost! And this time palpable enough, living in Perkovitz . . . it's the niece of your closest neighbor!"

He very heartily envied his brother for the eloquence he was working up to. Of course, you have to be quite limited in intellect to come up with such home-baked platitudes in front of such a wonderful creature. Meanwhile, that's precisely what happened with gusto. Frederick said: "Such weather in September – that's a blessing – the grapes are ripening – the beets and turnips are sweetening!" and looked at her with gazes that practically wrapped her in good will, and bowed down so deeply over her hands – that were resting on the table and playing with the Swedish gloves – that it seemed he was about to kiss them.

The woman appeared to be well aware of the spell she was casting. Only a clueless clown in some German comedy playhouse would fail to notice it, but instead of getting arrogant, she appeared a little embarrassed, a bit unpleasantly moved.

The person absolutely gloating at the barons' imminent misfortune, however, the one in whose mien was mirrored an expression of deeply malevolent triumph, was none other than Her Excellency.

Her very first concern, though, was to conceal her true feelings, and suddenly she started in with her loud, drawn-out nasal voice: "Now what's going on, my dear Ludwig? I've already asked you three times whether or not you've finally sold your wool, and I've gotten no answer. What in the

---

[22] Immanuel Kant (1724-1804), German philosopher.

[23] Voltaire (1694-1778), French author.

[24] Latin: "fate."

world is going on with you two? I don't know why you look the way you do, I swear! . . . One of you sitting like Amadis[25] on the rock of poverty and the other . . . Be careful, Fritz,[26] you're not looking so well today: as red in the face as if you were about to have a stroke."

It seemed to the barons as if they had been launched from seventh heaven down to earth with a single kick, and down to earth's most miserable region at that. They would have been very glad to assassinate the old woman at that point.

The latter continued: "By the way, we still have one bone to pick. I wanted to ask you to give your forester permission to hunt somewhere other than at my property line, at least from time to time."

"Give permission?" the brothers mumbled. "Your Excellency . . . indeed . . . ."

"Somewhere other than on the boundary line!" Her Excellency repeated sharply and with emphasis. "He patrols back and forth in front of my shed, day and night, and shoots whatever shows its head – whether it's a billy goat or a nanny goat.[27]

The barons yelled. Frederick's eyes were blazing and Ludwig's were shooting sparks. "I give you my word," said the latter, "that the forester will be fired if ever it proves to be the nanny goat."

"He's jobless then!" cried Her Excellency and stretched forth her scrawny hand imposingly. "The nanny goat was shot the day before yesterday!"

"Excellency!" responded Frederick, scarcely master of his emotions any longer, "I saw the carcass: it was a billy goat!"

"It was a nanny goat!" Her Excellency broke in with cold wickedness, and Frederick screamed with rage . . . that is, he wound himself up to scream with rage, but it remained at the stage of intent. One look from his lovely neighbor transformed his excitability into feebleness and his animosity into ecstasy. Terrified, she looked at him, then quietly and pleadingly whispered to him: "I ask you! Please have regard for the stubbornness of the aged."

"I ask you . . . ." It sounded like heavenly music, captivating and irresistible. Not only pacified, nay, blissfully he bowed his head before Her Excellen-

---

[25] In medieval romance: a knight-errant, model of the chivalric hero.

[26] Fritz is a nickname for Frederick.

[27] It's considered bad sportsmanship to shoot the female of the species (the nanny goat).

cy and said stoutly and ardently like a knightly martyr: "If Your Excellency commands, then it was indeed a nanny."

"There we have it!" said the aunt; her niece, however, put her hands together as if she were applauding: "Bravo! Bravo! You are so extraordinarily charming, Baron Gemperlein!"

"When we're so close, at least we make the effort . . ." he said with good-hearted naivete and, overcome by his grand, rapidly inflamed feelings, he added: "Please stay close by a very long time, Fräulein!"

At these words she lifted her head, blushing and with a roguish mannerism of protest. Scheber's eyebrows suddenly came together with delight in the middle of his forehead; Fräulein Ruthenstrauch in her window bay let out a giggle . . . But the lady of the house gave punishing looks to her two satellite workers . . . Scheber's face returned to its usual wrinkles of anxiety and concern. Fräulein Ruthenstrauch suppressed her giggling and canceled it at the same time by vividly clearing her throat.

Her Excellency rapidly rolled out another topic of conversation and then said, turning to her guest: "Shall we have our coffee in the gazebo, Clara?"

Thus the brothers learned that the niece of Frau von Siebert was named Clara. Frederick was extremely glad to learn that; he wasn't satisfied with this information alone, however, but in the course of the evening was able – cunning as he was – to find out through skillfully targeted inquiries and finely attuned questions that Clara was the daughter of the Frau Chancellor's brother-in-law, of Herr von Siebert, a colonel in the Saxon military. He rejoiced at the success of his research. This time Ludwig would not be able to accuse him of falling in love with a phantom; this time he was moving forward soundly, practically, logically with the preparations for possibly courting her in the future.

The gazebo where the evening meal was served was on a knoll opposite the one from which Castle Vlastovitz dominated the area. Clara exclaimed that it was beautifully situated, that with its white chimneys and high French roof it appeared very inviting, yes, one could even say imposing.

Frederick ventured his opinion quite blissfully that it seemed that way to himself at times as well. Vlastovitz was a dwelling place, he said, that actually left nothing to be desired . . . "With the exception of one thing, of course . . . yes, one . . . long sought . . . not yet found . . . it's lacking a . . . ."

"Stop!" Clara interrupted him, "Let me guess!"

"Good, good, make a guess . . . make a guess . . ." he quietly repeated and blinked his eyes at her expectantly.

"It would be a work of art to guess that!" said the Frau Chancellor dryly. "A wife is what's missing, the whole world knows that."

Clara assured everyone that she wouldn't have been able to guess it; she laughed, she joked, and Frederick, innocently laughing along, failed to notice the knowing looks of mutual understanding that the aunt and niece, secretary and social companion were sharing with each other.

Ludwig's face had darkened. He was ashamed of his brother; he had to hold himself back from yelling out to him: "They've gotten the better of you!" That wouldn't have been appropriate just now, though, so he said to Clara in a reproachful tone of voice: "You have a very jovial disposition."

She lowered her eyes and suddenly looked quite shocked. Only after a short pause did she answer: "Yes."

It's true she only said "yes," but in that one little word was embodied the frankest confession, the most charming penitence. Ludwig felt disarmed and said, in friendlier tones by now: "All we can do is congratulate you on it!"

"Isn't it true?" she said: "It's so good to be one of the people who thank God for having put the brightest light right next to the darkest shadows."

A quote, not exactly original, but very charmingly appropriate: he was forced to acknowledge it, she had found a witty retort, and the high opinion he had formed of her at first sight was restored. How very differently this heavenly creature spoke with him than she did with his brother! How well she knew whom she was dealing with now, how raptly she turned her attention to his dignified discussions! He rewarded the trust that her perceptive mind instilled in him by introducing the deepest questions with which his own intellect wrestled. He stipulated the three cardinal points of his convictions:

1. The only moral form of state is a republic.
2. There is no personal life after death.
3. The mother of all the evil that's ever been on earth is imagination.

Frederick shifted his weight back and forth in his chair, painfully embarrassed. Such an intelligent person, this Ludwig! But he has no idea of how to act around women . . . It just made you sorry, Jesus, really sorry for him . . . .

Frau Chancellor loudly asked what time it was; Fräulein Ruthenstrauch and the secretary yawned through their noses. It began to get cool and dark; the company returned to the castle. In the dining room the candles were already burning, and the servant went up to Her Excellency with the question of how many places should be set at the table . . . "Table settings? . . . For what? . . . ." the lady of the house interrupted him and then turned with undisguised impatience to the barons: "Are *you* going to stay for dinner *too*?"

She was not understood, for the brothers assured her as from one mouth that they were incapable of refusing such a gracious invitation.

"Now I've had just about enough of this joke!" Her Excellency said so loudly to Ruthenstrauch that the latter was horrified and cast a long sideways glance at the barons. No need to worry! All they saw and heard was beautiful Clara. The dinner was served and the remnants were carried off again; the obstinate guests still hadn't budged an inch.

Frau Chancellor finally gave the order for the barons' coach to be announced, the conveyance to which the horses had long since been harnessed. Then the brothers awoke as from a dream and took their leave – both as much in love as they had previously imagined such a thing possible.

5

For the first time in ten years the brothers spent a sleepless night. For the first time they dispensed with their morning ride on the following day; for the first time each of them ate breakfast in his room and then wandered off alone through the woods and meadows. They didn't come home for lunch, which caused Anton Schmidt such despair and the cook such agitation that they poured gravy instead of chocolate sauce over a Spanish wind torte and threatened to fire the kitchen maid who dared to smile at their mistake.

Having been informed about what had happened in the castle, Frau Kurzmichel spent the day in fear and dread and didn't have an answer for the question her husband kept repeating: "What to do? Where do we start?" In the face of things undreamed of, even the keenest intellect comes to a standstill.

That evening around eight, the Herr Steward proceeded to the castle as usual to give his report. It was as quiet inside as if it were only inhabited by mice. Nearly paralyzed with fear, Anton set out to look for his superior.

The rest of the house staff sat around the warm stove in the brightly lit kitchen, whispering and mumbling.

Kurzmichel, to be cautious, first wandered down through the entire suite of rooms. All of them empty, deserted, and eerily dark. The old man finally sat down on the black leather sofa in the antechamber and waited, the financial ledgers under his arm. The evening star winked in cozily through the wide window across from him, while light gray fog slowly rose up from the meadows on the valley floor and gradually intermingled with the heavy wreath of clouds lying immobile above the mountains. Kurzmichel began to consider everything that could have happened to the noblemen, and terrible possibilities presented themselves to him. Maybe they'd both been in an accident – maybe only one of them – maybe one of them because of the other... Kurzmichel had feared as much a thousand times with their temperaments, with their unquenchable thrill of battle!... Maybe they'd carried it to the extreme; maybe one of the brothers is now... No, the thought is unthinkable... Kurzmichel tries to exorcize the demonic ideas rushing at him by engaging in a peaceful intellectual activity and begins to recite his multiplication tables half out loud. At the same time, though, he is listening feverishly, tensely, for any sound from the stairs, and finally it seems to him as if steps could be heard coming from them. They slowly rise up the stairs; the door to the antechamber opens to let in an imposing figure, and the voice of Baron Frederick says: "Who's there? Why don't you light the lamp, you jackass?"

The steward doesn't feel himself addressed by the term "jackass," for his master obviously thinks he is the houseboy. But he can't get around thinking that the barons should use this expression, which is insulting to any person, somewhat less often.

"It is I, Your Highly Well-Born Gentleman," he says; "I've come, I'm here to give my report."

An unarticulated sound – the word "report" restated as a mumble with an accent, as if it signified something outrageous or unheard of. Frederick shouts at Herr Kurzmichel: "Talk to my brother about it!" and goes past him into the living room, slamming the door shut behind him loudly.

"Talk to his brother!...." Kurzmichel takes a deep breath and recovers, and as the houseboy with the burning candlestick stumbles in, lights the hanging lamp, and hurries off to spread light elsewhere, the steward hits himself on the head as if trying to punish it for the crazy ideas it had just nurtured in him.

Again the heavy door rattled in its hinges, and in strode Baron Ludwig. He carried his head as high and proudly as ever, buried both hands in the pockets of his long overcoat, and walked past Herr Kurzmichel just as absent-mindedly as had Frederick. "I've come to give the report," said the steward. "Talk to my brother about it!" yelled Ludwig without stopping, without even looking at him, and slammed the salon door shut behind him even more loudly than Frederick had done.

Herr Kurzmichel was acquainted with the rude manner of his masters, but was always sensitive and still felt injured by it. On returning home, he told his wife that a person doesn't have to consider something unpleasant to be pleasant just because it happens to him every day. The marvelous woman let stand the correctness of this observation and offered her husband the best consolation there is: she felt sorry for him.

The barons devoured their evening meal silently and hastily. After that they lit their cigars, pushed both their chairs back from the table, didn't exactly turn their backs on each other but a little to the side, and stared stubbornly into the air. Frederick was the first to allow a sound to escape by beginning to mumble: "Siebert . . . Siebert! Clara Siebert!"

"What?" asked Ludwig.

"Good family," Frederick continued. "A part of the oldest nobility in Saxony."

Ludwig replied with an unbelievably gentle voice: "Where did you get that from?"

His brother gave him a cursory glance: "I'm convinced of it."

"I believe that you're wrong there," said Ludwig as gently as before. "The Sieberts are middle class – peerage by meritocracy[28] doesn't count in your eyes, of course. They're very much middle class."

Frederick straightened his back, pounded sharply on the table with his fist and cried: "For all I care!"

A long pause ensued. Finally Ludwig spoke, breathing heavily but still with a reverent hush: "You're in love. I am too."

Painfully agreeing, Frederick nodded with his head. The word didn't surprise him; it was only the confirmation of a misfortune of which he was already aware.

---

[28] The German original word is "*Papieradel*" or literally "paper nobility," the call to peerage that comes by letter to those who are thought to have earned the privilege.

"Men must have the courage," Ludwig continued, "to accept things the way they are. True?"

"True," was the answer.

"But marry . . . she can only marry one."

"Also true . . . ."

"For you see . . . brother . . . ." Ludwig stood up, pressed the knuckles of his clenched hands on the table and appeared to be winding up to deliver a lengthy speech.

But Frederick prevented him from carrying out this intention by saying: "Dear brother, you don't need to expound to me on what is self-evident."

"So that's settled. Listen to one more thing . . . listen to me patiently a little more. Can you patiently listen to me a little more?" asked Ludwig.

"I'll see. Speak!"

"She can only marry one. But next comes the question: which one?"

"Yes, that's the question!" Frederick stood up as well, ran both his hands through his hair, and sat down again.

"I asked: Which one?" said Ludwig . . . "The answer to this question is the most evident on earth, and it is: The one she chooses . . . Let's leave the choice up to her!"

" . . . Her . . . the choice? . . . The choice left up to her? . . . Don't you think, dear brother, that she will choose the one who most vigorously pursues her? The one who offers her his hand first?"

"I believe, dear brother, that she will choose the one that pleases her better. What pursuit? . . . If the one who doesn't please her pursues her, then she'll refuse him . . . Then she'll refuse him . . ." he repeated, deep in thought.

When the brothers had departed from Perkovitz the day before, Ludwig had taken along with him the conviction that he'd made a very favorable impression on Clara. In the sleepless night, however, and during the solitary daydreams of the present day, all sorts of doubts had started to creep in. That she had recognized his intellectual superiority over his brother seemed to him a done deal. But couldn't precisely this superiority send a chill through her? Might not Frederick's naive and innocent personality be more to her fancy than his strict and unbending one? Hadn't she perhaps said to herself: "Now I could be a wife to you, but he's somebody I could control?" Who knows, maybe she's one of those women – they say there are such – who would rather rule than be ruled . . . .

The suggestion, therefore, which he presented to his brother, that of letting Fräulein Clara decide between them, came from a completely honest heart and from the sincere desire to make an end of the torturous uncertainty in which they found themselves – one way or the other.

Frederick, however, hesitated to say yes. He already knew ahead of time what answer Clara would give if the choice were left open to her; it seemed to him false, unfaithful, sneaky, to expose the poor devil, Ludwig, to certain disappointment and humiliation. On the other hand, even if he's told over and over: "She's not going to take you!" will he believe it? A hard battle raged in him. He would have given anything on earth to find another way of informing him, but he found none, no matter how much he struggled with it. So he said nothing, stubbornly remaining all the more silent the more earnestly and eloquently Ludwig tried to force him either to accept his suggestion or to make a better one!

While he sat there so dark, mute, and suffering, his hunting dog came up, laid its head on his knee, and began to whine. "Go away!" cried Frederick, and when the animal didn't obey right away, he gave it a rough kick. The dog let out a short, howling yelp and went over and sat down in the window bay; shaking, quietly whining from time to time, it followed Frederick constantly with loving, pleading eyes, and contentedly hammered its hard tail against the floor when it succeeded in getting its master to throw a glance its way. The latter grumbled: "Spoiled beast!," stood up, took a pillow from the sofa and tossed it over to the dog, who immediately shoved it into the corner with his snout and lay down on it.

Ludwig suddenly boiled up: "God in heaven! . . . Here I've been trying to talk sense into this person for half an hour . . . It's a matter of his happiness in life, as well as mine, and this person . . . is playing with his dog!"

Now Frederick went up in flames: "Have it your way! . . . Fine, then, let her choose! That's all right with me. But when the choice has been made . . . whoever makes recriminations is a coward . . . ."

"A pitiful coward!" Ludwig trumped him. "The one marries, and the other takes care of himself as best he can."

"His problem. It doesn't bother me."

"Me even less!"

"Make a note of it!"

The barons looked at each other full of bitterness and stormed out of the room in opposite directions. No matter how angry they still were, they found it a relief to have finally unburdened their hearts from the perplexing torture of not knowing what to do.

6

The next day, after the brothers had just returned from their morning ride, <u>H</u>err Steward had his presence announced to them. He reported that the messenger from the Perkovitz postal domain had just deposited a letter at Baron Frederick's address in the domain of Vlastovitz, and . . .

"Letter . . . " Frederick interrupted him, "from Perkovitz . . . where?"

Kurzmichel handed over a nice, decoratively folded piece of paper and then asked if he might take the opportunity to proceed with the report which had been missed the day before . . . .

But the baron wasn't listening to him. He had hastily broken open the small note, looked excitedly in all his pockets for his reading glasses since – woefully sad but true – he had no longer been able to read without his reading glasses for a year now. Not having found them, he stumbled into his room with giant steps.

"Who's it from . . . the letter? . . . ." asked Ludwig hollowly.

"From Her Excellency . . . ."

"From Her Excellency. . . ?!" and Ludwig hurried after his brother.

"An invitation!" the latter called to him. "Lunch assembled in honor of her niece and us in the little Rendezvous[29] Forest Castle. Her niece *and us* . . . do you understand? *And us* !"

"Aha!" said Ludwig and took the small letter from Frederick's hands. Its closing lines were much stranger than the beginning. Frederick just hadn't taken a good look at them in his frenzy of joy: "We have a confession to make to you; then we will drink coffee to our continued good friendship."

"Really? Is that what it says there?" Frederick rejoiced and hopped around in the room like a happy child.

For this one day the barons didn't complain about the rapid flight of time. One full hour the two of them waited in front of the castle for the coach

---

[29] "Rendezvous" is apparently the name of one of Her Excellency's smaller castles.

scheduled to arrive at three o'clock in the afternoon. Right on time the carriage arrived in the courtyard: a light Phaeton[30] harnessed with bays that the coachman guided from a rear seat. As soon as Frederick caught a glimpse of the horses, he rumpled his brow. "The Hannakers?[31] Who ordered the Hannakers to be harnessed?"

"I did!" answered Ludwig, swung himself up to the elevated coachman's seat, and took the reins. "Get in! Well . . . go ahead and get in!"

But Frederick kept standing next to the horses, looking them over with a hateful eye. "You're really going to make a grand impression with those," he said.

The bay horses had been the source of lively arguments between the barons for months. Ludwig, who, as Frederick put it, understood as much about horses as a barrel maker does about bobbins, had bought them from a farmer without informing his brother beforehand. As he had them paraded before the latter, proud of his good taste, Frederick yelled out while they were still a good ways off: "Nothing to them! Coarse blood lines!"

"What do you mean, coarse? . . . Nothing is coarse but arrogance. They cut a fine profile!" rebutted Ludwig.

"Profile . . . but no blood lines . . . and not even a profile . . . legs like spiders . . . backs that sway down . . . necks like deer . . . they're just nags!"

Ludwig had expended the most meticulous care and effort to have them put in stalls with straw all the way up to their bellies, to have them stuffed full of oats . . . he had exercised them, trained them, and gradually conditioned them . . . all in vain! They were poor draft horses and never improved: lazy when leaving the barn, temperamental when returning, easily spooked, nervous, wary of the terrain, in a word . . . worthless.

Ludwig was attached to them, though; he liked them, and because he hoped that Fräulein Clara would like them too, he had them harnessed up that day.

"Go ahead and get in!" he repeated, and despite Frederick's inner misgivings, he decided to do that. This was difficult enough for him! "On an occasion when you'd like to show yourself in the best light, when everything about you should carry the stamp of solidity and tastefulness, to drive up with a set of horses like that . . . that's just too much!"

---

[30] A carriage named after the son of the sun god in Greek myth.

[31] Horses originating in the region of the Hanna River in Moravia.

But he did it; he gave in. That poor fellow, Ludwig – about to face bitter disappointment, probably within the next hour – filled him with sympathy, and he let him have his childish whim.

They drove through the village. In spite of Frederick's urgent warning, Ludwig left the road at the end of town and took the path through the fields. This path was as bad as it could possibly be, and it turned treacherous in the forest blanketing the closest ridge, the one that formed the boundary to Perkovitz. At that point it followed a tiny stream and climbed steeply until it reached the summit, bordered by a heavy forest on the right and plunging precipitously toward the moist meadow bottoms on the left. It's true that a railing had been constructed at its narrowest point, but it only consisted of half-rotted birch branches and seemed much more to advise: "Be very careful!" than it did "You can trust me!"

Contrary to all of Frederick's expectations, the bays were performing remarkably well that day. They were moving forward lightly and cheerfully at a uniform trot as if they knew they had been entrusted with the honorable duty of guiding their masters into the arms of good fortune. Ludwig watched them with great love and didn't fail to call out flattering compliments to them. His face was beaming with joy. Now the path began to climb, and the weight of the coach became manifestly evident to the horses: both of them suddenly pushed against the wagon tongue, and one of them butted the other's neck with its head as if to say: "*You* do the pulling!"

Frederick, who had been sitting quietly next to his brother with his arms folded up until then, now spoke – very quietly but disdainfully to the extreme: "They're not going to make it up the hill."

"They will make it!" Ludwig declared.

"No way at this gait."

"Well then, at a different tempo!" exclaimed Ludwig and cracked his whip. The horses leaped into a gallop, and the coach moved along just fine for a bit further. But the effort expended by the Hannakers exhausted them all too quickly; they took a few more steps and stopped . . . the coach rolled back. Frederick blinked his eyes and let out a sarcastic "Bravo!" Ludwig whipped the backs and flanks of the horses with powerful blows: they quivered, kicked and . . . wouldn't budge an inch. The coachman climbed down and wedged a rock behind one of the wheels; in doing so he slipped and fell, got too close to the edge of the path as he tried to leap back up, and fell head over heels down the slope.

Frederick was laughing, Ludwig was swearing; he tossed the reins to his brother, sprang down from the coach, began beating on the bays like a mad man and screaming at them, foaming at the mouth with fury: "You beasts! . . . kill you . . . I could kill you!"

The animals, groaning under the blows raining down on them, reared up . . . everything shifted, the wheel with the rock propped against it broke apart, and the coach stood sideways to the path.

By this point Frederick no longer found the situation so amusing. "You fool, you just wait!" he cried out and tried to swing down from his perch, but Ludwig didn't give him the time. Senseless with rage, he just attacked the horses all the more wildly. They threw themselves backwards and struck the railing; it broke, and the entire *equipage*[32] took the same path that the coachman had already taken before it.

"Cheers" said Ludwig, gnashing his teeth . . . but in the very same instant, the consciousness of what he had done flashed through his mind with deathly terror, and a horrible shriek forced itself from his lips.

Pale as a corpse but with his eyes wide as saucers, he rushed to the edge of the slope. Down below lay the horses, tangled in reins and straps; there lay the coach with its wheels in the air . . . but of Frederick there was no trace to be seen.

In despairing leaps Ludwig bounded down the hill. The coachman came toward him limping. "Jesus, Mary! Jesus, Mary and Joseph!" he whimpered, and, paralyzed with fear, he stared at his master, who, with all the appearance of a dead man, was doing the work of ten live men.

He sliced through the reins and tore them free; when one strap wouldn't loosen right away, he shattered the connecting crossbar to pieces with a rock. One of the horses was pushing and straining against the carriage as it tried to struggle to its feet; Ludwig swung his fist at its head so that it fell back as if a bolt of lightning had struck right in front of it . . . Now the coach was free . . . Frederick could be seen lying beneath it, his face, with blood running down it, pressed into the grass. Ludwig leapt to his side. With enormous power he propped himself against the coach – half with his head, half with his shoulder – and carefully raised it, slowly, then pushed it off of the man who had been bearing its full weight until that moment.

---

[32] French: the entire complement of coach, harness, horses, *etc.*

This man, however, took a deep breath – he was alive! ... Ludwig wanted to bend down over him, to stretch out his arms ... but they dropped from fatigue, his knees were shaking: instead of the name he tried to pronounce, only a forced groan came out of his mouth. . . . Suddenly Frederick raised himself up on one knee; with his hand, he quickly wiped off the blood running down across his eyes from his forehead, saw Ludwig standing in front of him and . . . "There you have it! It serves you right!" he exclaimed with a voice that left no lingering doubt that the powerful Gemperlein rib cage had victoriously withstood the shock it had suffered.

He stood up, shook himself off, puffed and panted, pointed to the pathetically abused horses, covered with blood and filth, and said: "Don't they look nice!"

Ludwig still didn't move a muscle. His eyes, glowing under their swollen lids, were fastened on his brother with an expression of delight and of inexpressible love. "Are you all right?" he asked hoarsely and in an even tone.

Only now did Frederick give the man a good look; an astonished and sympathetic smile glided across his face, he pulled out his handkerchief, pressed it to the wound on his forehead and mumbled something that couldn't be understood clearly, but the word "jackass" was heard to issue forth somewhere in there. Then he took one of the Hannakers by what was left of the reins hanging from its bridle and climbed up the steep incline with the exhausted animal stumbling at every step . . . somewhat more slowly than this would have occurred on a different day. The coachman followed with the second horse; at the rear came Ludwig, his head lowered, carrying in his hand a broken coach lamp that he had mechanically picked up.

The little caravan silently entered the courtyard at Vlastovitz a half hour later. The horses were taken to the barn; arrangements were made to have someone retrieve the coach that had been left at the bottom of the gorge.

Frederick thought Ludwig should just change his clothes quickly and ride on over to Rendezvous; he himself would follow in a half hour. "It would be smarter if you went home and made yourself an ice pack," said Ludwig.

Frederick replied very gruffly that he hadn't just given birth. They squabbled a little and then went into the castle, each to his own room.

Ten minutes later, Ludwig's groom was trotting over to Rendezvous with a letter in his pocket for Fräulein Clara from the barons. Ludwig stayed home. He paced back and forth in his chamber, his head pounding. Every artery was beating feverishly; every thought that his seething brain conceived was confusion, torture, and pain! One thought – the worst of all – kept crowding out all the others: "I endangered the life of my brother . . . I came close to being his murderer . . . ."

The bell rang for dinner. He went into the dining room where Frederick was already waiting for him. The latter had a good appetite as he ate; they talked, smoked, even disputed – but it was all without true joy . . . Their hearts weren't really in it.

Much earlier than usual, Ludwig got up and said: "Good night!" He would have gladly added: "Sleep tight!" or have asked again: "Are you all right?" But Frederick would have gotten angry or laughed at him, so he let it be and silently left the room.

Frederick took a long, melancholy look at him going. His eyes filled with tears. "Poor fellow!" he quietly mumbled. Lost in thought, he cradled his head in his hands and remained in that position for some time. When he finally arose and entered his room with decisive steps, the glow of lofty and proud joy at a great victory lighted up his face – a victory of the noblest self-denial and of the purest willingness to sacrifice. Even as late as it was, Frederick sent a note by mounted messenger that same evening to Perkovitz, to Her Excellency, Frau von Siebert.

Meanwhile Ludwig was sitting at his desk, slowly and solemnly writing his last will and testament with sweeping gestures of his pen. In it he named his brother, Baron Frederick von Gemperlein, as sole heir of all his possessions in case he (Ludwig) should remain unmarried and childless, which, he added, might very well be the case. He closed this document with the words: "Wherever I may die, I wish to be buried in Vlastovitz."

After this deed was done, Ludwig felt somewhat more at peace. Nevertheless, he couldn't take it in the quiet indoors any longer; he heard the breath of Mother Nature in the open, cool air calling to him outside. It was dark: only individual stars were glittering in the sky; the wind was blowing through the trees, pushing the dry leaves across the white, shimmering sand of the pathways and rustling in the deep black clusters of bushes.

Ludwig went forward with determined steps. He wanted to walk each path in the garden one more time, to greet each of his favorite trees before taking his leave with a heavy heart.

You first, old noble fir in the meadow, the last of ten sisters transplanted from the forest. You were sickly for so long, and now you reach to the sky so proudly, full of health. And you, noble walnut tree, which Frederick never passes without saying: "Now that's a tree! . . . ." Then the araucaria near the larch grove . . . my hat's off to you! An evergreen with the soul of a palm – Nordic power combined with Southern beauty – it's an absolute miracle! . . . and you, cedar of Lebanon, young, exotic *Fräulein*, with your green satin hoopskirt on and the tender new shoots dressing up your treetop as well as hat feathers do the loveliest coiffure. Finally there's the hackberry tree. The uninitiated would go right past it and think it's an apple-bearing sort of tree . . . but the connoisseurs stand wide-eyed before it. They admire the moss-covered, iron-gray trunk, the slender limbs with branches fine as thread, the small silky-soft leaves. "In the botanical garden in Schönbrunn[33] there are lovelier hackberry trees, but nowhere else!" Frederick once said.

And he's right! . . . There may be lovelier things out there in the world, but nothing more beloved than what thrives, lives, blossoms and wilts right here. Pity, pity that I have to leave it. But under the circumstances that will soon – so soon! – come to pass, I, Ludwig can no longer live at Vlastovitz.

He climbs up the rise at the end of the garden one more time, from which vantage point the burial chapel can be seen across the way which his father ordered to be built. Through the grillwork of the window, a fiery pinpoint is shining, the light of the lamp burning over the coffin of his father – the first one to rest here.

A sad smile plays on Ludwig's lips; he is glad that in his will he expressed the desire to be buried in Vlastovitz. Frederick will certainly comprehend what that means . . . It means I'm returning to you, to the one I've so often hurt, whose life I even endangered once, but whom I *have* always dearly loved.

Very much at peace, almost cheerfully, Ludwig returned home. The windows of Frederick's bedroom were still illuminated, and behind the curtains a tall, dark shadow glided past at irregular intervals. "You're awake too – tortured by worries and anxious doubts. Wait! Just wait! Only a few more hours and you will be happy!"

At eleven o'clock the next morning, Ludwig dismounted from his horse in front of the manor gate at Castle Perkovitz. A servant, who appeared to have expected him, led him immediately through the *salle à terrain* to the door of the guestroom from which Fräulein Clara had stepped yesterday like a heavenly vision. The servant knocked; a dear voice asked: "Who is

---

[33] Schönbrunn is the imperial summer residence in Vienna, built in the late seventeenth century with sumptuous and expansive gardens.

it?" and called out, when the name of the visitor had been given: "He's welcome to come in!"

Ludwig stood before beautiful Clara, so apprehensive and emotional that it was impossible for him to utter a single word. But she didn't remain so self-assured herself. The cheery tone in which she had asked Ludwig to take a seat was transformed into a very dejected one after the first gaze into the baron's face.

She lowered her eyes, a light paleness flew across her cheeks, and she said hesitantly: "Herr Baron . . . it is . . . I pray you . . . ."

Her state of embarrassment most deeply touched and moved him. Oh, the cruel custom! That it forbids her to express unsanctioned feelings, that would be just fine; but that the purest feelings a person can have must remain unexpressed, that is pitiful! If Ludwig had been able to follow his feelings at that moment, he would have put out his arms and said: "Come into my heart . . . dear one!"

But that was not appropriate now, and so he gave her his hand and said: "I've taken the liberty to ask you to discuss things just between the two of us . . . ."

"Yes, yes," she interrupted him hastily, "in a letter which I opened, even though it wasn't actually addressed to me."

"How's that?"

"You see, my name isn't actually Fräulein . . . ."

"Oh," he exclaimed, "it's not really a matter of what your name is. Call yourself what you like. You are the niece of our honored friend and the most charming person we've ever come across. You are certainly also noble and good and will not abuse the trust that guides me to you and with which I tell you: You have made a strong impression on the best person alive – on my brother, Fräulein. I've come here without his knowledge, determined to sing you his praises. I don't intend to be any less honest with you than I am with him and implore you in your own interest: Allow his courting to please . . . ."

He spoke with such enthusiasm that she was unable to interrupt him, no matter how often she tried. When he ended up saying: "Don't pass up the opportunity to become the happiest woman on earth!" her impatience gave her the courage to say with determination: "But this opportunity has already been passed up, Herr Baron. I am married!"

He jumped up from his chair with an indescribable horror. "You're joking," he stammered; "That can't be . . . that's impossible!"

"Why not?" she asked. "Another person as well as your brother may have found me acceptable, for example my cousin, Karl Siebert, who took me across the threshold some years back. Why would you think that I've been an old maid up to now? For if you'll permit me to say so, I would certainly be a bit past my prime for a '*Fräulein*.'"

Ludwig looked at her with melancholy and said: "So beautiful, so charming, so witty, and . . . already married!"

"And if you knew how long!" she added, and all her cheerfulness and her good humor had returned to her.

"Excuse me, gracious lady," said Ludwig, "it would have been better if you would have had the decency to inform us earlier."

"Did you ask me about it? With what right was I to enlighten you about my family matters?" was her quick and ready response.

All he could say was: "Oh, gracious lady!" and took his leave with the proper respects. As he did so – strangely enough! – the pleasure of laughing at this strange man left her completely.

She hurried after him, caught up to him just as he was stepping back across the threshold, and said heartily and with warmth: "Farewell, Herr von Gemperlein!" In leaving she offered him her hand. Ludwig turned his head and acted as if he didn't see it; he just offered one more deep bow, and the door closed behind him.

In the vestibule Frau Siebert, just leaving her office on the ground floor, approached the baron.

"Well, what are you doing here?" asked Her Excellency. "Why did you come here yourself? Your ambassador has already received his answer."

"Who does Your Excellency mean?"

"Fritz is who I mean. He was here a half hour ago – courting my niece for you."

"Courting for me?"

"And how he was! If ever you want to marry again, don't do your own talking . . . let Fritz do it for you. I was completely shattered – regretted it not just a little – that I had to say: 'It is too late.'"

Ludwig grabbed his head with both hands: "This Frederick! He's a real human being!" he exclaimed.

From his voice there came such a powerful emotion that Her Excellency was almost moved by it; she struggled to quickly withdraw the unpleasant sensation, stepped right in front of Ludwig, tweaked his ear and said: "Take no offense! I'm almost sorry that we played this trick on you. Clara didn't want to have anything to do with it, but I forced her: I had to have revenge for my nanny goat."

"Your Excellency!" replied Ludwig, "I can tell you with assurance: it was a billy goat."

"No matter what it may have been, I'm going to spoil your forester's glee at hunting around my property line."

With that they parted . . .

A few months after this occurrence the brothers again began to draft all sorts of marriage projects.

"You really should marry now!" one of them would say to the other from time to time. They sometimes made observations about their fate.

"It is really strange," Ludwig once commented. "Just when I wanted to get serious with the Appleblossom girl, she was on her way to the altar, and when we thought about making that niece our wife, she had already been married ten or twelve or who knows how many years, and unless I'm very mistaken," he secretly appended, "she probably already had children at that point."

Frederick observed that everything in life repeats itself, more or less. The two of them were destined to have incredible love adventures: among the many still to come would be that very one, of course, that leads into the haven of marriage.

In spite of this visionary stance and in spite of good intentions to maintain their family with glory, neither of the brothers ever married. They passed over to the other side without leaving behind an heir to carry on their name, and so, as with so much beauty on this earth, the old family line of those named "von Gemperlein" died out.

Ludwig Anzengruber (1839-1889) began his literary career as a dramatist. After growing up in very modest financial circumstances and eventually finding work as a professional actor, he found sudden and resounding success in 1870 when a drama he had written, *The Priest of Kirchfeld*, played to enthusiastic audiences in Vienna. Its theme, the struggle of an honest village priest against self-righteousness and hypocrisy in the institutionalized church, fell on fertile ground in that time of Austrian *Kulturkampf*.[1] The astonishing success of this play on the Viennese stage encouraged Anzengruber, even before he received the respected Schiller Prize in 1878, to reach a larger audience among the reading public with works of prose having similar anti-clerical themes.

The Love Child[2] [1879] was a novella written in a casual and colloquial style meant to mimic the sub-standard German spoken by rural Austrian peasants in the late nineteenth century. The following English translation attempts to reproduce a similar level of language; note, however, that the use of this rustic vernacular does not point to ignorance or sloppy thinking on the part of the main character in any way. The narrator/speaker, brother of the "love child," is not a country bumpkin incapable of deep thought; rather, his homespun wisdom is couched in the language that was common around him. Like Will Rogers (1879-1935), the "Cowboy Philosopher" of America, Anzengruber's narrator indulges in a humorous and easily digested monologue whose unpolished words belie the depth of wisdom they contain.

The entire novella, despite the absence of stage directions, has the feel of a dramatic monologue. It is the sort of unilateral storytelling that might have been recorded word-for-word from the mouth of one of the village elders as he sat with other wizened peasants around a stove in a communal gathering. The narrator, to some extent, represents an anthropological preserver and transmitter of local lore as he recites from the oral canon of tales about individuals, living and dead, known to everyone in the village. The only hint at the audience surrounding the speaker comes in the very last

---

[1] German: "cultural struggle": suspicion and animosity against the Roman Catholic Church, paralleling that in Bismarck's newly unified Germany and often leading to laws limiting the power of the clergy.

[2] There is an important connotative difference between the German title, which translates directly as "*Sin Child*," and the English euphemism used here, *Love Child*, with the former directly showing a judgmental aspect of sin.

paragraph, where the narrator tosses in a casual reference to "all of us sittin' here."

An aspect of Anzengruber's prose just as central as his use of down-home dialect is the suspicious attitude towards the dominant religion of rural Austria, the Roman Catholic Church. It would be a mistake, however, to accuse the author of religious bigotry. Rather, he saw beyond the religious issue to portray the plight of a human being caught in the web of a cultural tradition, a tradition in which men and women can emerge as victims or victors.

Love Child emphasizes a family relationship, part and parcel of which is the destructiveness of a wrong career choice, aggravated by the mother's misguided attempt at atonement. While the cassock of priesthood, in the plot of this novella, doesn't appear to be a good fit for the narrator's brother, it is for very human reasons and personal foibles – not because of the institution itself – that the tragic mismatch occurs.

The Love Child

Ludwig Anzengruber

Well, sure, said Pechleitner, a smile creepin' up around the corners of his mouth and then vanishin' again just as quickly. Well, sure, that was a sad story with my dear mother back then; may she rest in peace. That's what I think, a real strange story. Thirty-five years ago it was: I was thirty at the time, Mama was carryin' all of forty-five years on her shoulders. Yep, go ahead and roll your eyes if you like; so what? There's nobody still alive to bear me out on this, but back then, at the time I'm talkin' 'bout, I could count on my fingers the number of people who even thought about how quickly my mother had matured and then were astounded at how long it took before she started to show her age. I was her first, the weakest among maybe a dozen brothers and sisters, and still I outlived 'em all; so just to get the story straight: I was the only one left thirty-five years ago, my dad had died three years before that, and so Mama and me, we lived alone on our little piece of land. We always did an honest day's work and things were goin' fine; well, I was at the peak of my powers and I'm not lyin' when I say she could just about do as much work as me, the only difference bein' maybe the way a woman is less able to work compared to a man anyhow. All at once things change, though; she starts shirkin' her duties, gettin' bigger around the middle, bigger and bigger, until finally she's totally good for nothin'. Now she was well known as a respectable widow, nobody dared to gossip about what was goin' on, nobody would'a listened anyhow! "The

Pechleitner lady's sick," people would say, "she's just got the dropsy."³ And that's how things stayed for quite a while.

So then I had all the work to do by myself, and one evenin' when I get back home dog-tired, what do I find? I thought I'd never get my eyeballs back in their sockets, never get my mouth shut from astonishment. The rooms are full of womenfolk from around these parts, the midwife's there; to make a long story short: all at once the old baby clothes layin' around forgotten in the closet were gettin' used again.

When it got dark the visitin' women lost themselves one after the other 'til finally it's just me standin' there alone, standin' at the window and drummin' on the panes, and the longer I stand there and drum the more embarrassed I get, and that's somethin' I sure don't need, God knows, so I turn around with a beet-red face and say: "You ought'a be ashamed of yourself, Ma; you ought'a be ashamed of yourself!" Since she doesn't say nothin' and doesn't move a finger, I take my pipe and leave; didn't wanna make tobacco clouds in the nursery of a newborn, you know.

When I was done with my pipe, I thought about it some. Talkin' about it after the fact doesn't do any good. So it was completely improper and stupid for me to be tellin' my own mother what to do. How would it even help if she listened to my preachin' and dealt with the mistake? If she wasn't ashamed before, what good would it do now afterwards? Just for her to feel bad about it? That wouldn't do nobody no good. Also I thought about when all those ladies shouted at me: "Your mother has had her a child!" None of 'em said: "You got you a brother!" All my days I've been rebellious against what such people have to say anyhow: what are they thinkin' 'bout with their long braids and their short minds? Do they think maybe I'm gonna hold it against the poor little innocent worm? And even if I didn't have a heart . . . just to spite the people out there I wouldn't blame him: he's my brother! To hell and damnation with those that wanna split up the children comin' from the same mother!

I went to the room nice and quiet-like, opened the door; the two of 'em were lyin' there sleepin', so I sat down next to the bed and leaned over to the baby – but first off I wiped my dirty mouth with my sleeve – and as a sign I wanna be his good friend, I give him a big fat kiss: that was just the thing, 'cuz I'd been goin' around for a few days without shavin' . . . so that

---

³ More recently called "edema," an illness where body fluids collect in the interstices of cells between tissue spaces, causing a visible swelling.

must'a scratched him like it was the curry-comb for my horse, and he let out a howl like you wouldn't believe. From that my mother wakes up, too, but when she sees me sittin' there next to the bed, she just turns over on the other side.

And the funny way that things go with me, again I get real embarrassed. I clear my throat for a while and say: "Just stay in your bed; all that twistin' and turnin' could be bad for you. And, if you wanna know what I think about it, what's done is done. And not everybody's strong. We're all made different, but everybody has his weakness!"

Then she slowly turns over halfway and looks at me from the side: no girl of seventeen who already knows but won't tell if the window latches to her room lock tight or open easy could give such a God-forsaken look as did my mother that very hour. In that sense women are all the same, whether old or young.

After Mama had recovered from givin' birth, we divided up the work like we'd done all the times before; it even seemed a bit more fun for us, 'cuz now it was also meant for little Leopold. In our concern for him we were always united and stayed that way up 'til the time he had shot up taller and people could start askin' us what he was gonna do when he got older; on that point Mama and me couldn't agree, not from the first time we talked about it.

It was one evenin' my brother was runnin' around with boys his own age in the village, me sittin' on the bench out front of the house and a'smokin' my pipe, and the old woman kept busy a little while in the front room, then she came out, sat down next to me, folded and straightened her apron for a while, and when it maybe seemed smooth enough for her, she starts up, but without lookin' at me: "My dear Martin," she said, "you're a good lad; I know that, and all the people around here recognize that; you've honestly done your share for Leopold – may God reward you for it – but it'd be sinful if you were made to suffer for your goodness, and an injustice cryin' out to heaven if your inheritance were reduced because of the boy."

The introduction seemed distasteful to me right away: it always makes me suspicious when somebody comes rushin' at me with a speech that puts my advantage right up front: that isn't customary in the world, since everyone puts his own self uppermost. Mostly by doin' so they're just tryin' to hand me a back scratcher to scratch their back with, or else they're tryin' to put blinders on me so I can't see what the fella next to me's up to. So I don't say nothin', take a deep puff from my pipe and wrap myself in a fog – like up on a mountain top that doesn't expect to see sunshine that day.

But that was unhealthy weather for my old lady; she started coughin'. "And you like to smoke that cheap stuff?" she says. "Well, better days are comin' when you'll be able to afford better, once we don't have little Poldy sittin' over the dinner plate anymore."

"Ah, let him sit over it as long as he likes," I said, "he ain't eaten me out of house and home yet, and I don't reckon he will, 'specially now that he's startin' to do his own share of decent work. He's thrivin' and I'm glad for it. I'm already an old fella, much older than he is; the boy's healthy and things would have to go awful wrong if he's not the one to see me put away in my grave, and then . . . Well, you know, Ma, I never got myself involved in marriage and I won't either."

"Don't say that," said my old lady, "somethin' like that could just come over you all at once."

I slowly took the pipe out of my mouth, gave my dear mother a wry wink and said: "I don't know about that, but if you say so, I guess I gotta believe it." I was just tryin' to tease her with that and also thought she wouldn't take it wrong, 'cuz I wasn't thinkin' mean thoughts any more than I was earlier at Poldy's crib, and I'd kept the same attitude towards her all through the years, but now I noticed she wasn't the same as earlier: instead of her tellin' me with a straight face that I should watch my mouth and keep it under control, like I was expectin', she lifted her apron and began weepin' under it.

That's the weirdest of all for me; I don't like to see anybody cryin', let alone me bein' the one to make 'em cry, and I didn't have an idea how I brought it about and why. It annoyed me to the tip of my soul that I'd caused it, 'cuz I wasn't aware of havin' any bad attitudes, so for all the world I wasn't able to say a word to make things better – even if one thing or another would've occurred to me, which wasn't the case. So I sat there and held my pipe by its stem, just as comfy as a kid bundled up in a sleigh and may not have looked very intelligent right then.

"Oh, my God," sobbed my mama under her percale apron. "Now it comes back to haunt me! My oldest son lets himself make crude sayings about me, and what will I have to listen to from the youngest, the love child, when he's grown and people get him all worked up, somethin' that's bound to happen. Yes, yes, there's only one way, one single way for my boy to stay unspoilt and for me to find peace and a little forgiveness for my guilt. It has to be."

"What has to be?" I ask.

"I have to give him over completely to our dear Lord God; he has to become a priest."

"He has to become a priest on *your* account?" I think. "Well, that's sure the easiest way to get rid of your own sins, if you can get somebody else to pay for 'em." But I didn't say that: who dares to say somethin' like that to his mother's face? So I bend over forward just a bit so I don't need to watch what kind of a face she makes when I make my speech, and I say: "If I was you, I'd hold off just a bit and think about it. Maybe that'd be too big an obstacle for Poldy, and he wouldn't get beyond it all the rest of his life. Just think: what if he has your hot blood . . . ."

All at once she stands up, goes to the door mumblin' that I shouldn't talk such dumb tripe, Poldy was still too young to have bad thoughts, and I was old enough to know that no one on earth would ever fall victim to such shenanigans unless somebody pushed him into it, and God's help and the supervision of righteous people would prevent that, no doubt. With that she had slipped inside, and all I can see is the tip of her skirt scootin' in through the door.

For as long as she could still bound across the fields and up the slopes as fast as a weasel and get her work done as quick as ever, for all that time – God knows – I was never able to see her have a bad conscience; but all at once she started to suffer from gout and had to lay around in bed all by herself for days on end while we were out in the fields, and that's prob'ly the reason that suddenly my unexpected brother started to weigh so heavy on her soul. At any rate, her words were all newfangled, so I didn't have to pay much attention to 'em to know someone else was talkin' through her.

I could just imagine who it was! It was our Poldy's guardian, the sexton at our parish, such a proper prayer brother; he was the one who first put her unto the pious idea – or the work pleasin' to God, whatever you wanna call it – and then kept on busily strengthenin' her resolve afterwards. I never was able to put up with those kind: they just love to put their noses in other people's business too much, and I think precisely someone like that who's serious about religion wouldn't have time for it and ought'a have enough to do just keepin' his own nose clean. Maybe I'm wrong, of course, and it could be when a religious man like that notices he's havin' trouble tendin' his own garden that he goes around shovelin' fertilizer on other people's fields: you gotta be careful, though, 'cuz afterwards they can come runnin' and say that ever'thing grew so well just 'cuz of their manure.

That with Poldy was a done deal: Mama had agreed to it, the guardian had agreed to it, and the boy – what all can't you talk such a dumb little kid into? – he'd also agreed to it. What could I do? I said: "Do as you like, but leave me completely out of things: I told you ever since I knew about this, and I'll tell you again, that as far as I'm concerned the boy could stay on the farm for as long as I live and beyond, for as long as *he* lives. If it all turns out a disaster, don't put even a grain of sand's worth of guilt on my shoulders!"

They made fun of me and told me not to worry about rubbin' my shoulders the wrong way; they wouldn't be puttin' any big sand grains of guilt of my shoulders, plus somethin' disastrous like that wouldn't ever occur in such a saintly cause so pleasin' to God.

And when everybody in the village heard that Poldy Pechleitner was gonna become a priest, they came on up to visit him and they made him real uppity; the elderly folk asked him not to forget them once he'd taken his vows, and to include them in his prayers; the children were concerned with findin' out if it's true that a priest walks and talks with the Lord above and with the blessed saints just like he would with anybody else? He let 'em keep their good faith.

Soon he didn't have a single thought in his head unless it had to do with his future clergy status, and nothin' was too good or too bad to remind him of it, no matter where he went. If he was walkin' through the garden and was lookin' at the shrubbery, then the black aphids on the elderberry bush were monks, the green ones on the roses and such were secular priests, and the ants runnin' towards 'em were laypersons, and when they felt around with their antennae so busy-like, then they were askin' for blessings and absolution. "Well, you know, dumb little boy," I thought, "the ants milk 'em, and you show me a priest who'd stand still for that! If you were to turn the tables around and let the aphids be the laypersons and the ants the others, then it'd look more like a proper parable."

He wandered around a whole summer and didn't do a lick of work, but when I was rakin' hay in the meadow with my day workers or was out harvestin' in the field, then it often happened that he suddenly stepped out from a bush and started preachin' out loud to 'em; that was just fine with the lazy people: they dropped their work, gathered around him, listened to him real reverent-like, and of course I couldn't take offense at such paragons of piety. Mama was of the same opinion and said that his nonsensical blubberin' went straight to her heart: if so, it must'a taken the shortest route, 'cuz the path that leads through the brain was way off to one side as a detour.

I was shocked, and not just a little, whenever I heard my brother get wound up from the other end of the field: "And in that day the Lord Jesus spake unto his disciples . . . ." Oh, yeah, the Lord Jesus did speak in that day, but my brother Leopold could speak *all* day. Right away all the hired help was gone; for a job that required a full dozen hands, I didn't know what else to do but stick my own in my pockets and wait 'til he said "Amen" over there.

It got to the point I was real happy when Fall came and Mama and the guardian set him down between them on the wagon and drove him off to the seminary. I shook his hand and said: "Poldy, be good, even if you're gonna be a priest!"

He laughed, and with that he was off.

It was meant to be; he had his fears and set off blindly for a goal about which he knew just as little as a school boy could know about it. It was better to say nothin' and let his courage help him cope. I always think there shouldn't be extra trainin' like they have for carpenters, weavers and tailors. Well, sure, whatever it is that makes a priest seem acceptable in the church, that's a hurdle he can get past with book learnin', but when somebody comes a'runnin' up to him with no more healthy spots in his heart, cryin' out: "Now help me!" then he really has to know what to do: he's gotta find the sorest spot, and it has to look like he's reachin' into heaven, takin' God's hand, and layin' it on that defect. That's somethin' you can't teach. I'm full of admiration for my own priest over there in his vestments, that old white-haired man who took the time to figure out the world first before he took his vows.

Well, whatever – men are generally so foolish they make the same mistake a hundred times, thinkin' that's the rule on earth; but when the rule comes a'knockin' at their own front door, then they hope for an exception. The doctor can be just as sick as his patient, but you won't find him tryin' to doctor himself.

If I'd a'known back then what path the boy was actually gonna travel down, I, as his own blood guardian, would'a chased the other guy and Mama from off that wagon seat and kept him with me.

Sixteen years old he was at the time and our mother's age was just the reverse, that is, for her the six went up front and the one behind. When opportunity knocked now and then, she drove to town and checked up on how things were goin' at the seminary for Poldy and whether he didn't have at least the start of a halo growin', even if it was just a little glow, like on a firefly – but up by his head, of course, and not where those worms have it, since it wouldn't have any saintly significance down there at all.

Two years he'd been away from home when Mama begged him free for a few days, brought him home, and that's the first time I saw him face to face again. At the same time there was a distant relative visitin' us, a buxom example of femininity who was the very image of merriment and health, and she's the one he liked to hang around with. In spite of his eighteen years he still looked childish enough, and he took advantage of that, foolin' around with Ursel, who was twice his age; she laughed about her "little cousin Poldy," as she called him, but I had my own thoughts about that.

I don't know when it was he said his first Mass, but there weren't enough wagons to be rounded up in the whole village for everyone who wanted to be there. So my old lady lived long enough to see that, and also she was able to see him assigned as an auxiliary to a sick pastor in a nearby parish. Now he was a real priest and it had taken him eight years to get there, and it was exactly in this eighth year that Mama lied down and died. At the very last there was somethin' she wanted to tell me – maybe who was Poldy's father – but she wasn't able to, and that was just fine with me; I never wanted to hurt her by askin', and to be acquainted with one more scoundrel or coward in the world was not exactly high on my list.

Leopold was there at the burial of Mama, as was the buxom farmer lady; some girls he'd run barefoot through the grain stubble with, years before, all flocked towards him: they claimed it was to express sympathy, but they actually just wanted to hear him say he still remembered 'em. He shied away from every one of 'em and wouldn't shake hands with any of 'em, no matter how affectionate they acted. Other than that, he looked like milk and blood; now he had a real unhealthy manner to him, no color, sunken cheeks, and his eyes deep in his face, too: he stared at the ground with 'em and didn't return anyone's gaze. I didn't like it. When he got on the wagon behind the corpse, I took his hand and asked: "What's the matter with you, Brother?"

"Nothin'," he said.

"There's gotta be somethin' wrong," I said.

At that he pulled a face as if he wanted to laugh, told me again that nothin' was wrong with him, and quickly added: "Don't you wanna come on over to Rodenstein sometime and visit our parish? It's pretty there."

"I'll come visitin'," I said. "God bless you, Brother."

"God bless you, Martin," he calls out and rides off.

The followin' Sunday I talk my oldest worker into stayin' home and watchin' the house while I walk over to Rodenstein. Now that's a goodly distance, and after climbin' through the woods up to the heights, you walk along under nothin' but white birches for about a quarter of an hour. That's no happy grove of trees for me. Even at the thickest spot the soil's loose, the trunks stand up all lonely from each other, the sun burns down through the sparse leaves, and the white bark looks like bleached bones. That day I hit it especially bad: there had been a downpour in the morning, and now glowin' hot rays of sun were piercin' down from a sky that didn't wanna take on any color; it was like ever'thing was under a veil, and a humid vapor rose up from the ground so's you could only work your way forward bathed in sweat and half breathless.

Of course, it would'a cost me an hour and a quarter of detour time if I'd a' wanted to walk around the mountain, but that path at least led through the forest where young tree growth was on both sides and branched together over your head so you went along through a kind of shadowed, leafy passage. Now I was already up on top, though, and I thought, "God protect every Christian person from a birch life path," and it came over me like a premonition: had my brother perhaps stumbled onto such a path, and wouldn't he be much better off somewhere else?

Dear God, how many things on earth make us want 'em, and our hearts can get so fascinated with 'em that our heads don't know up from down anymore. Toppin' the list of what boys want are girls, and for the girls it's boys. I had a sweetheart once myself; she was my playmate from the time we were kids and both of us were still a little young to seriously think that we could be thinkin' seriously of each other, but when she drowned in front of my eyes in the pond and when I sat at her bier all night as she lay there, stretched out, pale, cold, her happy eyes sunken under half-closed lids, I took it for an omen once and for all. I still have my sweetheart; don't think for a moment I put her away in the ground: since then, I've always imagined her the way she was while still alive, her look and color so sparklin', her touch and gestures so correct, and her walk so light afoot and dancin'. I haven't kept anything but the sight of her, but all this time that's been more than enough for me. If you ask for more, then right off the bat you get jealousy and bad feelin's in your own heart or else in someone else's heart towards you; get yourself sucked in, and things'll go badly. If you've got the sight of somethin', you've got it all . . . unless you want to actually own it, 'cuz what you get you can lose again, but ever'thing keeps. That idea came to me all by myself. Nobody said to me: "Thou shalt not want things!" Nobody said to me: "Thou shalt do without things!"

If I say to someone: "Be satisfied!" then, by doin' so, I make him dig around to find some reason why he ain't satisfied; and if he digs around long enough, no doubt he'll find one. If I tell him: "Go without!" then, by doin' so, I remind him that he could be actively wantin' somethin', and even if he doesn't know up 'til then what it is he wants, he'll find somethin' or other. I imagined for a long time I didn't have any wants, 'cuz I was always satisfied with just lookin', but then it occurred to me that *that* was precisely my want: I wouldn't even need to lose my eyesight, I'd just have to live in unpleasant surroundings where filthy people ran around under my nose, and then my life'd be ruined. Nope, nobody gets through life without wantin' things, and doin' without things can't be escaped, and there's no teachin' or preachin' that helps for it or against it. The world isn't here for wantin' things and the world isn't here for goin' without things: it's here – I think – for workin', and whatever happens to us between desire and denial shouldn't make us jealous and shouldn't ruin our lives.

Now the young fella sits down there at the parish and knows as much about all that as a two-day-old dog knows about the color of his belly.

I made it to Rodenstein; my brother was still in church, so I went in there and saw him standin' at the pulpit and heard him preachin'.

It wasn't bad at all how he thundered on about hell and damnation, and he must'a been doin' it quite some time, 'cuz the people were all sittin' there as if they had the fear of God in 'em. "Hey, dear Reverend brother of mine," I thought, "aren't you kind'a startin' at the wrong end? Why are you makin' people fear things? Fear and worry they get enough firsthand, from the time they prepare the field 'til when they get the harvest in under a roof and even beyond. Is it gonna be a year of blessin's or disaster? Are frost, hail, rot, drought, and fire comin', or will they stay away? And if so, will the surplus depress the prices or will the interest rates send 'em soarin'? No, my brother, fear is no reason to be sittin' in the parish church; comfort's what the people need, you ought'a be pumpin' up their courage: whoever can't get happy here on earth all the days of his life is sure as shootin' gonna be some sad fool in heaven."

And then he kept talkin' in the context of the devil as seducer and about all his evil impulses. Oh, my, if only you let all the temptations rise up out of everybody's own heart, maybe then you could deal with it and persuade someone to turn from his wrongful path right at the last minute; but don't plant some devil in him as an excuse, someone superior to his powers who he can blame for all his guilt. And as I listened to the boy tellin' about all the bad thoughts that come to a person and how they can overwhelm him, I just shook my head and thought to myself: "If you got these ideas from anywhere else than your books, then you'd better make the sign of the cross and just bless yourself for all you're worth!"

He didn't seem to have thought about that, though, 'cuz at the end he raised his voice in a mighty cry, drummed on the pulpit with his fists, and threatened ever'body there, sayin' the devil would get 'em – and the people said "Amen" to that. Now I've been told that "Amen" means as good as "So let it be done!" Well, if they were satisfied with that, then there wasn't a more good-for-nothin' person at any spot on earth than my soul-savin' brother in Rodenstein.

When he'd come down from the pulpit, I pushed my way through the crowd to the sacristy;[4] there he let me pull the priest robes off over his head. Then we went to the rectory[5] grounds which lay a little bit off to the side behind the church, open to the plaza.

It wasn't time to eat yet, so we went walkin' back and forth a while in the garden. "Well," said my clergyman brother, "today you've heard me again, only this time from the pulpit: does it meet with your approval now any better than the way I used to do it out in the fields?"

"Hmmm," I growled, "I really couldn't say; back then it was child's play with big people, and today it seems to me like people's play with big children."

"Can't you do a thing but criticize?" he laughed. "Well, your thoughts are duty-free; just try to ignore 'em."

"Nope," I said, "I'm not willin' to do that. I'm not gonna bad-mouth the way my brother does his work, no matter what it is you do; if you were a shoemaker, for instance, and let the whole village limp around in shoes

---

[4] A room or building attached to the church where sacred objects and liturgical necessities are stored and where the priest dresses in his vestments.

[5] The dwelling place set aside for the priest to use.

that were too tight, I wouldn't say: 'My brother's a rotten shoemaker!' But the people would prob'ly come around to noticin' that by themselves. How is it you preach that way you do?"

"Hey," he cried, irritated, "you try teachin' a farmer like me to preach!"

"Well, well," I say, and point to the spot where a person's heart sits. "So you don't get it from here? Do you think you can talk your way into people's souls with invented words and man-made thunder? Well now, what kind of souls do you all think the people have? It seems to me a fine sheep[6] out in front of the others that doesn't always wanna be ringin' his bell for the others to follow and would even stick his bell in a bag from time to time if he had one. Soon they'll all be as clever as you, and for as far as your parish reaches you'll have invented morals and man-made Christianity."

Then he lays his hand on my shoulder and says: "Martin, you don't understand all this. Tell me, rather, how it is that you farmers don't want to follow the example of Countess von Turnschart, who's known around these parts as the foolish countess but who manages her fields in a way that gives her two harvests a year from her depleted soil."

"The foolish countess," I say to that, "has an easy time harvestin' twice, and if we wanted to put more into a field than comes back out of it, we could all have the same results. But, brother, that's somethin' you don't understand."

All at once there's a cry: "Come an' get it!" And not far from the garden path is a woman standin' there, big and wide enough around for three of the normal kind, and she had a triple chin, too. She may have been a parish cook clean through at one time; now she was just a cook at the parish: no one could accuse her of bein' clean. Behind her a tall thing, skinny as a rail, came shootin' up, a girl 'bout sixteen years old; her face looked yellow and shriveled as a prune – just a coupl'a eyes were scorchin' out from inside it and she was tossin' her gaze around like a falcon. That was the only thing on her she seemed able to use to her advantage, 'cuz she didn't know how to stop her hands and feet from movin': they were awkwardly wigglin' and squirmin' with such jerks it was a cryin' shame.

When the fat one sees that my brother wasn't sayin' his farewells to me but takin' me by the hand, she comes closer, and Leopold says to her: "We have my brother Martin visitin' here today."

---

[6] The German word "Hammel" has a secondary meaning here of "oaf," which is no doubt intended.

"Oh my, your brother Martin," she said. "Well, of course he's invited to come along for a spoonful of soup."

I say it wouldn't be proper for me to come eat with 'em when the pastor himself didn't even know I was there, but the others told me he wasn't around at all; he was layin' in the sick bed.

"Chances are he won't even be there much longer," the fat one said and winked at my brother while the girl laughed to herself.

So the four of us went into the rectory the way we were and sat down at the table. I prob'ly don't need to mention that on that particular day my taste buds and belly had it good, 'cuz you don't eat bad and you don't eat like sparrows where the priests live.

In the evenin' as I was ready to leave and my brother was wantin' to accompany me part of the way, the fat lady takes me by the hand and leads me off to one side. "The old fella's on his last legs," she said, "and then your brother should have things good around here with us: they'll give him the parish for sure, 'cuz they're real happy about his eagerness."

"His fire an' brimstone eagerness?" I think to myself. "Well, okay, as long as his superiors are satisfied . . . ." I tell the parish cook that I'm somethin' of a talker myself and that I'm real happy to hear all that. With that, we turn around and I see the spindly girl whisperin' to Leopold.

We left, and when we had Rodenstein at our backs and arrived in the open fields, I said: "Are things really goin' that poorly with your pastor there?"

"Very poorly," my brother said.

"Tell me," I asked further, "did that fat woman arrive at the rectory 'cuz of him?"

"Yep," he answered, "she came with him back then, and he's been livin' with her for fifteen years."

"Uh-huh," I said, "and who's the skinny girl?"

"Her daughter," he informs me.

"So then, was she a widow before she took up workin' for the pastor?" I ask real dumb-like.

"Well," my brother said, smilin' to himself, "you don't really need to know everything."

"Fine, fine," I said, "but I do know she's pretendin' like she's even heavier in importance than she actually weighs, and that's sayin' somethin' for her. She acts like she's the one who owns the parish, along with ownin' the current pastor. You know, she told me you'd get the job for sure, and she thinks she'll be able to stay here."

"She just imagines whatever she wants," Leopold growled.

"Yeah," I say, "and would you want to have her keep workin' for you?"

"Well, you know," he said, "you're tryin' to count the chicks before they're hatched: I'm not gonna get the parish at all." And sayin' that, he looked more at peace with the thought of not gettin' it than with the thought of gettin' it.

While talkin' we had come to the bridge that goes across the Rodenstein millstream; from that point on I was gonna go on my way alone. A hundred and some steps further up the mountain was the mill: through the leaves we could see the white glimmer of its walls. They'd stopped the wheel; there was nothin' to be heard but the gurglin' of the water and individual bird songs here and there. The moon was hung up in the sky in front of us, a narrow, scarcely visible sickle, and behind us were dark crimson clouds above the sinkin' sun. I can't always pay attention to what kind'a face the world's makin' around me, but right then I could, and it all seemed so peaceful to me that I stood still for a long time, breathin' so easy that my chest scarcely moved, and thinkin' that life's actually quite a flatterin' thing.

As I was shakin' hands with my brother, I felt the boards under me move slightly, noticed that someone was comin' the opposite way across the bridge; before I can look around to see who it is, though, to let him past, I see my brother's eyes get big as saucers and the little red he has rushes to his face: so I turn around, and in front of us stands a girl, who, as I find out from givin' greetin's back an' forth, is the miller's daughter and is called Marie-Lisa.

Ah, yes, was that a girl! Every part of her as if turned on the lathe; her golden yellow hair billowin' up in waves above her forehead and fallin' down her back in heavy braids; from her large, cornflower-blue eyes she looked out intelligently and innocently into the world; her nose was bowed very slightly at the top and delicately rounded and lifted at the bottom; her mouth was charmin', no bigger or paler than a cherry; her whole face was as pink as a healthy apple blossom, not so rounded that the cheeks were 'bout to burst and not sunken, either; on her chin she had a little dimple; and her little head sat on a neck that was so full and yet so mobile . . . oh, my, if I could only tell you how it was! That's how it goes when an old codger like me tries to describe a young girl, but I'll never forget all my born days how the miller's Marie-Lisa in Rodenstein looked in her heyday.

Now she tugged at her apron a bit and said: "Father, since you're already here, don't you want to come visit at our house? My parents would be pleased to see you."

Then he squeezed my hand, and, without a word, he walked away with her on the path that led to the mill.

I watched both of 'em until they'd disappeared behind the trees, and then I walked on. I don't know what it was, but the whole way across I could never find the happiness I'd felt just a few moments before. When I was passin' through the birch forest on the heights, now bathed in moonlight so all the branches glistened like thickened bones, my brother and the birch life path went through my mind again. Indeed, the sun has to be down and the night cool, if you wanna walk across there without too much trouble.

The old pastor of Rodenstein was on his last legs, they'd said, but he measured his time well enough to make those legs still last a good three weeks, and only in the fourth did he die. I was invited by my brother to his burial, so I went over and watched it. The fat parish cook dabbed her hanky over her face a few times, and the spindly parish girl at least wasn't throwin' her eyes around like usual.

My brother consecrated the corpse. It's not really the custom for us Catholics to chase after the dead with more words at their grave, but my brother thought it would edify the congregation if he said a few words about the dearly departed, and so the people stood around the open grave, Leopold at the head, and he gave a sermon.

In the beginnin' he looked down into the open trench at the coffin, but when he wanted to impress on the hearts of those present what a good example the deceased had given, he raised his eyes and looked at us; all at once, in the middle of his homily, he stopped short and only with great difficulty was he able to find his way back into his text. I'd looked up at the same time with a sharp eye and knew what it was. Not far from him stood Marie-Lisa, listenin' reverently and keepin' her eyes fixed on him: just as if he can feel it, he looks quickly in that direction, locks eyes with her, and then forgets every other word.

The sun was high in the noon sky when we returned to the rectory; things were a little out of whack there that day and we had to wait for the meal, so we wandered around in the garden. My brother leaned over the fence between the bushes and his shadow fell across the narrow strip of grass runnin' along outside next to the sidewalk.

People passed by – always in single-file – and gave their greetin's: the miller came by as well, the miller's wife, and, as third in line, Marie-Lisa, who stepped up to the fence, placin' her little feet very carefully so as not to step on the head of my brother's shadow. She showed her white teeth and the dimples in her cheeks a little and said: "I made you confused today, Father. Please pardon me, but I just wasn't thinkin', and I won't stare at you again like that."

He said it didn't matter.

"No, no," she said, "Not for all the world would I want to start gossip among the people, especially now when you're probably next in line for the parish and it could harm you."

He shook his head.

"They do talk," she said, "and talkin' about it is all they ought'a do – without havin' a thing more to point to. If I'm not too lowly to give you a piece of advice, I'd like to give you one."

"Well, Marie-Lisa?" he said, takin' her hand.

She squeezes his hand but then quickly pulls her own away again, bends over towards his ear and whispers to him: "Don't get involved with those types there in the rectory." And then she was gone.

"What's she runnin' away from all at once?" I think. I turn around and see the parish girl standin' right behind us. As I watch the skinny thing that snuck up to us so unheard, it seems to me she wasn't any diff'rent than a starvin' cat.

She'd made her hands into fists and let 'em hang down at her hips, but she clenched 'em strong like they were crampin' up, and if I hadn't been standin' there, I reckon, she would'a shook those fists in my brother's face. Her black eyes were a little moist but her eyebrows were knitted in anger. One more step she takes towards my brother and raises her hand with the fingers spread out like she wanted to grab his arm, and from deep in her breast her voice comes out and she says: "Say, that was the miller's girl again, wasn't it?"

"Yes," he said and turned his back on her.

For a moment it looked like she wanted to break out in sobs, but then she laughs – it didn't sound no diff'rent than when a cat hisses – shows the tip of her tongue between her teeth, turns away and throws her elbows off to the side.

I stood there with my eyes poppin' out and the question on my lips how that cat got to the point where she could behave like that towards my brother; he must'a guessed what I was thinkin', though, 'cuz he lays a hand on my shoulder and says: "If you care for me as a brother, Martin, don't say a word about it!"

At the dinner table this time ever'thing's real quiet, and just as I'm startin' off for home later and my brother tries to leave the house behind me to accompany me, the fat old lady holds him back by his sleeve, pulls him into a corner, and then the two of them were angrily whisperin' at each other and battin' at each other with their hands at the same time. I wasn't able to hear a bit of it, except towards the end the old lady says louder: "There ain't no way you're gonna have her, and I don't scarcely think she'd ever wanna have *you*." After that they each whisper one more thing at each other and then we left.

Since I wasn't s'posed to talk 'bout what I really wanted to put into words, we tramped off down the path next to each other without talkin' much, only 'bout things like how red the field poppy was – and how blue the cornflower was – and how anybody who planted buckwheat this year just might've miscalculated – and how people on this earth were riffraff for the most part – each of us spoutin' off a little phrase every few minutes and then enjoyin' the long silence, 'cuz we both just wanted to think our own thoughts right then.

When we got to the bridge over the mill stream again, we shook hands: I went on straight ahead followin' the road, while he didn't go straight back to town but off sideways towards the noisy clatterin' mill.

That was the second and last time I visited my brother in Rodenstein. Until the decision came, of course, he sat there as warm and cozy as a regular pastor; and a regular pastor is just what they made him, but maybe Rodenstein seemed too fatty of a morsel for his young teeth and he was s'posed to practice chewin' on some stale bread first, so they installed an elderly clergyman there and my brother was sent a few miles further off to a small village in the countryside. He wrote me about all that, and he wrote it so short and to the point I thought to myself that earlier, when there'd been talk about the Rodenstein parish, he'd just pretended not to care, and now after the fact it upset and disappointed him tremendous-like or else he was ashamed that nothin' had come of it. After this one letter I didn't hear or see a thing from him for at least three full seasons of the year.

Then one day a letter arrives at my house – chicken scratchin's like the hens make in the sand – and I'm finally able to figure out from it that my brother's in bed seriously ill and he wants to see me.

What with findin' the place, stayin' a while and returnin', it could prob'ly take a whole day, so I didn't think about it for too long, made sure someone could take care of things around the house, and drove on over to Weissenhofen: that was the name of the place.

Crude is what it was there: crude air, crude soil, crude people. The little village was up on a mountain, about a dozen houses set along the steep road, that was all, and above it the church peered down from the mountain ridge and out across the wide valley. I've often been amazed that churches are sprinkled all across the countryside so lonely-like but also large enough for the whole community to fit inside . . . even if ever'body carried his house around on his back like a snail. Had there been a city around it at one time, or was one s'posed to grow there? Who can say? Were these long-forgotten locations of merciful grace from which, with time, first the miracles and then the pilgrims left until at last they were both gone? Who knows?

That's how magnificently huge the church was at Weissenhofen. Against the one wall, just around the right corner from the entrance, the rectory was attached like a small bird's nest against the bottom of one of the blocks of stone, and out in front of it was only a very tiny little garden. Prob'ly up at those heights nothin' would grow very good, anyhow.

That was a poor little excuse for a priest's dwellin', the very one I was walkin' towards: it did have a second story sittin' up top, but the whole thing was all so low and narrow with three little rectangular peep-holes up top, two down below and a narrow front door in place of the third one. When I open the door up, the first thing I see is the fat parish cook from Rodenstein and, as second, the starvin' cat. How nice that I had come, they said. The old lady made it clear to me my brother was kind of in a bad way, but I should go ahead and ask him if he wasn't gettin' all sorts of good care and keepin'. And the younger one jumps up to me, slaps my hands as if we'd been the best of friends all our lives, and says: "I hope we'll get him outta bed soon; I think sickness is disgustin', no matter who has it!"

And now she'll tell him I'm there, she says. With that she shoots up the short stairs and slams two doors shut behind her so loudly that a healthy person would wanna swear at her.

Meanwhile I ask the old lady if they were up there all alone, if there wasn't anybody else to help look after things?

She says to that: they were alone durin' the day for the most part, but towards evenin' the woodcutter would come up from the village; he rang the bells and he also served at the altar. If they ever needed anything, he saw to it.

"And," says I, "is my brother still able to say the Mass?"

"Indeed," she says, that's somethin' he'd been able to do day by day: from his room there was a door leadin' to a short passage where he could get to the pulpit in just a few steps, she tells me, and – by goin' down some stairs – to the middle of the church itself.

Then she's windin' up to give a long and loud proclamation 'bout how all that was only possible for my brother on account of the good care and keepin' he was gettin' – but then the young and skinny one hollers down and says that Leopold was expectin' me – so I say she should save the jabberin' for later and slowly climb up the stairs. I open the door and enter a tiny little chamber filled with rubbish, then I step up to the second door and knock on it softly; a voice as weak as if a sleepy child was speakin' it, says from inside: "Come in!"

I go inside, and right across from me is Leopold lyin' in bed. He looked like a paintin' of Christ on the cross. I stood there and didn't know what to say, and I turn around a little to pull the door shut behind me again; and when I'm facin' him again he sticks out both his miserable thin arms towards me, a couple of cries from deep in his chest get stuck in his throat, and then he starts to weepin' out loud like a child. So I tossed my hat in the middle of the room and went to him.

"Jesus, my Savior! Leopold, what's wrong with you?!" I yelled at him. All he did, though, was to run his narrow, translucent fingers through my hair – there was already a little gray in it – and he couldn't stop sayin': "You're like a father to me – Martin – You're like a father to me!" And from time to time he'd add: "Forgive me!"

But me, I didn't let out one peep about how dismayed I was at his livin' conditions and how much his appearance shocked me.

And when he'd quieted down some, I had to leave my arms lyin' across his bed sheets, and he squeezed and stroked my crude paws, the hands – he said – that had earned his daily bread for him when he was a little boy.

I sure had to pull myself together so's I wouldn't start cryin' myself!

All at once he leans back, looks at me real cheerful, and says: "I really wish I had hands like that, too."

"Well now," I say to that, "they're really not all that clean!"

He twitches his mouth just a teeny bit like he's gonna laugh, leans toward me some, and says quietly: "You don't understand me, Martin. What I'm tryin' to tell you is – I shouldn't have become a priest."

For a while we were both quiet, then he started up again: "Martin, then I never would'a gotten to know those others . . ." He just raised his hand a little and didn't even move three fingers, but I knew right away who he meant by "those others." "I never would'a gotten to know those others and maybe I would'a been received well at the mill in Rodenstein, and ever'thing would'a been fine, alright."

"Don't think about it," I say. Then we were quiet for a while again; and all at once he asks: "Did you know she got married?"

"Marie-Lisa?" I ask.

"Marie-Lisa . . ." he says to himself and then goes on talkin' in my direction: "Martin, you can't imagine how hard it is to run when you're stuck inside a sack; it takes a real effort just to keep yourself standin' up, and if someone comes along with loops to trap you, then you fall right over. For me the priest's cassock was a sack like that. When I was runnin' around outside as a kid, out there in my shorts, I was doin' things the way other people do 'em, but now I'm off to one side from ever'body, of no use to anybody, and upset at myself. Brother" – he yells – "I fell into disgrace, suddenly, like a wild animal into a huntin' pit, and I was ashamed of it, not like the worst sinner when he's done somethin' he planned outta sheer evil. And I wouldn't have stuck with it, if only ever'thing hadn't stayed so secret at first so no one shied away from shakin' their clean hands with me . . . but then I think I can find my way back out of it and belong to the world and ever'body in it again; only those others knew that right well, and they wanted to keep me for themselves, and so they acted bold and shameless so that ever'body in all of Rodenstein soon knew about it, from the forestry house at the one end to the mill at the other! From then on I didn't see another friendly eye, and the blue ones, oh, yeah, the blue ones, they were always turned away from me like I was the enemy. And 'cuz she was so angry at me, all at once she got friendly with someone she wasn't able to stand earlier. People shook their heads and prophesied that nothin' good would come of it. So the time came that I was s'posed to come to this parish here. I had enough worries to push me into the ground: my honor and peace of mind were squandered; those that had taken it from me were stickin' to me like burs; and I was s'posed to leave behind in Rodenstein the little bit of sunshine I had seen in my life – but when my concern for her, for my sunshine, was put on top of ever'thing else, I just had a breakdown and they took me and led me away here, and I let myself be led."

As my brother's talkin' like that, there's a knock at the door and a thickset fella steps inside and says: "Good evenin', Father" and takes a key from the wall and leaves again with it. It was the woodcutter, who'd come to ring the bells for *Ave*.[7]

A while after he'd left, my brother says: "And things haven't gone well for her, either."

Meanwhile the bells start to ring, and the women below pray out loud: "The angel of the Lord brought the message to Mary . . ." and I chime in up above. My brother didn't join in out loud or to himself, but just leaned back and stared in front of him.

After the bellringing, the woodcutter comes back in, hangs the key in its proper place and says: "Reverend, if there's maybe anything you'd like me to do . . . ."

My brother shook his head.

The woodcutter looks at him, scratches himself behind his ear, and asks: "Shouldn't I have one of the other priests from around here drop by? Maybe the one from Rohrhausen or from Goldsdorf? They're the closest, and the way's just as easy for the one as for the other."

"Leave me in peace, Woodcutter Veit," says my brother. "If I feel a need for one, I'll be sure and tell you."

"Oh my," says Veitel, still at the door, "for the sake of the people alone it ought'a happen, for the sake of the people! Well, good night, Father!"

"Yeah, yeah," growled Leopold, "so each of us ought'a listen carefully to what the other guy's doin', just like school boys learnin' to memorize somethin'!?" After that he stays as quiet as a mouse, quite a while, longer and longer, and when I take a little closer look, his eyes are shut and he's fast asleep; so I get up carefully from the chair, walk across the room on tiptoes and go downstairs to where the women are.

They made space for me to spend the night in the lower room on the ground level where they usually had their beds themselves. At first I didn't wanna accept it and said I'd be just as fine in the kitchen, but they said that wouldn't work; one of them always slept there lately to be ready in case my brother needed somethin', and if they'd have to come past me when somethin' was needed, then I wouldn't have a very restful night.

---

[7] The bells calling for prayer to the Virgin Mary, *Ave Maria*.

I also said I intended to look at the church next mornin', 'cuz I wouldn't want to drive back home without havin' been inside it.

The girl says that'd prob'ly be well worth my while. At that we said good night to each other.

In the middle of the night I'm awakened; the girl's standin' in front of me, has a small lantern in her one hand and in the other a big key.

My head shoots up and I'm wide awake: "Heavenly Mother! What's happened?"

"Nothin'," she says. "Come look at the church."

"Are you crazy," I say, "to be playin' these games with me? Didn't I say tomorrow mornin' would be soon enough for me to look it over?"

"Just come along," she says. "The church looks much prettier in the moonlight than at sunup, and it's a perfect time if you wanna see what you can only see now at the midnight hour."

"A spook, maybe?" I ask, perturbed. "I don't need to be there for that." With those words I turn over onto my other side.

She acts like she wants to leave and mumbles: "For all I care. So you don't wanna hear your brother preachin'?"

"Hear him preachin'? Now at midnight, to empty pews?" I yell, leapin' out of bed in one bound. "For the sake of our bloody Savior, tell me it ain't so . . . ."

"You come look for yourself," she says. "Let's not waste any more time, though; otherwise we could be too late." With that she puts the lantern away, places the key down next to it to get one hand free, tosses me my robe from the chair and helps me into it. I don't think I've ever seen any elderly lady as free of embarrassment as this young one.

Next she grabs the things again that she'd laid aside and we leave the house. Outside there's bright moonlight spread over ever'thing and the wind has picked up speed, blowin' sharply across the heights. The girl's walkin' in front of me; her free hair was blowin' over in front of her face, she was barefoot and didn't have a thing on her body but a nightshirt and also a robe that would first flutter out in the wind and then get blown back across her. She had to cover the light in the lantern with her hand: it looked glowin' red as if it was burnin' when I stepped up close but seemed to have gone out if I stayed a step further back. At that point the girl didn't look like a starvin' cat to me no more, but like a real-live witch, and that's the way she looked more and more after we'd gone around the corner, standin' in front of the large church door, and she pushed the key into the lock and

I was standin' right there next to her, lookin' at her face with the moon shinin' on it: she was clenchin' her teeth, her eyes were glistenin' and lookin' right in front of her, straight ahead, as if she was peerin' right through the heavy church door.

Once we had it open, we stepped inside. It was a large, beautiful house of God with richly decorated altars; stained into the windows were colored images – no doubt datin' from olden times – but with time individual panes had been broken out and in their place were now others made from some other color or even white, so that the depictions looked patched and full of holes.

I had scarcely looked around when the tower clock struck twelve rattlin' jolts: just then the little door up by the pulpit creaks open and Leopold steps out. Right above him a bright beam of moonlight had poured in through a white glass pane, laid itself out across the pulpit, struck my brother's face, and I could see his eyes were shut as if he were sleepin'.

"Jesus, Mary," I say quietly to myself. "He's sleepwalkin'." And I grasp the girl by her arm and ask: "How long has he been like this?"

"Ever since we've been here," she says. "From the very first night, as long as we've been here, he's been doin' it like this and always the same thing. I've never disturbed him at it."

Meanwhile he's kneelin' up at the pulpit, his folded hands in front of him on its padded edge, his head bowed over it, just as if in quiet prayer and to collect his thoughts as is common before a sermon. All at once he raises up, bends forward a bit as if the pews below were full of people and he wanted to survey 'em first, then he tosses both arms to the side and stands there as if to say: "Strike me dead if I give you any offense, but I can do nothin' else!" Well, that's not really what he said, but with a voice as you might speak in a dream he did say the words: "I don't know a thing!" And then again – throwin' his hands up toward heaven and then bringin' em back down as if he were pointin' to ever'thing inside and around the church – "I don't know a thing!" After that he turned around and left.

As for me, it sent shivers up my spine. "Poldy," I cry out, "is this how far you've come?"

Then the witch laughs behind me.

"How can you laugh at that?" I ask grimly. "Have you given up on faith yourself?"

Then she says in a harsh voice: "Do you think I don't know I'm the child of a priest? People like me aren't s'posed to even exist. If there was a God and mercy and all that, He wouldn't lemme grow up without both parents, or else His anger would have to destroy children like me. But I think I've grown just tall enough to reach up under your nose and so I'm not somebody who can be overlooked."

The next mornin' my brother's doin' real poor when I see him; on that partic'lar day he wasn't able to say Mass. I don't know if he knew about his sleepwalkin'; I didn't say I'd seen him doin' it, but 'cuz of that I sat next to his bed for a while not sayin' a word at all; then he started in to talkin' 'bout his childhood days: it was strange how he remembered the tiniest little details, and it seemed to me as if, right in the middle of talkin', he was surprised at it himself, too.

Since I saw that talkin' with me was cheerin' him up, I put off my trip home and stayed a while.

Bit by bit he proceeded with his life and we talked it over real good, from the time he was runnin' across the room and around the yard in his toddler clothes 'til when he went off to school – and then into the seminary and – to Rodenstein . . . .

The sun had already set by the time we got along in our cozy little chat to where we were now – in Weissenhofen.

"And that's where it ends," I said, "and there's nothin' more to tell."

"Yeah, yeah," my brother said pensively, "that's where it ends and there's nothin' more to tell."

I look at him.

He lets his head droop for a while . . . . "Martin," he asked me quickly all at once, "are you still there?"

"Near at hand," I say.

"Gimme your hand," he says . . . "Listen, Martin, I'm feelin' – I can't even tell you how it feels."

"Is it hard what's happenin' to you?"

"Not really," he sighed, "but it seems to me the end has come."

"Don't even think it!" I yell, tryin' to stand up to get some help.

But he holds me by my hand and won't let me get up. "Let it be," he says. "Don't turn those others loose on me. I'll get through this alone."

"Poldy," I insisted, "this ain't what's happenin', but if you think it might be, don't forget about God."

Then he squeezes my hand. "Brother of my heart," he says, "have a good life, have a real good life! Don't have any worries 'bout me. If I should end up somewhere other than just under the cool grass, I'm not worried.

I'm a'thinkin' we can come to an understandin' with that God in heaven, and we don't even need a reward for what we suffered on account of Him down here on earth."

"Brother, brother," I beg him, "don't be blasphemin'!"

"You understand!" he said and smiled a tiny bit. "For a long time I've had no more rev'rent thoughts than that one."

"Okay, okay," I agree, "it may be that I don't understand what you've been a'goin' through, but for now you ought'a try and take it easy," 'cuz I'd noticed that the talkin' was makin' him weak even if it wasn't no loud talkin', but still he'd been speakin' and speakin' almost without stop since early on. I was thinkin' we could talk him into things later on. Woodcutter Veitel was right: just for the sake of the people there he ought not to reject the last rites.

So it got quiet as a mouse in the room.

After about a quarter hour, I hear him sayin': "Yeah, yeah, so now we're together again, but you don't hafta squeeze me in your arms so tight." With that he throws his body over to his right side – he'd been a'layin' on his left – takes one deep breath, and it's all over.

From my chair I flew bolt upright, I bent over him; there wasn't a breath left in him. For a long time I wasn't able to close his eyes for him; that's how insecure I was feelin' with my hands, and I didn't want to touch him too hard. Finally I was able to get it done, though. Then I left; while I was still in the doorway, I looked at him one more time, the way he was layin' there so still, said "God bless you, Poldy," and quietly pulled the door shut behind me.

When I come down, the womenfolk shriek at once: "Dear Jesus! What's the matter with you? What happened?" They would'a had to been blind, too, if they couldn't have seen it from the way I looked. Then I say: "My brother's withstood it all now." It took a while 'til they figured out what it was they'd heard, but then the old one started to howlin' out loud and wanted to come to me, but I fended her off and she went runnin' up the stairs. The young one, horrified and real timid, retreated into one corner of the room and stood there without makin' a peep or changin' expressions, just like a hunk of wood. I went out the front door and walked, on and on, 'til I'd gotten back home.

On the second day after that was my brother's funeral, so I was in Weissenhofen for a second time – just like I'd been in Rodenstein twice. So I saw the two women one more time, but I haven't seen 'em since and don't know what became of 'em.

Right after the funeral I set off on the path home. All my thinkin' was directed at Leopold for the whole, long way. So I'd had to be there to see his death, too, just like with so many of my brothers and sisters! But I still think today it wouldn't have had to end like that if only Mama had let him live his life the way it would'a grown an' developed on its own. Children have to pay for the sins of their parents anyhow; for their inborn ones people can't do nothin', they're scarcely able to shuck off their bad habits, and it weighs down so heavy on their shoulders all their days that the people who get old have to watch it all afterwards. Mama must not have thought it to be such a big sin anyhow, 'cuz otherwise she never would'a brought a Poldy Pechleitner into the world in the first place; if she imagined afterwards that it *was* such a big sin, then she should'a seen to makin' things right with God on her own. Oh, yeah, he had to put on the priest's cassock, which is for sure a much bigger sack than the farmer's overalls and has plenty of room for other people's sins, too, but if the priest commits one himself, where does he find space for that?

If only I'd used my head better back then when the plans were bein' made for him: I did predict disaster and knew full well that Mama was an old lady – at an age when the conscience wakes up for many while the brain's fallin' asleep. He wouldn't have had to gamble away his faith, honor and peace of mind, 'cuz the farmer class doesn't play with such high stakes. Today the boy would still be runnin' around the farm alive and well where I could see him, and next to him – I couldn't ask for anything nicer – would be Marie-Lisa with her little ones, and he'd be sayin' "God bless you" to me and ever'one would be so concerned about their old uncle. Now there won't even be so much as a cat to blubber over me when I'm gone.

And that's the way things would'a been, like I say, I know that for sure, 'cuz Marie-Lisa, I saw her again one more time. Fourteen years after my brother's death it was, a year and a half ago. For business and for this and that I happened to be near Weissenhofen on All Souls' Day.[8] I think to myself: "I'll go on over there, say the Lord's Prayer at my brother's grave," and that's where I met her, Marie-Lisa, a fine figure of a woman, a widow for eight years already, and she hasn't married again up to the present day; next to her a little boy was standin' lookin' real serious with his big, blue eyes:

---

[8] November 2, the day when prayers are said for the dead.

he was the spittin' image of her. When I come up to the grave there, she wasn't exactly embarrassed, I can't say that, but she did turn a little off to one side as if we didn't need to pay attention to each other.

"Miller lady," says I, "maybe you don't recognize me anymore; I'm the brother of the fella lyin' here under the ground, and the fact that I'm meetin' you here – which makes my heart feel so odd, both happy and sad at the same time – you don't have a thing to be ashamed of 'bout that."

"No, I don't," she says, and we shake hands across his grave.

Oh, you poor love child, you, how wantonly your joy of livin' was destroyed! There's not much understandin' and pity in this world, even from one person to the next. I had to think of his two Gods, the one for earth, the other in heaven; it can't be much longer 'til I head out to the place of no return myself, and it'd be just fine with me if I happened to meet up with the Second One and was acceptable to Him. Well, no matter what happens, I'll find it out soon enough, just like all of us sittin' here will find it out. Would someone pass the matches on over to me? My pipe has laid around long enough: I gotta smoke out all the funny ideas that whirl around in my head so often now that I'm breathin' down on my seventies and don't have anybody to be happy 'bout it, and that includes myself for sure.

Peter Rosegger (1843-1918) was a native of the mountains of Styria.[1] His father was an illiterate farmer in the highland pastures, and the memories of Rosegger's youth in his forest home were to find echo and narrative detail in many of his later prose writings. Other than the sporadic tutelage of a wandering educator, he was largely self-taught; the possibilities for further formal schooling were limited by geography and financial realities. Too weak to take up the farming profession, he was first designated by his very religious parents to enter the priesthood, but this, through a chain of events, didn't work out. He became a tailor's apprentice, which allowed him to travel the surrounding areas of Styria, getting to know the land and the people. Gradually his talent for writing became evident, and various mentors and benefactors helped him to bring his first stories before the public. Orginal credit for discovering young Peter's talent must go to Dr. Adalbert Svoboda, editor-in-chief of the *Tagespost,* Steiermark's highly respected daily,[2] while later assistance came from Leopold von Sacher-Masoch and the publisher Gustav Heckenast.

Rosegger founded the journal *Heimgarten* in 1876, editing and contributing prose fiction to it for decades. He also voiced his concern in that publication about such topics as animal rights, the economics of mountain farming, Alpine environmental issues, and the politics of the day.

In an age of threatening industrialization and, for many people, of an involuntary alienation from nature, the call back to nature that Rosegger's writings represent was welcomed and even made him into one of the most popular literary cult phenomena of the day – on the one hand – and into a critically renowned author on the other: he received honorary doctorates from the universities of Heidelberg, Vienna, and Graz; honorary membership in the British Royal Society of Literature; and he was later nominated for the Nobel Prize (in 1913).

In the gripping tale entitled **Mary in Misery** (1881), two of Rosegger's earliest formative influences come together: the mountains of his home province and the Roman Catholic Church. The title of the novella can be seen as ambiguous, referring both to the name of a fictitious shrine to the Virgin

---

[1] "Steiermark" in German, a mountainous province in southeastern Austria of which Graz is the capital.

[2] My thanks to Dr. Gerhard Rosegger, great-grandson of the author, for his informative comments and suggestions, including this reference to Svoboda .

Mary situated in such a desolate wasteland that it can be called "misery," and to the name of a female penitent, also Mary, who suffers in misery of soul. As in many of Rosegger's forest tales, the narrator of this story is a proponent of taming the wilderness and taming its inhabitants without spoiling either. To make this vividly clear, a semi-wild "half-fool" of a hermit juxtaposes himself against the clearly devoted and talented priest of the shrine. Yet events transpire to show the young priest that the wilderness and desolation within his own soul need taming no less than does the wildness of the "blasphemer." At the same time, the earthly Mary is put in a position of potential mediation between earth and heaven and is inspired to accomplish selfless spiritual purposes for which she had earlier unsuccessfully petitioned the other Mary, Mother of God. Throughout the work, other metaphors and parallels tie together the loftiness of heaven by reference to the tops of the Styrian mountains.

The parallel between the theme of this novella and of Anzengruber's *Love Child* (p. 364) is striking: in both stories,[3] a young priest is assigned to a small chapel in the mountains, where an unpriestly attraction to a member of the opposite sex tempts him to overlook or abandon clerical duties in favor of his own love fulfillment. Though the outcomes can be called tragic in both cases, the nature of the tragedies differ greatly: where Anzengruber portrays a young fellow totally inappropriate for the clergy and who suffers both mental anguish of alienation from his true love interest *and* the mortal suffering that narratively underscores the blunder of his calling to the priesthood, this powerful novella by Peter Rosegger shows a priest who proves to be eminently well-suited to his calling and whose tragic love and loss only inspire him to further growth, insight, and service to his fellow beings.

---

[3] The two writers, Anzengruber and Rosegger, were well acquainted with one another and carried on a correspondence for nearly two decades (1871-1889).

Mary in Misery

Peter Rosegger

"It is not good that man should be alone"[4]: thus spake Jehovah and introduced Adam's companion to him.

That was the first love story. All mankind has lived love stories since then, all writers have written love stories, and all receptive souls have eagerly listened to love stories. Love has remained the same for the many millennia in which humans have been measuring their existence, just as a rose on a thorny bush in the wild has remained the same. Even if zealots have tried to suffocate love in the hair shirt of penitence, to bury it in hell; even if society, from the beginning, has concentrated on veiling it in milder forms ... love has remained the same, like a fiery flame that can be extinguished but never cooled. Where love reigns, there all barriers fall; there all the veils of civilization fall away, and the last becomes the first:[5] Adam and Eve.

The world is accustomed to concealing from view, lovingly, that type of love that grim rules have lovelessly forbidden. But in our case it has to be revealed, since it is as grand as the mountains in which it thrived. When we – you, dear reader, and I – stroll through the heavens someday, we will come face to face with a smiling couple that could only be joined together there, at the throne of God . . . . The love story to follow doesn't culminate in the grave, you see, nor in the marriage bed, but continues on over into Paradise.

---

[4] *Genesis* 2:18.
[5] Cf. *Matthew* 19: 30.

A Little Chapel in God's Temple

"Magnificent! Delightfully magnificent!" the Alpine traveler shouts for joy when he rises above the ridge of the last pastured foothills and suddenly sees the extensive, torturously sublime rock basin before him. But after he has dwelt in this region for only a few hours, for a day, he begins to feel as if the pure, thin Alpine air had turned to lead and were depressing his spirits. It is a great and intractable wasteland. The life that thrives here is by no means friendly to man. The gorges and depths lie in a bluish haze; the untamed waters bursting forth from mountain crags and over vertical cliffs, the bold overhangs of deeply furrowed and split rock faces, the stone bulwarks jutting ever further by the unremitting push of glaciers, the towering masses of ice inciting snow to avalanche and rocks and mud to slide into the hollows at every Föhn[6]: all these threaten the dark stand of fir trees in the depths, where a lake once stood. The lake was filled in with sediment; the forest grew from the fill only to share the fate of the lake someday. Gigantic fallen boulders are piled up beneath the sheer, gray faces of stone. The bearded vulture and the golden eagle soar in circles around the jagged pinnacles, scanning the area below for chamois[7] and large ravens after having annihilated entire races of black grouse and snow grouse. The populace of small birds has been totally murdered; only the Alpine lark is able to save herself in the dense foliage of the arolla pine, and the falcon avoids his enemies only by maneuvering as fast as an arrow in flight.

Frosts, storms, snow kill any plants and flowers that try to sprout in the black soil between the rocks. While invigorating summer breezes waft gently through far-off river valleys, sharp Alpine winds howl and whistle around the unyielding crags and peaks here; while mild, life-giving rain drizzles in the valleys, swirling snow precipitates out of dark fog masses here.

There is no friendly life form that flourishes in this stony wasteland; violence and destruction dwell in the high-towering and wide-domed massifs.

---

[6] German: a warm, dry wind from extreme altitude that descends along the north slope of the Alps; also known as *scirocco* in Italian.

[7] A goatlike antelope at home in the high mountains of Europe.

And yet, on the pale-green meadows of a protected mountain plateau, a human refuge stands in the midst of this wasteland. A few houses have been constructed with thick walls and with windows as tiny and deep as peepholes in a citadel. The roofs are battened down with beams and heavy rocks; chimneys – as wide and massive as small fortresses – protrude from the rooftops. And next to these citadels stands a church, built to be just as firm and secure. It's a Gothic church, and its slender white tower stands out like a milestone against the dark gray rock faces that fill the range of vision round about. The narrow, tall windows of the House of God have sturdy bars in front of them, not because of evil people – for whom there's nothing of interest in the sanctuary – but because eagles could break through the window and hack to pieces the colorful candlesticks prominently placed before the object of veneration at the altar.

A strange object of veneration hangs in the niche above the altar. The figure is decorated with jewelry and fine ornaments in the manner of a crowned queen; a totally shapeless face can be seen, brown as bark, and two gnarled arms stretch out to either side. It is a highly sacred figure, though – an image of the Virgin Mary – not made by human hands, like idols, but formed by the omnipotence of God.

It was centuries ago that a herd of sheep, grazing on this mountain, was found kneeling before a densely foliated arolla pine one Saturday evening. Within its gnarled branches could be seen a human likeness, recognized by the priests as an image of Our Lady, the Eternal Virgin and Mother of God. The divinely sculpted image was carried down into the valley and displayed in a magnificent monastery church. But it didn't want to stay down in the valley, and the sheep found it in the arolla pine foliage of the Alpine wasteland the very next Saturday evening. Then the sign from heaven was duly recognized, and the church and hospice were built on the tall mountain; soon pilgrims came from far and near, individually and in groups, laying their cares and all their suffering and faults at the foot of Our Heavenly Lady. But only those truly unhappy and miserable made the pilgrimage to the little chapel on the wild and desolate mountainside.

And the lonely shrine is called: "Mary in Misery."

Mary's Young Keeper

The church was affiliated with a splendid monastery situated way off in a fertile valley. This monastery was to tend and protect the site and hold in trust the offerings that pilgrims laid at its altar. The monastery was also required to keep a priest on the mountain during the summertime to contribute to the salvation of pilgrims. A few hosts and merchants always accompanied the priest to Mary in Misery to provide the crowds of pilgrims with the necessities of life, images of the saints, rosaries, and other objects of devotion. In the autumn, though, everyone returned to the valley: no human being remained in the heights, wild snowstorms howled around the forlorn walls, and Our Lady's font of mercy was frozen to ice.[8]

The monastery had elderly priests who were completely satisfied with a glass of wine, a pinch or a pipeful of tobacco, who gave the world nothing and took nothing in return, and who fulfilled their ecclesiastical duties each day in their standard, indifferent manner.

Such were the people assigned to provide pastoral care for the pilgrims at Mary in Misery.

But then, by and by, a time arrived when such people had died out in the monastery, when no one could be found who considered himself venerable and virtuous enough to serve up there in the Misery as Mary's devout keeper.

At this time, when the little Alpine chapel was in danger of becoming priestless, young Pater[9] Emanuel was living in the monastery. He had taken his vows only a few years earlier. He was a man of rare enthusiasm; whether at the altar, at the pulpit, in the confessional, or even in the social circle of his cohorts, he took his mission so very seriously, anywhere and everywhere, that all the exertions of his religious order seemed scarcely sufficient to him, and he took new and unique paths in trying to heed the voice of his conscience. He loved solitude, but he also sought out suffering people now and then. They were comforted at the very sight of him: he was tall and handsome and his youthful countenance mirrored traits of gentleness and dignity. He avoided the lawns of the monastery, though, where his clerical brethren bowled; and when he sat in the refectory – and everyone around

---

[8] Besides any metaphorical meaning, this may also refer to the basin of holy water.

[9] Latin: "father."

him was lighthearted and merry, since the kitchen and the wine cellar basically didn't permit any sadness – Pater Emanuel sat there silently and almost bored. It was well known that Emanuel could be jolly, lively, and witty at times, but that happy temperament arose from the bottom of his soul and didn't require any wine or Dutch tea. His only delight was in spiritual joy, whether it was to be found in a good deed or in the enjoyment of beautiful nature, open and free.

What the abbot[10] said one day at the dinner table had long been inevitable.

"Pater Emanuel!" the abbot called out in a somewhat joking tone of voice, "Would you like to be a pastor?"

The young priest laid his fork and spoon to one side and responded in the same tone of voice: "Sir, I am prepared!"

"The position at Mary in Misery is available."

At that, boisterous laughter broke out. The laughter was like ridicule directed at the poor little chapel in the Alpine wasteland. The abbot laughed along with the others.

Emanuel wasn't laughing, but, once the ruckus had ended, he did say: "If the monastery laughs at the shrine, then why don't we get rid of it? And if, on the other hand, we find it best to continue to maintain it, then the laughter is incomprehensible. Mary in Misery is no grand monastery like this proud, magnificent building of which I am honored to be a part; it is a stepchild . . . ."

"It's a milk cow!" yelled a bold face, red with wine.

"Where," Emanuel asked, "where do the faithful go on pilgrimage when their hearts are full of sorrow? To our monastery or to Mary in Misery?"

"So the answer is yes? You're ready for this?" the supervisor interrupted him; but now his voice seemed serious.

Before the young priest could think about it twice, he was up on the high mountainside in the midst of the boulders, seeing nothing of the world but stones and clouds. And what was to be found there . . . was poverty, and what the pilgrims carried in with them from far-off lands and regions . . . was sorrow and suffering.

The priest's quarters in the hospice were like a prison. A bit of the rock face peered in through two deep, barred windows, and just enough light came in through them to barely illuminate the crude, thin straw mattress

---

[10] The title given to the head of a monastery.

and the brown *prie-dieu*[11] and the wooden crucifix. The other corners of the little room didn't have much to show, but prominently displayed on one of the gray-washed walls was a collection of smoking pipes left behind by his predecessors.

The new pastor's food and other material needs were taken care of by an old caretaker who had lived on this mountain every summer for fifty-three years. The old woman was almost as ugly as the statue in the church, but she knew all about the hospice, the weather conditions, the household. This woman frequently had to instruct the young pastor about the long-standing customs in the house and in the church. Gertrude alone knew when Mass should be said, how long the sermon had to last, and at what point the morning, noon and evening bells needed to be rung. She knew ahead of time on which days most pilgrims would arrive, and where they came from, and what languages they spoke: there would be Germans, Slavs, Hungarians, speakers of French and Italian. Pater Emanuel, fortunately, was a good student of languages and could edify the people in their own mother tongues. Lady Gertrude reaped infinite advantages, though, from her superior experience. Thus she claimed that the clerical gentlemen who had been in Misery before the present *pater* had eaten nothing but bread and milk, as is only right and proper at such a holy place, except for church holidays when they added a little lard. Pater Emanuel didn't want to have things any better than his elderly predecessors and was satisfied with bread and milk, while the trusty housekeeper tucked away any savings from meat, pastries, and wine into her own pocket.

Only when the young priest went out with a shotgun in his leisure hours and returned with a hawk he had bagged, or even an eagle (since only birds of prey could be shot), only then was Lady Gertrude able to convince him that some hearty roasted poultry might not make a bad meal.

Emanuel might have sensed that the old lady was taking advantage of him, but for the sake of domestic tranquility he made no objections; he remained silent on the matter, didn't concern himself with the housekeeper, fulfilled his duties, and retreated even deeper into his own world of thought . . . And that was precisely what angered, insulted, embittered the trusty old woman so much: that this young *pater* was so pridefully aloof, so very arrogant – in contrast to the former priests, who had been so entertaining

---

[11] A desk or stool used for kneeling in prayer, attached above which is a rest for books or other reading matter.

and sociable – yes, there had often been exceedingly good times up here at Mary in Misery.

On days when there were large crowds, the young priest felt best: he realized who he was and what he was capable of; he comforted people in the confessional and edified them from the pulpit. With gladness and glowing enthusiasm, he spoke of Mary, the Virgin and Queen, to whom he poured out all the love of his youthful heart. With the grace, fire, and dedication of a divinely-sanctioned minstrel, he praised her beauty, her femininity, her celestial dignity, her mercy and love. – It had been the previous tradition that six candles would burn in front of the marvelous image of Mary's mercy above the altar during the sermons, but Emanuel always had the flames extinguished before he began speaking and only allowed the red votive vessel of "eternal light" to burn, its pale gleam laying a mysterious aura over the ugly, formless image.

It was also traditional at Mary in Misery that the priest would bless candles of red wax and keep them on hand to sell to pilgrims in the sacristy.[12] Each pilgrim took one of these candles home with him or her, for the belief was widespread that such candles – blessed and dedicated at Mary in Misery – would, if lit at the hour of death, lessen the fear of dying and neutralize the temptations of the devil. – Pater Emanuel dispensed with this source of secondary income. He distributed candles from the large supply on hand, yet he refused to allow himself to profit from the means of deathbed comfort for his fellow men.

Often the priest quietly watched the activities of pilgrims, who, while in front of the statue of Mary's mercy, didn't quite know how to express their veneration, their love, their pain of heart, their longing. Many lay for hours as if lifeless on the stone floor; others stood up straight and stretched out their hands, like Christ on the cross; still others slid on their knees around the altar. He saw one old man, crouching in a corner of the church, who had lit seven candles in front of him: he had seven beloved family members back home for whom he wanted to offer a burnt sacrifice here to the glorious Bearer of God. One little woman dragged a large rock in through the door, a rock she had pushed and lifted up the steep mountain with sweat and great effort; she had no other sacrifice, for she was a poor woman, and so, to fill the needs of her reverent heart, she laid the rock before the altar.

---

[12] A room in the church where sacred vessels and vestments are stored.

Then new crowds approached, singing and praying, letting their flags flutter in the Alpine wind, and they dipped low their crucifixes before the miraculous image. And many coins clanked in the stone offertory box standing next to the entrance, sealed shut with a number of iron bands around it. A prime part of it all, though, was confession, communion, repentance, and the offering up of every need and every deed in honor of Mary.

And when they had thus satisfied their urges and longings, they left again and had peace in their hearts.

Loneliness: Lone, Depressed

Pater Emanuel stayed behind in the wasteland, though; and on quiet, lonely days a mood arose in him like emptiness of heart and dryness of the spirit. His books were extremely uplifting and instructive, but they couldn't satisfy him. There was no garden to plant here, no trees or flowers to tend. Oh, here and there a blood-red bush of mountain clover blossomed, or some white lady's-mantle, and on the cliffs Alpine roses[13] went on display – but only for a short time. He dug up an extraordinarily delicate snow-white stone lily, along with its roots, put it in his room next to the window, and treated it with loving kindness. At length he gave it a little blue Alpine Bell[14] as a companion which was supposed to ring out lovingly in honor of the lily.[15] – Unfortunately, these delicate children of Flora had to suffer a violent death before their time, a demise under the hand of the bustling housekeeper. – "And it's just as well," Emanuel thought to himself, "that my fate doesn't speak the language of flowers."

Then he went out and improved the steep path leading up to the church, removed the stones, and dug runoff ditches for melted snow. At the most dangerous spots he widened the path and furnished handrails. Then he sank long poles along the path from point to point so that safe passage could be found in the event of a sudden blizzard. He also tried to dig a well, but his efforts were unsuccessful. The culinary water used on the mountainside

---

[13] Also known as *rhododendron*.

[14] Literal translation of *Alpenglöcklein*, known botanically as *soldanella*.

[15] Often used as an emblem of the Virgin Mary.

had to be hauled in from over an hour away where it tumbled down from the glaciers through a deep crevice in the rocks.

Every third day a delivery man came up from the foothills with groceries and newspapers. He turned the groceries over to Lady Gertrude, the papers to the *pater*.

The newspapers recounted the violence and scandals going on in the world and what people had to say about them. They left him as empty as did the Latin books lying on the *prie-dieu*.

What was left for the young, active man to do? He went out again and again to observe nature. He listened to grains of sand sloughing off the stone walls; he heard the thundering of avalanches and saw the white clouds of powdery snow behind the jagged peaks. And strips of fog hung from the highest summits, and in the high hollows lay the eternal armor of ice with its cracks and crevices. – Eternal armor! Hadn't he, the young priest, even dreamed once, after falling asleep over a book about geology, about magnificent jungles of tropical plants – fig trees and orange trees, palms and cypresses – growing wild up in the heights where the glaciers lay? A little lower down, the waves of the high seas had been beating on the rocks, in his dream, and mythological sea monsters had been cavorting in the yawning precipices where today the sun sets over endangered forests of fir.

It was a strange dream, one impossible for him to interpret by the book of books, the Bible.

One day Emanuel climbed up a goat path at great effort and danger until he reached the rock towers from which the hospice could be seen far below as if in a valley, even though it lay on top of a seven-thousand-foot mountain. Behind the towers began the waste regions of endless cirque[16] fields. That was where the bone-colored limestone massifs were found: gigantic stone conglomerates – pasted together, impassively flooded, hollowed out, etched, and weathered. Hollows, ditches, holes, canals, caves of the strangest shapes; anything resembling soil washed away. But in the scoops and hollows, here and there, stood silent black water without a living thing in it; it had come from rain or the glaciers and had found no outlet, no shaft through which to seep, to drain, to fall like other pools of water that reappeared at the cliffs below as springs or fountains and as cataracts in the gorges. It had to wait until the wind came along and lapped it up, or until

---

[16] Steep-walled basins carved out by glaciation and other forces.

the frost came and froze it solid. – Isn't the young man on the mountain called Misery waiting for a similar fate? – To be scattered, dried up, and blown away . . . or frozen solid.

As Emanuel looked down on his little chapel from these lifeless and comfortless heights, terror shot through him. Along the white, sandy path to the shrine was crawling and undulating a long, brown, hundred-footed lizard with a trembling red flame at its head. No, it wasn't a dragon, the sort of beast said by legend to have held sway over the mountain heights at one time long ago; it was just a crowd of cross bearers, with pilgrims' walking sticks and a red flag, on pilgrimage by foot toward the place of mercy. And that was what caused the priest's terror, for while he was supposed to be waiting for the pilgrims at all times down at the church, to greet them with the ringing of bells and a priestly welcome, he was now up on top of this inhospitable overlook and had no idea how he could get back down quickly.

When finally, after three hours, he arrived at the little church with his body bruised and bleeding like a martyr, he became aware of something edifying. Gertrude, the old housekeeper, was squatting in front of the altar, reciting Psalms and the litany to the newly-arrived pilgrims in her nasal voice and with her head wobbling, and, in the intervals while the congregation busily repeated the words, the trusty old woman openly expressed her indignation at the truant priest wandering around heaven knows where stealing the day from the Lord.

A gripping evening sermon from Emanuel made abundant restitution to the pilgrims for the old lady's devotional exercise. In this sermon, held under the open skies, the young priest directed the congregational gaze upward to the rocky peaks glowing deeply in the evening twilight. "All over creation," he cried, "we can feel God's presence, but here, in the sublime tops of the mountains, his visible temple is open for all to view. The Alpine head, covered with eternal ice, is his high altar. The glowing crags of rock are the candle holders with their sacrificial flame. The raging waters that course down from all ramparts of the mountain range signify for us the unquenchable fonts of mercy of our God. And that is, no doubt, the reason that man has constructed a temple on these heights, far from the cares of the world: because here, in the midst of nature's majesty, he is more receptive to the great and the sublime than down there in everyday life, and because only where the heart of man is collected and prepared does the spirit and the mercy of God overshadow it."

It had no effect on Lady Gertrude, though, and that very evening she watered down the *pater*'s milk for the first time. – "Oh dear," she giggled to herself, "Didn't I hear a lovely sermon today, about God and the mountains! – Oh, these young priests nowadays! They don't even find it worth their trouble to preach about Our Dear Lady!"

What Else Grows in the Branches of the Arolla Pine?

From that time forward, Pater Emanuel paid close attention not to stray too far from the church during his walks. He only went as far as one basin where an avalanche the previous spring had split rock and destroyed a stand of pine trees. Between the debris he found a crushed ibex[17] and a number of dead birds. At times he also climbed down to the "Ebony Eye," a small, dark lake that lay in another deep basin. Even if constant winds swept the heights and even if storms were raging, seldom as not, this lake stayed as smooth and unruffled as the top of a mirrored table; it had no apparent influx and no drainage outlet. When a leaf or a piece of wood was thrown in, the gently widening waves of water were the only movement on the lake: the object would glide on the smooth surface for a while, but suddenly it disappeared and was never seen again. Emanuel liked to play this game and concluded from the phenomenon that there were incredible depths and powerful currents hidden within the lake.

Once, the young man found on the mossy shores of the "Ebony Eye" a charming and strange violet inside whose petals a second violet was sprouting forth. This discovery filled him with thoughts and daydreams; suddenly a harmless steel-gray snake darted in front of him and reared its hissing head, as if in fearful protest of the ambiguous flower. But Emanuel boldly caught the beast with his bare hands and let it slither merrily across his chest and around his neck. And when they had both had their fill of the game, Emanuel let the snake go again. It shot into a nearby arolla pine, and at the same instant a human shriek of indignant terror rang out from among the branches.

---

[17] A type of mountain goat, *"Steinbock"* in the original German.

Emanuel gave a start. A head with dull brown hair raised up above the thick, tree-green foliage; a young man stood there, covered by pine branches up to his chest. His gray eyes flashed; his vividly reddened face wanted to smile, but it only managed a confused grin.

The young fellow was in traditional Alpine dress and looked good-natured but a bit roguish. He greeted the priestly gentleman.

"What are you doing here?" the priest called out.

"Oh, of certainty not, of certainty not!" was the answer of the man in the arolla pine. It was an anachronistic and misplaced negation.

Now Emanuel recognized him. He was a herder named Gaiser Bimmel[18] who lived as a hermit in a den in the forest: he made a living with his few goats and kept himself busy every summer by harvesting wild hay. Bimmel helped out at times as something of a sexton in the church on "Mount Misery" and enjoyed the reputation of a devoutly religious man as well as that of a half-fool. His ways of living and of expressing himself were strange, for they arose from other circumstances and motivations than those of other human beings. His ancestors, persecuted during religious wars, are said to have immigrated from northerly regions, and Bimmel's father is said to have attained a great and perfect intellect. He had died suddenly, and his son grew up in poverty and loneliness, and, not knowing anything better to do, he simply took up living with the animals of the forest and went wild. His manner of thinking was unique, and, independent of reality, it followed the paths of its own very specific logic. He didn't care about anyone, just as no one cared about him – he was the half-fool.

Now Emanuel stepped up to this young man, and, behold, he noticed at the feet of the latter – hiding in the bushes – a woman.

Now they were both speechless. The priest was trying to pull himself together.

"Gaiser Bimmel!" he finally said, "Is that what you call harvesting wild hay?"

The lad jumped out of the shrubbery and replied boldly and merrily: "Yep, that's harvesting wild hay."

"Come on out," Emanuel called to the woman still in hiding, "and tell me who put you together in the bushes like that!"

---

[18] The name "Gaiser" comes from the German word for "goat," and so the herder's name could be roughly translated as "Goat-Boy Bimmel."

"We grew up in the arolla pine, just like Our Dear Lady up there on Misery Mountain," Bimmel answered, winking.

The woman, now slowly emerging,[19] was young and full of vitality, but her much-too-tousled brown hair hung in her face. She picked up a stone and tried to throw it at the snake: "You horrible piece of trash, it's all your fault! Even if my mouth were nailed shut, I'd have to yell and scream when a beast from Hell like that ran across my hand."

But the little snake had long since slipped into a crack in the rock, and the priest said seriously: "I think the bright side of it is that the snake accomplished the opposite here of what the serpent did in the Garden of Eden."[20]

"Herr Priest!" the young man now raised his voice, boldly taking the girl by her hand, "What can a fellow do? That's my Ursel! . . . And we weren't doing anything wrong."

"If not, then why did you hide in the bushes?" the priest asked.

"Well, yeah, because . . ." said the goatherd, "because the Herr Reverend Father often gives such sharply worded sermons."

That was, to all appearances, the answer of a fool, but it embittered the man with the strict principles.

"You are a hypocrite!" he said energetically to the lad, "You want to look like a saint in front of people and act like a hermit, casting your eyes to the ground when you walk past women . . . and all that so you can secretly carry on your immoral life style. And in the confessional you don't say a word about it."

"Because it's my secret," Bimmel whispered with his head bowed.

"But the Lord God sees it, even if it's hidden!"

"That's just what I thought, too, when I kept it to myself."

"You're a blasphemer!" cried the priest. "People say you're a simpleton, but now I know you better: you're sly, malicious, maybe even more!"

"I thank you very much for the priestly lecture!" responded the lad and made a charming bow. "And . . . I was just about to say something . . . but don't be angry, Reverend Father . . . the reason you're up in arms so much about me . . . I think that's just because . . . ."

---

[19] The German verb in the original "*sich hervorwinden*" suggests an uncoiling as she came out, much as a snake might do.

[20] It is often assumed that the serpent's temptation of Eve (*Genesis* 3: 1-6) led to sexual transgression.

"Geezus and Mary! Stuff somethin' in your mouth, Bimmel!" the young woman cried, took the young man by the arm, and quickly pulled him away.

They disappeared in the forest ravine. Pater Emanuel heard the girl still yelling and arguing for a long time about the snake that she thought had caused all the trouble.

The *pater* cast one more deep and sharp look into the arolla pine needles, then he also left. He often stopped along the way. Up on a cliff between two weathered, gray stone faces, he saw a nest of falcons where there was a lot of lively activity. He stood in front of it for a long time, and later he regretted the way he had delivered his admonition to Gaiser Bimmel. He had been irritated, of course, but the rebuke could have been handled differently.

Mary's Assumption Day

Towards the end of summer, on the 15th of August, the Catholic Church celebrates one of its most luminous holy days. On this day the cult of Mary crescendoes to the glory of an almost demonic enthusiasm. It is the marvelous day on which, long ago, the Mother of Jesus, under the eyes of the apostles and accompanied by choirs of angels, ascended into heaven with body and soul.

Wherever a temple to Mary arises on the fruit-bearing plains, wherever the bell of Our Lady's chapel rings out in the forested ravines or on the tops of the mountains, pilgrims flow together to celebrate the day of commemoration with pageantry and heartfelt joy.

Pater Emanuel looked forward to this celebration with longing, but also with trepidation. The little church in Misery was festooned with pine wreathes and juniper branches inside and out; slender new candles were placed at the altar, and in such numbers that they nearly hid the sculpture of mercy from view. All the rooms of the hospice were made available, but when the crucifix-laden crowds streamed together from three sides of the mountain on the night before the holiday, echoing their prayers and hymns off the stony surroundings and arriving by the thousands with their flags flying, then the church and hostel were nowhere near able to contain all the guests. Hundreds of the tired pilgrims had to spend the night in the little merchant shops and on the stone floor of the House of God. At the same time there was a constant praying, singing, and sighing in all kinds of languages: the impatient Hungarian tried to outshout the German's "Hail Mary," the passionate Italian to outshout the melancholic hymn of the Slav – whoever yelled the loudest would be heard by Our Blessed Lady. At times an elderly prayer leader stood at the offertory box and warned about pickpockets in his already thoroughly hoarse voice. Another tried to create a passageway through the compacted human tangle for a woman who had fainted, for a half-trampled child.

On the night before Assumption Day, when the sun had already gone down but ever more crowds of pilgrims were still streaming in, Emanuel held solemn vespers; innumerable candles were flickering at the altar, on the walls, and even in the midst of the devout worshipers themselves. A thick, blue haze gathered in the rooms of the church, and the feverishly excited faces of all were turned towards the statue. – Today was the day. Whatever could be petitioned from the mighty Queen of Heaven at this hour and at this place, it was petitioned. Blessing for the fruits of the field, peace or fertility in marriage, health, riches, the release of poor souls from purgatory, bliss in the hour of death – and everything and anything else that arouses a wish in the human heart – was the object of prayer. One old maid prayed for a sick sheep just as fervently as did a young woman for her dying spouse. An old horse trader begged the Mother of God to keep secret the tricks by which he had outwitted his business colleagues. A sixteen-year-old boy approached Our Richly Merciful Lady about a mustache. – Who could count and measure the secretly held sufferings of the human heart, though, that didn't break forth in words and thoughts here, but which came out in streams of tears?

After the vespers, Pater Emanuel sat down in his confessional and listened, deep into the night, to the afflictions, mistakes, and monstrosities of the human soul. These had to be gruesome hours for the young man, since only faint traces of this world had floated towards him in his otherwise empty and lonely life. But of the sin-rousing urges that announced themselves to him through the confessional screen, strangely enough . . . he had already encountered all of them in his own soul. And he was supposed to judge the missteps of others? Men with deep wrinkles and snow-white hair were coming to him, seeking instruction and counsel. And many young souls caught up in the heat of living came to him as well, full of trust, revealing themselves to him right down to their innermost sanctum, to areas usually protected by the fires of shame.

With his head reeling, Emanuel finally got up from the confessional around midnight and tottered off towards his room. But he couldn't fall asleep with the witches' dance of human passions whirling through his brain. For the inanimate statue on the altar the pilgrims had brought loving hymns and charming flowers; but for him, alas, for the priestly human, they hadn't brought a thing but their own most bitter and ugly possessions, pain and sin.

He was particularly bothered, though, by one single penitent. She was a wide-eyed brunette of eighteen or twenty. For a long time she had knelt at the confessional, trembling and sobbing, before she was able to speak a single word. Then the young confessor had said she'd come from a very long and hard journey to seek help from Mary; she couldn't help herself anymore, she said, but she was terrified of herself, being void of any love, gratitude, or loyalty. – "My child," the priest had comforted her then, "Your sins are loosed by your recognition of them. From this moment on, since you've accused yourself of ingratitude and lack of love, that's no longer the way you are at heart. Go your way in peace!" And he had made the sign of the cross over the penitent; the latter had remained there, though, weeping on her knees at the step, until a group of scolding women pushed her out of the way so they could have their turns.

The young priest felt that this girl had left the confessional without being comforted. And when he finally closed his eyes, he saw her lying at his feet in a dream, with her hair let down, but much more charmingly and movingly than in depictions of Mary Magdalene kneeling before the Savior.

A long time before the sun poured out across the pinnacles and broad glaciers of the Alps, Emanuel was in the church again to fulfill his obligations to the reassembling crowds. The entire peak was full of people; everyone was pushing towards the House of God to see the image of mercy there. And as the bells rang out and the organ played in solemn tones, an absolute tumult arose as many tried to force their way through the entrance into the festival Mass. Feelings began running even higher, and, when the Mass was over, the wooden railing dividing the sanctuary from the area of public worship gave way to the crush; the people rushed to the altar to kiss the image of Our Lady, and suddenly voices were heard saying: "Lift it down, the holy image; carry it out into the open so that all can see it!" And the site was stormed, and the statue was taken from its dust-swirling niche.

Emanuel shook. How will the offensive image look in the open light of day once its decorations have been removed? – But the crowd yelled, howled, and wept with delight as the form that had grown from the pine branch was carried in triumph around the mountain peak. The jubilation and reverence of many became even greater, in fact, now that they had seen with their own eyes what they had so often heard in disbelief: that the image did not have its origins in the hand of man but had been formed by the omnipotence of God.

In their enthusiasm, they hadn't let the priest say a word, but the crowd quieted down and the image was back in its niche once again. Today the image had withstood the test by fire: the divine voice of the people had recognized it as authentic, and a conflict that had long been gnawing at Emanuel's spirit appeared to be resolved.

After the services, the priest lifted the chalice from its tabernacle to offer the Body of the Lord[21] to those faithful who had been cleansed by the sacrament of repentance. The people knelt in numerous, long rows, and Emanuel laid on each of their tongues the round, white wafer with the words: "Lord, I am not worthy for you to come under my roof; oh, but only say the word and my soul shall be healed!" Yet when he saw that girl with the black hair and the wide eyes, the way she knelt there with devoutly folded hands, her rosy lips modestly parted, and as she lifted her bright and childlike eyes to the priest until her long lashes sank back down in holy resignation ... then Emanuel's hand suddenly started to shake, and the host, even before it had touched the girl's mouth, fell to the stony floor. The girl gave a shriek: "Oh God, my God has forsaken me!" and fell unconscious into the surging crowd of people.

– –

Emanuel visited her in a cell of the hospice. She was lying on a straw bed, covering her face with her hands. The young priest stood there indecisively, for he didn't know if he had come as a priest or as a man.

"Are you feeling better, my child?" he asked, very tentatively.

---

[21] During communion, the host (wafer) offered to the faithful is considered to be the literal Body of Christ.

"It's you?!" cried the girl, astonished, looking up at the priest. "You, a man of the cloth, have come down to visit me in my misery? Oh, I'm miserable beyond measure, and you saw for yourself how the Great One, God, fled from me."

At once, Emanuel remembered the superstition among the folk that considered it an evil sign when the host breaks or, even worse, falls on the floor while a penitent is receiving communion.

"You good soul," he said, "what happened was my own fault. My hand was shaking; I didn't sleep very well last night. That scene with the statue of Mary was upsetting to me, too, and so the accident happened. I'm asking you to forgive me . . . If you have anything else at all on your mind that you didn't have a chance to say in the confessional because of the pushing crowd, now a servant of God stands before you."

Almost instinctively, Emanuel took this clandestine path to find out as a priest what he as a man wanted to know.

"It's very good of you," answered the girl and sat up in her bed, "and your goodness warms my heart again . . . I've often heard that there's a type of confession in which people can tell their entire past life to the father confessor, for isn't life itself a kind of sin? But even if not, I'd like to make this type of confession to you."

Emanuel was joyfully willing.

The girl got up and went over to bolt the door with its wooden latch, stroked the hair out of her pale face, and tried to kneel on a stool before the priest.

Emanuel prevented her from doing that: at a general confession it's the normal practice for father confessor and penitent to sit right next to each other like two friends, for a general confession is not just a time for self-accusation by the sinner, but also for a total disclosure of the human soul and for counseling with the pastor about how the errors and transgressions of this soul might be eradicated and settled through mediation.

Outside was the surging and the muted buzzing of the pilgrim crowds; a puff of wind rattled the little windows now and then.

Emanuel sat at a small table and propped his head in his hand. And the young stranger sat on the stool, and, after hemming and hawing and sighing, began to speak as follows:

"I really don't know, Reverend Father, how to begin. Often the idea goes through my head that my life is so wretched because of my parents' sin. In the city of Innsbruck they found me as a newborn child at the entrance to a church. From there I was taken to an orphanage. From the orphanage small children are given to private citizens that volunteer for it. Many volunteer because of the sum of money that is dispensed along with the children. A woman from out in the countryside got me, but she was, as people say, an angel maker: that is, she used the support money for herself and let the children die – dead children become angels in heaven; you know that, Reverend Father . . . But I had some hearty and stubborn life in me, and when my foster mother saw I wasn't about to die, then she thought – fine, all the better – she'd use me for work. She beat me and abused me and used me for hard work and let me go hungry. I didn't know anything better or anything worse, and I assumed that was the way things had to be. I did grow up all the same, and was happy about everything and sang like a lark . . . It's not from vanity that I say it, Reverend Father, but people have often said I have a lovely voice, and they like to listen to me sing."

The girl was quiet and looked at the floor. And when the Father Confessor asked her to continue telling about her life, she sadly lifted her eyes to him and asked: "Isn't it true, Father, Sir, it's not permitted for one human being to sell another? . . . I really must've been quite ungrateful to my foster mother and displeased her, just as I'm still ungrateful by confessing her sins instead of my own. But she did sell me."

The pain choked her; she could hardly speak.

"A handsome, tall man in a Tyrolean folk outfit, with feathers and a *Gemsbart*[22] on his hat, and with a full red beard, came into the house one day," she continued. "He was probably just joking when he asked how much the 'nightingale' cost . . .

"'For a hundred guilders and a good word she's yours!' cries my foster mother. Then a hundred guilders are in her hand, and . . . I'm the 'nightingale.'"

Emanuel had stood up and strode back and forth across the room several times with a bright red face . . . "Is it possible?" he mumbled, "In our country? Among our honest Alpine folk?"

"I didn't cry and didn't laugh; I went with the red-bearded man. We traveled far and wide: he played the zither while I sang an accompaniment. We earned money; he dressed me nicely and was like a father to me, protecting me when high-spirited men tried to make advances at me . . . That's

---

[22] German: a tuft of chamois hair used for decoration on Tyrolean hats.

how things went for several years. But when I got to be about the age I am right now, my companion said something to me one day . . . Reverend Father, I couldn't ever repeat it. I turned him down flat. You wouldn't believe what an awkward situation it made for me from then on: my master was sweet and crude to me, or even sanctimonious, but I can tell you that none of it did him any good. He keeps zithering, and I sing like before, and before long we've put together a pretty good pile of money . . . But I suppose I really ought to stop, Reverend Father, I see this isn't really a confession?" the storyteller interrupted herself, at the same time asking and begging with her eyes for permission to continue.

Emanuel took her by her hands and said: "I am your brother!"

The girl looked at him as if taken aback; she hardly knew what a 'brother' was. She got subdued and tentative, and the priest thought that finally the guilt of this charming child would have to be revealed, this child that had come as a penitent to the church in Misery and who now sat at his feet.

"On a trip into the mountains," the stranger finally took up her tale again, "we got out of the post coach because my master wanted to visit a nearby Alpine lake. I hadn't been aware up till then that he was a nature lover, but the lake was situated so beautifully between the forest and the stony cliffs, and had such peace and solitude, that both of us were very happy at the sight. My master had found a fisherman's rowboat. Nobody was around, so we got in the boat without any hesitation: my master unchained it and rowed it out into the deep water. And when we were out in the middle of the lake, then . . ."

The girl blushed and was silent. Emanuel raised his eyebrows; the wind was rattling at the window.

"I didn't know any other way to save myself," the penitent said, "so I jumped in the water . . . Having gotten out of his clutches, my will to live came back again: I remembered the words of an old soldier who'd said once that sinking people, who hadn't ever learned to swim, would have to keep their wits and keep moving to hold their heads above water. I followed those instructions for all I was worth, and at last, fortunately, I made my way to shore, hid in the bushes, kept an eye out for the cursing redbeard, and, even before he was able to get close, I ran away . . . ran away through the woods like a wild animal . . . Now I don't have a soul on earth to call my own; I'm utterly alone now. And the way things have gone in my life, I have to bitterly hate the only two people that ever did anything good for me. That hurts me. And what I'd like . . . oh, Reverend Father, you just can't imagine how much I'd like somebody I could love, really love from the bottom of my heart. Yeah, sure, you look at me so sternly when I say that, but I can't tell it to anyone else for as long as I live; I can only tell you, Reverend Father, since you are the Dear Lord Himself when people confess to you."

Emanuel busily tried to rebutton his collar that had sprung open; he couldn't get it done for the longest time, since his fingers were unsteady and made it difficult.

"In my need, though, a good thought came to me," said the girl. "Maybe if I can't find a man to love, I told myself, then I'll love the Blessed Virgin Mary! She's the one, you know, who saved my life when I was in the water. In thanksgiving I'll undertake a pilgrimage out into the mountains and up to Mary in Misery . . . And my own name is Mary, too, you see, and I'm in misery; so things couldn't fit any better than that."

She kept quiet and wept.

"Mary in misery!" said Emanuel with a feverish voice and lifted the girl up to him.

"Even that has turned out badly for me," responded Mary. "It's a horrible sin, and you'll never forgive me for it, but I can't keep from telling you during confession: Reverend Sir, a Mother of God like the one you have in your church is one I can never love."

"She can never love her!" The phrase echoed with horror through the priest's soul.

"And so then, I thought, I'd have to turn to God Himself, who is the essence of Eternal Love," the penitent said, "but it seems to me that God didn't find me worthy, since he'd rather be crushed underfoot on the dusty church floor than to enter into my heart . . . So now I'm all alone . . . and it hurts so bad!"

"You are not alone, my good child!" the priest whispered, and he laid his hand on the soft curls of her hair, and her head dropped down on his chest.

"Confession like this is good, I'm sure," Mary sobbed. "Now, at least, I'm feeling better . . . If only I could stay with you, you good Pastor Father!"

Now it was quiet. Outside, the rain was drizzling and the wind was whipping some drops against the window. The father confessor kissed the penitent on her forehead.

The housekeeper Gertrude down in the kitchen considered it just another of her helpful duties when she loudly complained about the *pater* who couldn't be found in the lodgings or in the church while the pilgrims were making the craziest racket. Nothing was going right in Misery anymore, and it was high time she informed the monastery so that things could change.

At the Edge of the Chasm

Late in the afternoon, when the ceremonies of Assumption Day were at an end, a large part of the pilgrims made ready to depart. They underwent their strange proofs of devotion one final time before the image; many of them seemed inclined to lift it from its place at the altar again, to carry it around the peak, and finally to carry it home with them to have the Divine Helper with them at all times.

Emanuel turned the agitated crowd back with stringent admonitions. Storming the image could be followed by stealing the image. It had been clear today what fanatically inflamed souls were capable of.

A burden was lifted from him when a large part of the pilgrims finally left, and he was happy to give them an official escort. Dressed in his surplice, stole, and biretta,[23] he went out with the crowds as far as the rock cliffs. There he granted them his priestly blessing and started back on the path home.

The rain had stopped, but strips of fog hung from the rock faces, and the mountaintops disappeared into the gray clouds. A gloomy atmosphere lay over the entire region, similar to the melancholy that troubled the heart of the young priest.

As he was walking on the moist sand path back towards the church, Mary, his strange penitent, met him. She had recovered and now, quiet and sad, wanted to leave the place again to which the road had brought her with longing and hope.

"And didn't you want to say good-bye to me?" the priest asked her.

The girl was hesitant in answering, but then she replied: "I couldn't find you anywhere in the church or your house."

---

[23] Ecclesiastical robe, vestment strip, and cap used ceremonially.

"So you did go looking for me after all?" cried Emanuel, but he tried to mute his voice during the exclamation, so the first words came out like a shout but the last more like a whisper.

"And you're leaving all by yourself, Mary? Now, when it'll be getting dark soon, and the storm clouds are threatening, and you don't know your way in the wild and dangerous mountains?"

"Once I'm down at the red pillar with the angel on top, then I'll be able to find my way easily. For people who don't know where they want to go, any path is the right one." That's what the girl said.

"To get to the red pillar will take three hours," replied Emanuel. "If you'd like, Mary, I can go with you for a ways and guide you past the dangerous spots."

That was one of those decisions again where Emanuel the man forgot about Emanuel the priest. He had usually held to strict fulfillment of duty, but his priestly duty, his office, and his efforts now seemed all at once so immaterial, so useless. He didn't see how mankind could truly be served with a Mary in Misery. Of course, certain pilgrims with their faith and trust, individually, may find true comfort for their heart at this consecrated place. The great majority, though, didn't worship God here the way Jesus taught. Nevertheless, Emanuel had always felt a deep reverence for the Image of Mercy; its age, the charming legend about it, and the common folk's love for it had made the sculpture, whose keeper he was, holy to him. But the admission of the poor girl, a stranger, that she was unable to love this Mary in Misery, expressed loudly and horrendously a feeling that the priest himself had always tried to repress within him. Since this confession of a poor, distressed soul from the people, the statue of Mary at the altar had become an abomination to him, and it drove him away; now, suddenly, as he stood in front of the departing girl, it occurred to him that he would be a much better shepherd if he were to accompany the helpless and inexperienced girl through the unknown dangers of the night than if he were to watch over the wooden object in its niche, now that most of the pilgrims had already left.

Mary accepted Emanuel's offer with anxious gratitude; the priest took his ecclesiastical vestments off and bundled them up together. And through the wastelands and into the night went a young man and a young girl.

They stepped over fallen rocks, where Emanuel had to guide his protégée by the hand; they traversed steep slopes where they were forced to hold each other arm in arm; they climbed along such narrow paths, threatened by chasms, towered over by walls of rock, that the girl, her sense of balance reeling, had to allow the priest to carry her with his strong arms over the treacherous passes.

Twilight had broken. The walls of rock echoed, from time to time, with the thundering of crashing avalanches that had been loosed by the rain. And suddenly the two hikers stood before a gaping chasm that a mud slide had torn away. Down below in the depths, murky waters were bubbling through the debris; the paths of the wild stream below and the hikers above had both been cut off.

Should they turn around and look for another way down the slopes? What else could they do? With great effort they started clambering down; they had to keep from falling by holding on to rock ledges and roots of shrubbery. Hugging tightly to each other, they started sliding several times until, finally, they were standing in the dense undergrowth of the forest that grew profusely in the ravine.

Quietly down through the rocks came the ringing of the church's evening bell. It was time for the priest to pray vespers in front of the shrine's candlelit altar. But now Emanuel couldn't leave the girl until she'd been guided to a safe path.

As they sat down on the trunk of an uprooted fir to rest a while, the girl suddenly broke her silence and said: "You know, Reverend Father, I can tell you I've never had a day like this all my life. Today my world is falling apart."

Without giving a reply, Emanuel forced himself to get up again and to pull the girl onward with him through the dark forest, quickly, with feverish haste. A menacing owl with its hoarse voice laughed at the pair of humans wandering down the wrong path.

Suddenly through the branches came the glimmer of a reddish light. A human habitation. Emanuel breathed easier. They soon stood in front of a hut built of uncut stones and mossy spruce trunks. A bit of smoke was wafting out the open door, for a lively fire was burning inside, in the middle of the dwelling. A few goats were sniffing about the fire and apparently wanted to try it out, to see if the little dancing flames weren't just as magnificent to eat as the green blackberry-bush leaves. The attempt came at the expense of a few soft little beard hairs that hung down from the chins of the bleating animals. But behind the rustic hearth sat Gaiser Bimmel and his Ursel.

It was too late for Emanuel to retreat, for Bimmel had already seen both of them and called out loudly to his companion: "Lord Geezus, Lord Geezus, Ursel, now the Misery Pastor has picked him out a woman, too!"

This statement shot like an arrow through the heart of the girl at the priest's side; Emanuel was struggling to collect his thoughts.

"Well, won't the dear Lord have somethin' to laugh about now!" the outdoorsman shrieked with laughter and ran both his hands through his hopelessly tangled, light-brown hair. "Of course he will," Gaiser added, "and I'm sure he'll enjoy himself."

"Who will?" asked Emanuel, mustering up as much dignity in his voice as possible.

"Why, the good Lord, of course! And for what reason? Because the young, crucifix-clean pastor has finally taken up with a woman."

Mary dashed out of the hut. Emanuel hurried after her. On a mossy stone she sank down, and he raised her up in his arms: "Mary, you poor, you good, you beautiful girl. Now the words have been spoken out loud that I wanted to keep buried in my heart for all eternity... I've left the altar, I've followed you, you are the lady's image in whom I want to worship my God. You shouldn't be in misery anymore. Mary, you dear soul, I'll stay with you!"

She had still wanted to free herself from his fiery embrace, but this effort was soon abandoned: a young woman like this can't struggle for long against a determined man and against her own heart. Soon she slung her arms tightly around his neck and tilted her head back so that her hair flowed[24] down over her black robe.

At that moment the lively and quite stocky Ursel wanted to leave the hut, but her man said: "Come on, let 'em have their arolla pine!" and they drew back further into their dwelling, and Bimmel lit a big pipe, smiling to himself. "If this is how things are," he mumbled, "I'll be going up Misery Mountain to church again."

"He called you a hypocrite and a blasphemer," the woman noted.

---

[24]The German verb used here, *"wallen"* is closely related to the verb earlier used, *"wallfahren,"* meaning "to go on pilgrimage."

"You know, Ursel," Gaiser said, "he just lit into me so loud 'cause he didn't have a woman of his own . . . I would've done just the same if I'd been in his shoes; he's been to college and I haven't been to college; he's handsome and sophisticated, I'm a bear from the woods; but there's a little drop of blood in everyone that makes us all the same."

The first kiss of love was still burning on Emanuel's lips when he tumbled into the hut, half tipsy. He laid a packet in Gaiser's hands and said with artificial calmness: "Dear friend, once I did you wrong as a man, but I had to act that way as a priest. Now I'm not a priest anymore. Look, in this little bundle are my priestly vestments. If you have the chance, take them up to the church tomorrow; please do me that favor."

The jolly fellow lifted up the palm of his hand and slapped it into Emanuel's so there was a clapping sound: "It's a deal. The habit will go on up. But, Sir, you really need a loden coat[25] if you're going to stay out in the forest."

"I'm not going to stay in the forest, Gaiser. But give me a loden jacket, and I'll give you this crucifix for it; it's made of silver. It can be something to remember me by, too; you probably won't be hearing from me again."

Emanuel and Mary wandered on through the forest. A rolling, wild sea was surging in their hearts, and Mary often stopped and asked the question: "But is it really God's will? Emanuel, I'm going to be your destruction."

"God showed me the way to your side."

"But if I were your destruction, or if the world lost a good and proper priest because of me," the girl said softly, "then I wish the largest avalanche would have already buried me today."

"We'll be happy, my dear soul. Nothing holds us to this land; we'll slip across the border to the Reich[26] and become man and wife."

Those were the words of Emanuel. The passion he had dammed up for so long made the inexperienced young man forget everything now and act like a boy. His heart was raging, his head reeling. From the living goblet of her mouth, at the first kiss of this woman, he had drunk deeply of this accursed intoxication. Scarcely twenty-four hours had passed since the girl had accused herself of lovelessness in his confessional. Oh, how narrow

---

[25] A heavy, wool Austrian coat, usually dark green in color.

[26] The German Reich north of the Austrian frontier, which, at the time of this novella, had been recently consolidated under Bismarck.

Mary in Misery 421

is the right path; perhaps the time might come soon when Mary would have to confess herself guilty of love.

In that same night, a last group of pilgrims started out from Mary in Misery to hike through the inhospitable region. The moon had risen, and so the most knowledgeable leaders thought they could risk making their way by night to make up for the excessive amount of time they had spent at the comforting place of pilgrimage. Taking various detours, the group reached the same forested ravines in which the pair of lovers were joyfully hiking. In order to make their way out of the mountainous wilds as rapidly and safely as possible, the couple joined up with the parade of pilgrims, unrecognized in the dark, without being particularly noticed. Long before the break of daylight they would have to come into friendlier terrain, and then Emanuel intended to take a separate path with his chosen beloved.

The pilgrims stumbled ahead slowly. Some of them quietly prayed, others coughed in accompaniment without a word or a thought, and yet others talked about the shrine and the impression it had made on them. There was also talk of the priest, who, they said, was so young and friendly, yet so devout.

"Now I know what it means to make a good confession," said one. "I'd been totally despondent because nothing on earth made sense to me. You can believe it or not, but I climbed up Misery Mountain with my rosary in one pocket and a piece of rope in the other: if I couldn't find any comfort up there, I told myself, then – God forgive me – I'd toss the rosary to hell and make a noose for myself. After the confession my heart felt so refreshed that I hung the rope next to the altar once and for all, as an everlasting remembrance of merciful Mary in Misery."

"And me," said another, "Why, I cried like a child for the first time in thirty years up there when the priest preached about the loving compassion of God. And I've made my mind up not to be fainthearted in my life anymore, no matter what happens to me. I'm going to try to fulfill my duties and leave everything else up to the loving compassion of God."

"The smallpox plague last spring ripped my husband and three children away from me," a woman reported. "I stayed back on earth with my youngest child. I couldn't find any comfort; I came to Mary in Misery. But praying in front of the Mother of God didn't really come from my heart, because I was constantly thinking, 'It's really a great injustice of our Lord that he let this disaster happen to me.' The priest was the first to give me any encouragement: even if what had struck me . . . even if it did hurt down deep in my heart – and it hurt so bad I couldn't begin to express it with a thousand tongues – it still basically doesn't mean much. My beloved ones, he said, had just gone on ahead of me a little hour or two and were faithfully waiting for me at heaven's gate, and at my death-bed they would hold out their hands: 'Come to me, dear wife; come to us, dear mother. We've already prepared a place for you! . . .' But even on this earth I still had the most beautiful and holy task, he said, that any person can ever have. I'd have to be both father and mother to my only child and use love and wisdom to make her into a good person. God meant well and didn't forget me . . . Now I'm sure that's the way it is, and I won't do any more complaining."

And an old man talked about the magnificent sermon the priest had held in the pilgrimage church about human passions and withstanding them. The greatest majesty and power on earth, he had said, was being master over yourself. This power was proof that we are children of God and will be the celestial inheritance through which we, by conquering earthly powers, might be able to return as heroes to God.

So they spoke, and so they edified each other in the afterglow of the priestly words. And from all that was said, the teaching emerged: do your duty; endure adversity with patience; rejoice in doing good; have no fear of death.

Emanuel and Mary walked along in the midst of those speaking. What they felt was not spoken, but it was a peculiar sort of pain that tore at the heart of the fleeing priest, the heart that had just found such ecstasy. While the pilgrims spoke, Mary had snuggled up close to her companion with a wild, almost feverish strength. Later she just held his hand and scarcely responded to his urgent finger squeezes.

The pilgrims had now become subdued and totally quiet at last, since they were passing the dangerous stretch of the *Riedwand*[27] rock face. But it was deepest night, and no one could see how narrow the footpath was; the only things visible at all were the black masses of horrifying rock overhangs that cut off the light of the moon. The thundering of rushing water could also be heard below, from deep in the chasm. The pilgrims held hands together in a long chain in order to walk carefully along the path at the edge of the cliff.

---

[27] The proper name of a cliff in the Austrian Alps with a precipitous drop that was carved glacially from a domed massif.

Emanuel placed his left hand in the hand of the man in front of him, and with his right hand he held on to Mary, who was walking along cautiously and quietly behind him. He whispered some words of encouragement to her from time to time, but the wild stream down below was roaring so loudly, and she may not have heard his words.

Now they all stood still to rest, and many a fearful woman secretly called on the protection of Our Dear Lady in Misery. The chain had dissolved for a moment, since most needed a free hand to wipe the sweat from their face. Mary's arm was missed for a little while, too, but soon Emanuel took the beloved hand again, the hand of the one with whom he wanted to spend the rest of his life. His hand-squeeze was returned with fervor.

Finally the dangerous stretch was past. The path leveled out and widened; the moon spread its glimmering veil over the hiking figures. As Emanuel turned around to pull his girl closer to him again, Mary was missing in the column; he was holding a strange hand in his own, and the face of an elderly woman grinned at him.

A terrified yell from his mouth, many voices calling: "We're not all here!" rang out in the rocks . . .

When the red dawn arose in the east, as the finches and thrushes started up their singing, Mary was found. She lay dashed and shattered at the bottom of the gorge, between wet, gray boulders in the wild stream. Her blood was still blushing red into the water.

Silently and without a sound, she had thrown herself from the chain of her companions into the chasm at the *Riedwand*.

In the deep forest, Emanuel – wild bushes and flowers growing profusely around him; bugs, spiders, butterflies, and merry birds flitting and fluttering around him – lay down and pressed his face into the cool moss, moss that had rarely been moistened by the dew of human tears, no doubt, such bitter tears . . . By now Emanuel had guessed everything and come to understand. He thought back on Mary's words: "But if I were your destruction, or if the world had to lose a good and proper priest because of me, then I wish the largest avalanche would have already buried me earlier."

The girl had recognized Emanuel's significance as a priest from what the pilgrims had to say, and had considered the unholy paths that Emanuel was starting to wander because of her . . . She had sacrificed herself . . . He had preached about conquering the passions, about self-denial and sacrifice; she had sealed the priestly teachings of her passionately beloved with her own young life.

The Blasphemer of the Shrine

A different man arose from the moss than the one who had sunk down to it hours before. A passionate young man had been buried here; a priest stood up. A priest after God's heart who had confirmed the teachings of his mouth with his deeds . . . Emanuel wanted to return again to Mary in Misery and be a faithful, strict keeper of the shrine that the people's faith and trust had chosen. Thus had fate decreed it as well, and perhaps the spirit of that strange woman, who also called herself Mary in Misery, would transfigure the stiff image in that church of mercy . . . And Mary, the martyr, who threw herself twice into the depths – once to save her innocence and a second time to save her beloved's freedom of conscience – she deserved to be buried up at the side of the church, the place where pilgrims who were accident victims had their final resting place.

In order to preside over this burial and to resume his office again in all seriousness, Emanuel returned to Misery Mountain.

New crowds of pilgrims had arrived, meanwhile, and in the sacristy was seen an unknown priest who was preparing to mount the pulpit in the inexplicable absence of the local clergyman. The church was filled to overflowing; and Emanuel, dressed in Gaiser's loden jacket, wanted to make his way unrecognized through the crowd to reach the sacristy and dress himself in the vestments of his order. But the priest was already standing at the pulpit with a red stole and black biretta. It was a young, suntanned face with light-colored hair, but the voice sounded strangely out of place. The sermon was short, for alarm soon swept through the House of God.

"You're all heathens, every one of you!" yelled the preacher so loud that the walls rang, "Up there is an image of idols. Images are not supposed to be worshiped. The Lord God has forbidden it!"

The bellow of a thousand voices in the church. The preacher had disappeared; he wasn't seen again. His surplice, biretta, and the stole lay in the sacristy: they were the same objects that Emanuel had given to Gaiser Bimmel, asking him to return them to the church. And of all the listeners, Emanuel was the only one to recognize the preacher; it had been the forest hermit, Gaiser, the one they called the half-fool in these parts.

For as long as the Church in Misery had stood – and prelates[28] and bishops had preached there – no sermon inside its walls had made such an impression as these very shrill utterances of the forest hermit. They wanted to stone him, the blasphemer of the shrine, but they couldn't find him: Bimmel had long since made his way through the rocks along the paths of the chamois and the ibex.

Emanuel was the one hardest hit by the blows of the strange speaker: he felt numb, since the long-germinating but innermost hidden thoughts of his own soul had been expressed so suddenly and so horribly out loud. But now there was no more secretive worry in him; his artificially repressed emotions had torn free and shaken his soul.

The first thing Emanuel had to do now, though, was to throw the robe over his shoulders and ascend the pulpit to quiet the crowd. This wasn't very successful, for today he couldn't find the right words to defend the honor of the shrine of mercy in light of this "crazy man" who had desecrated it. Most were so worked up and so torn away from their devout feelings that they left the place of pilgrimage without confession or communion and vowed never again to visit this church where the most vile blasphemer of God was not struck by lightning on the spot.

No sooner had Mary, the "accident victim" during pilgrimage, been buried at the side of the church than a decree went out from the monastery that relieved Emanuel of his post.

He hiked down the mountain, but he doesn't live in the valley anymore. The monastery doesn't want to call him an apostate, exactly, but it makes a point of never mentioning his name.

The Latest News

Many years have passed since all that.

Not long ago, a letter addressed to Gaiser Bimmel found its way into the high mountains. He was still living in his forest basin. The letter was from Emanuel, the one-time pastor at Mary in Misery, and its contents were as follows:

---

[28] Highly placed ecclesiastical dignitaries.

Dear Friend!

On the ground at the side of the Church of Misery, the side that looks toward sunset, you'll find two gray stones lying close to each other. Maybe moss is growing on them already. Braid a wreath of juniper and Alpine rose branches and lay it on the stones. You are a good person and will carry out my request. – Things are going well for me, body and soul; I'm living as a missionary in New South Wales, on the continent of Australia.

Gaiser shouted with joy as if long-awaited news had come from a beloved brother. He and his woman braided a wreath of juniper, Alpine rose branches, and all the evergreen plants found in the Alps. And even today the grave at the side of the church is always resplendent with fresh decorations.

The hospice is void of humans, though, and the shrine is neglected. The few pilgrims who do climb up to it soon leave again. The sad tones of the bell in the tower are unable to erase those words of the alien priest or to reawaken the people's trust.

From the rock faces two mountain spiders have made their way down to the abandoned church and have woven a triple veil over the niche where stands the divinely sculpted image that, long ago, so strangely grew from the arolla pine.

Ferdinand von Saar (1833-1906) can be called a representative and prototypical Austrian writer of the nineteenth century. Though he considered himself first and foremost a dramatist, his prose has been more successful.

Saar's narrative strengths centered around his ability to portray various strata of Austrian society as they existed in the late nineteenth century, whether they were the military (where he spent a number of joyless years himself), the theater world, the poor working class, the Jewish population, the nobility, or the outcasts. His keen eye was able to furnish images that a reader of today still finds convincing and historically accurate.

The fictional life of Johann Bacher portrayed in the novella *Tambi* (1882) is in many ways a self-portrait of the author. Like the Bacher he invented, Saar lost his father at an early age and had to see his mother struggle through years of poverty. Like his character, he had his own first play eventually rejected for the stage – after initial signs of critical success – precisely for its outmoded dramatic style and its plot deficiencies. Both the fictional and the real dramatist then fell into a frustrating writer's block. The similarities are not limited to outer circumstances, of course, since Saar was drawing on his own life experiences: the feelings about art and life, the mind-set and the psychological means of coping all run parallel between the creation Bacher and his creator Saar.

The title *Tambi* refers to the name of Johann Bacher's dog. When Bacher's inner world and even trust in himself have begun to fall apart, his only two remaining friends are a canine companion and then alcohol. Both prove to be elusive crutches, however, and the poor man's fate is sealed.

This psychological self-study is unflinchingly realistic and therefore – we'd have to say – extremely courageous. The author portrays his narratively reflected self as a demi-talent, or at least as one with serious defects, as someone doubting his own abilities, as a human being critical of his own essential nature and personality. The theme of a quasi-artist shown to be unsuited to life is reminiscent of Grillparzer's *Poor Fiddler* (a work also created through self-portraiture), and in both novellas the hero – or can we already say "anti-hero"? – finds himself unable to harmonize with the world around him.

Saar's outlook on humanity was a negative one. It's no accident that his prose seems to posit a narrative corollary to the philosophy of Schopenhauer, to present a literary argument for pessimism and resignation at one's lot in life. Saar consciously set about to set Schopenhauer to prose, though not as a bitter and vengeful activist. He came to believe at some point that the human condition was not reparable and that quiet acceptance of life's shortcomings was a natural outgrowth of such skepticism. Indifference to even the most alarming of human calamities is given narrative voice at the end of the novella when joyous sights, sounds, and smells– the songs of birds and other bright harbingers of spring – present themselves to the senses at the very moment that human worries are the heaviest.

Saar thought himself to be a transitional figure between those Austrian writers closer to the post-classical mold, such as Grillparzer and Stifter, and those modern authors of the early twentieth century who followed him, such as Schnitzler and Hofmannsthal. Perhaps he can be seen as something of a bridge between the two eras, although in his character portrayals – with their observant mimesis of the human psyche – he has to be considered an archrealist as well. Beyond the psychological realism and the philosophical resignation, though, Saar gives this novella symbols and structures that lend it a deeper artistic meaning and make it significant on more than one level.

It may be noted that both Saar and his wife took their own lives – she two years after *Tambi* was completed, he twenty-two years after her in the throes of depression over an incurable disease.

TAMBI

Ferdinand von Saar

I

    Years ago I decided to spend a winter in a rural setting, since I'd gotten bogged down in my work and needed to rest and collect my thoughts. So it was that I proceeded in late fall to a nobleman's estate whose owner had been a friend of mine for years. He himself, having spent part of the summer there, had already left with his family for Italy, but I moved into a small building next to the manor house and soon arranged my furnishings to feel right at home. My windows offered vistas on two sides. From the one side I looked out into the park; from the other the open landscape and a portion of the village lay before me. A true Moravian scene[1]. Endless fields with piles of beets and potatoes here and there, gently inclined hills, dark evergreen forests – all intersected by a railroad line and a lazy little river snaking through.
    During the first part of my stay I was outdoors a lot. An old horse enjoying his pension of oats in the manorial horse stalls was saddled for me, and I rode out to the surrounding estates and villages in the gentle rays of the late October sun, or else, a hunting rifle slung over my shoulder, I passed through the silent forests until they finally began to drip with November fogs . . . and with a reluctant jolt I took up my customary activities. From this point on I didn't leave the house again except for regular morning walks,

---

[1] This novella's setting is in rural Moravia, a former province of the Austrian empire now forming the eastern end of the Czech Republic. (See also page 319, footnote 3).

and by the time the Christmas snow lay on the fields, I'd finished a project that had long troubled me and to whose fortunate conclusion I was able to drain a glass of self-brewed punch on New Years' Eve.

New Years' Day was something I wanted to celebrate in my own festive way as well. It was an exceedingly hard but beautiful winter that year, and at that very time we were enjoying the most magnificent weather. The skies were transparent blue, and white crystals were glittering as far as the eye could see. I decided to hike to the ruins of an old castle in the mountains that was about two hours away by foot and that offered a splendid panorama of the countryside. I'd already enjoyed this panorama in summer a number of times but now wanted to get to know its winter charms.

After doing this and after having breathed in enough of the pure but biting air blowing about in the heights, I set out on the return path. It was past noon: tired and hungry, I went into the first village inn I came to. It was a dilapidated place, marked only by a few wood shavings attached over the door, as was the local custom. A few farmers were sitting in the main room with their cloudy beers; three wandering musicians were there as well, their brass instruments lying in front of them, intending perhaps to play some dance music later. The innkeeper, though, from whom I ordered a light meal, showed me across the hall to a small auxiliary room in which was to be found just a single long table.

At this table, with his back to the wall, sat a man dressed in city clothes who seemed to be asleep; at any rate, his arms were crossed and resting on the table top, and he'd laid his head on them. Next to him on the bench lay a brown dog who gave a short bark as I entered.

The man lifted his head, looked me in the eye . . . and stared at me as I did at him. This round, pale, and flabby face, now gradually turning a light shade of crimson, seemed so familiar to me that I involuntarily blurted out: "What's this? It's you, Herr . . . Herr . . ." I was struggling in vain for a name that had escaped me.

The man was visibly hesitant to give his name. Finally he said in a low, halting voice: "Bacher, if you please . . . Johann Bacher."

"Right . . . Herr Bacher! This is what I call a surprise meeting!" I sat down across from him and quickly sketched out the reasons I was spending the winter here. "But what brings *you* to this area?" I continued.

"This is actually my home," he replied, still very discomfited, "since I first saw the light of day in the nearby district capital where my father was a minor official. Since then, of course, I've gotten around to different places as well. For the present, though, I'm a scribe for the notary office in . . . ." He named a large village which, while belonging to the same local administration, was located a good hour by foot from where I was staying.

Before I continue with the story, though, I first need to backtrack a bit.

About a decade before, a literary genius had once again been discovered, a modern Shakespeare who was expected to usher in the rebirth of German drama. A heretofore totally unknown author living in Vienna had just published a tragedy said to be the most significant that had been created in this genre for many years; in fact, a certain pundit, who loved to greet almost all publications of contemporary literature with silence, went so far as to say in a sudden fit of enthusiasm that the work could only be compared – if at all – with *MacBeth* or *King Lear*.

As for myself, I didn't think much of all this. By then I'd already lived long enough to know how little was generally to be found lurking behind such puffy-cheeked praise. I considered it all to be more or less another shimmering soap bubble, many of which I'd seen rise and burst before. So I really had no desire to acquaint myself with the drama in question until finally driven to it by the urgent prodding of a lady within my circle of friends, someone who encouraged rising talent with an enviable zeal and not without a certain insight. It was with mistrust and discomfort that I picked up the book; it was with great interest and at times true pleasure that I read it to the end. Here, indeed, an unusual talent and moreover an independent spirit had expressed himself, one who'd truly taken the example of the great Briton[2] but – except for some minor similarities in form – had in no way descended to the level of imitation. The plot was not as fortuitous. The latter proved to be most unsatisfactory, treated almost as an afterthought. In individual scenes, certainly, a lively and nimble dramatic power made itself felt; yet precisely when it should have manifested itself – and in fact was required to manifest itself – it ceased completely or else transformed itself at climactic junctures into a feeble weakness that seemed to me an extension of the author's own nature. All told: an error-ridden but justifiable dramatic attempt. I shared my view with the lady and added at the end that the writer deserved

---

[2] William Shakespeare.

to be given warm encouragement in any case; how highly his talent was to be rated and to what extent it could be developed, on the other hand, were things only the future could tell.

I found that I wasn't alone in this opinion. Gradually, similar expressions began to be heard from various sides, even if not always so well-meaning. What's more, a certain theater director, all-powerful at the time and influential in literary affairs as well, had rejected the play for the stage with the comment that he always loved to make about similar productions: it was in the interest of the author that he didn't introduce the play to the public. The author should write him a new and better one.

This was taking a long time, though; in fact, the claim arose that Hans Bacher – this was what the author called himself or rather what his name was – would never bring forth another play. The one with which he'd succeeded in attracting some attention was one he'd written many years before, and since that time he'd been working on some magnificent but totally undramatic material that was consuming him intellectually, so to speak. At the same time, unfavorable judgments about the personality of the author himself were coming out bit by bit, as is customary. He was self-taught, it was said, and long past the age when he could learn anything; at the same time he was lazy and arrogant, and, above all, the criticism was made that he'd given up an insignificant enough civil service job[3] to devote himself completely to literary pursuits, whereby he – like many another demi-talent before and after him, overestimating his own capabilities – would inevitably have to meet his doom.

About that time I attended one of the evening gatherings sponsored by the previously mentioned theater director where a number of artists and cultural figures of both genders customarily got together. This time there was a very large number of people present so that the salon, not very large, was filled to overflowing. After I'd exchanged the usual short greeting with the host, who was sitting in a circle of men and women, I moved back to a window niche with a close acquaintance who happened to be there. Soon after, a man entered who was totally unknown to me. "That's the writer Bacher," my acquaintance said.

Since I was interested in the man, I closely observed him. He was about forty years old, short, rather corpulent, and was wearing a threadbare black

---

[3] With its lifelong tenure and guaranteed income.

jacket with sleeves so insufficient that they scarcely covered even the strikingly short arms that were inside them. Also striking to me was the shy, humble submissiveness with which the new arrival bowed in front of the director and some others present with whom he may have been acquainted, for a lot of ceremony wasn't usual here; this behavior also seemed very much at variance with the accusations of arrogance which had been raised against him. He took a seat on a chair which had just been vacated in the circle around the director; it was at the side of an elderly lady, an author herself, who took advantage of the opportunity to draw him into a conversation. He appeared to feel very distracted all the while, though, shifting back and forth uneasily on his chair and continually reaching for his forehead as if to gather his thoughts. The latter, along with his nose, exhibited high degrees of development; the lower half of his face, though, tapered off weakly. I couldn't judge his eyes: they were half concealed by heavily drooping lids.

His talk with the lady hadn't lasted very long when suddenly the director turned his head towards him and called out with his characteristically loud and raspy voice: "Well, Herr Bacher, how are things with your new play? Is it finished?"

The object of the interrogation winced, and his eyes shut almost completely. "No, not yet," he replied with visible effort while turning this way and that for embarrassment.

"What? Not yet?" cried the other, leaning far back in his easy chair. "Then it never will get finished, since to all appearances you yourself are finished!"

This inconsiderate comment in the presence of so many persons almost threw the poor writer off his chair. He turned pale as death; then he began to take on a stronger and stronger crimson glow in his mute shame. Fortunately, most of those present were long accustomed to such impromptu utterances on the part of the host and didn't think anything more about it, while the host himself immediately began to talk with the person seated closest to him about something altogether different. Just a very few looked at the stricken man with repulsion and, as it seemed to me, in part with smug satisfaction as well. I couldn't keep things to myself, though, and since right then an agitation was arising in the salon with some ladies making their preparations to leave, I walked up to the man, who was still struggling with shame and embarrassment, introduced myself to him, and said that I was very glad to get to know him since I'd read his drama with great interest . . . and whatever else I could say to ease his pain somewhat.

At first he appeared not to hear my words at all; bit by bit, though, he became attentive and his face brightened, a face which, on closer examination, bore the stamp of an exceeding good nature. He was obviously pleased to be with someone who wished him well and thanked me in rather laboriously chosen terms, but then his speech became ever more fluent and natural. He also mentioned his new play, on which, as he said, he was placing very great hopes, but complained that in spite of all his efforts it didn't seem to be falling into place. A few allusions to the subject matter which he let fall did, in fact, indicate to me that those who called his choice a bad one weren't exactly wrong. But I kept from letting this show in any way, for I knew that such concerns and objections can be misleading and confusing, but never convincing. I comforted him, rather, by emphasizing that I'd had similar, frustrating bouts of writer's block myself and supported him in his intentions of completely withdrawing for a time from the unfamiliar and distracting social life into which, as he put it, he'd become enmeshed completely against his will.

Finally I thought it appropriate to take my leave, and he used this opportunity likewise to leave unnoticed. We went down the stairs together; we said good-bye at the front door, and each of us went his way.

Soon after that, I went on a trip that kept me away far longer than had been my original intent. During this time I thought less and less about good Hans Bacher... and finally forgot about him altogether. Since I didn't see him anymore, even after my return, that's the way things remained. Only when suddenly another genius, an epic poet, had been discovered, one who promised to be a modern Dante, was I reminded of the lost playwright. But I couldn't get any information about him. Nobody knew where he was; people shrugged their shoulders and said they imagined he'd probably gone to his ruination somewhere.

But now he was sitting in front of me, visibly aged, with feeble, fallen features, his thin hair gray and wild at his temples, and, still disconcerted, he was moving his short arms about on the table.

"So now you're working in a notary's office," I said mechanically. "And how are things going..." with your work as an author? I wanted to ask, but stopped involuntarily.

He understood what I meant and made a dismissive gesture. "Oh, that's over with... completely over with. I don't think about it anymore and have given up all hopes in that regard."

"But why?" I interjected. "Not just because you weren't able to master that play that you had in mind earlier? Or have you finished it?"

"I haven't finished it."

"Well, maybe the theme itself was totally contrary to the dramatic form. Each of us has had to deal with similar false starts in his creative work. Perhaps you just took on more than you could handle."

"That I did! That I did! Oh, I was possessed by absurd arrogance. I wanted to create the ultimate . . . something never seen before! *Parturiunt montes* . . .[4] And not even a mouse was born . . . not even a ridiculous mouse!"

"You can't say that," I replied seriously. The work you first published is very noteworthy . . . It's an appreciable witness of your intellect."

"Appreciable!" He cried out almost involuntarily. "Who appreciates it? *You* perhaps, honored Sir, and a few other well-meaning people like yourself. Other than that, all it has brought me is scorn . . . or at least disregard. And maybe you can tell me yourself: what literary significance does such a rudimentary work deserve, an audition with so many holes poked in it? None! None at all!"

I held my tongue. No quick response was possible in the face of such a sharp and basically correct self-criticism. "Well now," I finally said, "Actually you're right. But nowadays who can stake a claim to true recognition, to indisputable significance? Goethe's saying is especially true for the arts: 'Woe unto you for being a grandchild.'[5] And in the end, any kind of greatness is only relative. Time shakes down everything and everybody . . . even the columns that have seemed to reach to heaven up till now. In any case, you shouldn't have gotten depressed, but kept on trying . . . ."

"As if I hadn't kept on trying!" he cried out. "Do you think that I've only had this one theme in mind . . . as people have been saying all around? No, honored Sir! In here . . ." He beat himself on the forehead with his hand, "in here there was plenty of life and action! An abundance of characters filled my head . . . but when I tried to grasp them, to set them free, they melted away . . . only to return time and again as haunting shadows. And finally,

---

[4] Latin: "The mountains went into labor . . . ." This quote from Horace alludes to the Egyptians under King Tachos who, when they first saw the small stature of their Lacedomenian ally, King Agesilaos, as he came down from the hills, allegedly exclaimed: "The mountains went into labor, and only a ridiculous little mouse was born." Bacher extends the metaphor to the "labor" of literature.

[5] Goethe's *Faust*, Part I, line 1977: *"Weh dir, daß du ein Enkel bist."*

recognizing my artistic impotence and turning my back on everlasting fame, I tried the most mundane and worn pathways of literature, but even there my intellect failed me. Oh, the director was right back then! I was finished . . . long since finished; I just didn't want to admit it to myself."

"But how is that possible?" I cried out.

"Yes, how is that possible? I asked myself the same thing again and again through dull and dreary days, through sleepless and fitful nights. 'How is that possible,' I groaned in despair as I looked over my first printed work, as the sheet of paper I'd laid out was just lying there, empty, and the ink was drying in my pen. And yet that's the way it was. Maybe the reason for it is some worn-out fiber in my brain or some circulatory disorder. But that leaves me in the dark, and a person is found guilty . . . guilty in the eyes of the world, is despised, ridiculed; and nobody has an idea of the pain such an unfortunate person has to endure . . . the dark night of insanity that starts to loom up before him! Oh, the things I've suffered!"

He covered his face with his hands and broke out in tears that he tried to restrain by force. But he wasn't succeeding: they streamed down in a passionate flow, uncontrollably.

Moved, I sat there and let him cry. The dog, a breed of dachshund who'd been lying curled up at his side till now, sleeping, stretched up full length and laid his front paws on his master's shoulder, whimpering.

Suddenly came wild, ear-splitting sounds: the brass players in the main hall of the inn had started their music. Bacher gave a start while petting the howling dog with one hand; with the other he pulled out a crumpled pastel handkerchief and hastily wiped his eyes and cheeks dry.

"Excuse me for showing my feelings like that," he said. "But I couldn't control myself. You're good and understanding and won't despise me."

"Certainly not!" And I shook hands with him.

"I'm not always that weak, either," he continued. "I've long since resigned myself to things. But now the old wounds were opened up again."

I expressed my regret that I, without wanting to, had been the cause.

"Don't worry about it," he replied. "The tears were good for me. When I'm by myself I can't cry, and since I've just poured out my heart to a man I respect, I'll be able to live out my unnoticed existence all the easier."

"So you're not altogether unsatisfied with your present lot in life?"

"Not at all; to the contrary. What I earn at the notary office is admittedly not much, but it's enough to keep me going."

"I'm glad to hear that. Excuse me for butting in as an uninvited dispenser of advice . . . but wouldn't it be possible for a man of your talents to arrange for a more advantageous position? Certainly something more suitable could be found, and if you'd permit me, in Vienna I could . . . ."

He recoiled in horror and put his arms out in violent resistance. "No, no!" he cried. "Not at any price . . . not even for the salary of a cabinet minister! How could I be seen there among those people? And besides . . . you overestimate my capabilities. I only have limited knowledge, unfortunately, since I wasn't able to finish my education. My father died when I was just a boy, leaving my mother behind poor, very poor. So I had to leave school prematurely and take a job in an office where it was more a matter of practice than theory. It was in the customs office.

"For a while, since my work was very much that of a subordinate follower, things went fine. But later, as I rose through the ranks and was expected to intervene in others' affairs, the failings of my character immediately came to light. Direct contact with other people confused me; I couldn't get a quick grasp of what my underlings were doing, and so offenses were committed which gave me the reputation of a lackadaisical and careless manager in the eyes of my supervisors, while I was actually just an anxious and clumsy person who took even the tiniest mistake to heart. And when they finally found out that I was a 'writer,' then things were finished for me. People turned recalcitrant, made difficulties and embarrassments for me on purpose, passed me over for a promotion I deserved . . . and I could see the day coming when they would just let me go. Consequently I resigned from the position myself just as soon as I had a little literary success. So it wasn't out of arrogance or even out of laziness, both of which I was later accused.

"Indeed, I was arrogant, as I've already admitted to you, but only in that one respect; beyond that, though, nobody could've been less pretentious than I was. And what left such a deep impression on me during the torture of my involuntary idleness was that without some activity I wouldn't be able to live at all. But it has to be a quiet, predictable, more mechanical activity like merely copying something down by hand. Anything else that imposes some kind of responsibility, requiring me to reach out beyond myself, makes me lose my head.

"It's peculiar," he continued after a pause, in a softer voice, since the music had stopped again in the meanwhile, "it's peculiar, but I had a premonition of that when I was just a boy. Whenever my fellow pupils would announce their hopes and dreams for the future, when the one wanted to be a soldier, the other a doctor . . . or even greater things, the quiet, predictable existence of a simple scribe, by contrast, was what I always found enticing. I had in mind the three legal clerks working for the lawyer in my small hometown. His office was located on the ground floor of the apartment house where we ourselves lived, and when I saw the three colleagues of various ages showing up at the stroke of the clock, peacefully writing near the windows, and then leaving again at the stroke of the clock, I considered their lot – at the time I had no dreams of literary fame – to be the pinnacle of good fortune.

"Well, I'd have been able to call this fortune my own soon enough, but it was my fate to attain it only after long detours, very long ones. Now I'm satisfied with it, though, and wouldn't trade my modest position for any other on earth . . . even if only because, as I've said, I couldn't handle anything else. From eight to six I fill up my sheets of paper with writing, except for a short break at noon; evenings, Sundays and holidays, though, belong to me and my dog." While saying this, he took the animal in his lap and hugged it as if it were a child.

To this resolute explanation there was nothing more to be said in appropriate response. I dropped the topic of conversation, therefore, and also turned toward the dog, which looked very handsome indeed with his yellow paws and similarly-colored spots above his intelligent brown eyes. "A good-looking dog," I said approvingly. "What's his name?"

"Tambi. When he was still quite small I bought him from a trainer who'd given him the silly name of 'Tambourl.'"[6]

"A common name for dachshunds."[7]

"Since he was already used to the name anyway, at least I kept the first syllable."

I tried to have Tambi come to me. He looked at me in a friendly way and wagged his tail, but he wouldn't come.

"Oh, he doesn't go to anyone," Bacher exclaimed. "He is faithfulness personified and would never leave my side."

---

[6] German: "little drummer."

[7] Despite the image of the short and fat dachshund today, its German name was taken from *Dachs* ("badger"), indicating the original tenacity and ferociousness of the breed before domestication.

"An admirable trait. Too bad the dachshund breed wasn't preserved in its pure form with him. He's much too high-slung, and I see he carries his tail rolled up, a sure sign of crossbreeding."

"That's exactly what the trainer said, which is why he left him in the house for the children. Though they didn't realize what they were doing, they tormented the poor beast quite gruesomely. In addition, a serious malady became evident in his ears. But that healed quickly . . . and now we're both happy!" Again he cuddled the dog, which responded by snuggling in his arms. "Just look how understandingly he gazes into my eyes: he knows we're talking about him. An absolutely unique dog! Quiet, gentle . . . and yet very protective. At the same time no trace of greed or gluttony; he has to be virtually invited to eat his little bit of dog food. He knows only *one* passion: hunting."

"Are you a hunter?"

"Me? Oh no . . . how could I do that? He hunts just for himself. And you should see the life, the fire that takes over in this otherwise so quiet animal! The excitement as he runs down the plowed furrows across the field, the way he tracks the scent, the way he takes off with his loud yelping after the rousted rabbit."

"And you just let him do that?"

"Why not? He really doesn't do any damage. Our bunny friend is always much faster, and so Tambi returns to me after a while, panting and foaming at the mouth."

"That's the way it goes right now because he's obviously still young. But once he's reached his full size, you'll find that he won't give up on the prey. What you've told me is evidence that the wild nature of dachshunds is a deep part of him in spite of everything, and once he succeeds in catching a rabbit, that'll bring out an untamable bloodthirstiness in him."

These words obviously had a painful effect on Bacher and made him pensive. "So you think . . . ?" he asked dejectedly.

"Absolutely. And in any case you have to prepare yourself for the eventuality that your dog could be shot one day or the other: the hunting laws in this region are very strictly enforced."

He turned pale. "That's what the forester told me, too. But I thought he was just trying to scare me and alienate me from the dog. People just can't watch anybody being happy with something, you know; in the beginning everyone laughed at the dog and ridiculed it . . . and now all at once he seems dangerous to them. The forester did say that he himself and his assistants wouldn't do anything to Tambi, but if he ever crossed paths with someone who didn't know him or went into another district . . . ."

"Then he's a goner, because only actual hunting dogs enjoy the right of protective exemption. And what's more, all foresters have a peculiar inclination towards blood lust for precisely such four-footed animals."

He rocked back and forth on his chair as if in despair. "But, my God, what should I do then? I can't keep the dog locked up in my room. And out in the open here . . . there are wild animals at almost every step!"

"You have to keep him on a leash."

"On a leash!" he cried out indignantly. "A creature created for unencumbered running, whose nature and instinct drive him to roam the woods and meadows . . . on a leash! Just think, sir, what that means! Now and then it might be appropriate, and I'm in the habit of doing it anyway in the woods, where Tambi could come across deer and upset or chase them. But at other times, all other times? To have to watch him strain forwards and sideways at every step, to have to feel him pulling at the constraining line almost to the point of choking himself . . . No! No!"

"Well, then you'll have to try a training program so he learns to obey your commands under any circumstances."

"But in his excitement when he's on a scent, he doesn't even hear my command."

"He'll hear it all right once he's been thoroughly disciplined a few times."

"Disciplined!? What do you mean? I'm supposed to hit him? That's something I can't do . . . I'd rather hit myself!"

"Excuse me, but that's a weakness . . . ."

"That may be, but it's just not possible for me. And besides . . . I hate all forms of discipline. I've felt too deeply in my own life what it means not to be able to follow the innermost drives of my being . . . to be tied up; whether internally or externally, it's all the same. Before I could force the dog to deny his own nature . . . I'd rather he . . ." He was terrified at the conclusion he was about to put into words, and abruptly stopped. "But there must be some other way . . . some way out of it," he continued after a pause, "I've often thought about it . . . ." And then he sank into thought, cupping his forehead in his hand.

It became very quiet in the small room, which by now had already darkened bit by bit. Tambi sat up on the bench and looked back and forth at us.

In the next room the music started up again. It'd just been an introduction earlier, but now it seemed the dance was actually beginning. Bacher looked up. "It's already late," he said, "I have to think about going home."

Since nothing was holding me back, either, we paid our small bill and left after casting one more glance into the main hall of the inn, where in fact the billowing skirts of several girls were whirling about.

Outside, twilight was just descending. The rosy light of evening was still lingering on the white peaks of distant ranges; above us in the deep azure of the sky, though, the first stars were beginning to twinkle.

Silently we walked through the silence of nature, while Tambi ran along the edge of the forest, sniffing.

After a good half hour we'd reached the road where our paths separated.

"Farewell," I said, "and do remember our meeting. Perhaps you can show up at my place sometime; your visit would be most welcome at any time."

"I'll feel free to do so in any case. Permit me to point out, though, that my time is measured to such a degree that perhaps it won't be very soon . . . ."

"I beg you not to feel any sort of commitment. We're rather close neighbors, and so we can safely leave it to chance to bring us together again." I offered him my hand, which he grasped with his own unique submissiveness. Then he left.

Meanwhile it had become night, and the crescent moon rising from behind a hill cast its magical light across the landscape. Suddenly in the distance behind me there arose a lively barking that faded away little by little. Tambi had apparently flushed out a rabbit.

II

What I had foreseen came about: Bacher didn't appear at my residence. Since I didn't miss him, either, I forgot about him again more and more. In addition, I was soon deeply engaged in my own work anew, for I'd committed myself to making the most of the winter in my *Buen Retiro*.[8]

---

[8] Spanish: "The good seclusion" or "good retreat," also the name of a park in Madrid adjacent to *El Prado* art museum.

About four weeks had passed since then, and it gradually became noticeable that spring was on its way. The thaw hadn't begun yet, but the cold spell had broken under overcast skies, and moist air was already slowly separating the snow patches on the fields and meadows.

Under these drab weather conditions, I'd left my house one morning and set out along a footpath between the river and the rail line. On other occasions I generally turned away from this footpath – that followed a large bend in the river – and continued along the shore. That way I would come to a bridge and cross it in order to return home again in a roughly circular manner by way of a high road on the other side. This day, though, I stayed on the footpath, lost in thought, without actually knowing or thinking about the fact that it led down through the lowlands to the town that Bacher had named as his place of residence. It was Sunday, and there was a deep silence all around; the church bells hadn't begun to ring yet. Out on the fields sat crows that would now and then flutter lazily up into the air; from time to time a light rain fell, blowing about and mixed with small snowflakes.

In these surroundings I'd already gone more than halfway to the village when suddenly, on a very large meadow lying before me, I saw Tambi merrily frisking along with his nose to the ground and his tail wagging back and forth. I looked around . . . and there was Herr Bacher, too, walking behind and following his dog's cavortings with amused eyes, not noticing me until we nearly bumped into each other.

He was so surprised – or rather so bewildered – that he almost totally forgot to say anything in response to my friendly hello. "Oh . . . you . . . honored . . . ," he said, gathering his wits. "So you've made it to our area now? Have you?" he continued quickly, blushing, "You'll excuse me that I haven't taken advantage of your gracious invitation yet, but . . . ."

"No excuses, please, dear friend! You don't need any as far as I'm concerned. I'm just glad to have met you on my walk and to see that things are going well for you and your best friend."

"Yes, we're both well . . . and he and I have good cause to be thankful to you, very thankful. You'll remember," he continued after a pause, "what an impression your recent words left on me and how deeply I took them to heart and pondered them. The whole thing was indeed a question of life and death for me and the dog, whom I can't lead around on a leash continually for years on end, you'll have to admit that; and to train him, to discipline him with violent methods like foresters and similar people do, that's something of which I'm totally incapable. So I had to find a way out of the dilemma. And I've succeeded. I've discovered a neutral ground for Tambi, a kind of domain, so to speak, where he can romp around to his heart's content and at the same time give in to a very innocent hunting delight without causing any damage. Just look at this meadow. You'll notice that it's quite large and surrounded on all sides by water. Behind us, the river sets a boundary to the terrain; in front of us, all along the entire meadow, is the millstream which flows into the river up there by the spillway. So Tambi can't break out anywhere; he's afraid to go in the water."

"That's very good," I said. "But you're forgetting about the bridge further up, and there's probably a plank laid down across the millstream somewhere."

"No, there isn't, there isn't," he assured me emphatically. "I've looked into it carefully. You can only cross right up at the mill. What's more, the only living things around here seem to be partridges; at least up till now no other animals . . . ."

He couldn't finish the sentence. For just then in front of Tambi, who was chasing around in circles, a rabbit popped up and began running straight towards us. When it saw us, it stopped for a startled instant and then took off to the right. The dog, running behind it, did the same; the rabbit turned to the right again and rushed straight towards the ditch where the millstream was. This had all happened as fast as lightning, and whether both animals had leaped across the not all-too-wide stream or had swum across it . . . in any case: there they appeared on the other side, flying across the nearby rail line, shooting up a deforested hillside and disappearing – with Tambi's shrill bark still reverberating in the air.

"There you have it!" I said to Bacher, who was standing there petrified and only now found the power to call out and whistle for him.

Suddenly two shots rang out, one immediately after the other.

Bacher turned white and began to shake violently.

"They've shot at the dog!" I cried out involuntarily.

"Do you think so?" he stammered. "Maybe at the rabbit . . . ."

"That's possible but not likely. It's not the time to be hunting right now. Do you want me to go check on things?"

"Please do! Please!" he cried and folded his hands.

I hurried across the meadow towards the mill, then across the dam, and climbed up the mostly snow-free slope, at which point a young man in a hunting outfit was just descending with a double-barreled shotgun slung over his shoulder. I saw him; he saw me as well, and he tipped his hat courteously.

"Did you shoot at a dog?" I asked him.

"I did!" he answered, stopping in his tracks. "He was chasing a rabbit into the hunting preserve."

"And is he dead?"

"Yes. Did he belong to you?"

"Not to me, but to an acquaintance with whom I was just conversing down there on the meadow."

He turned red. "I'm sorry. But I didn't see you gentlemen and didn't know the dog; I've only been employed here as an assistant for a week. But you know," he added, throwing out his chest and with a touch of defiance, "I was just doing my duty."

"Certainly. But maybe you didn't need to react so quickly . . . He was actually a hunting dog, you see . . . ."

"A hunting dog?" he replied contemptuously. "It was a bastard, a mutt. Up there in the preserve is where you'll find him." With that he tipped his hat again and left.

I rushed up to the preserve. At the edge of it lay Tambi, under a small spruce, his four yellow paws stretched out in front of him, his flank bleeding where a full load of shot had struck and torn into it. Crows had already gathered in a flock around him; they fluttered up cawing at my approach but immediately landed again a short distance away. With a painful shudder I looked at the carcass of the animal that had fallen victim to his own instincts and whose eyes now seemed wide open, glassy and staring at the heavens. Poor Tambi! Poor Bacher!

Now it was to *him* I had to bring the disastrous news. At the foot of the slope he was already crossing the dam and coming towards me, every bit the image of a soul inconsolable in his dread.

"Well? Well?" he asked in a monotone.

I made a sign with my hand.

"Dead?" he cried, "dead!?"

I gave a silent affirmation.

"My God! My God!" And he looked around as if into emptiness.

"Do you want to see him?" I asked after a pause.

"See him? I don't know if I can stand to look. But is he really . . . Isn't it possible he could still be saved . . . Perhaps we could still . . . ."

"It's all over," I said, "and there's nothing more we can do. It'll be best if we bury him up there right now. Is that all right with you?"

He gave no answer, but I could see that he wanted me to do the thinking and acting for him. So I went down to the mill and asked a boy to bring a shovel and follow us. Bacher could hardly stay on his feet; I had to take his arm to hold him up.

When we'd arrived at the top we stopped, and I pointed over toward the preserve. Bacher first threw a shy, fearful glance over to the spot where Tambi was lying; then, his eyes transfixed, he took a few quick steps forward . . . and turned away trembling with horror.

"Sit down on this tree stump for a while," I said, "I'll take care of everything else."

He did it mechanically and covered his face.

The small grave was quickly dug and quickly covered over again with grass and moss. We'd situated it under a young, free-standing Scotch Pine, and as a final touch I erected a small monument from colored pieces of syenite[9] laying about. Then I paid the boy, whom I asked to leave, came up to Bacher, and laid my hand on his shoulder.

He was startled, turned and walked toward the grave with his arms outstretched . . . .

I felt that he needed to be alone now, so I left.

III

A week passed without my having heard a thing from Bacher. Although there was actually no obligation on my part now, it seemed to me as if I ought to check and see how he'd been doing since the loss of his dog. So one afternoon I made my way towards the little town, and once there I was soon able to locate the notary office. As I entered, a young man with tousled yellow hair was writing busily at his desk, and when I asked him, he told me that Bacher hadn't shown up at the office for the past three days.

"Is he sick?"

"Not really," replied the clerk with a peculiar smile, "but . . . ."

"Well, then maybe I'll find him at his house. Can you tell me where he lives?"

---

[9] A granular igneous rock consisting mainly of feldspar but which includes other minerals, including hornblende.

"It's certain he won't be home. But you might find him at Herr Wassertrilling's."

"Who is Herr Wassertrilling?"

"The merchant over there . . . at the far end of the plaza."

I took my leave and went looking for the designated store right away; a teenaged Jewish girl was leaning against its entrance, looking at me with large black eyes. She was obviously the daughter of the merchant standing inside behind a heaped-up and messy counter, pouring brandy into small glasses for a few dissolute-looking men. When he sighted me he rushed outside towards me with servile bowing and scraping.

"Is Herr Bacher to be found here?" I asked most dubiously.

"Yes, indeed! Yes, indeed! Herr Doctor be's[10] in there at the wine tavern." So saying, he tore open the door of a partition to one side which was wallpapered with blue sugar paper[11] and from which emanated the strong stench of cheap alcohol. In this room, which was filled with all sorts of barrels, bundles, and balls, sat Bacher behind a bottle of wine at a small table. In the semi-darkness endemic there, he didn't recognize me right away, but when he did it wasn't a pleasant surprise that came across his face so much as an awkward displeasure. Nevertheless, he was just as obliging and subservient to me as ever.

"Pardon me for the surprise attack on you here," I said. "I just wanted to see how things are going with you."

"Oh, you're very kind. Things are going badly with me . . . very badly . . . but please, take a seat . . . ."

Herr Wassertrilling, who'd come in after me, pulled out the requisite second chair from a corner and asked if he might serve me some red wine, which I let happen. "I'll have someone bring some light, too!" the tavern owner cried, hurrying out.

Indeed, that seemed necessary. It was as dark as a cellar in there, since only a faint shimmer of light was entering through a small, half-opaque window pane in the door.

---

[10] Saar's portrayal of the Jewish merchant includes the latter's use of nonstandard German grammar.

[11] Literal translation of German *Zuckerpapier,* which was used by Viennese confectioners to wrap their cakes and candies, an item the merchant would have had readily at hand and which, used as wallpaper, underscores the poverty of the surroundings.

After a while the young girl showed up with a smoking petroleum lamp, placed it on the wobbly little table, and then left again, slowly swaying her hips.

Bacher had collected his wits in the meantime. He took my hand and said with a deep, heavy sigh: "Things are really going very badly for me . . . worse than you can imagine. I can't live without my dog!"

"Oh! Oh!" I interjected.

"That's the way it is! The way it is! Perhaps you'll understand me when I say that with him I lost *everything*. He was the only thing still holding me up, since he was the only creature on earth that loved me."

"Certainly a strong statement."

"Nevertheless a true one. But I don't want to be unfair and leave out one other person: my poor mother. Yes, my mother did love me," he continued pensively, "though in her own way. She always wanted me different than I happened to be, always tried to experiment with me, change and reconstitute me. Certainly it wasn't with harshness or severity like my father, of whom I only have faint memories . . . or with ridicule and scorn like the rest of the world: no, it was with that painful tenderness that's the most hidden and yet the loudest accusation. I think she died purely from the grief of having brought me into the world the way I am and not some other way; God bless her! So you see . . . that's it: I was never just right for anybody in my life. Everybody wanted to see me as somebody different than who I was; everybody wanted to give me advice, to guide me along new pathways, and since that never caught hold, they all ended up hating me.

"Oh, I had some friends down through the years . . . and I loved them all from the bottom of my heart in spite of their mistakes, failings, and weaknesses . . . even in spite of many hurtful practical jokes one or the other of them played on me. I accepted them the way they were, content with their positive side, with the good character traits they exhibited along with the bad – just like anybody does. But they wouldn't do the same for me. They picked at me, tormented and teased me, and preached about my shortcomings . . . loudest about the ones they possessed themselves to an even greater extent, until I couldn't take it anymore and the break came about.

"And then the women . . . Oh, the women! Never, not once in my life did I succeed in winning a feminine heart. It seemed as though the entire sex didn't see me at all – except with contempt after the fact. And if it seemed to me from time to time that I was causing someone to notice me and show some appreciation . . . before I knew it, right after the first conversation almost every time, it was all over, as if evaporated. One single woman – she's now long dead – seemed to have deeper feelings for me . . . but *she* gave up on me, too, looking at me with an expression as if to say: 'No, it just won't work!'

"And that's the way it went with my literary success as well, which was almost over before it'd begun; that's the way it was at the office – and so on, with everything and everybody – right down to the dogs! Yes, dear sir, right down to the dogs! From the beginning I loved these animals dearly, and it was my fondest wish to have one of them devoted to me. But to no avail! No matter how many dogs I may have brought home through the course of time, none of them could get used to me in spite of all the tenderness I could muster . . . and when I tried to be strict with them, they growled and bit at me. They all ran away, some earlier, some later. But my Tambi was the first one, the only one, who recognized me as his master, who wouldn't leave my side – who loved me! Oh, my Tambi! My Tambi!" The pain overcame him, and he broke out in tears as he had before in the village tavern.

I let him cry. After he'd calmed down somewhat, I said: "Well, you see, your yearning for a faithful and devoted dog has been satisfied. Who knows if maybe you'll also have the good fortune of finding a person who can return all that love that you've missed and gone without in your life till now."

He sat bolt upright. "A person!" he cried with a scornful laugh. "It's too late; I couldn't respond to a love like that any longer. In order to really be something to a person, we have to be able to feed the perception that *he* can truly be something to us, too. And I'm no longer in a condition to do that. People have long since become totally alien and worthless to me – mere phonies and phantoms!" He had no sense of how much hurt was contained in that phrase for me personally and continued, rapidly returning to his own pain: "If I had lost the dog in any other way, if he'd been stolen from me, if he'd succumbed to some disease, maybe I'd just humbly accept it and endure it as I've accepted and endured so many other things. But it was *me* who took my own dearest possession away from *myself*, and that thought is almost driving me crazy. I feel like a murderer. And aren't I? Tell me yourself – who killed him? The forestry assistant who didn't know him and who only brought him down out of a feeling of duty . . . or me, who in foolish weakness, in criminal stubbornness, turned my back on the warning of the forester and *your* kind exhortations? If I'd followed your advice and kept him on a leash . . . he'd still be alive!"

"Well, probably so. But it's precisely this point that provides a source of comfort if you look at it more closely. For the objection you raised back then is one I have to recognize today to its full extent. You were in fact unable to keep Tambi continually on a leash all the time. A single unguarded moment could have destroyed months of heedfulness and brought about the disaster. In addition, even the best trained dog can fall back into his instincts from time to time under specific conditions. So don't be so hard on yourself. The evil lay in the circumstances themselves. Around here, where the wild animals are looked after and protected, it's impossible for anyone who isn't a forester or hunter himself to keep a dog permanently if it has even the tiniest hunting drive. In a city you'd have been able to rejoice safely in your possession; in this area it just didn't work. That's what you have to tell yourself; you have to recognize the necessity of what happened, and then your pain will lessen more and more until finally you'll forget it."

"Forget it? Never! For that I'd have to get away from here . . . far away! And how can I do that? Oh, I don't even know how I'm supposed to keep living here anymore, where everything, everything reminds me of my loss, where I can't take a breath of air without breathing the memories in with it. When I wake up in the morning from a disturbed half-slumber, my eyes fall immediately on the chair next to my bed where Tambi used to sleep. In the office I can't write three lines without looking under the table, for that's where Tambi used to lie cuddled against my feet, not making a sound. If I go outside, I see him running across every meadow, every field, jumping out from behind every bush. I can't eat without thinking of the modest portion that went to him, and so the bite sticks in my throat. That's also the reason why I avoid the inns and all the other places I've ever been with him . . . and only in this dive can I take it, since I'd never set foot in here before. This is where I spend my days now . . . trying to drown my pain in miserable wine!"

He hastily emptied a glass of the cloudy red liquid which deserved an even sharper judgment. It was a beverage of true poison, the straightest mix of alcohol and fuchsin.[12]

---

[12] A water-soluble coal-tar derivative that forms deep-red chemical solutions and is mainly used as a dye.

"And then there's the nighttime! The night!" he continued. "Oh, you wouldn't believe what I endure! I shouldn't have looked at him lying there in his blood. Now I can't get that horrible image out of my eyes in the dark, spooky silence. I'm positively terrified of ghosts. And yet it would be my fondest wish for him to appear before me again . . . for him to jump up on my bed . . . ."

I admit that I found myself in an embarrassing dilemma. This was no case of unburdening emotions and feeling better, as it'd been before: I found myself across from a man who – spurred on by my presence – was just working himself deeper and deeper into a disturbed state. So I said: "Dear friend, I see with regret that for all my concern I can bring you neither consolation nor help. Your condition is a pathologically overwrought one for which there is only *one* doctor: your own determined will to liberate yourself at any price from this torturous and destructive mind-set. That's what I give you to ponder. You've already overcome so much . . . Be strong one more time!"

He was silent and appeared for an instant to breath more freely; but he quickly sank right back into his troubles. "Precisely because I've already overcome so much, I just can't do it anymore," he said numbly.

I'd looked at my watch in the meantime. "You're wanting to go already?" he asked in a tone that convinced me he had nothing against it.

"Oh, yes. It's time."

"If you'll permit me, I'll accompany you part of the way," he said, reaching for his hat and walking stick.

"I'd like that very much."

Out at the store I paid Herr Wassertrilling for the red wine I hadn't drunk, then we walked through the town and turned down the main road.

The sky was dark. A light wind was moving through the leafless tops of the tall poplar trees that stretched before us left and right; scattered dim lights shimmered in the distance before us.

At a pillar dedicated to a martyred saint,[13] glowing forth from the darkness with its white paint, Bacher stopped walking. "Here's where I turn around," he said.

"Farewell . . . and think about my words."

He said nothing in reply and shrugged his shoulders, sighing.

---

[13] Pillars with images of saints on top of them dotted the countryside of Moravia.

Soon he'd disappeared behind me, and I walked on alone through the night.

IV

Spring storms were raging across the countryside. As if before the heat of a fire, the remaining layers of white melted away from the heights, and round about there began a dripping, a drizzling, and a rushing, while the generally so lazy little river – into which all the released waters were flowing – shot along in a high and deep surge. Meanwhile it'd also begun to rain violently and continuously, so that the danger of flooding seemed likely and arrangements were being made to protect the areas along both shores as much as possible.

During this time a coach stopped in front of my residence, and an elderly man stepped out of it. It was the notary from the small town. He said that he was taking the liberty to appear in the interests of Bacher, who was now in the most regrettable state of mind. He didn't show up in the office anymore; he would spend half the day at the grave of his dog and the rest of his time in the so-called wine tavern of Merchant Wassertrilling, where he was giving himself over more and more to the drinking of alcoholic beverages. "Where's it all going to lead?" concluded the notary. "Right now, as far as I know, he's keeping himself going by pawning and selling off his few paltry belongings, and if this continues very much longer, it's certain to end up very horribly for him."

I was shocked at this news, but I wasn't surprised by it. I very frankly said as much to the notary, too, by referring to the tone of my last meeting with Bacher.

"Yes, I know," replied the notary, "that you looked him up a while back; at the time I was away on official business. But I'd still like to ask you to ride back with me and make one last effort. I've found he doesn't pay any heed to my words. You count for a lot with him, though, and maybe it would bring some success if you were to make a strong appeal to his conscience."

"Well, all right, I'll do it, although I fear that his seeing me will just drive him even deeper into his depression. For I am, as you may know, intertwined to some degree with the fate that befell him."

"He told me about that, and indeed it's a peculiar fate," the notary continued pensively. "He's been an unhappy person for as long as I've known him, someone who's brought a lot of worry on himself and others. The one most affected was his mother, whom I knew and who was a splendid woman. But in dealing with her son she proved to be excessively weak and may have pampered the willful boy much more than was wise. When Bacher had failed with his literary hopes, I met him by chance in the nearby district capital, the one where he'd spent his childhood, and since he didn't know what to do with himself anymore, I employed him in my office . . . and kept him, too, though he wasn't a very eager or reliable worker. Already back then I thought I noticed that he was drinking some, and I assumed it was to dull painful memories.

"After he got the dog, though, a marvelous change came over him. He became frugal and punctual, took a great deal of pleasure in his work, and, with such a talented head on his shoulders, he suddenly showed a very good grasp of concepts within this profession of mine, so much so that I had the highest of hopes for him and was already thinking of being able to make him my legal assistant in time. Then his dog gets shot and everything is finished and done . . . and now he's drifting toward his doom. But we can't let it get to that point; we have to try to save him at any price. Come along! It's exactly the time right now for us to find him in that merchant's store."

We climbed into the coach and drove down the road – with wind and rain pelting us from the side – to the small town, where we stopped in front of Herr Wassertrilling's store. We were informed that Bacher wasn't there. He would certainly be coming along later, though, because up till now he hadn't missed a single day.

We asked those in the tavern to let us know as soon as he made his appearance, and then we went into a nearby inn where the local dignitaries usually came together in the evenings.

After we'd waited there fruitlessly almost two hours, we went back to the store one more time. We were told Bacher still hadn't made his appearance.

"Then let's go check in his apartment," said the notary.

It had turned dark in the meanwhile, and we turned our steps towards a narrow little side street that consisted only of little shanty-like houses and that led out into the open fields. The notary stopped in front of one of the last houses and knocked on a dimly illuminated window. Part of the curtain raised; the notary called out a few words in a Slavic language, whereupon the door was opened and a woman appeared at the threshold, furnishing the gentleman accompanying me with information that was incomprehensible to me.

"He left very early this morning," the notary now said to me, "and hasn't returned home yet. Besides, I'm told he had a very bad night last night, continually moaning and lamenting."

I was silent. A dark foreboding was rising up inside me.

The notary seemed to have the same thought. "If only, if only he hasn't . . . ."

"I'm almost afraid he has."

We checked back one more time in the store and then returned to the inn, where the announcement had just been made that the river had left its banks and washed out the nearest bridge.

I looked at the notary and said: "Perhaps his return home was cut off because of that?"

"Quite possible if he was on the other side of the river."

"That's where the grave of his dog is, and you've already said . . . ."

"Absolutely right. We'll just have to wait and see what tomorrow brings. I do regret you having to drive back again with things still up in the air. If I didn't have relatives visiting in my house right now, I'd offer to let you spend the night there."

"That's very kind of you. But do you know what I think? I'll spend the night here in town, anyway, to be available first thing in the morning. We mustn't let Bacher slip past us again when he returns – as I still hope he will. They'll probably have a room for rent in this inn, won't they?"

"Certainly, but it won't look like much . . . ."

"That doesn't matter; I can put up with it this once."

We then joined in discussion with the rest of the guests, who were conversing very animatedly about the flood waters which – as a result of their safe distance from any human settlements – certainly held no terror and could only cause some damage to the more or less vulnerable agricultural areas. In the course of discussions ten o'clock came around, and those present left a few at a time, the last of which was the notary himself, promising to be there early next morning.

I sat there alone for a time; then I was guided to my room, which had been heated in the meantime. It was very sparsely furnished, in fact, but it was quite clean. Since the little room had probably not been inhabited all winter, there was a perceptible chill in spite of the fire crackling in a small iron stove, and I ordered some hot grog, which I received after an extended wait. Then I lit a cigar and walked up and down. From time to time I stopped at the window and looked out into the night that spread out with impenetrable darkness. The rain had stopped; round about was deep silence – only when I listened carefully for a while could I hear in the distance a muffled, eerie rushing and raging.

My imagination was fixed on Bacher, of course, and in my mind's eye it seemed as if I saw him in the darkness at the grave of his dog . . . and then again at the edge of the swollen flood waters, stumbling back and forth, confused.

The flames in the stove were long since extinguished and the candles had burned all the way down. Shivering, I threw myself on the bed fully clothed and tried to fall asleep, at which I finally succeeded.

It was about seven o'clock in the morning when I was awakened by sunshine streaming in. The skies had cleared, and the day was coming to life in the building, as it was downstairs on the plaza.

After some time, the notary came. "He hasn't returned home yet," he said.

"Well, it's still early," I replied. "If he spent the night somewhere in the area, there's really no way he could be back yet. I suggest we wait until afternoon before assuming the worst."

The notary kept me company at breakfast, then we both hiked to a nearby rise from which we could get a view of the flood.

The lowlands were partially transformed into a lake. A fresh wind was ruffling the shimmering water surface and swaying the treetops protruding from the deep water.

The meadow where Tambi had hunted for the last time was under water, too. The mill had taken on the appearance of Noah's ark. Involuntarily my eyes fell on the heights where the fatal shot had been fired. I pointed it out to the notary and said: "How would it be if we were to go take a look over there?"

"We'd have to take quite a detour to get there. If you'd like to go, I'll have my horses harnessed. In any case we can spend the morning doing that, and if Bacher hasn't arrived by the time of our return, I'll confide in the police captain."

We took his coach up the main road about a half hour to the next town, where we were able to cross the river without any difficulty. Then we got out and hiked up to the forest's edge, coming back along it on the far side of the river.

Under other circumstances this hike would have been enchanting. A fragrant, moist air was blowing at us from the whistling treetops; the early morning bird voices were twittering delightfully; and over the countryside lay the first glimmer of spring. But our mood was serious and depressed, and so we kept on walking pensively along the mossy path.

Finally we saw the plateau with the hunting preserve before us, its bright green sparkling in the sunlight. The area was quiet and empty, and the small grave loomed up lonely and deserted under the Scotch pine.

We walked towards it. "There's a hat on the ground!" I cried. It could be seen between some bare shrubs near the tree.

The notary lifted up the worn and thoroughly soaked head covering with his walking stick.

"That's Bacher's hat."

We called out his name with loud voices. But nobody answered; only a quiet, plaintive echo seemed to resound from the forest.

Now we were firmly convinced that the miserable man had sought and found his own death. Certainly, the possibility was still not completely precluded that he'd been trapped by the flood while returning home in the dark; the hat having been left behind where it was, though, appeared to speak against this assumption. Regardless of the cause, the fact remains that his corpse was found floating by the sluice gate of a nearby hammer mill[14] that same day.

---

[14] A mill that served to crush coal or break up ore under the beat of hydraulically-powered hammers.